STONEWALL OF THE WEST

STONEWALL OF THE WEST
PATRICK CLEBURNE AND THE CIVIL WAR

CRAIG L. SYMONDS

 UNIVERSITY PRESS OF KANSAS

Published by the University Press of Kansas (Lawrence, Kansas 66049), which was
organized by the Kansas Board of Regents and is operated and funded by Emporia State
University, Fort Hays State University, Kansas State University, Pittsburg State
University, the University of Kansas, and Wichita State University

Library of Congress Cataloging-in-Publication Data

Symonds, Craig L.
   Stonewall of the West : Patrick Cleburne and the Civil War / Craig L. Symonds.
     p. cm. — (Modern war studies)
   Includes bibliographical references and index.
   ISBN 0-7006-0820-6 (alk. paper)
   1. Cleburne, Patrick Ronayne, 1828–1864. 2. Generals—Confederate States
of America—Biography. 3. Confederate States of America. Army—Biography.
4. United States—History—Civil War, 1861–1865—Campaigns. 5. Georgia—
History—Civil War, 1861–1865. 6. Tennessee—History—Civil War, 1861–1865.
7. Helena (Ark.)—Biography. I. Title. II. Series.
E467.1.C58S9 1997
973.7′42092—dc20
  [B]   96-44624

British Library Cataloguing in Publication Data is available.

Printed in the United States of America

10 9 8 7 6 5 4 3 2 1

The paper used in this publication meets the minimum requirements of the American
National Standard for Permanence of Paper for Printed Library Materials Z39.48-1984.

CONTENTS

v

MAPS

(photographs follow p. 98)

ACKNOWLEDGMENTS

Because a portion of this project was completed during a year spent in England as visiting lecturer at the Britannia Royal Naval College, I am more indebted than usual to individuals at reference libraries and archives throughout the United States, England, and Ireland who took the time to respond to my many long-distance requests for help.

In Ireland, I benefited from the thoughtful and conscientious assistance of Tim Cadogan of the Cork County Library, who brought to my attention several obscure local histories as well as published accounts of Cork County election speeches; Kieran Burke helped me find material in the Cork City Library. During a visit to Pat Cleburne's boyhood home near Ballincollig, my wife and I were graciously received by the current mistress of Grange House, Mary O'Sullivan, who along with her sister-in-law, Nora Lynch, offered hospitality and history over tea. Walter McGrath and Denis Wilson of Cork have been enthusiastic pursuers of information about Pat Cleburne for many years and shared with me their insights and material.

In England, I benefited from the cheerful assistance as well as the friendship of Richard Kennell, Wendy Tomlin, and Mags Griffin of the Britannia Royal Naval College Library as they tracked down titles that were particularly obscure in that nautical clime. Paul Kerrigan of the Irish Military History Society gave me several important leads and maintained an interest in the project from the start. My colleagues in the Strategic Studies Department offered their collegial hospitality, provided a manageable work schedule, and helped me navigate the perils of the Public Record Office.

I could not have pursued this project from England at all without the assistance of literally dozens of librarians and archivists at institutions throughout the United States. Once again, first nod must go to Barbara Breeden, Flo Todd, and especially Barbara Manvel of Nimitz Library at the U.S. Naval Academy, who were tireless in their efforts to respond to my often unreasonable demands. Others who were willing to go the extra mile to assist me from long-distance were: Russell P. Baker of the Arkansas History Commission; Andrea Cantrell, head of Research Services at the University of Arkansas at Fayetteville; Tom Cartwright, curator of the Carter House Museum at Franklin, Tennessee; Bernard Crystal, curator of manuscripts at Columbia University; Christina Greene of the Special Collections Library at Duke University; Corina Hudgins of the Confederate Museum in Richmond; Jennifer Davis McDaid of the Virginia State Library and Archives; Michael Pilgrim of the National Archives; Julia Rather of the Tennessee State Library and Archives; Gail R. Redmann at the Western Reserve Historical Society in Cleveland; John H. Rhodehamel, curator of American History at the Huntington Library in San Marino, California; Bobby Robert of the Central Arkansas Library System; Richard Somers of the U.S. Army Military History Institute at Carlisle Barracks, Pennsylvania; and Christine Weideman, archivist of manuscripts at Yale University Library.

Others who offered ideas, advice, or pointed me to the occasional rare document include Carl H. Moneyhon of the University of Arkansas at Little Rock, Dianne Neal at the University of Central Oklahoma, Mark Hull of Huntsville, Alabama, Eugene Jones of Goose Creek, South Carolina, and a trio of Arkansans: Ron Fuller, Ivey Gladden, and especially Dewitt Yingling, who provided me with a number of valuable suggestions. Betty Ferrell of the Tullahoma Chamber of Commerce helped me locate and identify Ovoca Falls. The indefatigable Ed Bearss guided me through the Spring Hill and Franklin battlefields.

The members of the Works-in-Progress seminar in the History Department at the Naval Academy read Chapter 1; Dewitt Yingling read Chapter 2; and Tom Cartwright read the sections on the Battle of Franklin. I am particularly grateful to Albert Castel, Gary Gallagher, and Nathaniel C. Hughes, Jr., each of whom read the entire manuscript in draft. It is much improved for their comments, corrections, and suggestions. Nat Hughes also provided me with a copy of *Liddell's Record* and tipped me to other useful sources. I cannot let pass an opportunity to thank Howell and Elizabeth Purdue, who spent more than a decade hunting down Pat Cleburne materials for their 1974 biography, thereby making the pursuit of Cleburne materials immeasurably easier for subsequent scholars. Thanks, too, to my agent Jim Charlton, to Bill Clipson who rendered the eleven maps in the book, and to Mike Briggs who has been a supportive editor.

Very special thanks are due to five individuals with a personal interest in Pat Cleburne. Charles Cleburne Jordan of Minneapolis, who is General Cleburne's great-great-nephew, offered encouragement and generously shared his papers with me. William Pettus Buck of Birmingham, Alabama, great-nephew of Irving Buck who was Cleburne's aide and first biographer, sent copies of Irving Buck's papers as well as a diary kept by his sister. Ruth Duemler of Fresno, California, granddaughter of Patrick Ronayne Cashman, Patrick Cleburne's cousin, sent me a copy of a letter from William Cleburne to her grandfather. Doug Schanz of Roanoke, Virginia, generously shared copies of four Cleburne letters in his personal collection. And Michael D. Ronayne of Lufkin, Texas, provided genealogical information.

As always, my greatest debt is to my wife, Marylou, who traveled with me from Ballincollig, Ireland, to Franklin, Tennessee, who transcribed numberless nearly indecipherable letters, and who offered her usual cogent criticism of the text—not always received at the time with the thanks it deserved, but which I offer now.

PROLOGUE

At midmorning on 30 November 1864, after a week of seasonally cold and wet weather, the sun broke through the clouds scudding over central Tennessee and shone brightly down on a long column of men marching northward along the Columbia-Nashville Turnpike. The rifles carried at every possible angle identified the column as an army on the move, and the men stepped out in the manner of veterans who were accustomed to long marches. Yet these soldiers disdained any formal order and were attired in a wide variety of homespun ranging in color from faded gray to mud brown. Likewise, their weather-beaten hats of cloth or straw suggested little uniformity: some wore sadly faded kepis while others sported wide-brimmed "droopy" hats, which were distinctly unmilitary in appearance but effectively shielded the men from sun and rain alike. Not a few in the column walked barefoot and cursed the hard white paving stones of the turnpike. At a time of the year when armies would routinely be going into winter quarters, the Army of Tennessee was embarking on a desperate offensive into the heartland of the state whose name it bore.[1]

For the most part, the men were in good spirits. An army advancing is almost always happier than an army in retreat, and the men were advancing now through friendly territory. From the roadside, the civilian populace welcomed them as liberators: farm wives offered ladles of water, and old men urged them to "Push on, boys!" And push on they did, for they were chasing an enemy that was in full retreat. The signs of it were everywhere. One soldier counted thirty-four abandoned Yankee supply wagons along the road, the mules shot dead in the traces and the spokes smashed out of the wheels to render the wagons useless. On straight stretches of the road, those at the head of the column caught glimpses of the enemy rear guard barely two miles ahead.[2]

Despite the cheers from the side of the road and the scent of the chase, however, the men in the Army of Tennessee marched with the knowledge that

1

things had not gone well during the night. With the instinct of veterans, they knew that the enemy they were pursuing had slipped past them in the dark, escaping a trap carefully laid. Some had overheard their officers exchanging angry words that morning about missed opportunities and bungling. Others proclaimed confidently that their commander had let the enemy escape on purpose "in order to gain greater glory from whipping them in breastworks."[3]

Around noon, the head of the marching column reached a line of low, tree-covered hills. The turnpike rose gently to pass over the crest at a low point between two of them: Winstead Hill, the higher of the two, on the left, and Breezy Hill on the right. The retreating Yankees had posted a rear guard on both hills, and their artillery tried the range. Half a dozen shells exploded just in front of the advancing Confederate infantry; in response, staff officers directed the marching men off to the right and left. Skirmishers deployed and moved forward, and the enemy fled, giving up the high ground without a fight.

Almost the moment the two hills were in Confederate hands, a group of mounted officers spurred up to the crest of Winstead Hill for a view of the road ahead. Leading the group was a large, sad-eyed general with a full, brown beard who maintained his seat in the saddle by the use of straps and buckles, for he had only one good leg and the prosthetic he wore stuck out at an odd angle. Leaving the others behind, General John Bell Hood rode alone to the top of the hill and looked out over a flat, open plain toward the city of Franklin two miles away. What he saw was to all appearances an army in headlong retreat. The bluecoated soldiers he had been pursuing all morning were streaming back over the open plain toward the town which, from this distance, resembled an anthill that had been prodded with a stick. Some of the enemy soldiers occupied the earthworks around the town, built the year before in anticipation of just such an emergency. Others ran to and fro in apparent confusion as Federal wagons hastened to get across the Harpeth River and continue the flight north. Hood had no intention of letting them escape a second time. Rejoining the group of officers, he announced, "Gentlemen, we will make the fight." With that, he led the group back down the hill to a nearby farmhouse to write orders for an assault.[4]

At that same moment several miles to the south, Confederate Major General Patrick Ronayne Cleburne was lost in deep thought as he rode at the head of his division. At age thirty-six, Cleburne was two years older than Hood, though he looked ten years younger. At five feet ten inches and 150 pounds, he was lean and well muscled with a military bearing that was partly a reflection of his calm self-assurance and partly a habit from his years of service as a private in the British 41st Regiment in his native Ireland. His new gray sack coat was open at the throat, exposing a white linen shirt, and on his head was a general's cap with faded gold braid—the gift of a group of patriotic and admiring southern ladies. A thick shock of unruly dark hair stuck out above his broad forehead in what one soldier described as "bristly individuality," and crow's-feet crinkled at the corners of his steel gray eyes as he squinted in the bright sunlight.[5] ·

A reserved man by nature, Cleburne's grim countenance discouraged conversation at the best of times. Generally serious when there was work to be done, he looked particularly so now—his mouth a tight line, and his eyes cold and sharp. Only hours before, his friend and corps commander Major General Frank Cheatham had informed him that Hood was furious that the enemy had escaped during the night. Worse yet, Cheatham had told Cleburne that Hood blamed the debacle on Cheatham's Corps and specifically on two of Cheatham's division commanders: Major General John C. Brown and Cleburne. Apparently there had been heated conversation at breakfast about disobedience, insubordination, and an unwillingness to fight.

Such accusations were particularly astonishing with regard to Cleburne's Division, which had built a reputation as the hardest hitting, most dependable division in the army. In testimony to its prowess, it was the only division that was allowed its own battle flag, and veterans on both sides knew that where the blue flag of Cleburne's Division flew, there was the thickest fighting. The news that Hood now held him and his command at least partly responsible for the escape of the enemy the night before shook Cleburne deeply. He sent word up the column asking General Brown to wait for him, and he galloped ahead to find out what that officer had heard about the matter.

Cleburne found Brown quietly sitting his horse alongside the turnpike, and they rode together away from the line of marching men across an open field to talk privately. Brown had already received an earful that morning from Hood who was, Brown said, "wrathy as a rattlesnake." Pointedly, Hood had emphasized the importance of a vigorous pursuit, a message that carried an implied criticism, but he had not specifically charged Brown with responsibility for the errors of the previous evening. Nor had he mentioned Cleburne. Brown related all this to Cleburne and suggested that perhaps Cleburne had misunderstood. "No," Cleburne replied tersely, "I think not."[6]

After that, the road to Franklin ceased to be a joyous pursuit of the enemy for Cleburne; the winter sunshine brought him no solace. He was both hurt and angry—hurt that anyone could think him capable of doing less than his full duty, angry that he had to hear of the accusation from a third party rather than from the general himself. As he spurred ahead of his marching troops toward the line of low hills across the turnpike, at least half his mind was bent on a powerful determination to erase the accusations of his commander and to demonstrate his commitment to the cause.

He reined in at the foot of Winstead Hill and dismounted. To distract himself while he waited for his division to arrive, he squatted in the shade of a nearby tree and, brushing the leaves aside, used a stick to draw a checkerboard in the dirt and invited a staff officer to play checkers with him, using rocks and leaves as game pieces. The game was soon interrupted by the arrival of a courier from Hood who announced that the commanding general requested Cleburne's presence at headquarters. In the parlor of Harrison House at the base of Winstead Hill, Cleburne faced his putative accuser.[7]

Hood looked tired. He was often tired. Having lost the use of an arm at Gettysburg and a leg at Chickamauga, just getting through each day was something of a trial. He frequently took laudanum to ease the pain that was evident, even now, in his sunken, haunted, eyes. Hood was not a complicated man. He was exactly what Robert E. Lee had called him: "a bold fighter," and just the man wanted to lead a brigade in a desperate charge. Many thought he lacked the elasticity of mind necessary to command an army, but that was precisely where the fortunes of war and his own ambition had brought him. Jefferson Davis had given Hood the Army of Tennessee in July 1864 precisely because of Hood's aggressive instinct and because he believed—or at least he hoped—that such an instinct was exactly what the army needed. True to his character, Hood had abandoned the defensive tactics of his predecessor and attacked the enemy in a series of bloody battles outside Atlanta. When those attacks failed to drive the enemy from Georgia, he had conjured up the desperate invasion scheme that had led him to this line of low hills overlooking Franklin, Tennessee.

The previous night Hood had collapsed into bed utterly exhausted but confident that he had succeeded in trapping the Yankee army at Spring Hill. He awakened in the morning to the news that while he and the rest of the Confederate army had slept, the enemy had quietly escaped. As the commanding general, the ultimate responsibility for this incredible lapse was his. He also bore at least a share of the direct responsibility, for when he had been awakened in the night with news that the enemy was moving on the turnpike, he had turned the matter over to a subordinate and gone back to sleep. Then in the light of day he convinced himself that the true blame belonged to Cheatham's Corps and particularly to the divisions of Brown and Cleburne, the units that had failed to block the turnpike and thus had ruined his brilliant strategy. In a broader sense, Hood blamed the whole episode on the weakened spirit of the army. Cheatham, Brown, and Cleburne were proven combat leaders and he did not doubt their personal courage. But

Hood feared that their failure at Spring Hill was symptomatic of a deeper illness: the army had lost its heart. The fire was gone, and something needed to be done to rekindle it.[8]

Now all of those men—Hood, Cheatham, Brown, and Cleburne—stood together in the parlor of Harrison House. Also present was Major General William Bate who commanded Cheatham's third division and Lieutenant General Alexander P. Stewart whose corps had led the advance to Franklin. The Confederate cavalry commander, Nathan Bedford Forrest, was there too. Hood told his generals that the Yankees would not make a stand at Franklin—they were only putting up a bold front, he said, in the hope of slowing down pursuit. Though a full third of the Confederate army had not yet arrived, Hood was not going to wait for it. He would attack at once. All it would take was one good hard push, Hood insisted, and the town would be theirs. He ignored the difficulties of making a frontal attack over open ground against an entrenched enemy, and he may have done so deliberately to ensure that these men who had failed him (as he saw it) the night before would this time take the bit in their teeth. Without his putting it into words, it was clear to everyone in the room that the commanding general considered this an opportunity for the generals who had let him down to redeem themselves. Hood directed Stewart's corps to attack the enemy left, but he entrusted the direct assault—straight up the turnpike and across the open plain—to the divisions of Brown and Cleburne of Cheatham's Corps.[9]

Cheatham, Brown, and Cleburne received their orders in silence. It was the cavalry commander, Nathan Bedford Forrest, who spoke up. There was no need for such a frontal assault, he maintained. The enemy had his back to a river and could easily be outflanked. "General Hood," he said, "if you will give me one strong division of infantry with my cavalry, I will agree to flank the Federals from their works within two hours' time." Given this opening, Cheatham also spoke up. "I do not like the looks of this fight," he said. "The enemy has an excellent position and are well fortified." But Hood dismissed their objections. Driving the Yankees from Franklin was not his goal. They would only fall back to Nashville, he said, where they would have even better positions. He wanted to defeat them here and wipe them off the strategic map. He wanted not merely a success, he wanted a victory. What he left unspoken was his belief that a successful assault at Franklin would restore the fighting spirit of the army. The men—and their generals—needed to relearn the moral superiority of the offensive. They needed to be taught a lesson.[10]

Cleburne made no protest; his face betrayed no emotion. Along with the others he walked outside to where the horses were being held and prepared to mount. Hood followed him out and repeated his instructions: "Form your division to the right of the pike. . . . Give orders to your men not to fire a gun until you run the Yankee skirmish line from behind the first line of works, then press and shoot them in their backs as they run to their main line; then charge the enemy's works." Cleburne looked at Hood directly, as was his manner, and replied in a controlled voice, his Irish accent just perceptible, "I will either take the enemy's works or fall in the attempt." Then he turned his horse and rode off to lead his division in the last charge he would ever make.[11]

PART ONE

A STRANGER IN A STRANGE LAND

1
PAT CLEBURNE'S IRELAND

For the first twenty-one of his not-quite thirty-seven years of life, Patrick Ronayne Cleburne was a resident of Ireland. Before he wore Confederate gray, before he called himself an American, he was an Irishman. But he was an Irishman of a very rare type in the nineteenth century: part of a tiny but dominant class of well-to-do Protestants in a land peopled largely by poor Catholics. Such a distinction marked him in several ways. It meant that he had the advantage of a formal education, though it was abbreviated at age fifteen by his father's death; it made him comfortable in leadership roles despite an innate personal shyness; and it made him socially ambitious, a trait he brought with him when he emigrated to America in 1849. Cleburne's early years in Ireland also exposed him to fundamental social and political questions about self-government and the relationship between the laboring masses and the aristocracy. He could not avoid rubbing up against such issues, for the Ireland into which Pat Cleburne was born in 1828 was a powder keg with the fuse already lit and sputtering.

The issues that defined and divided Ireland in the 1830s and 1840s were both economic and religious. An exploitive tenant farming system and persistent famines since the end of the Napoleonic Wars kept the Irish peasants in a state of incipient starvation. More than half the population lived in single-room mud huts without any windows and frequently without a working door. Few of these primitive homes boasted any furniture; a survey revealed that in one village of 9,000 inhabitants, there was a total of ten beds. For these astonishingly meager residences (which they had to build themselves), the tenants paid land rents to mostly absentee landlords in England, rents that they earned by growing cash crops for export. If the tenants fell behind in their rents, they could be evicted and driven from the land at the point of a bayonet. Indeed, they could be evicted even when they paid their rent faithfully if, for example, the owner decided to turn the land over to pasture. Any improvements that the tenants had made on the land in the meantime belonged by law to the landlord. The result was that Irish peasants led a precarious existence, balancing constantly on the edge of ruin and starvation. A visiting Frenchman in the 1830s compared the existence of Irish peasants unfavorably with that of "Negroes in chains."[1]

In addition to their economic woes, Irish Catholics, who made up over 80 percent of the population, were politically disenfranchised as well. Although any freeholder (including Catholics) whose annual rent exceeded forty shillings was entitled to cast a vote, he could not vote for a Catholic unless the candidate was prepared to swear under oath that the invocation of saints and the celebration of the mass were both "superstitious and idolatrous." The official ban against government service by Catholics reinforced the view of most Irishmen that the British were *over*lords as well as *land*lords, a conclusion that many Englishmen would have acknowledged with satisfaction. This combination of economic poverty and political disenfranchisement created such a level of dissatisfaction that by the 1830s the English landlords began to fear open revolt. Although there had not been a violent uprising in Ireland since 1798, there was once again rumor of late night meetings and secret organizations.[2]

Into this volatile society Patrick Cleburne was born on St. Patrick's eve, 1828, the third child and second son of Joseph Cleburne, a doctor (the only practicing physician in rural Ovens Township nine miles west of Cork) and a Protestant—a member of the established Church of Ireland. Dr. Cleburne was not a wealthy man by the standards of the English gentry, but he occupied a level of society immeasurably above that of the Irish laboring masses. In addition to the status he earned from his profession and his religion, Dr. Cleburne had also married well. If anything, Patrick's frail and genteel mother was even further removed from the mass of Irish peasants than his father. Daughter of the prominent and well-connected Patrick Ronayne of Cork, Mary Ann Ronayne had grown up at Annebrook, a manor house near Queenstown (now Cobh), Cork's seaport. Patrick Ronayne was a member of the Cork Coursing (dog racing) Club and his wife a regular patroness of the Protestant Christmas Relief Fund. Indeed, there are hints the Ronaynes may have thought that the country doctor was a bit beneath their daughter. Still, at age thirty-one Mary Ann was well past the usual age for marriage, and Dr. Cleburne was at least a respectable match. She brought to the marriage not only her name and pedigree but also a dowry of £600, a substantial sum that yielded an annual income of £36 18s. to supplement the income Dr. Cleburne earned from his medical practice.[3]

The couple made their home in a twin-gabled two-story house called

"Bride Park," a name derived not from their recent marriage but from the fact that the house backed onto the River Bride just on the southern edge of Ovens Township. It was a delightful location atop a gently sloping hill less than two dozen yards from the river, a swift-moving stream that was deep enough for good fishing and just too wide to leap across, though stepping-stones behind the Cleburne house provided a convenient means of crossing dry-shod. Sometime during the next few years, Dr. Cleburne expanded the house, adding a third gable off the northern end where he established his surgery.[4]

Separated from the bustling city of Cork by the proverbial nine miles of bad road, the Cleburnes were effectively segregated from the cultural and social life of the city. They were not listed as patrons, or even on the guest list, of the many charity balls that punctuated the social calendar of the wealthy Protestants of Cork. They were, of course, relatively important personages in their own local community, but there was little social life for the couple in any case because their married life was dominated by Mary Ann Cleburne's almost constant pregnancies. She gave birth to the couple's first child, a son whom they named William, in 1824, had a miscarriage in 1825, gave birth to a daughter, Anne, in 1826, had another miscarriage in 1827, and was pregnant again in the winter of 1828. In a bedroom above Dr. Cleburne's surgery in the new wing at Bride Park, she suffered another difficult pregnancy but on 16 March gave birth to a healthy son, who was baptized Patrick Ronayne in honor of her father.[5]

While the Cleburne family grew larger at Bride Park, the twin issues of economic exploitation and religious disenfranchisement asserted themselves nationally. In the general elections for Parliament in 1826, candidates espousing Catholic Emancipation experienced unprecedented success. Conservatives were horrified when an advocate of Catholic Emancipation defeated the powerful Lord Beresford in an election in Waterford, and the issue came to dominate conversations in Cork as well when the death of Christopher Hely-Hutchinson forced a by-election there in December. Hutchinson's son John stood for the seat, and he turned the local contest into an event of national significance by announcing that although he was a Protestant himself, he believed the ban against Catholics should be rescinded. "I most sincerely believe," he declaimed at a public meeting in Cork, "that the passing of this measure would be the first great step towards a system of improvement and ameliorization which the circumstances of this country imperatively require, and I would, therefore, hail it as the opening of a new era for Ireland."

Aghast at Hutchinson's liberalism, conservatives put up their own candidate, Gerrard Callaghan, who had been born a Roman Catholic but became a convert to Protestantism while at school in England. With a convert's zeal, he charged that Hutchinson was no more than "the low and obsequious tool" of the Catholic Association, a group that advocated equal rights for Catholics but which had sinister and even revolutionary connotations for conservatives. Callaghan stated his own position boldly: "The Constitution was essentially Protestant, and it is impossible [that] a Roman Catholic can stand in reference to it, in the same position as a member of the Church of Ireland." "The ascendancy of Protestantism," he concluded, "should be upheld."[6]

The issue was thus openly joined, and it split Cork's Protestant community in half. Since voting was conducted publicly, all members of the community could see for themselves how their neighbors and fellow parishioners voted. The rector of St. Peter's Protestant Church was physically attacked and beaten when it became known that he had voted for the pro-emancipation Hutchinson. After the first day's voting, the conservative Callaghan led 388 to 312. The next day (19 December), Dr. Cleburne traveled the nine miles to Cork to cast his public vote for Hutchinson, thus proclaiming himself an advocate of reform. By the end of the day, Hutchinson had gained the lead, though the contest remained in doubt until 28 December when Hutchinson was declared the winner by a vote of 1020 to 969.[7]

The result of these elections profoundly shocked conservatives who feared that they presaged social revolution. They were even more shocked a year later when a Catholic, Daniel Patrick O'Connell, actually won election to the House of Commons from County Clare thanks to overwhelming support from the forty shilling freeholders. In London, members of both parties were alarmed by the apparent unraveling of their society. Elections that could be decided by the poor and ignorant threatened the very concept of rule by the propertied class. Could a threat to property itself be far behind? Nevertheless, they could not ignore such an evident electoral result, and in 1829 the House of Lords grudgingly joined the Commons in passing a Catholic Emancipation Act.[8]

These national events had no immediate personal impact on the daily life of Patrick Cleburne, who was only two years old when O'Connell finally took his seat in Parliament. But his father's public declaration of sympathy for the cause of Catholic Emancipation suggests that while the Cleburne home was one of relative comfort and privilege, the family was at least sensitive, if not actively sympathetic, to the lot of the downtrodden and disenfranchised.

Of far more immediate interest to young Pat Cleburne were the milestone events within his own family. His mother was pregnant again in the spring of

1829, though this time her health was so precarious that she decided to have the child at her parents' manor home, Annebrook. She delivered successfully, a boy who was named Joseph for his father, but her recovery was slow. She remained at Annebrook through the summer, confined most of the time to her bed, and she died quietly in the fall, exhausted at the age of thirty-seven.

The widowed Dr. Cleburne was left with four children: William now four, Anne three, Patrick at nineteen months, and the infant Joseph. Of necessity, the doctor immediately employed a governess to look after the children. She was Isabella Jane Stuart, a young woman only eighteen years old, who moved into Bride Park Cottage that winter. For Patrick, not yet two, Isabella became a surrogate mother, a relationship that was solemnized just over a year later in December 1830 when Dr. Cleburne, then thirty-nine, married the nineteen-year-old governess of his children. The new Mrs. Cleburne became the only mother Patrick ever knew. Throughout his life, he called her "Mamma" and solicited her advice even into adulthood.[9]

The new marriage was fruitful. A daughter, named Isabella for her mother, was born in December 1832. Patrick called his half sister "Issy," and she became his favorite sibling and most frequent correspondent. She was followed over the next nine years by three more boys: Edward (1833), Robert (1837), and Christopher, who was born in December 1841 when Patrick was thirteen, and who was called "Kit."[10]

Meanwhile, in April 1836, just past Patrick's eighth birthday, the Cleburne family took a big step up the social and economic ladder by moving from the gentrified comfort of Bride Park Cottage to an ancient and imposing manorial estate two miles to the east. The new Cleburne home was Grange House, a large, three-story Georgian house built around a fourteenth-century country home that was itself built on the foundation of a sixth-century abbey church. It was, by far, the grandest home in the parish, and the movement of the Cleburnes to this estate marked the metamorphosis of Joseph Cleburne, Esq., from country doctor to landed gentry. He leased the house and 205 surrounding acres of land for 100 years from John Hawkes for the sum of £230 per year, a huge sum at the time, the payment of which severely stretched the resources of the forty-four-year-old doctor.[11]

At least two tenant families lived on the estate and were included in the leasehold. They paid rents totaling ninety pounds per year to their new landlord, and Dr. Cleburne used the money to help offset his annual payment to John Hawkes. This made him a member of the most despised community in all Irish society: the middleman, vilified in the reform newspapers as "bloodsuckers" and "scoundrels." Such an emotional reaction was provoked by the tendency of middlemen to squeeze rent from their tenants in order to ensure

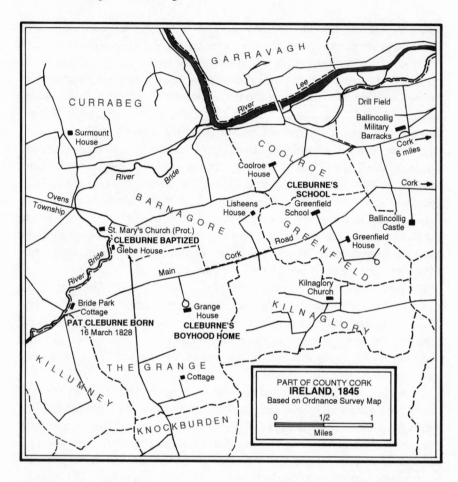

that those rents covered their own expenses, and for most of them profit was their only motive. But Dr. Cleburne was more interested in social position than profit. His tenant rents never covered his expenses, and he made up the difference with his doctor's fees. He therefore managed to escape the scorn generally heaped on middlemen by Irish reformers who considered such creatures to be "the most oppressive species of tyrant that ever lent assistance to the destruction of a country." Instead, Cleburne's forbearance earned him a local reputation as "the poor man's friend." [12]

Patrick's years at Grange House were among his happiest. He had a room of his own on the second floor over the front landing, half a dozen brothers and sisters for playmates, and 205 acres that he could wander at will. After his death, when biographers began to dig for scraps of information about his youth, a collateral descendant recalled that young Ronayne (as he was most

often called) was "full of fun and mischief." In the twentieth century a resident found his name carved high on the trunk of an ancient tree.

But his idyll could not last forever. In 1840, when Patrick was twelve, his
father decided he should go to school. Many Protestant landholders in Ireland sent their sons to England for school, but Dr. Cleburne was sufficiently
stretched maintaining his position at Grange House that such an expense
was out of the question. A few years earlier, the Reverend William S. Spedding had opened a Protestant school at Greenfield only a mile or so up the
road from Grange House. Though cheaper than boarding school in England,
Spedding's school was expensive enough; the fifty-pound annual fee included
room and board, even though the school was an easy twenty-minute walk
from Grange House. Patrick's older brother, William, had been one of Spedding's first students (along with Spedding's own seven children), and he had
successfully graduated to Trinity University in the summer of 1840. That fall,
therefore, when William went off to Trinity, it was Patrick's turn to go to
Greenfield.[13]

The twelve-year-old showed up for classes in the fall of 1840 with a box
bedstead and bedding, plus "two pairs of sheets and six towels." There is no
record of his daily routine at school, but a nearby school in Youghal advertised a regimen that was probably very similar:

6–7 A.M.	Study
7–8 A.M.	Recitation
8–9 A.M.	Morning Prayer
9–12 A.M.	Classes
12–1 P.M.	Recitation
1–3 P.M.	Classes
3–5 P.M.	Walking out in company with a master
5:30–6 P.M.	Dinner
6–7 P.M.	Study
7:30 P.M.	Tea
9:00 P.M.	Evening Prayers and Bed

From this tightly structured regimen there were two respites: a two-week
vacation at Christmas and a month in the summer.[14]

As to the content of his classes, young Cleburne embarked on a program
that emphasized "the several departments of English Literature in which
Mathematics and Composition hold a prominent place." Although Spedding
held an M.A. from Trinity College and had studied both Latin and Greek,
he did not emphasize the classical languages in his curriculum. Instead he

offered classes in such unusual subjects as "drafting maps" and (for an additional fee) "drilling." It may be that Spedding's role as chaplain to the nearby Ballincollig Military Barracks lent a particularly martial tone to the program of study at Greenfield School at the expense of the classics. If so, it certainly suited his newest pupil, who later in life maintained both an interest in all things military and a thorough dislike of languages, though the latter may well have been because he never had an enthusiastic language teacher.[15]

Outside classes, Cleburne played organized games and participated in daily exercise (it was one of Spedding's goals "to strengthen and establish the constitution"). Spedding also conducted classes in "deportment" and "arrangement at the table," the civilizing refinements that would mark his students as members of a privileged class. It is not known whether Patrick's father paid the extra fee for drill instruction, though Dr. Cleburne did have a remote connection to the military barracks himself as the on-call physician for the artillerists stationed there.[16]

Along with the rest of Spedding's students, Cleburne stood for his exams each December and June just before vacation. They were oral exams, conducted in front of Spedding and a trio of learned men, generally clerics, invited to the school for the purpose. The visiting scholars asked questions "in the various departments of classical and scientific education" and assessed each student's performance. The exams were an ordeal for young Cleburne, who was shy in public situations. Although Spedding announced that the results of these exams "afforded much satisfaction" to the examiners, it could not be disguised that his young charges were weak in the classics. Spedding knew that he could not hope to compete successfully with other boys' schools in Ireland or England until he could provide a better grounding in Greek and Latin, the fundamental components of a formal nineteenth-century education. In the spring of 1843, therefore, during Cleburne's third year at the school, Spedding hired another young tutor, William E. Marshall, a recent graduate of Dublin University, who was a classics scholar. Spedding rushed to the newspapers to advertise his new faculty member as someone who could teach both Latin and Greek. But young Patrick Cleburne never took a class from the new master, for late that summer Dr. Cleburne fell ill, and in the late fall, at the age of fifty-one, he died.[17]

His father's death was not only a personal catastrophe for young Patrick, now age fifteen and technically an orphan, it was also a financial catastrophe for the family. Deprived of her husband's income as a physician, the young widow (she was twenty-eight) could hardly hope to meet the annual payments on Grange House. She had the £90 that came from land rents and the £36 that continued to be paid to her stepchildren from her predecessor's dowry, but that could not be stretched to pay the £230 annual rent. Expenses had to be cut and at once. Patrick's older brother, William, returned from Trinity where he had been studying engineering, and Patrick dropped out of Greenfield School. Most likely the young pupil had mixed feelings about leaving school, later telling a friend that Spedding was "a man of harsh measures and forbidding manners."[18]

William became the putative master of the estate and was determined to make it a self-sustaining enterprise. For his part, Patrick appreciated that his continued presence at Grange House would be, as he told Issy, "little else than an encumbrance." Better to leave home and attempt to make his own way in the world. He accepted a proffered apprenticeship with Dr. Thomas H. Justice, a colleague of his late father, who had a thriving medical practice in Mallow, twenty miles north of Cork. As an apprentice, Patrick would earn no money to send home, but at least he would save his family the cost of his own board, as well as the fifty pounds per year that no longer had to be paid to Reverend Spedding. So at age fifteen, Patrick left the rural tranquillity of Grange House and Ovens Township for the bustling city of Mallow. It was the end of his boyhood; he would return to Grange House only for brief visits, and he would never again call the rolling farmland west of Cork "home."[19]

Mallow was a small town compared to Cork, but it was a metropolis compared to rural Ovens Township, and it was Patrick Cleburne's first experience of living in a city surrounded by people who were strangers. Here he was no longer the doctor's son, the young master from Grange House, but an aspiring apprentice, dependent from day to day on the goodwill or the bad moods of his employer. The specifics of young Cleburne's financial arrangement with Dr. Justice have not survived, but typically he would have traveled rounds with the doctor, mixed the various powders and medicines as required, and, if necessary, made deliveries, all in exchange for room, board, and an opportunity to learn about the practice of medicine. Fundamentally shy by nature, he did not make friends quickly or easily. A decade later he described himself as "constantly mingling with strange people and making few attachments," which could still pass as a description of city life. He lived quietly and within himself, dutifully fulfilling his obligations and observing life around him; it is almost certain that he was occasionally lonely.[20]

But Cleburne's diffident demeanor hid a surprisingly strong inner confidence in his abilities. He worked hard and learned quickly. Before long, Dr. Justice began to entrust the mixing of most medicines to his conscientious young assistant who now aspired to a career in the field. After only a year of service with Dr. Justice, Cleburne mailed a formal application for admission as a student to the Apothecaries Hall in Dublin. His application was rejected. Undeterred, he applied again in the spring but was again rejected. Disappointed, he remained in Mallow, watching, mixing, and learning but ambitious to make his own way.[21]

While the teenaged Pat Cleburne learned to mix medicines in Mallow, the political climate in which he lived reached a new level of volatility. Having obtained Catholic Emancipation, Daniel O'Connell and his supporters began a public campaign for a repeal of the Act of Union, the instrument that had combined the Irish and English Parliaments in 1801 to create the United Kingdom. What O'Connell wanted was an independent Irish Parliament. He was careful never to suggest complete independence from the Crown, and he was ever full of praise for Queen Victoria (whom he called "the darlin' little Queen"), but he was steadfast in his insistence that Ireland deserved its own parliament. In pursuit of this goal, he organized and hosted a series of mass public meetings in the early 1840s. These came to be known as Monster Meetings, not only for their size but because such a term suggested the feeling they engendered in Irish conservatives. The Irish upper class abhorred the ideal of repeal in part because of its character as a mass popular movement.[22]

Two of the largest of O'Connell's Monster Meetings took place in Cork in the spring of 1843 just before Patrick left the area for Mallow. The Butter Weighhouse in Cork was the scene of a large indoor meeting in May, and a month later more than half a million people showed up for a gigantic outdoor meeting on Sidney Hill just outside Cork. The influx of repeal advocates swelled Cork to five times its normal size. The show of support was awesome, and the Catholic *Examiner* praised both the public enthusiasm and the high tone of the meeting, congratulating attendees on the absence of public drunkenness. (The conservative Cork *Constitution,* meanwhile, sniffed that the meeting attracted only "the dregs of the city.") Addressing this huge assembly, O'Connell made a largely emotional appeal, casting the issue of repeal in terms of freedom and slavery: "Ireland! Land of my fathers. Ireland! Birthplace of my children. Ireland! That shall hold my grave. Ireland! That I love with the fondest aspirations, your men are too brave, your women are too beautiful and good, you are too elevated among the nations of the earth, too moral, too religious, to be *slaves.* I promise you that you shall be free!" O'Connell's speech provoked "the very ecstacy of joyous delirium" among his supporters and struck fear into the hearts of his opponents, who felt that his cause and his remarks were seditious. In October he was arrested, found guilty, and sentenced to a year in prison. Although his conviction was overturned after ten weeks, his spirit and his health were broken, and the repeal movement foundered.[23]

The teen-aged Pat Cleburne, living and working for the first time in a city away from his family, could not have avoided exposure to the issues of the repeal campaign. Did O'Connell's demagoguery repel him, as it did most upper-class Protestants? Or did he see this issue the way his father had viewed the emancipation question, as a matter of fairness and political freedom? O'Connell portrayed the "slavery" of the Irish using the same kind of rhetoric that southern fire-eaters would employ in the 1850s to protest the "slavery" of the South to the North. If the notion of national independence as a political birthright touched a chord in the young Patrick Cleburne, he left no record of it.

Whatever his reaction to the rise and fall of the repeal movement, Cleburne could not remain untouched by the next great crisis that befell the Irish. This time it was not politics—it was famine. Precarious as life was for most Irish, even the poorest generally had enough food to survive. They did not partake of the crops they grew for their landlords: the barley, wheat, and oats that were exported to England to make the breads and puddings of the working class there. Most Irishmen would not have known how to go about turning oats or wheat into palatable food anyway. They relied on the potato— roasted, boiled, fried, baked, or stewed, the potato was the staple crop that fed them all; about a third of the population relied exclusively on the potato. Then in the fall of 1845, some of the recently harvested potatoes began to show signs of blight—soft dark spots on the outside, signifying that the inside had turned to a putrid black mush. The culprit was a fungus, *phytophthora infestans,* whose spores were borne by the wind and which settled on the maturing crop, damp from the morning or evening dew. Within hours the fungus penetrated the tubers and began to spread with remarkable and terrifying speed.[24]

There had been small outbreaks of potato blight before, and it had caused terrible distress, but never before had it spread so widely, never had it so utterly destroyed the crop on which the Irish peasants depended for survival. Ironically, it was a good harvest year otherwise. The ships carrying grain left Cobh Harbor as usual, their holds stuffed with the fruits of a year's labor. But the Irish peasants did not eat the grains they harvested because that was how they paid their rent. Without rents, they would be forced off the land. They could not afford to *buy* the grain they grew, even if they knew how to grind, mill, process, and bake it into bread, which they did not. So the grain harvest was exported to England, and the Irish who had harvested it starved.

The government in London at first shrugged off the news of a potato blight. Tired of the constant tales of woe from Ireland, many Englishmen assumed that the real problem was the inherent laziness of the Irish. Finally, however, the evidence of widespread starvation became too overwhelming to ignore, and the government acted, establishing a program of public works, mostly the building of roads, to employ the needy. This program had two inherent flaws. First, it was not money the Irish needed but food. Even if they had money, there was hardly any food for them to purchase. Second, the program was to be paid for by taxes levied on the landlords. The logic of this was unassailable: the same people who enjoyed a lordly lifestyle off the rents collected by their land managers were to assume the responsibility of their station and help relieve their tenants from the threat of starvation. Taxes would therefore be levied in accordance with the number of tenants on an estate. As might have been predicted, however, many landlords responded to this news by driving their tenants off the land to reduce their obligation.[25]

The weaknesses of the government's policy became manifest almost at once. Local communities voted for an astonishing number of work projects, often authorizing new roads where none were needed; County Cork alone requested £600,000 for new roads. Hundreds of thousands of poor Irishmen set to work with a will, but when they were paid there was still nothing for them to eat. Moreover, landlords began to evict their nonpaying tenants off the land, turning them out of their homes with no more than the clothes on their backs. By the winter of 1845–1846, Ireland was filled with families that were both starving and homeless; Cork was clogged by 5,000 beggars who died at the rate of a hundred a week.[26]

Unlike the thousands of landless poor, seventeen-year-old Pat Cleburne did not go hungry. As a member of the gentry, he did not face the prospect of imminent starvation. But the potato famine did affect him, as it affected everyone in Ireland. Though there was plenty of illness in that bitter winter of 1845–1846, there was less money to pay doctors, and Dr. Justice found that his apprentice, who had been with him for two years, was a luxury he could no longer easily afford. Encouraged by these circumstances to consider other options, Patrick felt that he could not go home, for like other landlords in Ireland, the Cleburnes were burdened by the new taxes designed to relieve the distress of the truly poor. Patrick's brother William found that he could not easily pay the new levies and still manage the £230 annual rent. He might have raised the rents on his own tenants or tried to find new ones, but since no one had any money, it all seemed hopeless. Sooner or later, and probably sooner, the family would have to give up Grange House and find less grandiose quarters. As far as Patrick Cleburne was concerned, going home was not a realistic or acceptable alternative.[27]

With few options available to him, he resolved to travel to Dublin and present himself physically at the door of the Apothecaries Hall. He would convince the masters that his years of practical training in Mallow qualified him for admission. He made the trip by coach in the depth of the unhappiest winter in Irish history, arriving in cold, gray Dublin in mid-February 1846. But his determination was unavailing. The practical experience he had gained as an apprentice was insufficient to compensate for his inability to read Latin. The Reverend Spedding's emphasis on drill and mapmaking at the expense of the classics doomed the young aspirant to failure. He was again denied admission. Unwilling to return to Mallow, and knowing that his own family could not comfortably support him at Grange House, Cleburne made a life-altering decision. He decided to join the army.[28]

Patrick Cleburne had spent much of his youth living within a mile or two of the Ballincollig Military Barracks where his father was the physician on call and where his schoolmaster was the chaplain. He had almost certainly watched the public parades of the Royal Artillery Company in which the polished brass guns were drawn by teams of horses. And who could fail to be impressed by the soldiers, kitted out in their glittering blue and gold uniforms? Then, too, the command that Cleburne now joined, the British 41st Regiment of Foot, was officially assigned to the garrison of Madras on the east coast of India, 5,000 miles away and only thirteen degrees from the equator. The regiment had returned to Ireland in the summer of 1843 but was scheduled to go back to India again in the spring. The opportunity to wear a smart uniform and travel to an exotic land with a tropical climate where, as far as he knew, there was no famine was apparently irresistible.[29]

Cleburne enlisted in the British army on 27 February 1846, two weeks short of his eighteenth birthday. He lied about his age—understandable under the circumstances—but he also lied about his place of birth and his profession, which he listed as "laborer," the standard entry for the untrained and uneducated Irishmen who made up much of the rank and file of the 41st. He claimed later that he concealed his identity so that his family could not find out where he was. He told friends that he was ashamed of having failed to gain admission to the college of Apothecaries Hall and believed that he had disgraced his family. But whatever his motive, his decision to disappear into the ranks of the army without notifying his family was a self-indulgent act. His stepmother and siblings did not find out what had happened to him for nearly eighteen months, and they learned of his whereabouts only when a friend of the family, an officer in the 41st, informed Isabella Cleburne that

Patrick was a soldier in his regiment. Even then, when his stepmother and others wrote to him, Cleburne seldom replied. His lame excuse was that "the manner in which a soldier lives but ill suits him for a correspondent."[30]

If Cleburne had thought his enlistment would take him to the tropical climate of Madras, he was very soon disappointed. The worsening famine contributed to an increase of brigandage in Ireland as the starving peasants became desperate, and landlords called upon the army for protection. At the same time, many of the landlords insisted that the army evict unwanted tenants from their land. As a result, the 41st did not return to Madras but remained in Ireland as a reinforcement for the local constabulary. The men of the 41st were dispatched in small units across the countryside, marching here and there in response to constant calls for protection. Instead of escaping to warmer and less troubled climes, Cleburne found himself in the ranks of an army of occupation. Years later, describing his life in the British army to a friend, Cleburne claimed that "the life of a soldier on home service was nothing but a round of duties, monotonous and unromantic in the extreme."[31]

Neither did Cleburne's army service erase the loneliness he had felt in Mallow. He soon perceived that the British army was an institution deeply rooted in tradition and ritual. It was simple enough to survive so long as he behaved exactly like everyone else and did not expose himself to ridicule or persecution by betraying his inner feelings, particularly any sentimentality. To Issy he described army life as "a state of society where duty is paramount to every consideration, & kindred ties but little respected, where every feeling of a softer nature is accounted a contemptible weakness." A man who was already diffident by nature, he became even more so. A longtime friend wrote later that in the British army Cleburne "learned to govern himself." Concealing his feelings "from outward observation," he became a largely anonymous soldier in the ranks of the 41st Foot.[32]

After two years of relative anonymity in the ranks, Cleburne was promoted to the rank of corporal in recognition of his general good conduct. Though proud of his stripes, he did not keep them long. When the regiment was ordered out for drill not long afterward, the new corporal sought to avoid shouldering the heavy knapsack (which weighed over twenty pounds when fully loaded) by stuffing his with a pillow. Hours later, well into the drill period, Cleburne was horrified to hear the order, "Inspection knapsacks!" In recalling the incident years later, he was philosophical about it: "There was no help for it; the pillow was found and I was a corporal no longer."[33]

The weather was unseasonably cool in the spring of 1846. Though the frosty weather was doubtless cursed by the soldiers of the 41st who had to turn out for morning inspection in the predawn darkness, it was good news for the potato crop. The cold, dry air killed the fungus spores and nourished a hope that the potato famine was over. Unfortunately the cool spring was followed by a wet summer, and the ominous reappearance of the black patches on the maturing tubers foretold a renewal of the blight and another year of forced evictions, underfunded works projects, and desperation. Thousands died. Thousands more, stripped finally of the last of their hope, sold themselves to the captains of emigration ships, offering whatever they had left to secure a tiny corner of space in the crowded hold of a ship bound for Canada or America, ships that soon came to be known universally as death ships. They fled from one desperation into another, with no guarantee of a better life at the end of the voyage but certain that there was no hope left in Ireland.[34]

The sense of desperation touched the Cleburnes at Grange House as well. Although William had brought additional acres into cultivation, the harvest was poor and prices stayed low because so few could pay. The additional tax burden, designed to provide poor relief, took whatever profits there were. Patrick's stepmother concluded that further attempts to support the family by farming the lands around Grange House were hopeless. It had become evident, as William wrote to a cousin in America, that "the present high rent rates and taxes—accompanied by low prices and bad produce—would soon divest us of any property we possess." The social fabric was unraveling as well. Only a few miles away, several hundred desperate parishoners armed with pikes and scythes had seized the corn crop on the Colthurst Estate and had begun to carry it away when the constabulary arrived. A melee ensued in which several were wounded and a score more arrested. As matriarch of the family, Isabella resolved to move everyone to America—not on one of the aptly named death ships but as cabin passengers.[35]

She told Patrick of her plan during one of his infrequent visits home in the summer of 1849. Her proposal held forth the promise of both adventure and opportunity. Patrick could see for himself that "the prospects in this country are anything but good; and experience goes very far to prove that they will not be better." Moreover such an adventure would give him a chance to prove "somewhat more useful" to the family than he had been so far. He accepted the idea at once and even volunteered to go first, as a kind of scout. He wrote to Issy that "if Mamma has made up her mind to go, the best plan would be to go as soon as possible, but not without sending some of us in advance so as not to be wholly ignorant of the manner of business in that country."[36]

Of course there was still the matter of his obligation to the 41st Foot. The vast majority of Irish soldiers in the British army enlisted for life, and it was expected that anyone desiring to abandon his responsibility as a Queen's soldier would compensate Her Majesty's government for all that it had provided him. In effect, it meant purchasing a discharge. A year earlier such a requirement would have meant that Cleburne was trapped. But he had turned twenty-one in March and had thereupon inherited his share of the remnant of Mary Ann Ronayne's original wedding dowry, which gave him the twenty pounds he needed to buy his way out of the army. Though Cleburne was again promoted to corporal effective 1 July, he nevertheless left the army with hardly a backward glance. Four years later he congratulated himself that he had made good his escape. Had he remained in the army, he wrote his stepmother, "I would now be a poor servile mercenary without a will or a thought of my own, in some soul cramping fortress or barracks. . . . I should at best in my old age hold the commission of a petty officer, detested by inferiors, and looked down upon by superiors."[37]

Corporal Cleburne was released from his service in the 41st Foot on 22 September 1849. Twelve days later, he joined William, Anne, and Joseph on board the sailing bark *Bridgetown* in Cobh Harbor. Although 258 steerage passengers jammed the hold below the water line, these four paying customers occupied private cabins. For them, the seven weeks crossing the Atlantic was more of a holiday than a desperate flight from starvation. As the hills of his native land dipped below the eastern horizon, the twenty-one-year-old Patrick Cleburne said goodbye with few regrets. "The elements of decay and destruction," he wrote home to his stepmother some time later, "seemed to me to be so deeply seated in the heart of the body social or politic that to stay would only be to witness a lingering dissolution." Unwilling to try any longer to make his mark in such a society, he leaped at the opportunity to create a place for himself in the New World.[38]

His years in Erin had marked him. His three years under Reverend Spedding, his lonely two years in Mallow, and his anonymous three and one half years in the British army had made him wary and bequeathed to him the ability to adjust to new circumstances. The Patrick Cleburne who took passage for America in 1849 bore little resemblance to the nineteenth-century stereotype of the bluff and hearty Irishman. He was cool and reserved, for life had taught him that it was not always a good idea to draw attention to oneself. But his ambition continued to burn. In Ireland he had become intimately aware of how artificial barriers could kill ambition: barriers against Catholics in public office, against young apprentices who could not read

Latin, and against promotion into the officer corps from the ranks of the British army. He was going now to a land where he believed few such barriers existed. Quietly confident and fiercely ambitious, he eagerly looked forward to making his mark in America.

2
HELENA, ARKANSAS

Pat Cleburne was one of over 2 million Irishmen who emigrated to the United States in the early 1850s. Although he was unlike most of them in his social status and his religious affiliation, he was in other ways typical: eager for success, willing to go to great lengths to achieve it, and willing, too, to adapt himself to the mores and values of his new home. In America Pat Cleburne embarked on a determined campaign to achieve financial success, then social success, and finally political success. In the process, he became so thoroughly a part of his adopted society that in the midst of a national crisis, when his community believed that its very existence was imperiled, he joined his friends and neighbors and went to war to defend it.

He first espied the shores of his adopted country on Christmas Day, 1849, when the *Bridgetown* entered the mouth of the Mississippi and threaded its way upriver past the green swamplands on either bank to dock at the New Orleans levee the next day. With its Spanish-French-Creole heritage, New Orleans was the most exotic city Pat Cleburne had ever seen. Even so, of the four Cleburne siblings, only William planned to make this multicultural metropolis a permanent home. Before leaving Ireland, he had solicited a letter of introduction from the manager of the Ballincollig Gunpowder Mill to the president of the tiny Louisiana-based Carrollton Railroad who, he hoped, would offer him a job. The other Cleburnes saw New Orleans only as a stopover. They were bound upriver for Ohio, home of their distant cousin, Patrick Ronayne Cashman, who had written that there were opportunities aplenty in the great American Midwest for those willing to work hard and make their way.[1]

Patrick left first, taking passage for Cincinnati on a northbound river steamer. He was followed two days later by Anne and Joseph and not long afterward by William as well when he failed to secure the job he had expected in New Orleans. Reunited briefly in Cincinnati, the family soon split up for good. William found a job with the Union Pacific Railroad in Milwaukee, where he met and later married Eliza Thomisine, herself an Irish immigrant from County Limerick. Joseph, the youngest of the four, moved west to LaPorte, Indiana, to pursue another job opportunity. Anne stayed in Cincinnati, where she found work as a milliner. She, too, fell in love and soon married, becoming Mrs. James Sherlock and a lifelong resident of Cincinnati.[2]

Patrick also found work. He became a clerk in Thomas Salter's drugstore on Broadway, in one of the more elegant sections of Cincinnati, filling and delivering prescriptions and generally performing most of the tasks he had learned as a doctor's apprentice in Mallow. He remained in this job through the winter, sleeping and taking his meals in a public boardinghouse belonging to a Mrs. Hanson. With a population of over 115,000, Cincinnati was a thriving, bustling city with paved, tree-lined streets and handsome brick buildings. Patrick was pleased enough to have found work there, although it was a job with only modest prestige and with little hope of advancement.[3]

Then in the early spring, Salter told Cleburne of a job that proved to be just the opportunity he was seeking. Salter introduced him to a Mr. Freeman who had recently sold a drugstore in Helena, Arkansas, to two doctors. The doctors were looking for a man to manage the store, and they had asked Freeman to keep an eye out for a likely candidate. Was Cleburne interested? Indeed he was. He summarized his qualifications, and Freeman was sufficiently impressed that he wrote the young Irishman a letter of introduction. Armed with that letter but with no guarantees that it would get him the job, Cleburne booked passage on a southbound river steamer for Helena.[4]

The county seat of prosperous Phillips County, Helena was a small town (population 600) that was in the midst of a metamorphosis from frontier village to bustling commercial center. Founded only thirty years earlier, Helena was not much older than Cleburne himself, and it reflected the youthful bellicosity and respect for individual self-reliance that were characteristic of the American frontier. Cleburne described it as "the haunt of the most reckless, desperate, characters in the Mississippi Valley," a place where "pistol and bowie knife decided every quarrel." Here there were no old established families, and the social order was almost exclusively a product of personal wealth. Indeed, there were only two social classes within the white population: the rich, who made up the political and social elite, and those who intended to become rich soon—an ambition shared by the eager young Irishman who arrived in Helena with little to his name except a cowhide trunk full of old clothes, an army sword, and a pair of boxing gloves.[5]

Cleburne disembarked at Helena's busy waterfront along Front Street early on the morning of All Fools' Day, 1850. He was met by a thin, fragile-looking young man with a luxuriant beard and prominent ears who introduced himself as Dr. Charles Nash. After treating Cleburne to breakfast at nearby Fadley's Hotel, Nash escorted him along dirt streets to the drugstore on Rightor Street, only a short walk from the steamboat landing. There Cleburne met Nash's partner, Dr. Hector Grant, and the store's young apprentice, Joe Maxey. The two doctors explained to Cleburne that what they needed most was "a competent prescriptionist," but in addition they wanted someone who could manage the business end of the enterprise, for neither of them wanted to take time from his medical practice to supervise the day-to-day routine of running the store. Cleburne responded that he felt fully competent to act as an apothecary but admitted that he had "a limited experience in financial matters" and suggested that the doctors allow him to "take the position on trial for a month." As to his salary, Cleburne told them, "I will leave it up to you." They were impressed and offered him room and board and fifty dollars a month.[6]

Cleburne began work the next day, and he set to work with an enthusiasm that may have astonished (and almost certainly exhausted) his busy young apprentice. He completely reorganized the store, relabeling all the glass bottles "with fresh gilt edge labels" and redesigning the showcase in the window. By the end of the month Nash and Grant decided that they had just the man they wanted, and they made the appointment permanent. Indeed, Cleburne and Nash soon became fast friends. Although Dr. Grant was married and lived several blocks away, Nash was a bachelor and shared a room with Cleburne above the store so that the two men were roommates as well as business associates. Theirs was a mutually beneficial relationship. Cleburne adopted Nash as his mentor in a determined campaign to advance himself not only economically but also socially. In exchange, Cleburne stood up for his employer more than once in confrontations that, in frontier Helena, might have become life-threatening.[7]

On one such occasion, Nash was threatened with bodily harm after he had been instrumental in organizing a public protest against a visiting Mormon missionary. As a result of Nash's efforts, the missionary was ordered to cease his public exhortations and leave town, and he came into the drugstore promising to "get even" with Nash. Cleburne was present, of course, and thinking that the man was about to reach for a pistol, he leaped over the counter, grabbed the startled Mormon by his coat, and threw him bodily out of the store, saying, according to Nash, "If you ever come in again I will serve you worse."[8] For his part, Nash sponsored Cleburne in what passed for polite society in Helena. The fluid society of frontier Helena provided as much opportunity as any town in America for an ambitious young immigrant. The aristocratic pretensions of Virginia or South Carolina had not made their way west to Arkansas where membership in the upper class depended more on one's individual effort and talent than on family lineage. But Cleburne suffered from two particular handicaps in his campaign: he was painfully shy—particularly with women—and he was Irish.

Irish jokes were as much a staple of American humor in Arkansas as they were in Boston or New York, and Irishmen fresh off the boat were often the butt of popular jokes. Local papers occasionally filled the space between news stories with anecdotes about simpleminded Irishmen (inevitably named Pat) who liked to drink, fight, and steal but whose shenanigans seldom brought them any benefit, for they were also laughably naive. The humor tended to be good-natured rather than vicious, but the effect was to reinforce a popular stereotype that made Cleburne's campaign for acceptance and social position an uphill struggle. The following, from a contemporary Helena newspaper, is representative:

> Two Irishmen were in prison—one for stealing a cow, the other for stealing a watch. "Mike," said the cow stealer one day, "what o'clock is it?"
> "Och, Pat, I haven't my watch handy but I think it's near milking time."

Cleburne not only spoke with an Irish accent, he bore the archetypal name of "Pat." Although he was occasionally the victim of jokes or pranks, he made each such occasion a learning experience, and he never made the same mistake twice.[9]

He learned one lesson soon after he began working at the drugstore. In June, when the summer harvests were coming into town, Cleburne noticed several wagonloads of a large green fruit that he had never seen before and asked the apprentice, Joe Maxey, what it was. Maxey told Cleburne they were watermelons and that Cleburne should buy one, for they were delicious. Cleburne purchased a melon from a farmer and asked Maxey how to prepare it. Seeing his opportunity, the apprentice responded mischievously, "You must stew it." Cleburne accordingly got out the brass kettle and started a fire in the stove. He cut up the melon and dropped the pieces in the steaming water. As it began to bubble, Cleburne asked Maxey about serving this delicacy. Spinning out the hoax, Maxey told him, "Put it into dishes and eat it with a spoon." Cleburne served out several portions, and when Grant and Nash came into the store, he proudly announced that he had prepared a special treat. The astonished doctors viewed the product of Cleburne's efforts with undisguised disappointment, and they remonstrated that no one should ever stew a watermelon. At that, Maxey dashed out the door laughing with Cleburne hard on his heels.[10]

Such incidents demonstrated to Cleburne how much he had to learn, and his first eighteen months in Helena were marked by a personal campaign not only to fit in but to advance himself economically and socially. In the best tradition of American immigrants, he studied the society of which he had become a part in order to learn its mores and values. Then he internalized those values and made them his own—or at least most of them. He learned to ride, to hunt, and, when necessary, to fight. But he did not drink. He tried social drinking with his new associates but found that he could not do it; drinking made him lose control over himself. "Instead of making Cleburne jovial," Nash recorded, "it made him angry, and, as he said, crazy." After one drinking bout in particular, Cleburne threatened to kill Nash for waking him, and only later, after he had sobered up, did he realize how close he had come to murdering his patron. Distressed by such episodes, and determined not to be marked down as merely another drunken Irishman, he became a teetotaler.[11]

The first objective in his campaign of self-improvement, and a necessary precondition to social advancement, was economic success. Having arrived in Helena with but a few dollars to his name, Cleburne worked hard to make the drugstore a thriving concern. He managed to save most of his salary, for he had few expenses. For a year he lived rent-free above the store, and when Nash married Francis Epps (Dr. Grant's sister-in-law) in April 1851 and moved to a house in town, Cleburne moved as well, becoming a full-time boarder in the Nash household. He might have sent a portion of his salary back to Ireland, but there is no evidence that he did so. When, in December 1851, Dr. Grant announced that he wished to sell his interest in the store, Nash encouraged Cleburne to buy it, and Grant willingly accepted terms that made it possible. Cleburne paid Grant $350 as a down payment, with the balance of $1,150 to be paid over the next twelve months. Cleburne thus leaped from clerk to entrepreneur, a huge step up the economic and social ladder. The next month, the Helena *Southern Shield* announced the new company of "Nash and Cleburne, Wholesale & Retail Druggists." They advertised "Drugs, Medicines, Chemicals, Perfumeries, Paints, Oils & Dyestuffs" and invited the public to "call and see us." Cleburne's hand was evident in the boast that "our store has been newly fitted up, and new fixtures added."[12]

Cleburne's investment was nearly wiped out in the fall of 1852 by a fire that consumed more than half the town. Helena was built mostly of wood, and its citizens lacked the means to fight a large-scale fire. As a result, Cleburne and the rest of the population of Helena could do little more than drag their most valued possessions down to the riverbank for safety and watch the town burn. The fire was eventually quenched by a driving rain, but that same rain also ruined much of what had been saved from the fire. The drugstore was badly damaged, but like other businesses in town, Nash and Cleburne rebuilt and life went on. Cleburne was philosophical about it. To his step-mother he wrote, "I have no reason to complain."[13]

Cleburne began to advance socially as well, although he was handicapped by an innate personal shyness that was particularly evident in mixed company. Indeed, the presence of young women often reduced him to speechlessness. That shy exterior, however, sheltered the soul of a genuine romantic and more than one contemporary described him as "dreamy" or "absent minded." He idealized women and endowed them with almost mystical qualities. As a result, even a casual encounter with a young lady became elevated in his mind to the status of a great romance. To one young woman with whom he shared an afternoon walk in May 1854 he penned an insipid and guileless poem:

> Tell me, do your footsteps still
>   Rome to yonder shady hill
> Where the sweet May apple flowers
>   Neath the pretty dogwood bowers
> Where the Mock bird's varied song
>   Echoes sweet th[r]o woods among
> First we met near yonder hill
>   And fancy paints that meeting still[14]

He had more success in his campaign to secure membership in Helena's emerging political elite. He attended the small Episcopal Church, a natural enough decision for someone who had grown up in the Church of Ireland but desirable as well because it was attended by the "respectable and influential members of society." He joined the literary club, where he read books on history and biography, and he became a member of the town's debating society, where he rubbed shoulders and exchanged opinions with the county's lawyers and politicians. He formed a chess club and became its first president. Finally, he sought membership in Helena's Masonic Lodge.[15]

Nationally, the Masons were a prestigious Protestant social and political organization whose past members included both George Washington and Thomas Jefferson. In Helena it was the premier men's club and "nearly all the respectable male members of the town" belonged, so that for Cleburne membership was an essential step toward full acceptance in the community. Nash sponsored Cleburne's application for membership, and he became a member in good standing in 1852 soon after making the jump from shop clerk to shop owner. He was particularly committed, never missed a meeting, and quickly became a leader in the local lodge. He was elected master early in 1853, and later that year he "took the sublime degree of Royal Arch Mason" conferred upon him at a special ceremony by Arkansas luminary Albert Pike.[16]

Each summer, the Helena Masonic lodge joined with lodges from Mississippi for an annual convention, and the delegates chose a prominent member to deliver the keynote speech. In 1853, Cleburne won a close vote to be selected as the principal speaker at the June convention. It was his first public speech, and it is easy to imagine that he was nervous. In a forceful and direct style, he offered a talk dominated by high-minded platitudes about the principles of the Masonic order, "Brotherly love, friendship, charity, and truth," and he managed to please the audience. His friend Nash thought he "acquitted himself handsomely."[17]

By the end of his first eighteen months in America, Cleburne had carved out a comfortable and respectable niche for himself in Helena. No longer the butt of Irish jokes or the victim of pranks, he had become co-owner as well as manager of the drugstore on Rightor Street, a prominent member of the Episcopal Church, grand master of the Masonic Lodge, and had made a successful debut as a public speaker. It is a tribute to the success of Cleburne's campaign that in its story on the Masonic convention the Helena *Southern Shield* commented that although the principal speaker was "from over the water," he was "thoroughly Americanized."[18]

Of course the most elevated personages in Helena were not the town merchants, however successful or Americanized they might be; the richest citizens of Helena were all cotton planters. Arkansas in the 1850s was in the midst of a transformation from a frontier society to a cotton culture, and even those who made their money in other enterprises often invested in cotton land and the construction of a "great house." Cotton production in Phillips County increased fivefold during the decade (from 5,165 bales in 1850 to 26,993 in 1860). One modern analyst has calculated that of the 128 persons in Phillips County during the 1850s who could be defined as "elite," 126 were landowners and 127 were slaveowners. Even Nash and Grant bought cotton plantations nearby, in part because of the enormous profits that could be made growing cotton. But men also sought membership in the cotton aristocracy for the social cachet that it brought, for cotton was the currency of social as well as economic success.[19]

That being the case, it is noteworthy that the socially ambitious Cleburne did not seek membership in this elite society. Tempting as it may be to see in this some evidence of his disdain for human slavery, the answer seems to lie elsewhere. First of all, entry into the ranks of the planter class required a significant capital investment, and although Cleburne's economic status rose steadily through the 1850s, so did the price of land and slaves. Successful as he was, he never quite reached the economic plateau that would have allowed him to adopt the life of a planter without considerable risk. In addition, Cleburne had grown up on a gentleman's farm in Ireland and he may have remembered how difficult it had been for his brother and stepmother to make the Grange a going concern after his father's death.[20]

Cleburne did not record his private views about "the peculiar institution." He did express sympathy for "the stately sullen red man" who had experienced "unutterable woes" while being "driven before the mighty machinery of civilization to the foot of the Rocky Mountains." But nowhere in his few surviving papers from this era is there any reference to his views on slavery. Most likely, he did not think about it one way or the other. Slavery was an inherent part of the society he sought to join, one more American curiosity to be noted and acknowledged. Philosophical discussions about the blessings or evils of slavery were simply not current in Arkansas in the early 1850s; there was none of the shrill defense of the institution that characterized the more mature cotton cultures east of the Mississippi. One historian has concluded that "few people in Arkansas vigorously defended slavery—most of them merely accepted it as a part of the pattern of life." Cleburne seems to have done exactly that.[21]

Despite Cleburne's apparent unconcern about the whole issue of slavery, he was nevertheless a young man particularly susceptible to high-minded or emotional appeals. Fundamentally a romantic, he was almost completely lacking in guile or cynicism. It is not surprising, therefore, that when Helena was swept by a religious revival in the summer of 1853, Cleburne found it both moving and personally meaningful. Like many others in Helena, he fell under the spell of the Reverend Thomas R. Welch, an evangelical preacher who dominated many of the revival meetings that summer.[22]

Only a year or two older than Cleburne, Welch was both a magnetic personality in the pulpit and an affable individual in person. Welch and Cleburne soon became close friends; Welch joined Cleburne's Masonic Lodge and became its chaplain, and Cleburne attended at least some of the revival meetings in the woods outside Helena where a rude altar and rough log benches constituted the church. The simplicity of it affected Cleburne who saw a romantic purity in the notion that people could "worship God beneath his own ethereal roof." He found the whole experience strangely moving and described the scene rhapsodically: "They kneel beneath the old forest trees, while the gay paroquet shrilly cries in the lofty branches." In the wake of this experience, Cleburne became a vocal supporter of the temperance movement, and he changed his loyalty from the reserved Episcopalians to Welch's more evangelical Presbyterians, although he later returned to the Episcopal fold.[23]

Cleburne continued to be an indifferent correspondent, but that fall, when he learned that his twenty-year-old half brother Edward had died of disease on a merchantman off West Africa, he wrote a consoling letter to his stepmother that reflected his newly strengthened religious beliefs. "No son of Adam finishes his destine [*sic*] here," he wrote. "This world is but the opening scene. Yourself and Edward and the remainder of us will meet in immortality. . . . The only voice of comfort . . . is that true firm faith which tells of the not distant future when the tombs shall be burst and mothers shall take again their children to their arms."[24]

When he wrote that letter in October 1853, Cleburne was still "driving away at the Drug business." Sometime over the winter, however, he decided to abandon the drugstore and commit himself full-time to the study of law in the hope of gaining admission to the bar, which he had come to perceive as "the best avenue to distinction and civil importance" in his adopted country. Since Nash had no interest in running the store alone, the partners agreed to sell. The sale took place in April 1854, four years almost to the day after Cleburne's arrival in Helena, and he pocketed $3,000, his share of the proceeds. The money might have made a down payment on some good cotton land and a few slaves to work it, but Cleburne planned instead to live off his nest egg during the two years that he calculated it would take him to gain admission to the bar. The firm of Hanley and Alexander agreed to open its law library to him, and Cleburne said goodbye to the drugstore, though it continued for another two years to be known as "Nash and Cleburne's," and he continued to board with Dr. Nash and his family.[25]

For its size, Helena had a remarkable number of lawyers; one authority described the town as positively swarming with them. Hanley and Alexander on Elm Street was one of five major law firms in town, and there were a half dozen other attorneys who practiced independently. One reason for this plethora of lawyers was the large number of cases resulting from legal squabbles over land deals. Then, too, Helena was still a wild and wooly frontier town with more than its fair share of shootings and stabbings. Things had quieted down a bit in the four years since Cleburne's arrival; he no doubt intended to be comforting when he reassured his stepmother in the fall of 1853 that "there have been only three fights in which deadly weapons were used this year." Such an environment suggested that despite the plentitude of lawyers, there was likely to be enough business for one more.[26]

Cleburne got on well with both his law advisers. Thomas B. Hanley, known to all as Judge Hanley for his experience on the circuit court bench, was a leading Whig and perhaps the best known attorney in town. An avid reader of history and a small "d" democrat, Hanley was an admirer of Napoleon, and since the Anglophilic Cleburne reserved his admiration for Wellington, they often engaged in lengthy arguments about which of the two was the better soldier. Cleburne also got on well with the younger partner, Mark Alexander, a Virginia Whig "with the brightest prospects," who had recently migrated to Arkansas to make his fortune.[27]

That summer while he studied law, twenty-six-year-old Pat Cleburne experienced a political awakening even more powerful and life-changing than his religious renewal the previous summer. He had never been particularly political. Although he had been aware of the momentous issues that overshadowed daily life in his native Ireland, he had never been an active participant. He called himself a Whig largely because his father had been a Whig, because both of his law tutors were Whigs, and because he was aware that in America as in Ireland the "best" people were Whigs. But his adoption of the party label did not suggest any deeply held ideological principles. Events during the summer of 1854 changed all that.

The first event was the arrival in Helena of yet another lawyer, a man who would make an indelible mark on Arkansas politics and on Pat Cleburne. Thomas C. Hindman was the same age as Pat Cleburne, but in almost every other respect he was completely different. A veteran of the Mexican War where he had earned the rank of colonel, Hindman had been admitted to the Mississippi bar in 1851 at the age of twenty-three and had actively campaigned for Jefferson Davis in his bid for the governorship. Seeking new political fields to conquer, he moved to Helena in June 1854, two months after Cleburne began reading for the law. A dynamic and mercurial personality in a diminutive package (he was barely five feet tall), Hindman attracted a coterie of loyal followers and secured a public following with his dramatic oratorical style. With his "long flowing hair greased back" Hindman was a pugnacious political scrapper who seemed to one observer to be "perpetually anxious to have a duel." Even his political foes conceded that he had energy and talent, but they also charged that he was motivated entirely by personal ambition, and they feared his sharp tongue and hair-trigger temper.[28]

Cleburne probably first met Hindman at the Helena Independence Day picnic in 1854, a daylong community celebration punctuated by numerous public speeches by local leaders. After a series of scheduled speeches about freedom, independence, and economic growth, a Whig politician from Mississippi named James Alcorn mounted the podium to offer a distinctly partisan address. The crowd thought that a Democrat should make a reply, and Nash was one of several men who called upon Hindman, who had already delivered a talk on the benefits of railroad construction, to take up the challenge. Hindman thereupon delivered a two-hour extemporaneous harangue that was even more partisan than Alcorn's. At the end of it, the Democrats in the audience were cheering and the Whigs squirming.[29]

Not everyone in town appreciated Hindman's invective. The next day, he was outside Fadley's Hotel discussing the previous day's speeches with several others when a Whig lawyer named David Badham taunted him, calling him "my sweet scented individual." True to his combative personality, Hindman "made a grab" at Badham, and when he was physically restrained, he flung abusive insults instead. Badham felt he had to respond and sent a formal challenge through his friend and fellow Whig Mark Alexander, Cleburne's legal associate. Hindman accepted the challenge and chose bowie knives as the weapon. At this point, Badham and Alexander may have begun to appreciate that they had cornered a wildcat. Badham was likely to be badly cut up, if not killed, in a knife fight with the fierce and wiry Hindman. They sought some way to call off the fight without a loss of honor, and Alexander appealed to Cleburne to play the role of peacemaker.[30]

Cleburne succeeded in effecting a reconciliation on this occasion, but Hindman could not stay out of trouble, for, as a contemporary noted, "Hindman had a wonderful talent to get into fusses." In January, he managed to offend the Whig editor of the *Arkansas State Gazette,* Charles C. Danley. In consequence, two of Danley's friends confronted Hindman in the statehouse in Little Rock, and after an acrimonious exchange, one of them drew a pistol. Hindman drew his own weapon and fired at both men, hitting one of them in the arm. He was arrested and tried but found not guilty by reason of self-defense. The sympathetic *Democratic Star* claimed that "Hindman not only did right in shooting . . . but acted prudently as any reasonable man could under the circumstances."[31]

Prudent and reasonable, however, were words that few others would use to describe Thomas C. Hindman. He was confrontational, uncompromising, and unrelenting. In comparing him to Cleburne, Nash claimed that "there was never two men more dissimilar." Yet that spring Hindman and Cleburne became not only friends but close political associates. Cleburne, the shy and reserved lifelong Whig, became the leading lieutenant of Hindman, the fire-breathing Democrat and street brawler. Two events led to this remarkable association: the passage of the Kansas-Nebraska Act, which sounded the death knell of the Whig Party, and the emergence of the Know-Nothing Party in Arkansas.[32]

The Kansas-Nebraska Act was the brainchild of Illinois senator Stephen A. Douglas, who hoped by its passage to encourage the construction of a transcontinental railroad from Chicago to the West Coast. He sought to avoid the whole question of the status of slavery in Kansas and Nebraska by suggesting that the residents of those territories be allowed to vote for or against slavery at some unspecified future moment, a doctrine called popular sovereignty. But southerners noted that popular sovereignty would not work in Kansas and Nebraska because the Missouri Compromise of 1820 banned slavery from those territories. How could there be a fair test of popular sovereignty, they asked, unless both slaveholders and nonslaveholders were allowed to emigrate there? Needing southern support for his bill, Douglas conceded the point and added a rider to his proposal that repealed the exclusionary clause of the Missouri Compromise. He was not worried about this concession because he was convinced that slavery could not prosper in Kansas or Nebraska anyway due to the climate. Still, the Kansas-Nebraska Act had the effect of opening up territories to slavery where previously it had been banned. The passage of the act renewed the national debate about what role, if any, the national government should play in legislating about slavery in the territories.[33]

The political ramifications of the Kansas-Nebraska Act were enormous. It tore the Whig Party in half, with a southern wing ("Cotton Whigs") supporting the act, and a northern wing ("Conscience Whigs") opposing it. Most of the latter soon joined the new Republican Party, which announced its unqualified opposition to the extension of slavery into any of the western territories. Other former Whigs, casting about for a new political home, joined the American Party, better known as the Know-Nothings.

Nationally, the Know-Nothing movement grew out of the disgruntlement of Americans who feared and resented the recent influx of foreign immigrants, especially German and Irish Catholics. It began as a collection of nativist organizations with names like the American Brotherhood, the American Protestant Association, and most commonly, the Order of the Star Spangled Banner. Collected under a political umbrella as the American Party, the movement's objectives included barring Catholics from public office and excluding immigrants from the right to own land. Membership was selective, and meetings were characterized by secret handshakes and rituals so private that members were cautioned not to reveal them to outsiders. If asked about them, they were to respond simply, "I know nothing."

Although the origins of the Know-Nothing movement date back to the 1840s, it first appeared in Arkansas in the fall of 1854 when Albert Pike, a former Whig and the man who had confirmed Cleburne in his status as "Royal Arch Mason" only the year before, helped to organize it. Pike was motivated primarily by the need to find a new political home after the collapse of the Whigs. He attended the Know-Nothing national convention in Philadelphia in February of 1855 and convinced party leaders that the organization had no future in the South unless it committed itself to a platform plank asserting that Congress had no authority to legislate on the question of slavery. Having secured this objective, he returned to Arkansas and sponsored a series of public rallies in Little Rock that demonstrated the potential appeal of the new party.[34]

The demise of the Whigs also left Cleburne without a political home. Unsurprisingly, he found the doctrines of the Know-Nothings repugnant and personally threatening, and when Thomas Hindman launched a vigorous campaign to discredit the new movement in the spring and summer of 1855, Pat Cleburne became his active and enthusiastic lieutenant. In May Hindman organized the Phillips County Democratic Association, and Pat Cleburne became one of its charter members. In a series of picnics and barbecues that summer, Hindman and Cleburne lambasted the Know-Nothings as antiforeign and anti-Catholic and labeled them the heirs of federalism and its elitist doctrines.

Their most effective weapon was the charge, frequently advanced and just as frequently denied, that the Know-Nothings were somehow associated with abolitionism. They could make this charge credible because in April the Know-Nothing Party reversed itself on the question of Congress's authority to legislate on slavery. The party's unwillingness to stand up foursquare for states' rights opened it up to the exaggerated charge of abolitionism. As early as March 1855, the Helena *Democratic Star* insisted that "the absorption of know nothingism by abolitionism is thorough, complete, and irremediable." Democrats claimed (incorrectly) that "there is not a know-nothing in the whole state—not one! that is not also an abolitionist." Hindman and others asserted that the political defense of slavery was crucial to Arkansans because slavery was a means of maintaining upward mobility for whites. The Know-Nothings openly advocated closing the door of opportunity to outsiders, and by charging them with abolitionist sentiment, Hindman made it appear that they sought to close that door to current residents as well. As Hindman explained it, the defense of slavery was intrinsic to the defense of social democracy.[35]

In July, Hindman organized a large outdoor rally officially hosted by the ladies of Big Creek and Planters Township. Then when he learned that his father had passed away, he left town to attend the funeral, and the job of delivering the principal address fell to Pat Cleburne. It was his first appearance as a political speaker and the role did not come naturally to him; even his friend Nash had to admit that "Cleburne was never a stump speaker." But though he lacked Hindman's flamboyant style, Cleburne was "earnest and impressive," and the friendly audience "crowded around him to drink in every word he said." He made three points: First, he borrowed a page from his father's political philosophy by asserting that the proscription of Catholics from government was "unwise, unjust, and unconstitutional." Second, he argued that similar legislation aimed at foreigners, including Irishmen, was also unconstitutional—an argument that had a particular poignancy presented as it was in a mild Irish lilt. Finally, Cleburne repeated the charge that know-nothingism was little more than a front for the abolitionists. The first two points were surely his own, and he had more right than most to speak to them. The third point was almost certainly suggested by his political mentor. Cleburne's speech was a great success, at least as reported by the biased *Democratic Star,* which called it "one of the most interesting and telling speech[es] we ever listened to." Soon afterward, Cleburne was elected secretary of the Phillips County Democratic Association, and in September he delivered another major address, again asserting the unconstitutionality of discriminatory legislation against Catholics and foreigners.[36]

That same September, Helena was visited by a yellow fever epidemic, brought to town by infected passengers on a river steamer from New Orleans. When the disease broke out in Helena, most of those who could fled town. But Nash, Grant, and one other doctor stayed to tend to the sick. They asked for volunteers to help in caring for the stricken, and both Hindman and Cleburne agreed to do so. While the overworked doctors applied whatever ministrations they could, Hindman and Cleburne prepared meals, carried water, and provided moral support. Their courage and commitment were noted by the survivors and contributed significantly to their growing reputation as community leaders.[37]

Cleburne and Hindman were both spared from the disease, and they were soon back on the campaign trail. The very next month, they sponsored a huge outdoor meeting hoping to attract as many as 10,000 people, a significant proportion of the population of eastern Arkansas. By now most of the former Whigs in town had been forced to choose between the Know-Nothings and the Democrats, and both Judge Hanley and Mark Alexander joined Cleburne on the arrangements committee. Cleburne hired a full brass band from Memphis—a guaranteed draw—and the affair was a great success. Cleburne's brass band led the parade from town out to the meeting grounds, where Hindman presided over a two-day political festival marked by "martial music, banners, and artillery." The crowd cheered its approval of several formal resolutions denouncing the Know-Nothings, endorsing the Kansas-Nebraska Act, and demanding strict enforcement of the Fugitive Slave Law. Hindman addressed the crowd in what one newspaper called "his usual nervous style."[38]

That December, Judge Hanley accepted an appointment to the state supreme court, and a month later Cleburne was admitted to the Arkansas bar. These two events made possible the advent of the law firm of Alexander and Cleburne, whose newspaper announcement declared that the firm would "attend all the courts in the first circuit of this State, and the various courts in the western counties of Mississippi. Special attention paid to the collection of debts in any part of Arkansas." Cleburne proved to be a competent lawyer, although he was occasionally inclined to argue issues on the basis of general fairness rather than on the points of law.[39]

If anything, Cleburne's emergence as a lawyer increased his political profile. He invested most of his remaining savings in a joint venture with Hindman to buy the *Democratic Star* for $1,000. They renamed it (significantly) the *States Rights Democrat,* and the first issue came out in March 1856. They declared that their aim was "to publish the best possible paper," but their first objective was to acquire an outlet for their campaign against the Know-Nothings. "The position of the *Democrat* upon all questions shall be bold and fearless," the paper declared in its first issue. "Endorsed as it is by the Democracy of Eastern Arkansas, it has nothing to fear from such a course; and any other in these times when *treason* stalks abroad in public places, and direct attacks are made upon the life blood of the Constitution, would be unworthy of our patrons as of ourselves, and false to that country which we love."[40]

Cleburne's campaign to discredit the Know-Nothings in Arkansas won him a substantial local following and helped confirm his status as a community leader. But his close association with Hindman also embroiled him in the rough-and-tumble politics of frontier Arkansas, where opponents were occasionally inclined to move the debate from the podium into the street. On 24 May 1856, Hindman asked Cleburne to arm himself and accompany him to dinner at Fadley's Hotel because he had heard that one of their former colleagues, a man named Dorsey Rice, was angered over Hindman's public reference to him as a "mulatto" for having changed his allegiance from the Democrats to the Know-Nothings. Cleburne pocketed a pair of pistols and willingly went with Hindman. On their way to the hotel, they met Rice and two others in the street. Rice demanded that Hindman apologize. Characteristically, Hindman responded instead with a burst of verbal abuse. What followed was a scene that could have come straight from a Hollywood western: Rice drew a gun and fired, the bullet creasing Hindman's right arm and striking him in the chest. Hindman managed to fire several shots in reply before he slumped to the ground. At almost the same moment, one of Rice's associates fired at Cleburne who was also hit in the chest. Cleburne drew both his pistols and fired at the only man he could see clearly, Rice's brother-in-law James T. Marriott. When the smoke cleared, Hindman, Cleburne, and Marriott all lay in the street badly wounded. Hindman soon recovered, but the wounds of the other two appeared to be mortal.

Friends carried Cleburne into a room above a dry goods store and laid him on a bed. The bullet that struck him had passed through his right lung and lodged so near his spine that Nash was afraid to remove it. Instead he waited, hoping for a general improvement that would allow the operation. After three days, news arrived that Marriott had died in terrible agony. For another week it seemed that Cleburne would die as well. He lingered near death for ten days with Nash at his bedside most of the time. The bullet was eventually found and safely removed and Cleburne did recover, but he was never the same. Five years later he confessed to his half brother Robert that "my lungs have never been well since I was wounded. I catch cold on the smallest provocation and an hour's excited debate in the Court House will sometimes fill my mouth with blood." He often wondered if he would be "a permanent invalid."[41]

After they recovered, Cleburne and Hindman were exonerated by a grand jury for their part in the gunfight, and they refused to press charges against Dorsey Rice. The affair actually improved Cleburne's social and political standing, for most of Helena's townspeople saw him as the victim. Cleburne himself justified his participation in this frontier fracas as the consequence of simple duty. Hindman had asked for his support, and he felt that he could not decline such a request. Once pistols had been drawn, he had no recourse but to defend himself. "I had either to defend myself or run," he asserted. Yet he did feel remorse, even guilt. After all, the man he had killed had never fired a shot, although he had been holding a gun. For years afterward, Cleburne told his friends, he recalled the event only with deep uneasiness.[42]

Despite the severity of their wounds, Hindman and Cleburne were back on the campaign trail within a month. Cleburne spoke at another rally of the Phillips County Democratic Association in July. This time he attacked the Know-Nothing Party as "false to its own promises, pledges and obligations." By now, his stump style had evolved into something more characteristic of frontier politics. Although he continued to rely mainly on "plain, sound, practical argument," local papers noted that he delivered his remarks in "a withering and blasting manner." Cleburne's own *States Rights Democrat* asserted that he "made one of the best speeches we have heard in this canvass," and claimed that his rebuke "was so evidently merited" that any Know-Nothings present "would have been compelled to . . . repent upon the spot."[43]

The Democrats swept to "a brilliant victory" in the 1856 elections. Arkansas went solidly for Buchanan in the national race, and the Know-Nothings made no further inroads against the Democrats. Apparently satisfied with this triumph, Cleburne scaled back his commitment to local politics, and the *States Rights Democrat* ceased publication. Hindman, however, was just getting started. Elected to Congress in 1858, he began almost at once to seek the Senate nomination, challenging the powerful coterie of Democratic Party bosses known as "the family." He tried to "out-southern" his opponents by calling for strict enforcement of the Fugitive Slave Law and the unlimited expansion of slavery into the West. He even flirted with filibustering, hoping to expand slavery into Mexico and Central America as well. Failure to secure any of these goals, he argued, should be a cause for secession, and he soon developed a reputation as "the apostle of dis-union."[44]

Although Cleburne continued to support Hindman with his vote, and even acted as best man at his wedding in November, he ceased to be Hindman's principal acolyte. From the beginning, Cleburne's political activism had been a response to the threat of know-nothingism in Arkansas rather than the product of political ambition. In 1857 he returned full-time to the practice of law, and increasingly he turned his energies to the far more lucrative enterprises of land speculation and railroad promotion. Congress had granted to Arkansas some 7.5 million acres of "swamp and overflow" land that had been sold to the public for as little as twenty cents an acre to raise money for the construction of levees. A savvy investor could pick up a large tract at a bargain rate if he scouted the land beforehand and knew when to file his claim. In addition, Cleburne became an active proponent of railroad schemes, and he lobbied hard in 1859 for an extension of the St. Louis and Iron Mountain Railroad south to Helena. That same year, Cleburne's law partner, Mark Alexander, was elected circuit court judge, and Cleburne practiced law independently for some months before forming a new partnership with Barry Scaife and Learned H. Mangum, an 1857 graduate of Princeton University. The new partners advertised themselves as "collecting and land agents" for eastern Arkansas and kept busy filing claims and counterclaims over disputed land titles.[45]

Although no longer as politically active, Cleburne could not avoid the national trauma of the presidential election in 1860. In April, he served as a delegate to the state convention in Little Rock where his friend Hindman sponsored a resolution requiring Arkansas delegates to leave the national convention in protest unless the party adopted a platform plank for a national slave code. When later that summer northern Democrats refused to accept such a plank, half the Arkansas delegates joined Alabama fire-eater William Lowndes Yancey in a southern walkout of the party's convention in Charleston, South Carolina. The crisis split the party. Southern Democrats nominated their own candidate at a convention in Richmond, while northern Democrats nominated Stephen Douglas, author of the Kansas-Nebraska Act, at their convention in Baltimore. The Republicans nominated Abraham Lincoln, and a fourth party entered the contest when John Bell of Tennessee accepted the nomination of the Constitutional Union Party.

In Arkansas, the election soon became a contest between the southern Democrat, John C. Breckinridge, and the compromise candidate, John Bell; a few of the Democratic Party faithful stuck by Stephen Douglas, but no one voted for Lincoln, who was not even on the ballot. It was a bitter and rancorous contest. Hindman campaigned hard for Breckinridge, branded Douglas a traitor, and insisted that Lincoln's election should be the signal "for immediate disruption of the union." Although Breckinridge narrowly carried the state over Bell, Lincoln won the national race without the support of a single southern state. Hindman and like-minded revolutionaries across the South talked of secession, and the nation hovered on the brink of catastrophe.[46]

That winter Cleburne labored long into the night in his office, often alone, right through the Christmas season. To his half brother Robert who had emigrated to the United States with the rest of the Cleburne clan in 1856 and had settled in Newport, Kentucky, across the river from Cincinnati, Patrick confessed: "I never spent a more gloomy Christmas. . . . My partners were participating in gaities [*sic*] I did not feel like sharing. I have been invited to twenty parties this Christmas and have not attended one." The winter was a gloomy one for the nation, too. Lincoln was elected but not yet inaugurated, and speculation ran wild about the course he might take. South Carolina did not wait to find out. It chose delegates to a state convention and left the Union on 20 December. Mississippi was the next state to leave, declaring its separation from the Union on 9 January. From his office window in Helena, Cleburne could look across the river at what was now putatively a foreign country. Whether Arkansas followed Mississippi's example depended largely on what policies the new president-elect adopted. "I hardly know what to say to you about politicks," Cleburne wrote to Robert. "The fever of revolution is very contagious. . . . My own opinion is that the first blood shed on Southern soil in a collision between the Federal troops and the State authorities of any Southern state will be the signal for civil war."[47]

Cleburne hoped that the Union could be preserved, but only if the federal government proved willing to grant the South what he called "the full measure of her constitutional rights." Failing that, he hoped "to see all the Southern States united in a new confederation and that we can effect a peaceable separation." But even if it did come to war, he had no doubts about his own course. He had committed himself to Arkansas. During his ten years in Helena, he had become more of an Arkansan than he had ever been either an Irishman or an American. "These people have been my friends," he explained to Robert, "and have stood up to [for] me on all occasions." For him and for his brothers as well, scattered as they were up and down the Mississippi Valley, the determination of personal loyalty in this crisis was not the product of ideology. Each of the Cleburne brothers reflected the outlook of the society in which he lived: William in Wisconsin and Joseph in Indiana were for Lincoln and the Union; Robert in Kentucky hoped his state could survive a precarious neutrality; Patrick in Arkansas was for states' rights. It was not the South that Patrick Cleburne supported or even states' rights, and he had no personal investment in slavery. It was Arkansas. He confessed as much to Robert in that cold and foreboding January of 1861: "I am with Arkansas in weal or woe."[48]

3
COMMAND

Several months before the 1860 presidential election, in the last peacetime summer of his life, Patrick Cleburne helped to organize a militia company in Helena. Named in honor of Archibald Yell, a former governor who had been killed in the Battle of Buena Vista during the Mexican War, the "Yell Rifles" was one of many such companies founded all across the South in that crisis summer. Determined to defend home, hearth, and the principle of self-government, the 115 volunteers were for the most part the town's elite. Cleburne noted with some pride that "the majority are the young planters of the county," and membership in the Yell Rifles carried with it a certain community status. It was therefore a mark of social distinction and personal respect, as well as an acknowledgment of his three and a half years in the British army, that the members of the Yell Rifles elected Cleburne their captain.[1]

He adapted easily to his new role. Although often described by contemporaries as "very bashful" and "naturally timid," Cleburne was nevertheless completely at ease issuing commands on the drill field. Cripplingly shy in most social situations—particularly with women—he was an altogether different person in the company of men and participating in those activities that nineteenth-century Americans considered the domain of men: lodge meetings, politics, and military drill. Throughout the fall, as Lincoln's election was predicted and then confirmed, Cleburne supervised the Yell Rifles in afternoon drill, calling out cadence and instructing his enthusiastic volunteers in the manual of arms. Though he had labored for more than a decade to eliminate all traces of an Irish accent from his speech, old habits reasserted themselves on the drill field. One veteran later recalled the "peculiar intonation" of Cleburne's commands. In giving voice to the order "Forward march," for example, he pronounced the first word "with remarkable distinctness," while the second emerged in a long rolling brogue. The result, as the veteran later rendered it, was "For-ward MAR-R-R-C-H!" Even during inspection, Cleburne betrayed his Irish roots when he commented on the cleanliness of a soldier's rifle "bar-r-r'l."[2]

Cleburne's leadership of the Yell Rifles not only confirmed his social prominence in Helena, it also helped to sharpen and intensify his attitude toward the continuing national crisis. The defiant tone of much of the discussion that accompanied the frequent drill sessions led him to adopt an equally defiant view, which reflected community sentiment. As hard as he had worked to absorb the cultural values of frontier Helena, so did he now adopt the truculent tone of his friends and neighbors toward the imagined tyranny of the Lincoln government. "I have been elected . . . captain of the volunteer Rifle Company of this place," he wrote to Robert in January 1861, "and I can say for my company that if the stars and stripes become the standard of a tiranical [sic] majority, the ensign of a violated league, it will no longer command our love or respect but will command our best efforts to drive it from the state."[3]

Later that month a telegram from Little Rock relayed a rumor that a river steamer filled with Federal soldiers was on its way to the Arkansas capital to reinforce the Federal arsenal there. This prompted Helena's civic leaders to offer the governor the service of the local militia companies, including the Yell Rifles. Arkansas's governor, Henry Rector, was a strong advocate of states' rights, but he could hardly call up the militia to undertake a preemptive military action against a United States arsenal. His adjutant therefore responded to Helena's offer of military forces by replying that the governor had "no authority to summon you to take possession of a Federal post," though he did offer the pledge that "should the people assemble in their [own] defense, the governor will interpose his official position in their behalf." Helena's civic leaders interpreted this message as a thinly disguised appeal for help, and they decided at once to dispatch the Yell Rifles and the Phillips Guards to Little Rock.[4]

The two companies of militia boarded a steamer at the Front Street wharf in Helena and set off down the Mississippi. Sixty miles downriver, the vessel entered the mouth of the Arkansas River and breasted the current toward Little Rock where it arrived on 5 February. Cleburne marched his company of planters' sons through town to the governor's mansion where, much to their surprise and disappointment, Rector greeted them coolly. He praised their patriotism but asked them to make no attempt to seize the armory. Disappointed not to be more fulsomely received, they marched to the capital grounds where other militia units were already encamped. More arrived during the night, and by the next day the capital grounds were crowded with as many as 1,000 armed men from a dozen different militia units, each under widely varying—and sometimes nonexistent—discipline. Little Rock's citizens were alarmed, and they petitioned the governor to do something.

For Rector, the situation was both a problem and an opportunity. Expressing a concern that was partly feigned and partly real, he warned the Federal commander of the arsenal, Captain James Totten, that he could not control the actions of the growing number of armed men in the city and urged Totten to avoid a bloody confrontation by turning the Federal arsenal over to state authorities. Totten agonized only briefly before agreeing, and he evacuated the building on 8 February. Following this bloodless victory, the Yell Rifles went home the way they had come, satisfied that they had helped to drive the Yankees from Little Rock.[5]

That same February, the Arkansas legislature authorized a popular referendum to determine whether the state should hold a convention to discuss secession. By a nearly 2 to 1 vote, the electorate decided that it should, and the convention met on 4 March, the day that Abraham Lincoln took the oath of office as the sixteenth president. Even though seven other states had already declared their separation from the Union, most of the Arkansas delegates preferred to wait. Lincoln's inaugural address was a carefully phrased appeal for national unity, and most Arkansans were willing to see if his deeds matched his words. Thus began a curious five weeks of uncertainty, a twilight period during which Arkansans granted the Lincoln government conditional toleration. So long as his administration made no overt move against the states that had already declared their secession, Arkansas would remain in the Union. Any effort to coerce the South, however, would lead to secession. The uncertainly ended on 12 April with the bombardment of the Federal garrison in Fort Sumter and Lincoln's subsequent call for volunteers. Governor Rector sent a defiant reply to Lincoln's request for Arkansas troops, and the state convention, which had adjourned until August, went back into session. Virtually everyone expected an early vote to secede.

Secession sentiment was at flood tide in Helena as well, and the Yell Rifles drilled more frequently and more seriously, anticipating both secession and war. As one of the first militia units to organize, Cleburne's company was armed with the newest type of shoulder arm—rifled muskets that fired the .58-caliber minié ball—but many newer units lacked arms altogether. To address the deficiency, state and local governments across the South ordered arms and munitions, some from northern arms dealers. When news arrived in Helena that a cargo of arms consigned to Arkansas had been seized by local officials in Cincinnati, the city council was furious and resolved to retaliate by seizing the first Cincinnati-owned vessel that passed on the river.

On 25 April, the *Queen of the West* was forced to shore by a cannon shot fired across its bows. The vessel was indeed Cincinnati-owned. As fate would have it, it belonged to Thomas Sherlock, whose brother James was married to Patrick Cleburne's sister. These unlikely circumstances placed Cleburne in an awkward position.[6]

Loyalty was important to Cleburne; it was an attribute much admired on the Arkansas frontier where friends and neighbors were expected to stand by one another. Dutiful to this frontier credo, he had stood up for Nash on numerous occasions, and he had stood by Hindman to the extent of taking a bullet that had nearly killed him. In much the same way, he stood with his community when it was threatened by war largely because, as he explained to his brother, "these people have been my friends." His loyalty was not to abstract doctrines—he had no ideological pole star—but to his friends and neighbors; he was gratified that they acknowledged his "unswerving loyalty." When the city fathers declared the *Queen of the West* forfeit, however, Cleburne was torn between loyalty to his community and loyalty to his family. The extent of his anguish was evident in an uncharacteristic display of public emotion. He pleaded with town officials to relent, claiming that Sherlock was "a good Southern man," and he requested the release of the vessel "as a favor to me." He actually broke down and wept in an impassioned effort to obtain the vessel's release. Perhaps embarrassed, town officials agreed to allow the steamer to proceed after its captain promised that the boat would not be used in the Federal service. Patrick described the event in a letter to his half brother Robert in the hope that his demonstration of personal goodwill might deter his family members from active support of the Union cause. "I thought of you all when I did this thing," he wrote, "that it might make you a friend in the crisis which is now upon us."[7]

Only two days after this public display, Cleburne and the Yell Rifles went off to war. With Cleburne riding at their head, the company marched from the courthouse to the Methodist Church, where the minister blessed them in a special service that was so well attended the crowd spilled out into the street. Chagrined perhaps by his emotional display two days earlier, Cleburne's response was brief and delivered in a voice so low it was barely audible. After marching to the landing, the troops and the admiring crowd were regaled by another address, delivered at much greater volume by Cleburne's friend Tom Hindman, who had resigned his seat in Congress to form his own "legion" of soldiery. The ceremonies completed, the troops filed aboard the waiting steamer, bound upriver this time toward the real war.[8]

Pat Cleburne and the Yell Rifles disembarked at what was rather grandly designated as Camp Rector, really no more than an open plain on the west bank
of the Mississippi a half dozen miles upriver from Memphis. There he ordered
his command to pitch their tents among those of dozens of other volunteer
militia units from across eastern Arkansas and western Tennessee. Almost at
once most of these companies were grouped into regiments—ten companies
to a regiment in accordance with standard army practice—and elections were
scheduled to choose regimental commanders. The troops from Helena—the
Yell Rifles and the Phillips Guards—were regimented together with eight
other units with such colorful names as the Jefferson Guards, the Napoleon
Grays, and the Monroe Blues to form the 1st Arkansas Volunteer Infantry.
From the outset, Cleburne was the leading candidate to command the amal-
gamated regiment. He did not campaign for the job, for he believed it would
be inappropriate to do so, but it was soon evident that there was no other
individual who possessed the confidence of the men. "All the companies appear determined to elect me colonel," he wrote Robert on the eve of the election, and he was duly elected without opposition on 8 May, thus leaping in
one step from captain to colonel. Though he could not have been surprised
at the outcome, he claimed to be suitably sobered by it. "This is a fearfully responsible position," he wrote, "and I dread the honor but intend to turn my
whole attention to it and do the best I can for the cause I am embarked in."[9]

   Although the men in the ranks chose their regimental commanders, higher
authority selected the generals. In Arkansas that higher authority was exercised by a three-man military board chaired by Governor Rector. The board
was the creation of the state convention, which remained in session even after
voting for secession on 6 May (with only one negative vote), acting as a kind
of transition government. The military board appointed James Yell as a major
general, placing him in command of all state forces, and named two others,
Nicholas B. Pearce and Thomas H. Bradley, as brigadier generals: Pearce to
command forces in the western half of the state and Bradley to command
those in the east, including the troops gathering at Camp Rector.[10]

   Bradley was a sixty-five-year-old planter from Crittenden County, "a fine
specimen of an old Southern planter" but with no military experience. Worse,
from the point of view of many, was the fact that he had been "a Union man
to the last moment." When he showed up at Camp Rector in the third week
of May claiming command authority, he met skepticism and even hostility
from the Arkansas troops he was to command. The men at Camp Rector
had signed up for military service with their friends and neighbors, and they
expected to serve under men they knew and trusted. As far as they were concerned, this General Bradley would have to prove himself before they would

grant him full loyalty. Cleburne may have shared in the general skepticism—
he was bound to consider the popular mood in making his own evaluation—
but he dutifully reported to Bradley, thus demonstrating a public respect
even if he withheld his private judgment.[11]

Eager, perhaps, to assert his authority and demonstrate his capacity for
command, Bradley was in camp barely a week before he ordered a reconnaissance in force in response to unverified rumors that a force of Yankees was
advancing on Bearsfield Point. Since Cleburne's 1st Arkansas regiment was
the most advanced in its training, Bradley selected it to lead the expedition.
Cleburne dutifully mustered his regiment, but Bradley's poor staff work became evident almost at once. The supplies he ordered proved inadequate,
the order and even the route of march seemed random, and patrols found
no evidence of enemy forces. To the men, the entire expedition seemed di-
rectionless and purposeless. Worse yet, when Bradley ordered a withdrawal,
he not only abandoned much usable material, he failed to account for a detached scouting force that was left behind. The Arkansas troops arrived back
in camp much the worse for wear to be greeted by the jeers of the Tennessee
troops who were not under Bradley's command.

It was more than proud men could bear. They were furious at Bradley, and
a few even suggested that he was more than incompetent—he was a traitor.
Some of the captains in Cleburne's regiment urged him to arrest Bradley and
assume command. Again torn by conflicting loyalty, Cleburne had to choose
between obedience to appointed authority and what he saw as his obligation to his men. When a few days later the scouting party that Bradley had
neglected to recall returned to camp bearing the news that there never had
been any Yankees at or near Bearsfield Point, Cleburne posted a guard on
Bradley's quarters, in effect placing him under arrest. Then he sent a remarkable telegram to his former law tutor, Judge Hanley, who was a member of
the state convention in Little Rock, a telegram that was startling in its terse
brevity: "Arkansas forces returned from Bearsfield Point between two suns;
a quantity of material abandoned; scouting party of picked men abandoned;
no enemy nearer than Cairo; we are the laughing stock of the Tennesseans."
He ended this remarkable report with the curt demand: "Answer." Equally
astonishing was the telegram sent the same day by one of Cleburne's company commanders, Captain Charles H. Carlton of the Jefferson Guards, to
a friend in the state capital. "We have deposed Bradley," Carlton declared,
following this bald announcement with the demand that the military board
"appoint Col. Cleburne and satisfy [the] regiment."[12]

Cleburne's extraordinary decision to place Bradley under arrest and act in
his place was reckless in the extreme. And he reported his actions not through

the chain of command—to the governor or to the military board that had granted Bradley command authority—but to a friend and presumed ally who could be counted on to present the circumstances to the state convention in Little Rock in the most favorable light. It was not ambition that motivated him to take this desperate action; he was impelled by the outrage of his officers and a genuine conviction that Bradley was a menace to the safety of his command. He may even have convinced himself that Bradley was guilty of treason. But whatever his motives, his personal sense of loyalty to the regiment led him to commit what amounted to mutiny. He kept Bradley under virtual arrest, ignoring his orders, and refusing to allow him even to communicate with Little Rock unless he promised to leave Camp Rector. Accepting that condition, Bradley sent his own telegram to the military board forlornly informing the members, "I have been suspended from my command; I am coming to Little Rock." [13]

When Bradley arrived in the state capital, he preferred charges of mutiny against Cleburne and five others, and a court-martial was scheduled to meet in Mound City in mid-June. Cleburne escaped a close scrutiny of his behavior, however, mainly because Bradley decided that a court-martial was more likely to expose his shortcomings than restore his military position. He therefore left the matter up to Gideon Pillow, commander of the Provisional Army of Tennessee, to take whatever action he thought appropriate. Pillow, who remembered Cleburne favorably from Helena, had troubles enough of his own without borrowing more, and he allowed the matter to drop. Bradley resigned his commission in humiliation.[14]

This remarkable episode illuminates much about the nature of military command in Arkansas in the spring of 1861 and even more about Cleburne, whose commitment to his troops superseded his sense of responsibility to a military board in Little Rock or the pretensions of an unpopular militia general bearing its commission. As a regimental commander, Cleburne was a strict disciplinarian who brooked no mutiny within his own unit, but he believed that a commander was not only responsible *for* his command, he was responsible *to* it as well. He asked a great deal of his men and, as events would prove, did not hesitate to order them to risk their lives in desperate acts of valor on the battlefield, but he was not willing to ask them to indulge a general whom he deemed incompetent. In this case, at least, loyalty down proved more compelling than loyalty up. It was not the last time that such a view would land him in trouble.

The Arkansas Military Board sent James Yell to replace Bradley, but the complications of command became even more chaotic in June when Jefferson Davis, as provisional president of the Confederate States, appointed Brigadier General William J. Hardee to command that portion of Arkansas north of the Arkansas River and west of the White and Black rivers. Hardee was a professional career officer with impeccable credentials, best known as the author of the army's official manual on tactics. Still, in a culture where "states' rights" was a popular battle cry, the appointment of a "national" commander to supersede Arkansas officers was a sensitive issue. If the troops at Camp Rector had looked upon Bradley as an outsider, what kind of reception would they give this native of Georgia? [15]

Perhaps contemplating that question himself, Hardee traveled first to Little Rock to obtain the blessing of the Arkansas Military Board. Initially skeptical of turning Arkansas troops over to this Georgian, Governor Rector and the other members of the board were converted by Hardee's tactful diplomacy as well as his glittering military reputation, and they agreed to transfer to his command authority the seven regiments of infantry, one regiment of cavalry, and five batteries of artillery that were putatively under their own control. But there were conditions: no troops would be transferred to Confederate service without their consent, and each company was to be offered the option of accepting service under Confederate authority or of staying in Arkansas as local defense troops. Moreover, for any troops who did agree to transfer to Confederate service, Hardee would have to sign a receipt. [16]

James Yell, who stood to lose most of his command authority if the troops in eastern Arkansas transferred to Confederate service, campaigned hard to convince the men to oppose the transfer. Cleburne campaigned equally hard for amalgamation. His bitter confrontation with Bradley had soured his view of state military leadership, and he had been impressed when he met Hardee briefly in Memphis. Then, too, he may have concluded that eventual success in the war required a unified army. Whatever his motives, he was only partly successful. Overall, about 60 percent of the Arkansas troops at Camp Rector (1,800 of 3,000) agreed to serve under Confederate authority, although within Cleburne's regiment the percentage was slightly higher as eight of the ten companies voted to fight under the stars and bars—a total of 488 officers and men. The transfer to Confederate service became official on 23 July 1861, two days after other Confederate forces fought and won the Battle of Manassas, which the Yankees called Bull Run, in faraway Virginia. [17]

Cleburne was delighted with the new commander. The forty-five-year old Hardee was every inch a professional soldier: tall and distinguished-looking with his dark hair turning to gray, he exuded a calm confidence that Bradley had lacked. And Hardee was equally pleased with Cleburne, whom he came to rely upon as a friend and ally in camp as well as his strong right arm in battle. The two men developed an immediate rapport that soon became a friendship. Dr. Nash, who knew both men, believed that "Hardee's friend-ship for Cleburne was not born of a military character alone, but from the high merit of a moral man." They had the kind of relationship where each felt comfortable enough with the other to share humorous stories and even to offer the occasional jibe at the other's expense. Hardee's chief of staff wrote, "Cleburne's attachment to Hardee and his admiration for him as a soldier were well known to everyone acquainted with him." In time, Cleburne would serve Hardee as best man at his wedding, and Hardee would offer the tearful eulogy at Cleburne's funeral.[18]

Just prior to Hardee's arrival, the growing Confederate force at Camp Rector moved to Pittman's Ferry on the Current River just below the Missouri bor-der, where the task of turning armed citizens into soldiers began in earnest. The men were certainly fierce enough—many carried bowie knives and pis-tols in their belts in addition to the rifles on their shoulders—but they were unaccustomed to military discipline. Hardee was more amused than offended upon his arrival when a private on picket duty invited him to dismount and join him for dinner. Daniel Govan, a Mississippian who had moved to Ar-kansas just before the outbreak of war, wrote his wife that "it will require energy and dispatch to place this command in condition to take the field." Hardee soon discovered that Cleburne's 1st Arkansas regiment was consider-ably more advanced in its training than the others. Partly this was because it had been among the first to be organized, but in addition, Cleburne had already begun to put his particular stamp on the unit by mandating a daunt-ing regimen of drill and enforcing a high standard of discipline.[19]

Cleburne was a hands-on commander. He not only personally conducted regimental drill, he also supervised battalion drill and frequently superin-tended company and even squad evolutions as well, a daily regimen that often kept him on his feet from first dawn until well past nightfall. A fellow offi-cer later recalled, "I cannot remember that I ever saw an officer who was so industrious and persistent in his efforts to drill and instruct the men under his command." Although the schedule he set for the men left little time for leisure and provoked some early resentment, the troops could not help but notice their commander's constant presence and his evident interest in their progress. They also began to take pride in the fact that their level of perfor-mance and standard of discipline outstripped that of most other units. More-over, Cleburne not only imposed high standards on the men in the ranks, he also accepted as a matter of course that the counterpart to discipline was responsibility, and he held himself and his officers to equally high standards of professional conduct. At least one veteran was impressed by the fact that Cleburne "required . . . his subordinate officers to keep up a constant course of drill, discipline, and study."[20]

As involved as he was with the smallest detail of the daily routine, Cleburne nevertheless managed to remain a somewhat distant and enigmatic figure to his troops. He was not prone to engaging in idle banter, and an admirer admitted that "he had no mercuriality, no folly, no frivolity about him." His orders were simple and direct, often blunt, and those who did not know him well saw him as grave and forbidding, unsophisticated, and even rude. There was, on occasion, "an abruptness of manner and an impatience" toward those who were unable or unwilling to see what needed to be done. There was little subtlety or circumlocution in his command style. One officer recalled that "he abhorred the vague or undefined," and another noted, "When he acted his course was always in straight lines."[21]

However distant and direct, Cleburne nevertheless won the confidence, and even the affection, of the men in the ranks by living up to his own work ethic and by his manifest concern for the soldiers' comfort. He fought hard to ensure that the men were properly uniformed and shod. On one occasion during the winter of 1862–1863, when there were several inches of snow on the ground, he learned that a soldier in his command had been placed under arrest for refusing to turn out for work detail. Enquiring into the affair, he discovered that the soldier had refused the duty because he had no shoes. Cleburne quietly ordered him released and then rode off to visit army headquarters. The next day the army quartermaster delivered a wagonload of shoes to his command. On another occasion that same winter, Cleburne's inspector general, Major Joseph K. Dixon, kept the troops standing at "right dress shoulder arms" while he gave instructions to the noncommissioned officers. Cleburne sent his aide to suggest quietly to the major that he put the troops at ease. When that proved unavailing, Cleburne interrupted the instructions with an order given in a loud clear voice: "Major Dickson [*sic*], bring the men to order arms while you give those instructions." The command provoked a loud whoop from the men in the ranks, and no doubt brought a blush to Dixon's cheek. Weeks later, when the troops were still teasing the major about the incident, Cleburne interfered again to put a stop to it, "Boys, I don't believe I would worry him any more, as he is sorry of it."[22]

This stern but compassionate style of leadership made it difficult for anyone, officer or infantryman, to harbor any lasting bitterness against their demanding commander. Even when Cleburne was forced to chastise a soldier for one shortcoming or another, he almost never did so in a way that left lingering resentment. He never imposed the kind of physical punishment that was common elsewhere in the army, such as bucking and gagging. His standard penalty for minor transgressions was to require the guilty soldier to carry a fence rail for a mile. The troops always knew that someone was in trouble when they heard Cleburne's stentorian; "Arrest that soldier and have him carry a rail!" On other occasions he was remarkably gentle. During one arms inspection, as he moved along the rank of soldiers, he took a rifle from one of the men and examined it closely. After handing back the gleaming weapon, he looked carefully at its owner. "I hope I do you no injustice, my man," he said quietly, "but I don't believe you have washed your face in several days." [23]

Cleburne also helped to offset his own severe demeanor and his commitment to strict discipline with an ability to see the lighter side of things. An officer without a sense of humor can be a commander, but he can never be a leader. Cleburne was never the glad-handing, pat-you-on-the-back kind of leader, but he often used what one veteran called "his quiet, kindly humor" to take the sting out of a reproof. During one regimental drill, he began a command sequence by calling out, "By the right of companies . . . ," and a junior officer anticipated his next command by stepping out in front of the ranks to order a right face. Cleburne stopped in mid-order to reproach him. "Hold on there, Captain," Cleburne called out, "you don't know but that I was going to say by the right of companies into the moon." Chastised, but smiling, the captain resumed his position.

In the end, though Cleburne's experience in the British army provided him with a useful foundation of professional knowledge, it was his personal command style that made him both respected and popular with the troops he commanded. In a letter recommending another officer for promotion, Cleburne listed what he believed were the requisite attributes of an effective commander: "judgement, knowledge of the military art, and knowledge of human nature." It was this last quality that he exploited more successfully than many of his peers. He took his responsibilities as commander seriously and imposed a strict regimen of drill and discipline; at the same time he did not take himself too seriously, and his evident commitment to the rank and file, manifested daily in a hundred small ways, made him both popular and effective. His former law partner Learned Mangum, who served as a volunteer aide, wrote, "Although he was rigid in the enforcement of discipline, the soldiers whom he commanded loved him as a man, and trusted him implicitly." As one veteran of his command recalled years after the war, Cleburne "always looked to the comfort of his men, and was dearly beloved of them." [24]

While Cleburne drilled, instructed, and cajoled his troops into the semblance of a military unit, various generals in the theater began to contemplate an early offensive. In the western part of the state, Generals Nicolas Pearce and Ben McCulloch made plans to move into southwestern Missouri, while across the Mississippi Gideon Pillow developed his own plan to capture St. Louis. Hardee declined the invitation from Pearce and McCullough to cooperate in their campaign, noting that the proposed movement was well outside his command area, but he did agree to participate in Pillow's attack on Federal forces in eastern Missouri.[25]

In the last week of July, Cleburne's 1st Arkansas led Hardee's demibrigade of two regiments (about 1,000 men) across the state line into Missouri arriving at Greenville, some forty miles south of the railroad terminus at Ironton, on 4 August. Pillow, meanwhile, moved his 3,500 men across the Mississippi to New Madrid, sixty miles southeast of Greenville. After this promising start, the campaign broke down. Once across the river, Pillow became excessively cautious, convinced that he was about to be outflanked by a Federal river squadron. Hardee sent out small cavalry patrols to cut the railroad to Ironton, but they failed to do so. He then called upon Major General Leonidas Polk, the newly appointed theater commander, to order Pillow to move to Ironton, but Polk declined, noting that his command authority stopped at the Mississippi. The resulting lack of coordination brought the campaign to a halt. In the western part of the state, Pearce and McCulloch fought and won the Battle of Wilson's Creek on 10 August, although their victory was largely barren of important results. Meanwhile, Hardee's forces, including Cleburne's 1st Arkansas, remained largely immobile at Greenville.[26]

Cleburne continued his regimen of daily drills, and constant rumors of enemy activity kept the regiment in a serious frame of mind. In the second week of August, in response to a report that Federal forces at Ironton were advancing, he led his regiment and one artillery piece northward to meet them. Once his force was deployed, he learned to his great disgust that the crew of his single field piece had broken into the home of a nearby resident—a woman whose husband was in the Confederate army—and plundered it. Cleburne ordered the six men under immediate arrest. No sooner had he done so when "breathless scouts galloped up" to report that the enemy was close at hand and advancing. Amidst the general preparations to meet the expected attack, Captain Calvert, commander of the artillery piece, approached Cleburne to request the temporary release of his crew so that they could work the gun. Instead, Cleburne ordered him to take his gun to the rear, and in a voice loud enough to be widely heard, he declared that "*his* men expected to fill honorable graves and not to rest side by side with thieves." The

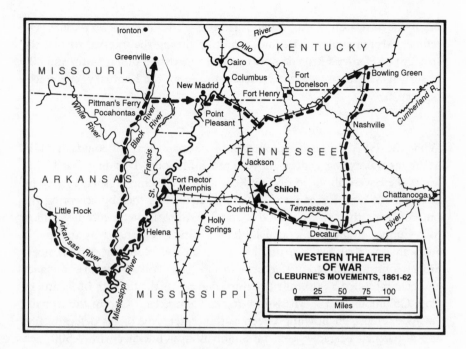

expected Federal attack never materialized, but Cleburne's men never forgot the lesson. One of them recalled later that the "moral effect" of Cleburne's announcement was profound.[27]

Another incident that took place while the 1st Arkansas was at Greenville had a less happy resolution. A handful of Federal prisoners had been brought into camp by a young lieutenant who was charged with guarding them in the town hall that Hardee and Cleburne used as a headquarters. One night Cleburne's sleep was interrupted by someone shouting wildly that the Federal prisoners were escaping. He bolted from his bed and, pistol in hand, rushed to the door where he spotted a dim figure dashing down the hallway. He fired and the man fell. After a lamp was lit, it turned out that the wounded man was the Confederate lieutenant who had brought in the prisoners. He had dreamed that his prisoners were escaping and still half asleep had run down the hallway shouting. Cleburne was distraught and begged the badly wounded man for forgiveness. The lieutenant granted it, but soon afterward he died — the first man Cleburne killed in the war was a fellow officer. Though he spoke of it only to his closest friends, Cleburne regretted the incident for the rest of his life.[28]

In the third week of August, with the campaign into Missouri at a dead stop, Polk ordered Hardee's force to return to Arkansas. Cleburne's regiment began the retreat on 28 August and arrived back at Pittman's Ferry on 2 September. More recruits had come into camp during the interval so that the strength of Hardee's Brigade now totaled more than 5,000 infantry and 800 cavalry. It was just as well, for events across the river in Kentucky were reaching a crisis.[29]

While the 1st Arkansas marched back to Pittman's Ferry, Leonidas Polk in Memphis was eyeing Federal movements in Missouri. Deciding that Union forces there were about to occupy Kentucky, he preempted such a move by ordering his own forces into Columbus, Kentucky, thereby accepting the onus of being the first to break that state's self-proclaimed neutrality. Union forces under Brigadier General Ulysses S. Grant responded by occupying Paducah, and Kentucky's neutrality was at an end. Soon thereafter, Albert Sidney Johnston arrived in Kentucky to supersede Polk in overall command, and he established a 300-mile defensive line across the breadth of Kentucky from Columbus on the Mississippi to the Cumberland Gap in the Appalachians. He selected Bowling Green as the centerpoint of his defensive line and dispatched Brigadier General Simon Bolivar Buckner with 4,500 men to occupy and fortify the town. Of course Buckner could not hold Bowling Green indefinitely without reinforcement, and as a result orders soon arrived at Pittman's Ferry for Hardee to bring his command from Arkansas to Kentucky.[30]

Hardee determined to march his brigade overland from Pittman's Ferry to Point Pleasant. The overland march might be slower than a movement by river steamer, but Hardee believed it would help toughen the brigade, and he ordered Cleburne to move with his regiment "as soon as practicable" to reconnoiter Chalk Bluffs Road which passed over the marshy Cache Bottoms. Cleburne dutifully set off on 17 September with his own regiment plus a company of cavalry. The road was barely passable. One soldier called it "without a doubt the worst road, if the track which we travelled could be called a road, that my eyes ever beheld." Nevertheless, Cleburne reported that the road was "practicable for the march of an army," and the rest of Hardee's command followed. Once the brigade arrived at Point Pleasant, the entire brigade ferried across the river where the men climbed aboard railroad cars for the 175-mile ride to Bowling Green.[31]

The train carried them south first, back into Tennessee on the Mobile and Ohio Railroad to Humbolt, then north on the Memphis and Charleston, across the Tennessee River bridge to Clarksville on the Cumberland River, and on to Bowling Green. They passed "through a beautiful country" of fields and rolling hills covered with trees. It may have occurred to Cleburne as the train rumbled northward that this was the same railroad that led to Covington and Newport, across the Ohio from Cincinnati where his stepmother, sister, and two of his half brothers lived. What had become of them? The last he had heard, Joe was planning to join the Union army and Robert was wavering, hoping that Kentucky could preserve its neutrality. Had they joined Lincoln's army? Were they, even now, in the ranks of the army he was rushing to fight? [32]

Cleburne arrived in Bowling Green with the rest of Hardee's brigade in mid-October and found the city crowded with arriving troops and homeless refugees. Situated on a series of low hills on the southern bank of the Barren River, Bowling Green was the linchpin of Johnston's defensive line. Connected by rail to the Confederate logistic base at Nashville and to Polk's force at Columbus, it constituted a salient jutting into central Kentucky. It was, moreover, a salient whose flanks were vulnerable. Too distant from either Nashville or Columbus for effective mutual support or reinforcement, the city could be turned on either flank. The Confederates had only a small army in the Appalachian highlands to guard the right of Johnston's extended line, and the left flank was wholly dependent on two forts guarding the Tennessee and Cumberland Rivers: Fort Henry on the Tennessee and Fort Donelson on the Cumberland. Ironically, the greatest strength of the Confederate position at Bowling Green was that the Federals had no idea of Johnston's weakness.[33]

For his part, Johnston was keenly aware of the precariousness of his position, and he was therefore considerably relieved when the arrival of Hardee's Brigade made possible a reorganization of the troops at Bowling Green into what he called the Army of Central Kentucky. Johnston named Buckner and Hardee as division commanders in this new army, and Hardee, in turn, nominated his three most senior regimental commanders to lead the three brigades in his division: Cleburne, Hindman, and R. G. Shaver. For Cleburne this was another dramatic step upward since promotion to brigadier general was likely to follow.

His new command consisted of four regiments: his own 1st Arkansas, now under Lieutenant Colonel A. K. Patton, the 5th Arkansas, the 6th Mississippi, and the 5th Tennessee. His new status as a brigade commander also entitled him to a staff. While Captains Charles H. Carlton and Benjamin F. Phillips took up the principal administrative duties of the brigade, Cleburne named two young lieutenants from his adopted hometown as his aides-de-camp. One was his former law partner Learned H. Mangum, and the other was Judge Hanley's son Steven. Both young men proved intensely loyal to their commander and remained with him for the rest of the war.[34]

Cleburne advanced his new command to the rim of an open valley five miles north of Bowling Green, a site that afforded an unobstructed view to the north, reporting to Hardee that his position was "sufficiently advanced to give us warning of an enemy's approach." His greatest problem was the lack of sufficient cavalry to scout the countryside for intelligence of enemy movements. He tried to solicit information from the locals, but the area of Kentucky north of Bowling Green was pro-Union in sentiment, and none of the residents would admit to any knowledge of Yankee dispositions. Cleburne wrote to Hardee, "I will keep a sharp lookout myself." [35]

Aware that his small army at Bowling Green was vulnerable to a determined Yankee assault, Johnston ordered his commanders to put up a bold front by conducting frequent patrols into no-man's land. Whenever the troops were not drilling or participating in divisional reviews (held once a week), they conducted forced marches to nearby towns. Even after the glorious October weather gave way to fits of lashing rain in November, the daily drill and occasional forced marches continued. Cleburne adjusted relatively easily from the hands-on style of command he had mastered as colonel of the 1st Arkansas to the more remote role of brigade commander. He continued to be an active drillmaster, supervising not only brigade drills but regimental and battalion drills as well. Those who were not used to such an active regimen of drill or Cleburne's strict application of the rules were somewhat taken aback at first. One private recalled that the brigade commander "was plain [and] unassuming, but resolute and determined. Everyone soon learned his orders must be obeyed." [36]

Cleburne's first opportunity to lead an independent expedition against the enemy came in November. In response to intelligence reports that Federal forces had occupied Jamestown, Kentucky, seventy-five miles to the east, Hardee dispatched Cleburne in command of 1,600 men with orders to "attack and destroy them." Johnston hoped that this foray deep into central Kentucky would help convince the Federals that the Confederate force at Bowling Green was larger than it was, and Cleburne was encouraged to promote the impression that his command was merely the van of a larger force. Cleburne set out on 9 November following a route that led his command into unfriendly territory across broken, hilly countryside perfectly adapted to ambush. At first the residents appeared to welcome the Confederates; the people of Scottsville offered the soldiers an "enthusiastic reception." But as the column advanced deeper into Kentucky, the march took on an eerie aspect. "We did not find a friend along the whole road," Cleburne reported, "houses were closed and [the] countryside apparently deserted." One of the few residents he encountered was an old woman who stood in the road with an open Bible in her hands, proclaiming loudly that she was "prepared and ready to die." Nothing Cleburne said could convince her that they did not mean to kill her.[37]

At Jamestown, the advance guard chased away some forty or fifty Yankee cavalry. It was evident, however, that there were no significant enemy forces in the vicinity, although the population was "bitterly hostile" and Cleburne could find no one who could or would tell him anything about the strength or location of the Federals. Finally, late at night, a local resident was ushered into his presence who claimed that the countryside was full of Federals: 3,000 at Campbellsville, another 3,000 at Columbia, and 300 more at Lebanon. If so, Cleburne never made contact with any of them. He put his brigade back on the road the next day, marching by a different route back toward Bowling Green.[38]

At Tomkinville, Cleburne decided to stage a dramatic entrance into town. After scouts assured him there were no enemy forces there, he ordered the regimental bands to the front, unfurled the colors, and had the men fix bayonets. The brigade then marched into Tomkinville in full panoply. But the gesture was apparently wasted, for the town was all but deserted. Cleburne was "astonished at the utter silence and desertion." He saw only two people, both of whom immediately fled. At once suspicious, he ordered the bands to retire and sent out skirmishers. But his men found no sign of either enemy forces or townspeople. He bivouacked his brigade in a field near town, and within a few days most of the women and children returned but few men turned up, presumably because they were off serving with the enemy.[39]

Throughout the march, Cleburne did what he could to convince the local population that Confederate forces were there to protect them rather than to plunder them. When locals complained that men under his command had stolen private property, Cleburne paid for it out of his own pocket. When his patrols found trunks and other articles hidden in the woods by locals for safety or dropped in haste as the population fled, he ordered that they be placed on the porch of the nearest house and labeled "returned by Southern soldiers."[40]

Cleburne and his brigade returned to their bivouac north of Bowling Green on 15 November. Although they had been fired at twice from ambush, the only casualty was a man who had fallen from a wagon, and Cleburne reported to Hardee that he did not believe Federal forces in central Kentucky posed an immediate threat. Indeed, a local resident whom Cleburne suspected of being a northern spy claimed that the enemy was "falling back . . . in consternation" and that "they seemed frightened." Although Cleburne was skeptical, the report was true. His advance had stirred unreasoning panic in Federal headquarters, and Federal forces in central Kentucky were beating a hasty retreat back to Louisville and Cincinnati in what came to be known as "the Wild Cat Stampede."[41]

After Cleburne's foray in mid-November, there was little activity on his front through the holiday season. He even managed to get away to Nashville for two days to purchase some new uniforms. Elsewhere in Kentucky, however, the Rebel position was under serious attack. The defeat of a small Confederate army in the Battle of Mill Springs on 19 January uncovered the right flank of Johnston's long Kentucky line, and two weeks later the troops at Bowling Green learned of the fall of Fort Henry on the Tennessee River, which exposed their left flank. The fall of Fort Henry was particularly ominous, for it suggested that the river forts guarding the Confederate left-center were unreliable. If Fort Donelson on the Cumberland River also fell, the army at Bowling Green would be cut off. On 7 February 1862, Johnston and his newly arrived second in command, Pierre G. T. Beauregard, decided to evacuate both Bowling Green and Columbus.[42]

The Confederate army began its retreat on 11 February. Hardee's Division, including Cleburne's Brigade, remained behind with orders to act as a rear guard and to destroy the accumulated supplies that could not be hauled away. Those supplies, plus the hundreds of sick who could not walk, filled the few available railcars. Three days later, as Federal artillery shells began to fall about the rail yards, the men of Cleburne's Brigade joined the exodus southward. They marched along the Louisville and Nashville Pike with their backs to the enemy while a cold rain mixed with sleet beat about them. The road was "slopy and disagreeable" and by the time they arrived in Nashville, eighty miles to the south, late on the evening of 16 February, they were "worn out, hungry, and tired."[43]

Nashville offered no haven or even a respite. The much dreaded news of the surrender of Fort Donelson arrived in the city that same night and made a further withdrawal necessary. As the men of Cleburne's Brigade prepared to board railcars for the trip south to Murfreesboro, the disappointed civilians of Nashville perceived that they were about to be abandoned to the enemy. Public order broke down, as mobs surged through the streets pillaging what the army left behind. Some civilians taunted the soldiers for running away; a mob outside Hardee's headquarters called the generals cowards and shouted for them to come out. With such taunts still ringing in their ears, the soldiers crammed themselves into the few available railroad cars, "having just enough room to turn around," and rolled slowly southward. Nashville was the first

Confederate state capital to be lost to the enemy, and it was lost without a fight.[44]

At Murfreesboro the troops passed around the rumor that the army would make a stand there, but after a week's rest, the retreat continued, this time on foot. Rain mixed with wet snow plagued them every step of the way. The rain made it hard to keep a fire going long enough to cook a meal; nor was sleep easy to find as strong winds knocked over the tents and provoked mad scrambles to secure flapping canvas. Johnston reported to Richmond that the army was in "good spirits," but Braxton Bragg reported more accurately that "confidence is lost on all hands."[45]

The fourth of March was the first anniversary of Lincoln's inauguration as president. On that day Cleburne was with his brigade at Shelbyville, Tennessee, on the Duck River, where his command constituted the rear guard of the army. That day, too, Cleburne received official notification of his promotion to brigadier general. The news was gratifying to be sure, but the army's circumstances did not encourage self-congratulation. His commitment to discipline and his rigorous work ethic had brought him promotion; he had won the respect of his men and the confidence of his superiors. But he had not had an opportunity to demonstrate his most salient characteristic as a commander: a reckless disdain for personal danger in the face of enemy fire. A brigadier general he might be, but after a year in uniform, he had not yet participated in a major battle.[46]

He would not have long to wait.

4
FIRST BLOOD: SHILOH

The bloody two-day Battle of Shiloh in April 1862 was Pat Cleburne's first experience with Civil War combat on a large scale. Despite his three and a half years in the British army, his year in Confederate gray, and the new stars on his collar, he had never led a large number of men in a desperate fight. He did not shrink from the prospect. He believed unreservedly in the justice of his cause and the innate superiority of his troops, and he had no doubt about the final outcome. Even as he and his men slogged southward through Tennessee and eventually into northern Alabama, he continued to insist upon a level of discipline and readiness that was unsurpassed in the army. He felt confident that when the time came, he and his command would be ready. His confidence was not entirely well-founded; despite his dedicated regimen of drill and maneuver, neither he nor anyone else was prepared for the unprecedented maelstrom of violence that occurred in the woods and fields near Pittsburg Landing beside a small country church called Shiloh.

After the fall of Fort Donelson, Federal forces followed up their success by mounting a river-borne invasion up the Tennessee River. Far from acting as a barrier, the Tennessee was instead a liquid highway for the Federal flotilla that used it to move swiftly and with relative ease into the Confederate heartland. After the fall of Fort Henry, Federal ironclads had steamed southward to destroy the railroad bridge that linked Bowling Green and Columbus, an event that had hastened Johnston's decision to give up Bowling Green and withdraw southward. But the Federals did not stop there. In early March, Braxton Bragg, who commanded Confederate forces near the crucial railroad junction at Corinth, Mississippi, reported that upwards of 30,000 Federals had come ashore at Pittsburg Landing on the west bank of the Tennessee less than two dozen miles from the Mississippi state line. Having lost Kentucky, the Confederates seemed to be on the verge of losing Tennessee as well.

Within the command circles of the Confederate forces retreating from Nashville, it was the newcomer Beauregard who saw an opportunity in the developing situation. Full of both confidence and imagination, the hero of Manassas convinced the demoralized Johnston that they should move their forces to Corinth to join with Bragg and pounce on the Federal army at Pittsburg Landing before it could be reinforced. Johnston hesitated, fearing to uncover Chattanooga, but eventually Beauregard's infectious enthusiasm captured his imagination; his mood swung dramatically from deep pessimism to unrealistic optimism. The Confederate retreat turned into a concentration of forces preparatory to an attack. It was a rather desperate gamble, but these were desperate times. As Hardee's confidante, Cleburne was aware of this plan almost from its genesis. When he received orders to move his brigade from Decatur to Corinth by rail, he knew that it was part of an elaborate plan to concentrate Confederate forces from four states for a decisive counterstroke. As much as anyone, he looked forward to the chance to redeem the long retreat with a victory.[1]

Cleburne arrived in Corinth in the third week of March. The small town near the railroad junction was merely a reference point for the sprawling army camp. By the end of the month, Cleburne's was one of fifteen brigades—a total of nearly 40,000 men—encamped in and about Corinth. His brigade remained in Hardee's Division, now redesignated as a "corps" in the new organization of what Johnston labeled the Army of the Mississippi. Cleburne's friend Hindman held a rather curious assignment as the commander of Hardee's other two brigades (those of R. G. Shaver and Sterling Wood). Polk's force from Columbus constituted another corps, as did Bragg's force of six brigades from Louisiana, Alabama, and Mississippi. A fourth corps was entrusted to the Kentuckian George B. Crittenden, although he was soon replaced by John C. Breckinridge after Hardee found Crittenden and one of his subordinates drunk on duty.[2]

In the general reorganization, Cleburne's brigade was augmented to a total of six regiments. He kept his old regiment, the 1st Arkansas, though it was now redesignated as the 15th Arkansas (despite Cleburne's protests) because another unit claimed pride of place as Arkansas' first regiment. He also retained the 6th Mississippi. The rest of his men were Tennesseans. The 5th Tennessee, like the 1st Arkansas, had to give up its number to another unit and became the 35th Tennessee.[3] New to the brigade was the 2d Tennessee under the capable leadership of Colonel William Bate who, like Cleburne, had enlisted as a private the year before and been elected to a colonelcy.[4]

All this reorganization was more impressive in theory than in reality. Many (some said most) of the Confederate troops at Corinth were virtually undisciplined. Bragg, whose penchant for discipline bordered on obsession, went further and asserted that "part of this army is in a state of chaos." Even so, having uncovered Chattanooga and Georgia to the Federals in order to achieve this concentration of force, Johnston was committed. The attack would go forward, and as soon as possible lest the Federals manage to concentrate their own forces. Somewhat unrealistically, Johnston issued orders to all corps commanders to have their forces ready to move by 6:00 A.M. on 3 April. Each man was to carry five days' cooked rations and 100 rounds of ammunition. Hardee's Corps would lead both the order of march as well as the subsequent attack, and Cleburne's Brigade would lead Hardee's Corps. The army would march to the vicinity of the Federal camp during the daylight hours of 3 and 4 April and launch a surprise attack at dawn on the fifth.[5]

Alerted by Hardee sometime after 2:00 A.M. on 3 April, Cleburne ordered reveille for 6:00, and his men spent the early morning hours cooking their five days' rations. Beauregard had told Hardee orally that his corps should be ready to move by noon, but at 8:00 A.M. Bragg, in his capacity as Johnston's chief of staff, told Hardee to move "as soon as practicable." Cleburne started his brigade out of camp just before noon, but even then the chaotic circumstances in much of the rest of the army caused delays as Cleburne's men threaded their way out of Corinth. The rest of Hardee's Corps did not move until after 3:00 P.M. when Hardee finally received written orders. Polk's corps left that evening, and Bragg's own corps got a late start due to an error by a staff officer. The result was that the Army of the Mississippi, like its namesake, became a meandering river of men flowing sluggishly toward the Federal force at Pittsburg Landing. It was not an auspicious beginning.[6]

The object of the first day's march was Mickey's Farmhouse, about halfway to Pittsburg Landing. Just as Mother Nature had seemed to mirror the somber mood of the troops during the long retreat from Kentucky, so now did she now turn a benevolent face on the soldiers as they advanced: the day was clear and bright, the roads relatively dry. Since Cleburne's was the lead brigade, his men stepped out unobstructed by other units on the road, and within a matter of hours they had crossed back into Tennessee, the event provoking cheers from the Tennessee troops who made up two-thirds of Cleburne's command.[7]

Near dusk, one of the divisional guides reported that a spring just off the main road could provide fresh drinking water for the troops. Cleburne therefore turned his column off onto a side road and ordered his men into bivouac near the spring. He visited the camp of each unit and made a series of formal speeches. He told the troops that they would most likely be engaged in a great battle within the next twenty-four hours. "Do your duty as good soldiers," he told them, "and you will gain a great victory which will restore you to your families and homes." He urged the Tennessee troops to think of the coming battle as a fight for their "homes and firesides." A private from the 23d Tennessee was impressed and wrote later that "Old Pat was an eloquent talker."[8]

Cleburne had his men up early on 4 April, and before the sun was very high above the horizon he had them back on the main road marching toward Mickey's Farmhouse. After only a mile or two, however, he found the road blocked by the baggage wagons of Polk's corps, which had passed the turnoff to the spring during the night and gone into camp on the main road ahead of him. Since Hardee's Corps was supposed to lead the advance, Polk's men now had to clear the road to allow Cleburne's to pass. Wagon drivers whipped their teams off onto the shoulder of the narrow roadway, but Cleburne's wagons and artillery had to maneuver past them with some care. Cleburne began to fear that he would arrive late to the jump-off point assigned to him. Although he could not have known it, other units in the advance were having even more serious difficulties. After their late start, the men of Bragg's Corps encountered delays on the narrow road assigned to them which proved inadequate for their baggage train, and on his own Bragg decided to change roads, a decision that caused more delays and confusion.

Cleburne arrived at Mickey's Farmhouse early in the afternoon on 4 April, on schedule after all, but the rest of the army trailed out behind him on converging roads all the way to Corinth. Bragg's corps in particular was hugely behind schedule; and as a result there was little chance that the planned battle could begin the next morning. Even so, an unplanned battle almost began that afternoon. At about 3:30, as Cleburne's men waited in the shade of the trees for orders, they heard firing in the woods in front of them. Two companies of James H. Clanton's 1st Alabama Cavalry, which had been screening their advance, came dashing back through the woods pursued by 150 or so bluecoated horsemen. Cleburne's men raised their rifles and as the Federals appeared over the crest of a small rise, they delivered a full volley at close range. So stunned were the Federal troopers that several who survived the fusillade were unable to stop their momentum; one rode into the line of Rebel infantry and was taken prisoner. The rest wheeled about and galloped back the way they had come. It seemed likely that the chance of catching the Federal army by surprise had evaporated. Even so, when his men went into bivouac that night, Cleburne cautioned his regimental commanders to avoid the use of bugles or drums so as not to alert the enemy, whose main camp was only a few miles to the east.[9]

When Cleburne settled his brigade down for the night, a gentle rain was falling. During the night it increased in intensity—a "cold drenching rain," one soldier recalled, "which made it very disagreeable." Expecting a fight, the men had marched from Corinth without tents, and as the rain began pounding down in earnest at about two o'clock in the morning, many of them scurried about to find more sheltered places to sleep. Of course, the rain turned the roads once again into sloughs. Hardee had told Cleburne to move at 3:00 A.M., and Cleburne dutifully roused the troops at that hour. But in the pitch-dark, with the rain bucketing down and the roads in a terrible state, it was evident that any advance under such conditions would lead only to chaos. He decided to wait until first light.[10]

There were the usual noises to be expected when 3,000 men rose from sleep and assembled for battle, but Cleburne had ordered silence in the ranks and for the most part, his discipline held. Elsewhere in Hardee's command, there were more serious problems. Inevitably, a few of the men worried that the rain had ruined their store of powder, and to test the charges in their rifles, they pulled the triggers on their muskets "to see if they would go off." By five o'clock, the eastern sky had grown lighter though the roads remained hopeless. Cleburne continued to wait. Finally a little before seven, he ordered his forces to begin a cautious advance. Soon they were so close that Cleburne could hear the drums and bugles from the Federal encampment. Some of his soldiers later claimed that they could hear the Federal officers shouting out commands as the Yankees conducted early morning drill, apparently oblivious to the presence of a large body of enemy forces nearby.[11]

It was the morning of 5 April. In accordance with the original battle plan, Cleburne deployed his six regiments of infantry in position for an attack. At that hour, however, Hardee's Corps was the *only* one in position. On Cleburne's right, the two brigades under Hindman's command had arrived during the night, but the rest of the army was still in motion, lumbering haltingly toward the attack positions assigned them in Beauregard's battle plan. Indeed, although Cleburne did not know it, Beauregard was beginning to lose his nerve. Cleburne's skirmish with Federal cavalry the day before and the undisciplined firing of infantry muskets that morning had convinced him that all hope of surprising the Federals was now lost. It was Albert Sidney Johnston who took the bit in his teeth. Having decided that he would attack the Federal army at Pittsburg Landing, he refused to be deterred despite mounting evidence that the enemy must surely have tumbled to the Confederate plan by now. "I would fight them," he muttered to an aide, "if they were a million." It was clear, however, that the attack could not take place that morning. Cleburne received orders to wait where he was until the rest of the army could join him.[12]

Once again he ordered his six regiments into bivouac. To the 15th Arkansas, the troops whom he had trained personally, he assigned the crucial role of advanced skirmishers with orders to keep a sharp lookout. Behind them, he placed the four Tennessee regiments and the 6th Mississippi in a north-south line facing east. Since his brigade constituted the extreme left of the Confederate line, he placed his left-hand regiment, the 2d Tennessee under William Bate, slightly to the rear in echelon formation, in order to guard his exposed flank. By ten o'clock all his men were in position, and like their commander, they settled down to wait.

For men anticipating battle, the wait was excruciating. It was no less so for Cleburne. Although he had spent a lifetime learning to disguise his inner feelings, his taut nerves were evident in his repeated orders throughout the day to form up, each time in the expectation of an imminent order to advance. Each time, he received another order to wait, and the men stood down again. Anticipation peaked just past noon when Beauregard appeared in person, surrounded by his staff. In a short impromptu speech, he urged the men of Cleburne's Brigade to "shoot low" and press the enemy hard, reminding them too not to cheer his remarks owing to the proximity of the enemy camp. Beauregard rode on, and the waiting continued. The afternoon passed slowly. Bragg's Corps, which was to form the second line of the Confederate advance, began to fall in behind them in the early afternoon, but the last division did not arrive until almost five o'clock. By then, it was evident to all that the battle would have to be postponed until the next day.[13]

For the second night in a row, the men of Cleburne's Brigade lay down on damp ground. They were too close to the enemy lines to light fires, but at least there was no rain and the night was clear and cool, ideal for sleeping. Cleburne, too, slept on the ground, if he slept at all. A few minutes before five the next morning, he and his men took a breakfast of cold meat and hardtack, and once again he deployed his six regiments for the expected fight. On his right were Hindman's two brigades, first Wood's and then Shaver's, and beyond them, Adley H. Gladden's Alabama Brigade of Bragg's Corps, added to the right flank to extend the front to Lick Creek. On his left, however, beyond Bate's 2d Tennessee regiment, there was only an open flank. Since the battle plan called for a broad continuous front, Cleburne was determined to ensure that his own advance was closely coordinated with that of Wood's Brigade on his right. Any gap between the two units might be exploited by the enemy. In order to oversee the effective correlation of the advance, he placed himself near the right flank of his front line, between the 23d Tennessee on the extreme right and the 6th Mississippi.[14]

At about a quarter after five, Cleburne heard the sounds of skirmishing to his right, and it grew gradually in intensity until about 6:30, when orders finally arrived for the long-anticipated advance to begin. Cleburne dispatched couriers along the line to relay the orders, and the brigade moved forward "silently and grandly." As if in promise of a glorious culmination to the frustrations of the past two months, the morning was bright and clear, "a typical spring morning," one soldier recalled, with "the air fresh and bracing." The ranks advanced as steadily as the terrain and tree cover allowed, with anticipation growing at every step.[15]

Cleburne spotted the enemy camp about a quarter mile ahead. The rattle of musketry to his right was now pretty general, suggesting that Wood's Brigade was fully engaged; he could hear drums in the enemy camp beating the long roll as the Yankees reacted to the unexpected assault. Before he could come to grips with them, however, he first encountered a more prosaic obstacle: a small stream flowing right to left across his front. It was Shiloh Branch, so small it was not even on any of the maps, but which had overflowed its banks in the recent rainfall and spread out into a marshy lowland "filled with undergrowth and tangled vines." Unwilling to let this minor obstacle disrupt the continuity of his battle line, Cleburne tried to force his way through it, and he spurred his horse into the tangle of bushes. Cleburne's horse was "an ungainly gray steed of peculiar power," but it shied at the wall of brush, and when its hooves were grabbed by the treacly mud of Shiloh Branch, it panicked. Despite Cleburne's urging, it reared back in fright and threw its rider. Cleburne fell full length into the mud. He was not hurt, and he was up at once climbing back into the saddle, but it was evident that the swampy morass could not be overcome by sheer will. He could not go through it; he must therefore go around.[16]

The ground was firmer to both the right and the left, and as the men advanced, the swamp acted as a wedge dividing Cleburne's command into two unequal halves. The three Tennessee regiments on the left, and most of the 15th Arkansas, moved further left, leaving the swamp to their right. The two right-hand regiments, the 6th Mississippi and the 23d Tennessee, moved to the right in order to maintain contact with Wood's Brigade. Cleburne went with them. In effect, the swamp cut off two-thirds of his command before he even encountered the enemy. He now led only two regiments, fewer than 1,000 men.

Emerging from the woods into an open field, Cleburne and his two regiments prepared to assault the enemy camp and, just beyond it, an improvised breastwork of logs and hay bales. Although utterly surprised by the Confederate onslaught, the Federals in front of Cleburne's two regiments were in a

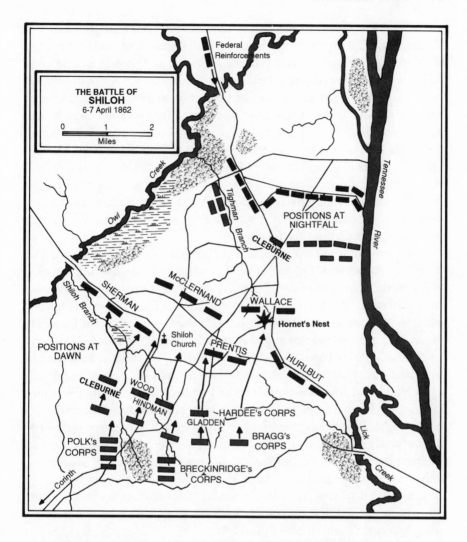

THE BATTLE OF
SHILOH
6-7 April 1862

0   1   2
Miles

Federal
Reinforcements

Owl Creek

Tighman Branch

Tennessee River

POSITIONS AT
NIGHTFALL

CLEBURNE

Shiloh Branch

SHERMAN

McCLERNAND

WALLACE

Hornet's Nest

Shiloh
Church

PRENTIS

HURLBUT

POSITIONS AT
DAWN

CLEBURNE

WOOD

HINDMAN

GLADDEN

HARDEE's CORPS

BRAGG's
CORPS

POLK's
CORPS

BRECKINRIDGE's
CORPS

Corinth

Lick Creek

naturally strong position: they held the high ground with an open field of
fire in front of them. One veteran of the 23d Tennessee who looked up at
the Federal line later wrote that the position was "virtually impregnable to a
direct attack." Impregnable or not, a direct attack was exactly what Cleburne
ordered. Placing himself in their midst, on foot now with his sword drawn,
he ordered the two regiments to charge. The men responded with enthusiasm. An observer later reported that "General Cleburne's brigade moved
in fine order" over the open field. The bluecoated soldiers in front of them
began to fall back, giving up their campsite where breakfast fires still smol-
dered. Cleburne rushed forward to lead a pursuit.[17]

The moment of anticipated victory did not last. The breastwork that was the target of Cleburne's assault was manned by three Ohio regiments from the division of Major General William T. Sherman. Although the attackers had the advantage of surprise, the defenders had the advantage of both numbers and position. Before the men of the 6th Mississippi and the 23d Tennessee could reach the enemy line, they were torn apart not only by the well-directed fire of the bluecoated infantry but also by unseen Federal artillery. Cleburne ordered his own artillery, under Captain John Trigg, to open fire on the enemy guns, but the Federal guns were better sited and Trigg's battery had no visible effect. Clearly at a disadvantage in firing at an enemy he could not see, Trigg limbered up his guns and cantered off to find a better position. Somewhat forlornly, Cleburne later wrote, "I had no artillery under my command from this time forward." [18]

It was now nearly 8:00 o'clock, and Cleburne could hear the sound of battle all around him. Off to his right, the men of Wood's Brigade were well into the fight, and he could hear the Rebel yell resounding through the trees. Although the swamp on his left cut him off from the rest of his brigade, he resolved to do what he could with the two regiments at hand. He ordered the men to re-form and charge again. "Boys," he called out, "don't be discouraged. Fix bayonets and give them steel." By now the Federals had recovered from their initial shock, and the renewed Confederate assault was again blasted by close range musketry and artillery. Urged on by their commander, the Confederates pressed their attack, but once again sheer will was not enough. Those among the attackers who were still standing recoiled from the storm of minié balls and artillery. Among the fallen were both regimental commanders and both of their seconds in command. In the 6th Mississippi, only sixty men managed to re-form; the senior surviving officer was a captain. In his official report, Cleburne noted, "It would be useless to enlarge on the courage and devotion of the Sixth Mississippi. The facts as recorded speak louder than any words of mine." [19]

Miraculously, Cleburne himself was unhurt. But he could see that his two regiments were incapable of further offensive action. Perhaps in frustration, perhaps in desperation, he mounted and galloped around the swampy morass that had split his command in half to try to find the rest of his brigade. He found it at about ten o'clock pinned down by what he described as "a murderous crossfire." He quickly learned that after having been cut off by the swamp, the three regiments had continued to advance until they encountered the defensive line of a Federal division. They had fired a volley and drawn first blood, but they faced a superior and steadily increasing fire and were soon "terribly cut up." Most of the officers of the 2d Tennessee, includ-

ing every company commander as well as the gallant Colonel Bate, had fallen
to the fierce Federal fire. Like the 6th Mississippi, the 2d Tennessee was all
but leaderless.[20]

Cleburne saw that there was little he could do until the arrival of reinforcements from Bragg's Corps. He watched the firefight for some minutes, then
decided that he could be more effective back on the right after all. Again he
put the spurs to his horse and galloped back around the swamp to the shattered remnants of the 6th Mississippi and the 23d Tennessee. The survivors of
those two regiments, perhaps two hundred men altogether, may have considered Cleburne's reappearance a mixed blessing. Nevertheless, when he called
on them to renew the advance, they responded. Cleburne lined them up and,
as he subsequently described it, "advanced directly to my front, through the
enemy's encampment." By now the Ohio troops who had fought off the first
two of Cleburne's impetuous attacks had begun to perceive that they faced
a general assault by the Rebel army; their left had been turned by the steady
advance of Wood's Brigade. Thus when they were struck by Cleburne's men
for a third time, they abandoned their position and fled. Satisfied at last that
the men of the 6th Mississippi and 23d Tennessee had done their duty, Cleburne dismissed the exhausted survivors and sent them to the rear, willing to
admit that they were "unfitted . . . for further service."[21]

Now a brigade commander without a command, Cleburne again prepared
to ride around the swamp to see how things went on the left. En route, he
ran into Hardee to whom he reported the circumstances and condition of
his troops. Hardee ordered him to round up the stragglers who had stopped
to loot the Federal camp, and Cleburne dashed off to obey. He found the
assignment frustrating. The men were reluctant to respond to a commander
not their own and reacted sluggishly and with apparent regret, even resentment. Their numbers were not great in any case, and after several hours of
attempting to put together a force that would prove useful in the fight—the
sound of which could still be heard to the east—he gave up and returned to
his own command.[22]

Cleburne rejoined his three Tennessee regiments on the extreme left of
the Confederate line at about two o'clock. Though the advance had moved
swiftly on other parts of the field, here the Federals had a nearly 2 to 1 advantage in numbers and were still holding their own. The 2d Tennessee was
badly disorganized, as was the 15th Arkansas, part of which had been cut off
by the swamp. But the 24th and 5th (35th) Tennessee regiments were mostly
intact, and Cleburne knew exactly what to do with them. "On reaching the
ground I ordered an immediate advance," he wrote later in his report. He was
delayed briefly by a Confederate battery that was firing across his intended

line of attack, but as soon as he got that sorted out he "pushed directly forward." In a few minutes, his men encountered the enemy front line. Cleburne urged his men forward in a sharp engagement that lasted about a half hour until suddenly the Federals gave way. As elsewhere on the field, their left flank had been uncovered and they had to fall back to prevent encirclement.[23]

Cleburne's instinct was to go after them, but his men were not only badly reduced by casualties, the survivors were all but out of ammunition. Moreover, the swamp and the thick woods had scattered them so that there was little unit cohesion left. Cleburne reluctantly halted the advance and regrouped his forces while a fatigue party went back to the brigade wagons for ammunition. Matching their commander's zeal, the volunteers "carried boxes of ammunition on their shoulders up and down the steep hills for more than a mile." As soon as they returned and cartridges were distributed, Cleburne again ordered an advance.[24]

With no more than 600 men, Cleburne pushed ahead. He "continued to move forward until checked by a heavy fire of artillery" from not only the enemy field guns, but from the Federal gunboats in the Tennessee River, which were firing large caliber shells into the woods in the hope of stopping the Rebel onslaught. Confronted with this new terror, Cleburne's men took cover briefly, but when there was a lull in the firing, he ordered them forward again. He was still pushing them forward at dusk when a courier arrived with the news that General Johnston had been killed and that General Beauregard had ordered the attack to be halted.[25]

With the fall of darkness, the two armies gradually fell silent and the combatants staggered into temporary bivouacs. Cleburne himself returned slowly to one of the enemy campsites that had been overrun that morning and was soon asleep in a Federal tent. It rained again during the night, heavy at times, so that the sound of it briefly drowned out the plaintive calls for help from the wounded. To add to the general misery, every ten or fifteen minutes the Federal gunboats threw a round or two of explosive ordnance in the general vicinity of the Confederate encampment. Some of the shells fell among the men of Cleburne's Brigade, but others landed indiscriminately among the wounded of both sides. Outraged, Cleburne later wrote, "History records few instances of more reckless inhumanity than this."[26]

Cleburne most likely went to sleep that night determined to resume the advance with the first light of dawn. Instead he awoke to the news that the Federals were themselves advancing, "pushing forward and driving in our pickets." He assumed at once that Buell's army had arrived and realized that "we had a fresh army to fight." Nevertheless, he had already determined to order a forward movement when a courier arrived from Hardee with orders "to advance on the Bank Road." Cleburne mounted and rode among the men, ordering them to form up. He directed them to fire off the rounds in their rifles that almost certainly had been ruined by the night's heavy rain and to reload with fresh powder and shot. Of the 2,700 men who had gone with him into the fight twenty-four hours earlier, only about 800 were now left to answer the roll. He could not help noting the dramatic contrast. "My brigade was sadly reduced," he wrote later. "Hundreds of my best men were dead or in the hospitals." Even so, he had little doubt about how he would employ his reduced command. He moved the men forward until he found another line of Confederate infantry facing east. It turned out to be part of Breckinridge's Reserve Corps, and Cleburne deployed his own small brigade to extend its left.[27]

He could see the enemy's front line in plain sight. He could see, too, that "it stretched beyond my left as far as the eye could see." Cleburne's left flank was completely in the air. Worse, he could see a large number of troops in that direction who were crossing a small clearing and heading for his own rear. They might be Confederates falling back to re-form, but they might also be enemy troops, and if that were the case, he would soon be completely outflanked. He watched them through his field glasses, but smoke obscured the field. As he watched, Major John Kelly of the 14th Arkansas, from Wood's Brigade, rode up to tell him that the troops were Federals. Cleburne thereupon ordered the six-gun battery of the Washington Artillery to open fire. Federal artillery responded, and soon found the range; enemy shells fell among the Confederate cannoneers killing several of the horses and wounding a few of the gunners.[28]

While Cleburne was awaiting the outcome of the artillery duel, and wondering if the Federal forces on his left rendered his position completely untenable, an officer from Breckinridge's staff rode up with orders to move forward at once and attack the forces in his front. Hardly one to question an order, especially an order to advance, Cleburne nevertheless questioned this one. He told the staff officer that he was "completely without support and outflanked on the left and would be destroyed if I advanced." The staff officer answered that the orders came from General Bragg, that they were positive orders, and that Cleburne must immediately obey.[29]

Again Cleburne ordered his now regiment-sized brigade to advance, but the forward movement had barely begun when the renewed fire of Federal gunners on the left compelled a halt. Cleburne ordered his men into a shallow depression where they would be protected from the shelling while they awaited the outcome of the long-range artillery duel. Even here the men were not entirely shielded from injury; the shells screaming overhead cut limbs from the trees that fell among the men and killed several of them. Gradually, the fire from the Confederate guns slackened and the Federal gunners gained the upper hand. Even so, Cleburne gave the order to advance and "the whole line of infantry charged the enemy." Their advance was slowed by the thick underbrush that again broke up the unity of his line. Hundreds of bullets whined through the trees to clip off branches overhead or thud softly into the yielding body of a soldier. Cleburne advanced more or less blindly; he could not see very far in any direction and was reduced to the effective role of company commander. "I could not see what was going on to my right or left but my men were dropping all around before the fire of an unseen foe." Ed Cowley, the town clerk from Helena who had replaced Cleburne as captain of the Yell Rifles, fell dead, shot through the head. Cleburne himself continued to be spared. The pace of the advance slowed and then stopped altogether. Outnumbered, unsupported, and targeted by an unseen foe, Cleburne ordered a withdrawal. The experience made him bitter, and he directed much of that bitterness toward Bragg who had ordered the foolish attack. A month later his pique was still evident in his official report: "My brigade was repulsed and almost completely routed in this unfortunate attack."[30]

Once the withdrawal began, unit integrity all but collapsed. Only the 15th Arkansas, the regiment that Cleburne had drilled personally from the first days of the war, rallied to his call. With a few score men, Cleburne occupied the reverse slope of a low hill and attempted to act as a rear guard. When a Federal unit advanced across his front, Cleburne could not resist ordering a counterattack as he led about 60 men over the crest of the hill. His furious charge temporarily halted the Federal pursuit, but it resulted in the death of Lt. Col. Patton who had succeeded Cleburne to the command of the 15th Arkansas. Patton had been the last surviving field officer in the regiment. With 58 men now left of his original 2,700, Cleburne started for the rear.[31]

"My brigade was now completely scattered and disorganized," he later reported. But he did not quit the field. He tried to rally small groups of stragglers and form them into lines to resist the further advance of the enemy; he directed the removal of those too injured to walk; and he rode among the abandoned Federal camps, determined to destroy what could not be carried away. He was still at it after sunset when Hardee ordered him to fall back and he began the long retreat back to Corinth.[32]

Shiloh was a disaster for the Confederacy. Needing a decisive victory to reverse the momentum of events in the West, the best the southern army could achieve was a partial success on the first day and a devastating defeat on the second. It was not for lack of trying. Albert Sidney Johnston gave his life in the fight, refusing medical attention while he slowly bled to death from a superficial wound, and over 10,000 men—nearly a third of the army—were killed, wounded, or missing. It was little consolation that Federal losses were even greater; the losses sustained by both sides in the two-day fight (nearly 24,000) dwarfed those of the celebrated Confederate victory at Manassas where some 3,500 had fallen.[33] Afterward, southern newspapers would criticize Beauregard for halting the battle at dusk on 6 April when victory (they asserted) might still have been achieved. For their part, northern newspapers criticized the Union high command—especially Grant, who arrived on the field only after the battle was well under way—for being surprised in the first place and for failing to carry out an effective pursuit that might have destroyed what was left of the southern army. Whatever validity there may have been to either claim, it was clear that the Confederates had thrown everything they had into a supreme effort to hurl back the Federal invasion and had failed.

They failed because of a hopelessly flawed tactical plan and because of ineffective field management at the top. Sending Hardee's Corps to lead the attack may have had a certain logic since it was the most seasoned unit in the army, but deploying each corps across a broad front, one behind another, meant that corps commanders had little effective direction of their commands once the battle began. As a result, the battle developed piecemeal as opposing Federal and Confederate units fought dozens of fierce engagements almost entirely unconnected with one another.

It might fairly be argued that Shiloh was a disaster for Pat Cleburne, too. Nearly every officer in his brigade above the rank of captain had fallen. In his first exercise of command leadership in a major battle, he had led his command almost to its annihilation. His response to nearly every tactical circumstance was to attack. Three times on the morning of 6 April, he threw the two regiments under his immediate control against the enemy line. The power of his personal leadership is evident in the fact that the men continued to respond to his urgings even after it became clear that their chances of achieving a decisive success, or even surviving the charge, were slim. But Cleburne's dogged determination suggested a certain inflexibility in his tactical imagination. After the war, a friend described Cleburne as a man "of methodical habits and military precision of movements." A fellow officer characterized him as "brave and considerate in danger, but slow to conception." Likewise, Hardee recalled that Cleburne's approach to problems suggested a similar systematic approach. "Before expressing an opinion . . . or coming to a decision," Hardee wrote, Cleburne "wore an expression as if solving a mathematical problem." Such a temperament did not contribute to innovation in the midst of battle. At this point in his professional development, Cleburne's principal strengths were commitment, reliability, self-discipline, and personal courage. These were very real strengths to be sure, but without the ability to respond and adjust to changing circumstances, he was doomed to suffer disappointment.[34]

When confronted with the unexpected obstacle of Shiloh Branch, Cleburne first tried to force his way through it, and when that proved impossible, he had veered off to the right with the two regiments closest to hand while allowing his three left-hand regiments to go forward on their own. Did he have other options? He might have sent an aide to Tom Hindman, who commanded the two brigades on his right, to suggest that Hindman assume temporary command of the 6th Mississippi and 23d Tennessee while Cleburne stayed with those on the left. With hindsight, it is evident that such an arrangement would have allowed Hindman the opportunity to exploit more effectively the weak points in the Federal line, making unnecessary the repeated and costly frontal assaults against the well-sited soldiers of Sherman's division. The notion probably never occurred to Cleburne, for it would have seemed to him like an abrogation of his responsibility. To him, leadership meant assuming responsibility and setting an example, not finding someone else to do your work for you. Given that, there seemed no option but to charge, and charge again, until the Federals broke.

Twelve hours of slaughter had apparently cooled Cleburne's ardor for the tactical offensive. When the courier from Bragg arrived on the morning of 7 April to order him once again to charge the enemy, this time in circumstances so unfavorable as to appear suicidal, Cleburne had remonstrated, though when he was told the orders were positive, he had obeyed. So did his men. Although there were instances of skulking and even cowardice at Shiloh, it is noteworthy that by and large the volunteer soldiers Cleburne commanded felt the same compulsion as their commander to do their duty. Personal courage under fire was one of the most honored of manly virtues in the nineteenth-century South, and at least at this point in the war, standing up at close range and exchanging bullets with the enemy until one side or the other broke was the essence of war. A private in Cleburne's Brigade who survived the battle later recalled with pride that Shiloh "was the best stand up give and take fight in the open field we made" in the war. Like that veteran, Cleburne took satisfaction in the steadfastness of the men he commanded. Still, there was a limit to his aggressiveness. He remained embittered by the memory of Bragg's "unfortunate" order to attack on 7 April and held him responsible for the destruction of what was left of his command.[35]

The tragedies and disappointments of Shiloh did not harm Cleburne's reputation in the army. His personal gallantry and unflagging energy throughout the two-day fight impressed his commanders. Hardee singled him out for special praise in his battle report: "Brigadier-General Cleburne conducted his command with persevering valor. No repulse discouraged him; but after many bloody struggles he assembled the remnant of his brigade and was conspicuous for his gallantry to the end of the battle."[36]

Cleburne's courage, and that of his men, could not be doubted. His brigade had lost 1,043 killed, wounded, and missing out of 2,750, nearly 38 percent. The 6th Mississippi had been all but destroyed—its losses at Shiloh (300 of 425) turned out to be the fourth highest rate of loss by any unit in any battle of the war. But his brigade had fought piecemeal, and in spite of Cleburne's nearly constant orders to advance, nowhere did it achieve a decisive breakthrough. In his official report, written six weeks later, Cleburne felt compelled to offer what almost might be considered a defense of his command: "This was the first battle my men were ever engaged in. They led the advance of our army on Shiloh and engaged and repulsed the enemy's cavalry the Friday before the battle. They fought in the foremost line both days and were never rested or relieved for a moment."[37]

The same was true of Cleburne's own performance. In his first fight he had behaved gallantly and with unsurpassed determination and perseverance. Alas, gallantry, determination, and perseverance had not been enough.

5
THE KENTUCKY CAMPAIGN

The Confederate army that marched back to Corinth after the Battle of Shiloh was not only beaten, it was heartbroken. Many of the rank and file, and not a few of the officers, believed that they had won a convincing victory on the first day of the fight, only to have the cup of success dashed from their lips the next morning. The loss of so many of their comrades—a third of their number—was deeply felt, as was the death of General Johnston. Exhausted from two days of fighting, the men were both tired and hungry. Their rations had been consumed, and they slogged southward with the bitter taste of defeat in their mouths and no other provender to replace it. To add to the general misery, it began to rain, gently at first, then harder as the night darkened until it became a steady downpour.

Cleburne rode among them, a captured sack of cornmeal draped across his saddle pommel as spoils of war. Separated from his command, even unsure as yet how much of it had survived, he rode disconsolately among the long line of marching men while munching periodically on a sheet of Yankee hardtack softened by rainwater. He was on the brink of exhaustion. As his horse plodded southward, he fell asleep in the saddle more than once, only to be jarred awake by the occasional flash of lightning or when jostled by another refugee on the crowded road. Arriving at a small stream, he paused to let his horse drink, and both horse and rider fell asleep where they stood until they were again swept southward by the river of retreating soldiers.[1]

Cleburne regrouped his shattered brigade at Camp Hill near Corinth, a place they had left with so much hope only a week before. Stragglers arrived over the next several days, and the reports from regimental commanders indicated just how severe the losses in his brigade had been; the 15th Arkansas was so decimated that it had to be consolidated with the 13th Arkansas. The news from elsewhere in the Confederacy did little to lift the pall of defeat that enveloped them. On the same day that the Federals had counterattacked at Shiloh, Union forces had compelled the capitulation of Island Number 10 in the Mississippi above Memphis, thus opening that river to further Federal advances; and on 29 April, news arrived in Corinth of the fall of New Orleans four days earlier. One soldier in Cleburne's Brigade noted in his diary that "a dark cloud" seemed to hover over the South. Even the good news had a bitter edge. Major General Earl Van Dorn arrived in Corinth with 14,000 reinforcements, veterans of the war in Missouri, but their presence was a reminder of the Confederate defeat at Elkhorn Tavern in March and of the fact that Missouri, like Kentucky, had been lost to the Federals.[2]

As soon as possible, Cleburne reinstituted his regular regimen of drill and inspection. The most immediate need was to fill the sadly depleted ranks of the officer corps. William Bate and Benjamin Hill, the wounded commanders of the 2d and 5th (35th) Tennessee regiments, would both recover, but Patton's death left the 15th Arkansas leaderless until Lucius Polk, one of Cleburne's compatriots from the Yell Rifles and the nephew of the bishop-general Leonidas Polk, was elected in his place as commander of the 13th-15th consolidated Arkansas regiment. Other vacancies were filled in the same way as new captains and majors won election. The democratic spirit spread even to those units whose officers had survived the fight and in a few cases the men decided to replace existing officers with new ones. This suggested a dangerous precedent. Might not soldiers vote out of commission any officer who demanded more of them than they thought appropriate? It also created the problem of what to do with officers who were not reelected. Did they return to the ranks as privates, or were they freed of their service obligation as a result? Cleburne put these questions to Hardee, but he could not answer either and passed them on to the army commander. Eventually it was determined that officers could be elected only in newly organized units. Henceforth officers lost in combat would be replaced by the next senior officer in the unit, and serving officers would not be subject to recall by popular vote. Inevitable as such a policy seems in retrospect, it is noteworthy that the war was seventeen months old before it was solemnized by a command declaration.[3]

As the brigade came slowly together again, Cleburne began to consider what lessons the Battle of Shiloh offered for future operations. The fight near Shiloh Church had resembled not so much the kind of stand-up give-and-take battle that had characterized Napoleonic warfare as it did large-scale bushwhacking in the wilderness. In such conditions, Cleburne believed that company-sized units of sharpshooters, intelligently deployed, could have a disproportionate effect on the outcome. During April he visited the camp of each of his regiments and discussed his idea with the officers. Assured of their support, he explained the plan to the rank and file. The five best shots from each company, he told them, would be detached to form special companies of sharpshooters. These units could be deployed in advance of the brigade as skirmishers, used to outflank an enemy position or to shoot down enemy gunners working artillery pieces. It is an important insight into Cleburne's command style that he took the time and trouble to explain the reasons behind his innovation to the rank and file before implementing it. Moreover, the creation of sharpshooter companies offered not only the promise of greater tactical flexibility, but the shooting contests that were used to select the members also provided the men with a useful activity in camp that helped to improve morale.[4]

Morale continued to rise with the improving weather as April turned into May, though conditions in camp remained poor. Provisions were scarce, and the water supply was inadequate for an army that had grown to 50,000 men with Van Dorn's arrival. Fortunately, an astonishingly cautious Federal advance from Pittsburg Landing gave the Confederates a badly needed respite. Only after nearly a month had passed did active patrols become necessary as the Federals edged closer. Cleburne's Brigade took its turn on picket duty in the first week of May. His men stayed out for three nights in intermittent rain before being relieved. Cleburne was unimpressed with the fieldworks, and it seemed to him that little was being done to improve them. "I think some of the Genls. ought to come out and see how these works are being done," he wrote to Hardee. "Had we been attacked up to this time, I think the work done of no value."[5]

Cleburne was concerned that the Federals were working their way around the flanks of the defensive lines to occupy a high ridge running southward from Farmington three miles east of Corinth. He ordered a reconnaissance which obtained the information that the Yankees were encamped fourteen miles back of Farmington where, according to a black slave in the vicinity, they were "thick as bees." Cleburne passed the intelligence up the chain of command to Beauregard who had already decided to strike them. While Hardee advanced toward the Federals on the Farmington Road, Earl Van Dorn's newly arrived Corps would attempt to find the Federal flank. Cleburne's Brigade led Hardee's Corps on a night march out the Farmington Road and encountered the enemy at 10:00 A.M. on 4 May. His men drove the Federals back several miles before halting, though the flanking force never appeared because Van Dorn had lost his way. Worse, instead of occupying and fortifying the ridge, Beauregard ordered Hardee to fall back to his lines around Corinth.[6]

Three weeks later, the glacial Federal advance on Corinth had moved to within a few hundred yards of the Rebel entrenchments, and Beauregard authorized another reconnaissance. On 28 May, Cleburne marched four undersized regiments (totaling about 800 men) out the Farmington Road while Van Dorn attempted once again to find the Federal flank. Cleburne ordered two regiments under Colonel Sidney S. Stanton to advance on his right. Stanton wanted to join his two regiments with Cleburne's to make a continuous front, but Cleburne was in too much of a hurry. He looked over the position briefly and decided, as he said later, that "it was not advisable." He dispatched Hanley to Stanton with orders to advance, waited a few minutes "to give the message time to reach Colonel Stanton," then ordered the brigade forward "in loud and distinct tones."[7]

Cleburne accompanied Colonel Hill and the 5th (35th) Tennessee as it advanced. As at Shiloh, "the undergrowth was so thick" that Cleburne "could not see twenty paces." Each regiment had to move forward more or less independently. Hill's men approached a large house that appeared to be abandoned, and they "rushed forward with a loud cheer to storm the place." Instead of an easy victory, however, "they were met by a heavy fire of musketry and artillery." Far from being abandoned, the house was the headquarters for an entire Federal division, and Hill's men soon became the target of its concentrated fire. Cleburne "waited with painful anxiety" for Stanton's two regiments to come up on his right, but it was soon evident that Stanton had not advanced at all. Worse yet, Cleburne also discovered that one of his own regiments, the 24th Tennessee, had not advanced either. As a result, the 5th (35th) Tennessee was left alone to face the fire of what was evidently a vastly superior Federal force. Furious, Cleburne rode back to learn the reason why.

He found the commanding officer of the 24th Tennessee, Colonel R. D. Allison, "dismounted and with his uniform off," which did nothing to calm Cleburne's mood. In a cold fury, Cleburne demanded to know why Allison had failed to advance. Allison tried to defend himself by claiming that a creek blocked his path and that the undergrowth was too thick, but Cleburne peremptorily overrode him. "At length I got him to move forward," Cleburne recalled, and the 24th Tennessee approached the scene of the fight. Once there, however, the regiment "fired one ineffectual volley, and then most of the men, especially on the right, ran away."[8]

If anything, these disappointments only increased Cleburne's determination, and he rallied his two remaining regiments, the 2d and 48th Tennessee, for another assault. Though it was not part of his orders to bring on a general engagement, his blood was up and he had become frustrated, if not angered, by the apparent unwillingness of both Stanton and Allison to join in the attack. He was poised to lead a charge when a courier from Hardee arrived with orders to call off the fight and withdraw. The engagement had cost Cleburne's Brigade more than eighty casualties in exchange for the intelligence that the "abandoned" house was strongly held after all. Worse yet, Van Dorn had once again become disoriented in his abortive flank attack, and nothing came of the offensive.

This skirmish, known as the fight at the Shelton House, was Cleburne's first independent command of a battlefield. Significantly, it is one of only five engagements carved in stone on Cleburne's monument in Helena. Yet his management of the field was anything but a model of the military art. He had failed to ensure Stanton's cooperation before moving forward, and as at Shiloh he exercised effective control over only a small portion of his command. The result was another piecemeal fight in which his personal enthusiasm and bravery were clearly evident, but in which he failed to coordinate the various elements of his command against the enemy. Cleburne, however, had no doubts in his own mind about where the blame belonged for the disappointments of the day. He saw Stanton and Allison as the culprits and sharply criticized both of them in his official report, claiming that Stanton "failed to obey my repeated order to advance" and that Allison "showed none of the qualities of an officer." Soon afterward, he relieved Allison of his command and replaced him with Major Hugh Bratton.[9]

That night (28 May) Beauregard decided to evacuate Corinth, though his decision was largely unrelated to the outcome of Cleburne's skirmish at the Shelton House. The slow but inexorable advance of the enemy was finally threatening to invest the town, and the dearth of good drinking water at Corinth made a siege unacceptable. The little water available was so bad that the men had to hold their noses while they drank to avoid gagging. A veteran of Cleburne's Brigade wrote that "our camp at Corinth proved very disagreeable and unhealthy," and another recalled with even more candor that "Corinth was a sickly hole." But the evacuation of Corinth would be difficult, for the opposing armies were in almost constant daily contact. The skirmishers exchanged not only shots but insults. One saucy Federal picket called out during a lull, "I say you damned conscripts, are you tired of drinking sassafras tea and singing Dixie yet?"[10]

On the night of 29–30 May, the Confederates left their camp fires burning, crept out of their campsites, and marched away to the southwest toward Baldwin. Several of the brigade and regimental bands were left behind to play tunes—somewhat nervously, perhaps—before they also departed. It was a well-conducted operation, and Beauregard quite literally stole a march on the enemy. One of his aides wrote home that "it was a splendidly executed move," though he exaggerated when he claimed, "We did not lose a man or gun," for they lost plenty of both. Hundreds deserted in the confusion, hundreds more threw away their rifles on the march.[11]

The army rested at Baldwin for a week before moving on to Tupelo in June. There, with the army safely beyond the reach of an immediate attack, Beauregard decided that he needed a rest. Though one of his aides wrote home that the army commander looked better than he had in months, on 14 June Beauregard notified Davis that he was taking leave and going to Bladen Springs for the sake of his health. He left three days later without waiting for a reply. Davis was disgusted. He had never particularly liked or trusted Beauregard and had sent him west to serve under Sidney Johnston in the hope that he would cause less trouble there than in Virginia. He had never anticipated that Johnston's death would leave the flamboyant Creole in command of the army. The president therefore reacted swiftly to Beauregard's message, charging him with abandoning his responsibilities and placing Braxton Bragg in command.[12]

Bragg was forty-five years old when he assumed command of the army at Tupelo. He was a tall man with a full brown beard flecked with gray and thick, bushy eyebrows that extended all the way across his prominent forehead so that he seemed to be constantly glowering at the world. A foreign visitor to the camp at Tupelo described him as having "a sickly, cadaverous, haggard appearance." Bragg's principal characteristics as an army commander were an unbending commitment to rigorous discipline and an untrusting, dyspeptic outlook on life. In the prewar army he had won a hero's plaudits for the performance of his artillery battery at the Battle of Buena Vista, but at the same time he had also earned a reputation as "the most cantankerous man in the army." Once in command he soon alienated many of his subordinates, though he got along well enough with Hardee, the only one of his corps commanders whom he believed was worth anything. At Tupelo Bragg put Hardee in charge of drilling the army, an appropriate assignment for the author of *Hardee's Tactics*. For his part, Cleburne might have been willing to give Bragg credit for placing Hardee in such a responsible position, but he continued to harbor doubts about the new army commander, perhaps remembering that it was Bragg who had ordered his division to renew the attack on the second day at Shiloh.[13]

Compared to Corinth, where the opposing armies had been in nearly constant contact, camp life at Tupelo was positively serene, even dull. Throughout a period of hot, dry weather, the army's morale improved along with its standard of hygiene and the quality of the rations. Fresh water was now plentiful, and the men made a concerted effort to wash the fleas out of their clothing. They even got fresh bread—a genuine luxury—thanks to the construction of bake ovens. But the army did more than wash and eat and fight mosquitos; under Hardee's direct supervision, it drilled. "We are drilling very hard," one soldier wrote in his diary in late June, "the discipline of the army is very rigid indeed." So evident was Hardee's hand as drillmaster that many believed he had been placed in command of the army.[14]

As it turned out, Tupelo was only a temporary camp. After all, June was the heart of the campaign season and no time for an army to go into permanent quarters. But where to go? Bragg considered launching some kind of an attack to regain Corinth, though such thoughts were soon supplanted by a scheme that grew out of the mind of Major General Edmund Kirby Smith, commander of the small Department of East Tennessee. A hero of the Battle of Manassas where he had arrived on the field in time to save the day, Kirby Smith found his new job an unpleasant one. East Tennessee was thoroughly Unionist in sentiment, and Kirby Smith had only about 9,000 men in six small brigades to defend the department. In spite of that, he was eager to go on the offensive, and he began to bombard both Bragg and Jefferson Davis with letters suggesting a joint invasion of Tennessee and Kentucky. After some wavering, Bragg succumbed. On 21 July he wired Davis that he would move to Chattanooga, and he began the movement two days later.[15]

Cleburne's Brigade was among the last to leave, presumably because Bragg wanted a reliable rear guard. Five days after the evacuation began, Cleburne's men crowded aboard the railcars for the long trip to Chattanooga. The train rumbled southward through the alluvial Mississippi countryside, past Meridian, all the way to Mobile on the Gulf of Mexico. The men were cheered at many of the small towns, and they leaned out the windows grinning and waving to acknowledge the accolades. At Mobile, they left the train and marched through town to the Pearl River docks to steamers that carried them across the river to another terminus where they boarded a train that took them northward to the Alabama state capital at Montgomery. There they changed trains again for the trip to Atlanta and then finally to Chattanooga. Such a convoluted route was necessary not only because the Federals occupied the direct rail line to Chattanooga, but also because of the limitations of the South's rail transport system. Long train trips invariably required frequent changes, for even when the rail lines connected, different routes frequently used different gauge rails. In spite of the difficulties and the circuitous route, Bragg's army arrived safely in Chattanooga during the last week of July, with Cleburne's Brigade arriving on 1 August.[16]

While the troops were still en route, Bragg met with Kirby Smith to hammer out the details of their coordinated offensive. They agreed that Kirby Smith would advance from Knoxville through the mountains of east Tennessee into Kentucky and that Bragg would move northward from Chattanooga into central Tennessee. Though the twin thrusts were strategically complementary, they took place in separate departments; coordination of the two offensives depended entirely on voluntary cooperation. Nevertheless, Bragg agreed to supply Kirby Smith with reinforcements, specifically pledging to him the brigade of Colonel Preston Smith from Cheatham's Division and Cleburne's Brigade from Hardee's Division. Thus it was that only days after his arrival in Chattanooga, Cleburne received orders to have his men cook two days' rations and "proceed by rail to Knoxville, Tenn., with all possible dispatch, and report to Maj. Gen. Kirby Smith for temporary service." Pointedly, Bragg noted that Cleburne's men should carry 100 rounds of ammunition each and be "prepared to take the field and meet the enemy at once." After another train ride, Cleburne reported to Kirby Smith in Knoxville on or about 7 August.[17]

Kirby Smith was delighted with his two new brigades, and he took advantage of their arrival to reorganize his army into four divisions. Carter Stevenson commanded by far the largest division, with some 9,000 men at Knoxville. Harry Heth and Thomas Churchill commanded smaller divisions of about 3,000 men each, and Kirby Smith lumped Cleburne's and Preston Smith's Brigades together to form another small division, naming Cleburne as its commander. Cleburne in turn selected Benjamin Hill of the 5th (35th) Tennessee, who had behaved so well in the skirmish at the Shelton House, as the temporary commander of his old brigade. Cleburne thus became an acting division commander, though his "division" consisted of only two brigades and a total of 3,000 men, about the same number he had commanded at Shiloh.[18]

Kirby Smith's plan to outflank the Federals holding Cumberland Gap was to use Stevenson's full-size division to feint at the Federal army, thus freezing it in position, while his three smaller divisions, with Cleburne in the lead, marched though Rogers Gap to occupy Barboursville, Kentucky, on the Federal line of supply. The Federals would thus be forced either to give up their position or capitulate. The movement began on 13 August with the departure of John Scott's cavalry brigade, and Cleburne's undersized "division" left at dawn the next morning.

The weather was hot and dusty in mid-August, and the roads were poor. "The face of the country is rugged and broken," one veteran confided to his diary, "and we frequently have long ridges to climb over rough rocky roads." At Big Creek Gap, the ascent was so steep the horses could not pull the artil-

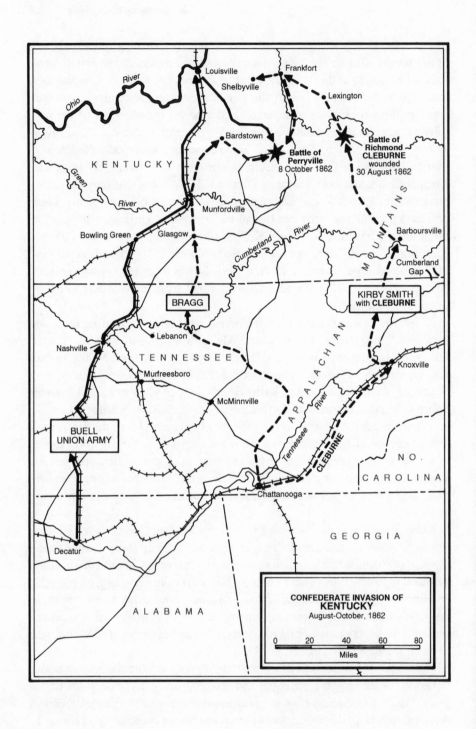

Louisville
Frankfort
Shelbyville
Lexington
Ohio River
KENTUCKY
Green River
Bardstown
Battle of
Perryville
8 October 1862
Battle of
Richmond
CLEBURNE
wounded
30 August 1862
Munfordville
Bowling Green
Glasgow
Cumberland River
Barboursville
Cumberland
Gap
BRAGG
KIRBY SMITH
with CLEBURNE
Lebanon
TENNESSEE
Nashville
Murfreesboro
McMinnville
Knoxville
BUELL
UNION ARMY
APPALACHIAN
Tennessee River
CLEBURNE
NO.
CAROLINA
Chattanooga
GEORGIA
Decatur
ALABAMA

CONFEDERATE INVASION OF
KENTUCKY
August-October, 1862

0   20   40   60   80
Miles

lery up the slope, and the men had to take hold of long ropes and manhandle the guns over the high spots. Even so, morale was high now that the army was advancing. The scenery was spectacular, and the men believed they were stealing a march on the enemy. They threw themselves into the march with the enthusiasm of zealots.[19]

Despite the difficulties, and the added disincentive of traveling through a countryside that was thoroughly Unionist in sentiment, the men covered sixty miles in fifty hours and arrived at Barboursville with empty haversacks and tired feet. A good rest would cure the tired feet, but there were no rations to be found. To make good time across the mountains, the army had left its wagons behind. Barboursville, like most of Appalachia, was loyal to the Union and therefore hostile to the Rebel invaders. Cleburne's men encountered no local hospitality and had to subsist on apples and green corn they plucked from the fields. One veteran said the men were turned out to "graze" in the cornfields like animals.[20]

The move over the mountains successfully outflanked the Federals in the Cumberland Gap and forced them to fall back. Kirby Smith sent Scott's cavalry ahead to reconnoiter, and Scott soon reported back that he had overtaken elements of the Federal army and captured a Federal supply train of 130 fully loaded wagons. Kirby Smith ordered Scott to hold his position and directed Cleburne "to move up at once" in support, emphasizing that Cleburne was to move "as rapidly as possible."[21]

Accordingly, Cleburne had his men up early on 27 August and on the road by 3:00 A.M. in order to put as many miles behind them as possible before the heat of the day. Late that afternoon, he gave the order to fall out and make camp, though he had his troops up and back on the road again before dawn the next morning. Finally on the afternoon of 28 August, the troops leading the advance encountered an enemy picket line, and Cleburne gave the order to halt. The men set up camp so close to the Federal position that when dawn broke on the 29th, the Confederates were astonished to find bluecoated pickets within their lines, though not nearly as astonished as the pickets themselves, who were instantly taken prisoner.[22]

Kirby Smith had given Cleburne specific instructions about where to post his division—five miles from the foot of Big Hill just south of Richmond, Kentucky—and after daylight Cleburne moved forward cautiously to the designated spot. At about 5:00 that afternoon, he heard the unmistakable sound of artillery ahead, and soon afterward Scott rode into Cleburne's lines to report that the enemy was very close—which was hardly news—and that the Federals seemed to be satisfied to remain where they were to await battle. Scott assured Cleburne that he had left a substantial cavalry picket on the road ahead just in case. Still, with "an unknown force" in his front, Cleburne decided "as a matter of precaution to form line of battle facing the supposed direction of the enemy." He called his regimental commanders together and gave them precise instructions about the disposition of forces in case of alarm. "I had scarcely dismissed them," Cleburne recalled, "before firing and yelling was heard in our front, and almost simultaneously a multitude of stragglers, consisting of part of Colonel Scott's cavalry, brigade, sick men, baggage wagons, servants leading horses, came flying in the utmost consternation, closely pursued by the whole of Colonel Metcalfe's command of United States cavalry." The Federal horsemen came pounding up the road assuming that they were in pursuit of a force of Rebel cavalry. Colonel Hill later claimed that he could hear the Yankee commander cry out, "Charge and shoot down the rebels."[23]

Cleburne quickly formed his line, careful to leave the road clear. He waited until the Federal troopers were within twenty-five yards, then two companies of the 48th Tennessee "fired on the enemy's advance" and threw the cavalry "into utter confusion causing a pell mell retreat." Suspecting that only a small force was in front of them, the Federal commander dismounted a regiment and advanced on foot. The sun had set by now and it was growing dark. Still not suspecting that there was anything in front of them more substantial than a cavalry picket, the Federal skirmishers moved cautiously forward. Cleburne sent a company of his sharpshooters to the front and they began to pick off the Federal troopers one by one. Unwilling to endure such punishment from an unseen enemy, "the whole force of the enemy precipitately retreated." Cleburne's men took some thirty prisoners. That night while Cleburne's men "slept in line of battle without any supper," a staff officer brought Cleburne new orders from Kirby Smith—he was to attack the next morning.[24]

The morning dawned "warm, clear and beautiful." One of Cleburne's soldiers declared later, "No brighter sun ever scattered the mists of early day." In accordance with orders, Cleburne advanced his division in battle order and after only a mile or two he found the Federal force "drawn up in line of battle in a fine position near Mount Zion Church, about six miles from Richmond." He deployed Hill's Brigade to the right of the pike with Preston Smith's in support just behind it, and he ordered out skirmishers, personally selecting the positions for his special companies of sharpshooters. He even went forward with the sharpshooters from the 13th-15th consolidated Arkansas regiment to assess their impact. By the time Kirby Smith arrived on the field at about 7:30 A.M., the firing was already "brisk."[25]

Kirby Smith determined at once that Cleburne faced at least a full Federal division and thought it unlikely that a frontal assault could be successful "without a disastrous loss." He therefore ordered Cleburne to "hold the enemy in check" while Churchill's division, coming up the road behind Cleburne, found a route to the enemy flank. Cleburne ordered his artillery to slow its rate of fire and left the fight to the skirmishers and gunners. The sharpshooters "popped away at them for an hour," causing serious losses among the Federal gunners but making no attempt to advance. Frustrated by these tactics, the Federal commander, Brigadier General Mahlon Dickerson Manson, decided to seize the initiative and ordered an attack of his own against Cleburne's right flank. Cleburne responded by bringing up a Tennessee regiment from Preston Smith's Brigade and sending the 13th-15th Arkansas to the right as well. The sound of the fight grew in intensity, and Cleburne decided that the Federals had staked the outcome of the battle on their effort to turn his right. If so, he calculated, they must surely have pulled troops from their center. Instead of responding defensively to the Federal threat, therefore, he decided to launch an attack of his own. He brought up the rest of Smith's Brigade to secure the right, and he prepared to lead his own brigade, now under Hill, against the Federal center. He galloped off to ensure that Smith's troops could hold, then raced back to the center to organize the counterattack. As he passed down the line, he reined in at the sight of Lucius Polk being helped to the rear. Stopping to inquire about his friend's condition, he was gratified to learn that Polk was only slightly wounded. Much relieved, Cleburne opened his mouth to reply, but his head jerked violently to the right as a minié ball pierced his left cheek, smashed two teeth in his lower jaw, and exited his open mouth. His aides must have suspected the worst, but in fact it was only a slight wound, and Cleburne was fully prepared to go on with his duties. He later joked that he "caught the ball in his mouth and spat it out." The wound proved to be more of a problem than he first thought, however, for within minutes the swelling and bleeding in his mouth made it impossible for him to speak.[26]

He stayed on the field long enough to witness the results of his counterattack against the Federal center. The Confederates burst through the weakened Federal center and began a pursuit that led them to the outskirts of Richmond, Kentucky, where they compelled most of the Yankee army to surrender. A veteran of the brigade claimed later that this attack was "the most gallant charge" ever made by Cleburne's command. But Cleburne did not participate in it; he reluctantly turned command of the division over to Preston Smith and retired to a field hospital where doctors sewed up his torn left cheek.[27]

Cleburne's conduct at the Battle of Richmond suggested that he had matured significantly as a field commander since Shiloh. He was certainly as keen as ever, and his disdain for personal danger was still very much a part of his battlefield persona. (Kirby Smith noted in his report that Cleburne had engaged the enemy "without waiting for Churchill's Division.") But this time, Cleburne also demonstrated both tactical innovation and insight—first by an effective use of sharpshooters and artillery and then by recognizing the opportunity presented by the Federal attack on his right and organizing the counterattack that won the day. He had successfully coordinated an attack by his two brigades, and though his facial wound prevented him from witnessing the culmination of that attack, the subsequent victory was surely as much his as it was Kirby Smith's. The forces under his command had routed an enemy more than twice their number, and at the end of the day the Confederates took over 4,300 prisoners, General Manson among them. Altogether, it was as complete and decisive a victory as any in the war to date.[28]

While his men cheerfully pursued the fleeing Federals to the outskirts of Richmond, Cleburne took up temporary residence with a farmer who agreed to let the wounded Rebel general convalesce in his home. Though Cleburne's wound was not life-threatening, the swelling and bleeding in his mouth made eating uncomfortable and speech impossible. He could not shave, and soon a beard began to sprout through the slowly healing wound. He spent much of his convalescence composing his detailed battle report while the events were still vivid in his mind. Kirby Smith awarded the men of his command a well-earned day's rest, issuing both fresh rations and in many cases new uniforms from the stock of captured Federal stores. As a result, many of those in Cleburne's command were outfitted with new blue wool trousers. Then his small division was effectively broken up, with units dispatched in various directions. Two regiments, including the 13th-15th Arkansas, marched toward the Ohio River and temporarily occupied Covington, Kentucky, across the river from Cincinnati, where Cleburne's brother and mother still lived.[29]

Elsewhere in Kentucky, Bragg's forces were also moving north, and they reached Glasgow on 14 September. Two days later, Bragg's army forced the capitulation of the Federal garrison at Munfordville, an event that compelled Buell to evacuate Bowling Green. Bragg briefly considered striking at Buell but decided that it was more important to unite with Kirby Smith for a joint assault on Louisville. So far the campaign had been a tremendous success. With the twin thrusts into Tennessee and Kentucky, the Confederacy had regained the initiative and reversed the course of the war in the West. After his seizure of Munfordville, however, Bragg lost both his nerve and his momentum, dispatching units over the countryside to occupy a series of outposts almost like an army of occupation. From Glasgow, he issued orders for the two brigades he had loaned to Kirby Smith—Cleburne's and Preston Smith's—to return to his command and occupy Shelbyville.[30]

By this time, Cleburne's wound had healed sufficiently to allow him to speak, and he set out to rejoin his command. He found his brigade encamped on the Georgetown-Shelbyville Road on about 23 September. Previously clean-shaven, he now sported a three weeks' growth of beard, not only because it had been too painful to shave but also because the facial hair helped to conceal the scar on his left cheek. His subordinates discovered that the wound affected his speech pattern as well. The loss of two teeth gave his speech a harsh sibilance that was most noticeable when he raised his voice on the parade ground or in battle. One soldier described it as "a hissing sound" that was particularly evident "when he spoke hurriedly or angrily."[31]

Cleburne arrived in Shelbyville with his brigade on 25 September and reported his resumption of command to Bragg. In reply, Bragg ordered him to hold his position at Shelbyville, and "if pressed by the enemy, fall back to Frankfort." At the same time, Bragg ordered other forces to occupy Shepardsville, Mount Washington, and Taylorsville. Cleburne's Brigade thus constituted one of a half dozen Confederate outposts spread out in a semicircular screen across central Kentucky. Behind that screen, Bragg planned to preside over the inauguration of Richard Hawes as Confederate governor of Kentucky in the state capital of Frankfort. Bragg's dispositions surrendered most of the advantages the Confederates had won on the Richmond battlefield. In effect, he relinquished the initiative back to the Federals, giving them a much-needed respite during which they consolidated their forces at Louisville. Leonidas Polk, who commanded one wing of Bragg's army at Bardstown, was concerned enough to wire Bragg that "it seems to me we are too much scattered," and Kirby Smith warned Polk that "our commands . . . are too far apart and beyond supporting distance."[32]

Cleburne's position at Shelbyville was precarious not only because of the curious disposition of the Rebel forces in Kentucky, but also because the Federals could use the railroad system north of him to concentrate forces quickly on his front while he could move only by the roads. His brigade numbered barely a thousand men; the 13th-15th Arkansas, now under its fourth commander in less than a year, contained fewer than 200. Moreover, he was low on supplies and had to order the men to live off the land, which offered slim pickings at the end of a campaign summer. Finally, none of his men had been paid for more than nine months. Almost plaintively, Cleburne asked Bragg, "Is there any way by which I can get some pay for my men?"[33]

Toward the end of September, Cleburne's pickets reported hearing trains arriving and departing half a dozen miles to the north, and a few days later, on the first of October, they brought the news that the enemy was approaching "in force" less than five miles away. Cleburne roused his command and dashed off quick notes to Bragg and Polk to report that the enemy was advancing and that, as instructed, he was falling back on Frankfort. Bragg received Cleburne's note the next day. At about the same time he received one from Polk that he, too, was under assault and was falling back on Harrodsburg. Bragg decided that the enemy advance against Frankfort was the Federal main effort and that the force probing Polk's lines was no more than a diversion. He therefore ordered Polk to advance and drive off the enemy.[34]

Startled and confused by Bragg's orders, Polk called a conference of his commanders. He told them that Bragg wanted them to attack, then he explained to them why he thought such a move was unwise. Loyally, they concurred in his decision not to obey. Polk thereupon wrote Bragg that circumstances made "compliance with this order . . . impracticable." Instead of advancing, therefore, he fell back, intending to join forces with Kirby Smith somewhere near Harrodsburg. Thus the Confederate forces would be unified *before* a battle rather than in the midst of one.[35]

In compliance with previous orders, Cleburne hastily withdrew his own force from Shelbyville, falling back on Frankfort where he arrived on 2 October. There he received orders to join Polk's movement to Harrodsburg, where he came back under Hardee's command as part of the division commanded by Simon Bolivar Buckner. The two wings of Bragg's army were now unified in the vicinity of Harrodsburg and Perryville, but they were dangerously separated from Kirby Smith's force, which was some twenty-five miles to the north near Versailles, Kentucky. In effect the Confederate forces in central Kentucky were divided in half: 20,000 at Perryville and another 22,000 under Kirby Smith at Versailles. Bragg himself was at Frankfort, and he continued to believe that that city was the objective of the Federal army. He therefore ordered Polk to deal quickly with the Federals at Perryville, then march north to fight what he presumed was their main body. He ordered Polk to "give battle immediately."[36]

At noon on 8 October, a courier arrived at Cleburne's headquarters with orders to form up "in line of battle east of the Harrodsburg and Perryville road." Cleburne was to cross the small creek to his front and "support the brigade of Brigadier-General Johnson" in its attack. Cleburne moved his brigade quickly along the Mackville Pike northwest of town and arrived atop the high ground above the small rivulet known as Doctor's Creek at about 2:30. His vantage point offered him a panoramic view of the battlefield. Buckner's

Division, to which his own brigade was attached, held the center of the Confederate line atop a ridgeline overlooking the creek bottom. Buckner arrayed his three brigades one behind the other with Bushrod Johnson's in front, then Cleburne's, then that of St. John Liddell. To their right was Frank Cheatham's Division and on their left Patton Anderson's. Across the nearly dry creek bed, atop another ridgeline, were the entrenchments of the Federal army.[37]

As Cleburne directed his regiments into line, the battle was already joined. On his right, Cheatham's Division marched down the hill, crossed the creek bed, and assaulted the Federal line. Bushrod Johnson's Brigade, directly in front of Cleburne, advanced in support of Cheatham, but Cleburne's orders were to remain where he was as a reserve. He watched the men of Johnson's Brigade as they moved down the long slope of open fields in front of him and crossed Doctor's Creek before ascending the far bank into the teeth of the Federal fire. A member of the brigade later wrote that the scene was a "battle like you see in pictures. For a mile we could see them, their splendid looking lines. Flags flying, bands playing." As Cleburne watched, Johnson's men moved up the far slope, then slowed, and finally stopped as the smoke from thousands of muskets filled the valley.[38]

At about 4:00, Cleburne received orders to go to Johnson's support. Having witnessed the earlier attack, the men in the ranks were under no illusions about their assignment. "We had a full view of what we were expected to do," one recalled. They came under fire as soon as they started down the slope, and Cleburne ordered them to double-time. They reached the dry creek bed at the bottom of the slope where the fold of ground protected them, and Cleburne ordered a halt while he conferred with Johnson. That officer professed an eagerness to renew the advance but declared that his men were out of ammunition. He would therefore have to withdraw to resupply and suggested that Cleburne's Brigade should take over the front line. Cleburne agreed.[39]

Cleburne sent the 13th-15th Arkansas off to the right to take position behind a stone wall that ran alongside the Mackville Pike. From there, the Arkansans could partially enfilade the Federal line. Then as Johnson's men fell back, Cleburne's Brigade moved forward. By now the Federals had abandoned the crest of the ridge and were sheltering behind it, which meant that they could not fire into any attacking force until it crested the hill. To exploit these circumstances, Cleburne ordered his standard-bearers to the front with the skirmishers and placed his brigade in line of battle about ten paces behind them. When all was ready, he ordered them forward. As his men started up the slope, they were shocked to come under fire not from the front, but from the rear. Confederate gunners behind them noted the division's blue battle flag and the blue trousers on the men in the ranks, and opened fire. Cleburne at once ordered the brigade to fall back to the creek bed and sent a courier dashing back to tell the rebel gunners to cease firing. The artillerists were reluctant to believe they had made such a mistake but agreed to hold their fire.[40]

That problem resolved, Cleburne again ordered his brigade to advance. A participant called it "the grandest advance in line of battle I ever witnessed." Hardee described it in his official report as a charge of "great impetuosity." Shielded from the direct fire of the Federal line until they crested the hill, the Confederate infantry advanced at right shoulder shift until they were nearly at the top of the slope. Bullets flew overhead with their characteristic whine that led more than one soldier to duck instinctively. Riding amidst the ranks of infantry, Cleburne was a conspicuous target, and minié balls filled the air around him; one of his young aides riding alongside him was shot dead.[41]

As the brigade's battle flags topped the crest of the hill, the Federals "emptied their guns at the line of skirmishers." Casualties were severe within the thin line of standard-bearers and skirmishers, but in the next moment Cleburne's main line, advancing ten paces behind them, emerged through the smoke while the Yankees were still reloading. The Rebel line halted and at Cleburne's command leveled their rifles and fired a deliberate volley at a range of less than 100 yards. Then the brigade charged "with a rush" and drove forward "up and up in resistless charge, and soon dislodged the line of Federals." The attack, Hardee reported, was "irresistible, and drove the enemy in wild disorder from the position nearly a mile to the rear."[42]

Cleburne's men pursued them, whooping the Rebel yell. One veteran recalled the moment with relish: "As their line broke, we had them, and gave it to them in the back. It was a hot evening, and the grass being dry, [it] caught fire, and the flames spreading to a barn just to our right. Rather than burn, out hustled a lot of blue coats to surrender." The charge and pursuit soon disrupted the order of battle. As the brigade moved across the Mackville Road and into a cornfield, the units became separated from one another, and Cleburne called a temporary halt to re-form. When he renewed the advance, his lines were raked by fire from a Federal battery to his left. One artillery shell exploded near Cleburne, killing his horse and spilling him onto the ground with a leg wound. He was up again almost at once, leading the advance on foot despite the wound in his leg. The steady progress compelled the Federal battery to limber up and dash for the rear, and the brigade continued to move forward until it encountered a new line of Yankee infantry.[43]

Cleburne "advanced to within 75 yards of this line," but his impetuous charge had taken him well beyond the brigades advancing more slowly on either side of him so that both of his flanks were exposed, and his men became the target of Federal enfilading fire. The 800 men under his immediate command were "in the center of the battle unsupported on either flank." Even so, Cleburne ordered his men to hold their exposed salient against repeated counterattacks by the enemy. As darkness fell, it became difficult "to distinguish friend from foe," and the firing briefly sputtered out until St. John Liddell's Brigade came up on Cleburne's right to fill the gap between Cleburne and Cheatham and force the Federals to quit the field, fleeing "in the utmost confusion." With some satisfaction Cleburne surveyed the battlefield. It was a bright moonlit night—bright enough to read by—and hundreds of shoulder arms abandoned by the enemy lay scattered on the field glinting in the moonlight. Though Cheatham's Division had borne the brunt of the fight, Cleburne's Brigade had driven the deepest into the Federal lines. That the Rebels held the field after dark was due in large part to the efforts of his command.[44]

The euphoria of the evening's success evaporated quickly. Bragg had assumed all along that the Federal force at Perryville was the weaker of the two Federal probes. By late evening, however, the evidence was overwhelming that the opposing army at Perryville was the Federal main body—nearly 60,000 men with Buell in personal command. Under such circumstances, Bragg could not continue to invite battle; he would have to retreat at once. Bragg later claimed that the Federals were "heavily reinforced" overnight, but in fact he had misunderstood the situation from the beginning. In any event, he issued orders that same night for a withdrawal. Cleburne did not record his reaction to these orders, but after the sacrifice his brigade had made to win the battlefield, it is likely that he would have felt great disappointment, at least, in being ordered to give it up so easily. A few of the men in Cleburne's Division privately described Bragg's decision as "cowardly."[45]

The Confederate army fell back to Camp Dick Robinson near the confluence of the Kentucky and Dick rivers. There Bragg's force was united finally with Kirby Smith's. Even so, the scarcity of provisions and the superior numbers of the Federal army led Bragg to advocate a general withdrawal from Kentucky. He had been cautioned by Jefferson Davis not to risk the army in an unequal contest with the enemy so far from his base, and he believed that it was time now to evacuate the state before the onset of winter made a withdrawal impossible.

The retreat began on 13 October. It was slowed by the crawling pace of thousands of wagons filled with muskets. Bragg had brought 20,000 stand of arms with him to supply the recruits that he had expected to flock to the Rebel standard once his army had established itself in Kentucky. Now those arms had to be carried back again, unused, along with thousands more that had been captured from the enemy. At Big Hill south of Richmond, Kentucky, it seemed likely that all these weapons would have to be abandoned.

The road over the heights was so steep, and the teams so exhausted, that it appeared unrealistic to expect that they could be salvaged. It was Cleburne who came to the rescue. He took command of the train and employed the 1,500 men of Heth's division to work in teams hauling the wagons up the hill by hand. He pressed others into duty, setting an example by his personal energy and enthusiasm, and managed to save the entire train.[46]

Even so, the move south was hardly a happy one. The army retreated through pro-Union territory. In many of the towns the women and boys hurled insults and even stones, and occasionally the retreating column was fired on from ambush. Rations were scarce, and the troops survived mainly on biscuits and onions. To add to the general misery, the weather turned prematurely cold. The first frost of the season came on 18 October, and on 26 October—the day Cleburne's Division reached Knoxville—a heavy snow fell in the mountains.[47]

As at Shiloh, the early success of the Kentucky campaign made the final disappointment all the more bitter. Many of the officers and men, Cleburne among them, blamed Bragg both for badly misjudging the situation at Perryville and for his unwillingness to stay in Kentucky and fight it out. For his part, Cleburne had earned new laurels during the campaign for his aggressive impetuosity. Buckner praised his "gallant services" at Perryville and insisted that "his conduct was in every particular entitled to the highest praise and is deserving of promotion." Hardee noted that Cleburne had "led his brigade with his usual courage and judgement." Once again, however, he had demonstrated more courage than judgement. His ability to infuse his subordinates with enthusiasm, his eagerness for the offensive, and his personal courage and stubbornness in battle remained the principal hallmarks of his leadership. Even his success in taking charge of the wagon train during the retreat was largely a product of his personal energy and charisma. Cleburne had proven himself a great *leader;* it remained to be seen if he could also be a great *commander.*[48]

Major General P. R. Cleburne. (Reproduced from the Collections of the Library of Congress)

Bride Park Cottage where Patrick Cleburne was born (in the room on the upper right) on St. Patrick's Eve, 16 March 1828. That room (indeed everything to the right of the drainpipe) had been added to the original structure by Dr. Cleburne in the 1820s. Bride Park was a comfortable cottage appropriate to Dr. Cleburne's status as a country doctor and member of the gentry. (Courtesy Nora Lynch, Ballincollig, Ireland)

St. Mary's Athnowen (Protestant) Church, in Ovens Township, County Cork, was only a mile downstream from Bride Park Cottage. There the infant Pat Cleburne was baptized in the Church of Ireland. His father was a vestryman in the church and is buried in the churchyard. (Photo by the author)

Grange House, where Patrick Cleburne spent much of his boyhood, was an imposing manor house whose foundations, at least, dated back as far as the sixth century. As a scion of Grange House, young Patrick would have been treated with deference by the tenants on the land. This 1986 drawing is based on an original map of the estate. (Courtesy Nora Lynch)

Cleburne's boyhood idyll was shattered not only by the death of his father in 1843 but by the onset of the potato famine two years later. In this newspaper sketch, starving Irishmen gather outside a workhouse in 1846 during the depth of the famine. The resulting social and economic crisis encouraged the Cleburnes to emigrate to America in 1849. (Mansell Collection, London)

The first known photograph of Patrick Cleburne taken in Helena, Arkansas, when he was a successful businessman and an aspiring lawyer at about age twenty-five. Cleburne was active in the Masonic order in Helena and enjoyed brief notoriety as an outspoken opponent of the Know-Nothings during the campaign of 1856. (Confederate Museum, Richmond)

Helena, Arkansas, as it appeared during the Civil War but looking much as it did when Cleburne arrived there in 1850. The opportunities available to an ambitious young immigrant in this wild and wooly frontier town appealed to the young Pat Cleburne, and he made his mark here, rising from a salaried apothecary to become a well-known lawyer and Democratic politician. (*Chronicles of Arkansas*, courtesy of Ivey Gladden, Helena)

Dr. Charles E. Nash was Cleburne's first friend and business partner in Helena. They were roommates for some time in a small apartment above the drugstore, and afterward, Cleburne boarded with Nash and his wife. Nash remained a lifelong friend to Cleburne and was his first biographer.
(From Nash, *Biographical Sketches*)

Thomas Hindman, the feisty and confrontational Democratic politician, was Cleburne's unlikely political ally during his brief sojurn into politics in 1856. Cleburne stood up with Hindman in a street fight in July of that year, taking a bullet that nearly killed him. Hindman and Cleburne both subsequently served in the Army of Tennessee, each commanding a division under Braxton Bragg.
(Library of Congress)

William J. Hardee was Cleburne's immediate superior through much of the Civil War. From the first summer of the war, Hardee became Cleburne's mentor, friend, and advocate. Though very different temperamentally, Hardee and Cleburne became fast friends as well as comrades in arms. One contemporary likened their relationship to that of Napoleon and Murat, an analogy that the Anglophilic Cleburne would probably not have appreciated. (Georgia Department of Archives and History)

Braxton Bragg commanded the Confederacy's western army from the summer of 1862 until after the debacle on Missionary Ridge in November 1863. Though unquestionably a man of military ability, his morbid and inflexible personality alienated his subordinates and condemned him to failure. (National Archives)

Joseph E. Johnston was popular with the rank and file but a disappointment to Confederate President Jefferson Davis, who concluded that he lacked the will to fight. Cleburne admired Johnston and was disheartened when Davis replaced him with Hood, in part because in elevating Hood, Davis passed over Hardee. (National Archives)

John Bell Hood replaced Johnston in July 1864 and immediately assailed the advancing Yankees in a series of pitched battles outside Atlanta. During the subsequent campaign into Tennessee, Hood was disappointed that Cleburne's Division did not block the road at Spring Hill, and he ordered the charge at Franklin that took Cleburne's life. (Library of Congress)

Aside from Hardee, Lucius E. Polk was Cleburne's closest friend in the army. Polk moved to Helena in the early 1850s, about the same time Cleburne did, and became a planter. An original member of the Yell Rifles, he moved up through the ranks to command a brigade, thanks in large part to Cleburne's recommendations. A nephew of Leonidas Polk, he was a bitter opponent of Braxton Bragg whom he believed had maligned his uncle in official reports. Polk was badly wounded in June of 1864 and had to leave the army.
(Library of Congress)

Daniel C. Govan was a Mississippian who moved to Helena just prior to the outbreak of war in 1861. Not a member of Cleburne's Yell Rifles, he raised his own company of volunteers, which eventually became part of the 2d Arkansas. Promoted to brigadier general after Murfreesboro, Govan was in the forefront of all Cleburne's battles from Chickamauga to Franklin.
(Library of Congress)

Hiram B. Granbury, another native Mississippian, moved to Texas in the early 1850s and after the outbreak of war became colonel of the 7th Texas. Granbury led the brigade of Texans in Cleburne's Division during most of the campaigns in 1863–1864 including Missionary Ridge, Ringgold Gap, and Pickett's Mill. Replaced briefly by James A. Smith, who led the Texans in the Battle of Bald Hill (Atlanta), Granbury returned to the command in time to die at the head of his troops at Franklin. (Library of Congress)

Mark P. Lowrey, the fighting preacher, was the son of Irish immigrants. In command of the 32d Mississippi, he fought well at Chickamauga and was promoted to brigadier general soon afterward. Lowrey commanded Cleburne's Division at Jonesboro when Cleburne commanded the corps. Alas, a misunderstanding of his orders led his troops in the wrong direction and ruined whatever chance there may have been for a Confederate victory. (Library of Congress)

The best-known photograph of Cleburne, probably taken in January or February 1864 during one of his trips to Mobile. A local newspaper reporter described him as "a tall and rather slender officer, with erect form but slightly bowed shoulders, a finely shaped head, with features prominent and striking—the firm set lip, betokening resolution and will." (Confederate Museum, Richmond)

Susan Tarleton swept Cleburne off his feet during Hardee's wedding at Bleak House in January 1864. Utterly smitten, Cleburne pursued her with the same single-minded intensity he applied to everything he did, and in March, she agreed to become engaged. After Cleburne's battlefield death at Franklin, she wore mourning for a year. (Courtesy Old Soldier Books, Gaithersburg, Maryland)

Cleburne's body, plus those of five others, lay on the porch of the McGavock House near Franklin, Tennessee, after the battle that took his life. The other bodies were those of Brigadier Generals John Adams, Hiram Granbury, and Otto Strahl, plus Granbury's chief of staff, Colonel R. B. Young, and Strahl's aide, Lieutenant John H. Marsh. From Franklin, Cleburne's body was carried by wagon to Columbia on the Duck River. Interred there briefly in the paupers' section, he was soon moved to the small churchyard at Ash Hill, the plantation of Lucius Polk. After the war, his remains were moved one more time to Helena. (Photo by the author)

The monument in Helena marking Cleburne's final resting place, erected in 1891. At its dedication, General George Gordon asserted that "a truer patriot or knightlier soldier never fought and never died." (Photo by Ron Fuller)

PART TWO

THE ARMY OF TENNESSEE

6

CLEBURNE'S DIVISION

After the retreat from Kentucky, Bragg's dispirited Army of the Mississippi moved westward in slow stages from Knoxville to Chattanooga and then northward by rail into middle Tennessee, arriving at Murfreesboro in the Stones River Valley in late November. By then it had undergone significant reorganization. Jefferson Davis had removed Mississippi and Eastern Louisiana from Bragg's command theater to create a new department for John C. Pemberton, who assumed responsibility for the defense of the Mississippi River. In partial compensation for this loss, Bragg attempted to integrate Kirby Smith's Army of East Tennessee into his own command by designating it as a third corps in what he now called the Army of Tennessee. The name stuck, but the organization did not. Kirby Smith left almost at once for Richmond to complain about Bragg to anyone who would listen, and when he returned, he stayed only briefly before leaving for good, announcing that he was unwilling to serve under an officer whom he considered incompetent. Polk and Hardee, who harbored serious doubts of their own about Bragg's competence, remained in command of Bragg's other two corps.[1]

Hardee's Corps was also reorganized. The senior division commander, Simon Buckner, left Tennessee to command the Confederate garrison at Mobile, and his departure created a vacancy for a major general. Buckner recommended Cleburne, a nomination that Hardee embraced with enthusiasm. It was a striking recommendation for several reasons. To begin with, two of the four brigadiers in Buckner's Division—Sterling Wood and Bushrod Johnson—were senior to Cleburne, and both of them had performed well during the Kentucky campaign. Johnson, moreover, was a West Point graduate which Cleburne was not. Finally, Cleburne was not a native-born southerner. If he were promoted, he would become the highest ranking "foreigner" in the Confederate army. Hardee nevertheless lobbied hard for Cleburne's selection, and Bragg, who was aware of the exceptional performance of Cleburne's command at Richmond and Perryville, wrote a strong endorsement asserting that Cleburne was "young, ardent, *exceedingly* gallant, but *sufficiently* prudent . . . and the admiration of his command." Jefferson Davis had to make the final decision, and though he was initially dubious, he finally acceded, as much to gratify Hardee as from conviction.[2]

Cleburne's promotion to major general and the permanent command of a division went into effect in December. It was a significant jump in both responsibility and authority. There were forty-seven brigadier generals in the army but only twelve major generals. As a division commander, Cleburne would be expected to demonstrate not only effective command leadership, but also to accept some share of the responsibility for the army's long-term strategic planning and decision making. In combat, his role would be more that of a chess master than a warrior; his new job would require him to manage his forces from the rear rather than to lead them from the front. Instead of four regiments, he would now command four brigades: Bushrod Johnson's Brigade of five Tennessee regiments that had led the attack of the division at Perryville; Stirling Wood's Brigade of Alabama and Mississippi troops; St. John Liddell's small brigade of Arkansas troops; and Cleburne's own brigade, which, thanks largely to his strong endorsement, would now be commanded by his friend and protégé from the Yell Rifles, Lucius Polk.[3]

Cleburne was also entitled to a larger staff. It was headed by Major Calhoun Benham, a thirty-nine-year-old former lawyer from California who had previously served both Sidney Johnston and Beauregard as a volunteer aide. Benham stayed with Cleburne throughout the war and proved to be a quietly competent administrator and a loyal champion of his commander. Another new member of the staff was Captain Irving Buck who also had served on Beauregard's staff. As Cleburne's assistant adjutant general (AAG), Buck would be responsible for divisional correspondence and official reports. He was young at age twenty-two, but no more so than many other staff officers throughout the army. Nevertheless, Buck's twenty-one-year-old sister Lucy, who called him "Irvie," found the notion of her brother in such a capacity to be nothing short of astonishing. "Captain Irving A. Buck," she wrote in her diary, "how ridiculously it does sound." Like Benham, Buck proved to be a competent and reliable administrator and an invaluable source for historians as well, since his frequent letters home offer rare glimpses into life at divisional headquarters.[4]

As for the rest of the staff, Cleburne kept both Hanley and Mangum as his personal aides-de-camp but found that he now had to deal as well with a chief of artillery, a chief of subsistence, and a quartermaster—all majors—plus a half dozen captains and lieutenants, a staff of twelve altogether. He generally gave them their head, allowing them to perform their administrative tasks without a lot of direct supervision. Buck wrote home that "General Cleburne and staff are a very pleasant set of gentlemen and allow me to write things my own way." For Cleburne, this was not so much a management technique as it was a recognition that his own strengths lay less in administration than in personal leadership. As for the general himself, Buck wrote, "He is quiet, has little to say, and any one to see and not know him would take him much sooner for a private than a Major Gen'l." Cleburne's quiet manner and stoic demeanor nevertheless inspired both admiration and affection among members of the staff, and as a group they proved both reliable and fiercely loyal.[5]

Cleburne's disdain for the symbols of rank was not merely an affectation; he genuinely preferred the common and familiar to the elaborate and ornamental. It may be that he was a bit intimidated by the exalted levels to which he had ascended, and that he deliberately sought more modest and, to him, more comfortable circumstances. When the staff officers hired a French cook (at forty dollars a month) to prepare gourmet meals for them, Cleburne told them jokingly that they lived "so d——d well" he would not mess with them any longer, and he took most of his meals with the division's medical officer, Dr. John M. Johnson, "a well-educated, thorough gentleman, full of good humor and witticism." Even more revealing was the presence at divisional headquarters of the general's clerk, Charlie Bailey, an irreverent Arkansan, who treated everyone from private to general with the same offhand familiarity. Bailey had a habit of peppering his speech with vivid profanity, which was a source of mirth to many members of the staff but which Cleburne chose to ignore. "He swears as long and loud when he is sitting beside General C as when we are alone," Buck confided in a letter home. "But with all he is one of the merriest best hearted fellows in the service and the life of our headquarters."[6]

Another aspect of life at divisional headquarters is revealed in a story told by St. John Liddell, the Louisiana planter who commanded one of Cleburne's four brigades. Cleburne, it seems, kept a pet raccoon at headquarters. At night, according to Liddell, the raccoon would "push its way under the cover of somebody's bed" for warmth. Occasionally the visit was unwelcome and it would be kicked out again, but it merely found another bed whose occupant was more hospitable. "One night, however, everybody seemed unfriendly to him and kicked him away. After trying all the beds, the poor fellow stopped and set up a most pitiable cry," which induced some softhearted staff officer to take him in.[7]

Buckner had been a popular commander, but Cleburne's appointment was welcomed in the division by officers and enlisted men alike. There is no evidence that either Johnson or Wood harbored any resentment at being passed over for command by a foreign-born, volunteer officer who had come up from the ranks. Cleburne's reputation as a fighting general, his evident work ethic, and his modest demeanor all helped to ensure his acceptance by the division. As popular as Buckner had been, Cleburne soon won over the affection of what for the rest of the war would be called Cleburne's Division.

The dominant issue in the army that fall, one that very soon eclipsed any lingering controversy about Cleburne's promotion, was the mounting groundswell of hostility toward Bragg. From the moment the army began its retreat from Kentucky, officers and soldiers alike began to voice their dissatisfaction with the performance of their dour and humorless army commander. Kirby Smith took the early lead in fomenting this discontent, castigating Bragg in letters home as early as mid-October, though by the end of the month most of the senior officers in the army were sounding a similar note. Even Hardee, almost Bragg's last ally among the generals, decided that Bragg had committed "unpardonable errors" during the campaign, "errors which any man of good practical sense . . . ought not to have committed." He wrote to Richmond asserting boldly that "Bragg has proved a failure."[8]

Cleburne was not inclined by temperament to conspiratorial discussions about the wisdom or competence of the high command. For the most part he was content to accept his orders and execute them as forcefully as possible. At the same time, however, he was not insensitive to public feeling. Once before, in siding with his regiment against the bumbling General Bradley in Arkansas, he had proved that he was capable of deliberate insubordination — even mutiny — if he believed the safety of his command was in jeopardy. Bragg was no Bradley, but Cleburne had experienced firsthand the army commander's tendency to make startlingly wrongheaded decisions, and in many cases those decisions had cost his command dearly. It was Bragg who had ordered Cleburne to make the fruitless attack on the second day at Shiloh; it was Bragg who had so badly misunderstood the disposition of forces at Perryville as to order an attack by fewer than 20,000 men on an army of nearly 60,000; and of course it was Bragg who had ordered the retreat from the field at Perryville after Cleburne's men had sacrificed a third of their number to break the enemy line. Already skeptical, therefore, of Bragg's judgment, Cleburne became more so when Hardee, his friend and personal mentor, expressed doubts about Bragg's fitness for command. The historian of the Army of Tennessee, Thomas L. Connelly, has written that Hardee "combined direct criticism and innuendo to demolish Bragg's reputation with the junior officers of the Second Corps." If so, none of Hardee's officers was likely to be more susceptible to such innuendos than Cleburne.[9]

Bragg's officers were not his only critics. The southern press was as quick to assail a loser as lionize a winner, and that fall many southern papers began to attack Bragg openly. Some of their stories included the assertion that Bragg had lost the confidence of the army. Combined with Kirby Smith's trip to Richmond, the widespread attacks in the press forced the government to pay attention to the command crisis in the Army of Tennessee. Davis called Bragg to the Confederate capitol in late October to allow him to present his side of the story. There, Bragg told Davis that the dissatisfaction in the army stemmed from a few malcontents (which was not the case) and that the army was generally in good spirits (also not true). The president was nevertheless inclined to give Bragg the benefit of any doubt, and he determined to sustain him in command. At the same time, however, Davis appointed General Joseph E. Johnston, recovering from wounds he had received in the battles near Richmond, as overall commander in the West with vague supervisory authority over both Bragg's army in Tennessee and Pemberton's army in Mississippi. Davis's conception was that Johnston would command neither army directly but would shuttle reinforcements back and forth between Bragg and Pemberton at need. Bragg, however, would remain in command of the Army of Tennessee at Murfreesboro.[10]

Johnston arrived in Murfreesboro in the first week of December. He was thin and erect with a receding hairline and a small gray goatee. He talked with Bragg, Polk, and Hardee and then, apparently satisfied, returned to his headquarters in Chattanooga. The very next week, the army had an even more distinguished visitor when on 12 December Jefferson Davis arrived to assess the army's mood for himself. Cleburne missed seeing the commander in chief, for he was twenty miles west of Murfreesboro leading a Confederate column toward Franklin, which a Federal force had attacked that morning. Even so, the president's visit would affect Cleburne's career in two ways: First, Davis brought with him the confirmation of Cleburne's appointment as a major general. Second, and less happily, Davis made it clear during his visit that Bragg still had the confidence of the executive even if the rest of the army had its doubts. Indeed, Davis decided that Bragg was so well situated at Murfreesboro, it was safe to detach Carter Stevenson's Division from the army to reinforce Pemberton in Mississippi.[11]

Cleburne not only missed out on the president's visit, he also missed the social event of the camp that season: the wedding of cavalry chief John Hunt Morgan to local belle Mattie Ready. Nor did he attend the "gala" Christmas Eve ball held in the Murfreesboro courthouse festooned with captured Federal flags hung upside down. Although Hardee attended both events, Cleburne stayed at his headquarters near Eagleville twenty miles to the west. Social events involving mixed company were not his favorite in any case; he would rather lead a desperate charge against the enemy than engage in polite social conversation with ladies whom he did not know well. However, his Christmas was gladdened by a visit from his youngest half brother, Christopher. "Kit" Cleburne, now twenty-one years old, had ventured south from Cincinnati in November to volunteer his services to the Confederacy. He may even have asked his brother for a position on his staff, although one authority claims that Patrick declined to offer his sibling a staff post, urging him instead to make his own way by enlisting as a private and working his way up. In any case, Kit enlisted in Morgan's cavalry in November 1862, just prior to Morgan's wedding.[12]

The holiday festivities at Murfreesboro masked a dangerous strategic situation. Bragg's army was not as secure as the president believed or as the active social calendar suggested. The army's sole link with its base at Chattanooga, more than a hundred miles to the south, was the single track of the Nashville and Chattanooga Railroad. In addition, with the departure of Stevenson's Division Bragg's army was reduced to a total of about 35,000 men, and barely thirty miles away was a Federal army under William S. Rosecrans with a strength almost exactly double that. Finally, Bragg compounded the situation by a dangerous dispersal of the resources he did have. As in Kentucky, he positioned the various elements of his command in a broad semicircle fifty miles across, with Hardee in Eagleville, Polk in Murfreesboro, and McCown's Division—the only surviving remnant of what had been Kirby Smith's Corps —at Readyville. He did not worry much about these dispositions, however, because he was convinced that Rosecrans would not move from Nashville.[13]

The day after Christmas, a cold, overcast day with threatening rain, Cleburne and three of his four brigades were at College Grove between Eagleville and Triune twenty-four miles southwest of Murfreesboro. His fourth brigade—Wood's—was four miles to the north at Triune serving as a divisional advance guard. In midmorning Cleburne received the first of a series of reports which suggested that contrary to Bragg's expectations, Rosecrans's army was on the move. Fifteen miles to the west a Confederate outpost at Franklin was overrun by a strong Federal column, and Wood reported that another Federal column was advancing from the north. If pressed home, these movements could drive a wedge between Hardee and Polk, splitting Bragg's army neatly in half. After forwarding these reports, Cleburne received a preliminary warning from Hardee to prepare for a sudden evacuation, and the next morning Hardee ordered him to move at once to Murfreesboro.[14]

On 27 December, Cleburne's men marched all day through a drenching rain, "bogging along," as one soldier put it, "in deep mud several miles on a bad road." They arrived at the outskirts of Murfreesboro after nightfall and drew rations of crackers and bacon. The next morning, Hardee ordered Cleburne to cross Stones River and deploy his four brigades in an east-west line facing north about 800 yards behind Breckinridge's Division just north of town. There, they constituted the right wing of Bragg's semicircular defensive line, while the two divisions of Polk's Corps—commanded by Jones Withers and Frank Cheatham—held the left. John P. McCown's Division would constitute the army's reserve.[15]

It was not a strong position. The most obvious weakness was that Stones River cut Bragg's army in half. The river was fordable at several places, but the water was cold in late December and shuttling troops back and forth would be both difficult and time-consuming. Bragg felt obliged to cover both sides of the river, however, because he was uncertain of the direction from which the enemy threat was likely to come. Rosecrans could approach along the line of the Nashville Pike, but he might also employ the Wilkinson or Franklin Pikes to the west or the Lebanon Pike to the north. For most of three days, therefore, Bragg considered his options while Cleburne's men remained in their bivouac north of town.

Then late on 30 December, Hardee and Polk were called to Bragg's headquarters to receive new orders: Bragg had decided to seize the initiative and attack. While the frontline divisions on both sides of the river remained in place, Cleburne's Division would move quietly from the right to the left to bolster an attack by the army's reserve division under John P. McCown. Supported by Polk's two divisions, McCown and Cleburne would drive in the Federal right wing and fold it back like a jackknife blade until they cut the Nashville Pike behind the Federal front lines. Bragg appointed Hardee to exercise overall tactical command during the attack, and he declared that it would begin at dawn.[16]

Cleburne got his orders late in the afternoon. The sun was already setting as his men broke camp and began to march southward through "a cold pelting rain." Cleburne halted the column at the fords over the river to await guidance from Hardee's staff officers who could direct him to his assigned position. It was well after dark when the nearly 6,000 men in his division began taking off their shoes (most removing their trousers as well), in order to wade through the bone-chilling water of Stones River. In the rain and pitch-darkness, the men encountered "many difficulties" crossing the river. Once across, Cleburne deployed them in line of battle as best he could by reference to the line of camp fires marking the location of Cheatham's Division on his right. Somewhere in the dark to his front was McCown's Division, but no camp fires marked its location, for Bragg had ordered that troops of the attacking force were not to light fires for fear of alerting the Federals. Cleburne rode forward and discussed the coming fight with McCown's brigadiers; then he met with each of his own brigade commanders to ensure that their forces were properly placed. It was well past midnight by the time he lay down on wet ground in the rain to await the dawn.[17]

Hardee had told Cleburne to attack at first light, which he estimated to be about 5:00 A.M. Cleburne therefore ordered his brigadiers to rouse the men at 4:30. Without fires, there would be no coffee (or even the coffee substitutes that had become common in the army), and the troops were assembled quickly and ready to move well before the sunrise. Cleburne deployed his division into line of battle with Johnson's large brigade of Tennesseans in the center, Liddell on the left, and Lucius Polk on the right. He placed Wood's Brigade behind Polk in a second line as a reserve. In Bragg's conception, McCown's Division would spearhead the attack and execute a gradual right wheel pivoting on Cheatham's Division. Cleburne would follow in the same way, thus providing the kind of attack in depth that could carry the advance all the way to the Nashville Pike. Cleburne passed the instructions on to his brigadiers, emphasizing that as their men moved forward, they should adjust their gait, "stepping short on the right and full on the left . . . gradually wheeling to the right."[18]

At 5:00 A.M., though not yet full daylight, Hardee told Cleburne to begin the advance, and the division moved forward on a front nearly a mile wide, swinging to the right like a huge gate. The terrain was much more suited to defense than attack: stands of mixed cedars were interspersed with open meadows while outcroppings of large limestone boulders littered the ground. There was some gapping and bunching during the advance, and Cleburne had to send staff officers dashing to and fro to keep his brigades in proper alignment. The morning haze lay thick over the ground; it was a "cold and frosty" morning, and the men could see their breath. Because his command constituted the second line of the advance, Cleburne did not deploy skirmishers. The line advanced for more than a mile without incident. Then his men began to encounter a few Federal skirmishers and soon afterward a line of Federal infantry. How McCown's men had passed over this ground without encountering such a force was a mystery Cleburne did not have time to consider. He threw his brigades into the fight that was welling up on his

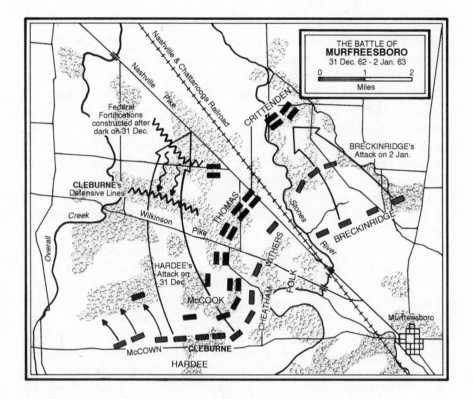

front. Despite the previous night's discomfort, the men rushed forward with enthusiasm, and as they did so, they took up the Rebel yell. A witness to the charge, a soldier from Cheatham's Division, claimed later that "Pat Cleburne's men could beat the world on a yell."[19]

Midway through the fight, Cleburne discovered the explanation to the mysterious disappearance of McCown's Division. McCown not only had started off late, he had headed in the wrong direction. After their initial successful encounter with the Federal right flank, McCown's brigades pursued the retreating Federals off to the west and nearly out of the battle. By the time McCown got his division reoriented and moving northward, it was on Cleburne's left flank. McCown told Liddell, commanding Cleburne's left-hand brigade, that his men were pretty badly cut up and that it might be better if Liddell took the lead. He did so, and McCown's men then fell in on his left. As Cleburne's men pitched into the Federals, McNair's Brigade of McCown's Division came up on their left and joined the fight. Cleburne reported that the fight was "short and bloody, lasting about twenty-five minutes, when the enemy gave way."[20]

When the Federal line broke, Cleburne's men instinctively pursued. The Yankees had established a second line not far behind the first, but the momentum of the Rebel charge broke this line too, and as the bluecoats fled, the Rebels bounded after them, their cold and hunger temporarily forgotten. Cleburne encouraged the pursuit, but he also had to ensure that the uneven advance of his units did not create gaps in the front line. It was not easy. One soldier described the terrain of "limestone rocks, gnarly cedar trees, [and] stub arms sticking out of the ground" as "almost impassable," especially for artillery. The alignment of units became even more haphazard, and Cleburne became concerned that the advance was "not very orderly." When his brigades ran up against a new Federal line near the Wilkinson Turnpike about 9:00 A.M., the disciplined volleys of the bluecoats checked their pursuit and they halted to reorganize.[21]

The biggest problem was that as in the battle at Perryville, Cleburne's front line had outrun the advance of Cheatham's Division, and it was receiving enfilading fire from the right. At Hardee's direction, Cleburne threw Wood's Brigade—his only reserve—into the gap. Wood's men, too, were temporarily halted by a battery of Federal artillery, and Cleburne ordered his sharpshooters forward to pick off the Yankee gunners. The sharpshooters proved less effective here than at Perryville and had to withdraw. Cleburne's artillery had more success. Although the Yankees had double the number of guns, two of Cleburne's batteries unlimbered boldly on the pike itself and engaged the enemy cannon. With a continuous front reestablished, the division soon moved forward again, driving the Federals back through the clumps of cedars toward the Nashville Pike.[22]

McCown's error in heading west before turning north and then east meant that the two Rebel divisions were now advancing not one behind the other as Bragg had envisioned but side by side on a front that was ten brigades wide. The benefit of this was that the Confederate line overlapped the Federal right by more than half a mile. When Cleburne and McCown renewed their advance at about 9:30, they swept forward like a giant scythe against the startled Federals of Alexander McCook's XX Corps. On the other hand, every soldier assigned to the Confederate attack was now in the front line. If it faltered before it reached the Nashville Pike, there would be no reserves to throw into the fight.[23]

After the fight along the Wilkinson Pike, Cleburne sent Wood's Brigade back to allow the men to replenish their depleted cartridge pouches. He now exercised direct command over three of his own brigades plus Preston Smith's Brigade of Frank Cheatham's Division, which had become intermingled with his own. A half mile beyond the Wilkinson Pike, these units ran into another

Federal line where, as Cleburne later reported it, the enemy "made an obstinate and destructive resistance." For nearly an hour, the issue was fiercely contested at close range, and Lucius Polk's Brigade (formerly Cleburne's) suffered particularly heavy casualties. The attackers had "to mount a very high cedar fence, and then charge." One veteran recalled, "They gave us more than we expected, but we kept on." Finally, the Yankees were dislodged and "driven from the cedars."[24]

Again Cleburne pursued. Hardee had told him to "push the enemy" and "give him no time to rally," and that is exactly what he intended to do. It was early afternoon by now and his men were tired. They had been awake most of the night, catching only a few hours of sleep on the cold ground with no dinner, and they had launched their attack at dawn with no breakfast. Since then they had carried the burden of the attack for over eight hours. Now less than a half mile from the Nashville Pike, they encountered yet another line of Federals, the fifth of the day. Summoning one more effort, Cleburne's brigades again charged the enemy line, and once again they drove the defenders from their positions back through a cedar break and onto the Nashville Pike. Here was the Federal main line of supply and communication. If Cleburne's men could hold it, the Federal army would be in serious jeopardy of being cut off and destroyed. Some of the men from Johnson's Brigade stood on the turnpike itself. But like a wave rushing up a sloping shore, the impetus of the Confederate advance had run its course; the men had reached the end of their strength. Cleburne later described the moment in his report: his men were "almost on the Nashville turnpike, in rear of the original center of Rosecrans' army, sweeping with their fire his only line of communication with Nashville; but it was now after 3:00 o'clock; my men had had little or no rest the night before; they had been fighting since dawn, without relief, food, or water." Even he knew that he could drive them no further.[25]

The Federal high command realized its peril and sent its reserves to hold the turnpike. "At this critical moment," Cleburne wrote, "the enemy met my thinned ranks with another fresh line of battle." It was too much. His line broke, the men fleeing as quickly as they could for the protection of a cedar break about a quarter mile to the rear. Smith's Brigade could not be rallied at all, but the other three (Johnson's, Liddell's, and Polk's) halted in the modest protection of the tree line. Hardee had detached Wood's Brigade to guard the army's ammunition train, which was reportedly threatened by a Federal cavalry probe. Cleburne had fresh supplies of ammunition distributed to his three remaining brigades and waited in some anxiety to see if the Federals would continue with their counterattack. With no supporting artillery at hand, his ability even to maintain this advanced position was uncertain.

Very soon, however, it became evident that the enemy was satisfied to have regained the turnpike and had no intention of advancing further. The two forces studied each other across a quarter mile of open ground.[26]

Although Cleburne's instinct was to attack, he could see that his men had given him all they had and that to attack under these circumstances would be suicidal. Even so, the notion of giving up before reaching the final goal was almost physically painful. His state of mind at the time was still evident a month later when he composed his official report and penned the rhetorical question: "Ought I to again advance?" He sent Major Benham to ask Johnson if his men could reclaim the road. Johnson replied carefully that such an undertaking would be "very hazardous," thus confirming what Cleburne already knew. Still, he could not bring himself to accept responsibility for calling off the advance. He sent a courier to Hardee to ask for guidance. Hardee knew his protégé well enough to know that if Cleburne was in any doubt at all about attacking, it was probably not wise to order him forward. Hardee later claimed in his own report that another attack "would have been folly, not valor." Hardee ordered Cleburne to hold the ground he had gained, rest the division, and await further orders. Cleburne set out pickets and prepared to bivouac what was left of his division in line of battle, a quarter mile west of the Nashville Turnpike.[27]

Almost certainly, the arrival of a fresh Confederate division, or even a fresh brigade, would have allowed the southern army to hold the Nashville Pike and secure the victory. In his subsequent report, Hardee wrote almost wistfully, "If, at that moment . . . a fresh division could have replaced Cleburne's exhausted troops and followed up the victory, the rout of Rosecrans' army would have been complete." But there were no fresh Confederate troops west of Stones River. McCown's troops were as used up as Cleburne's, and those of Withers and Cheatham—Leonidas Polk's two divisions—spent the afternoon making a series of futile attacks against the center of the Federal line, a strong point called the Round Forest, where the Federals had concentrated their artillery. That left only Breckinridge's Division of Hardee's Corps that remained inactive east of the river. For much of the morning, Breckinridge believed that he was about to be attacked himself, and by the time he determined that such an assault was unlikely and sent reinforcements over the river, it was too late.[28]

For the second night in a row, the men of Cleburne's Division went to sleep without the benefit of camp fires or hot food. Having discarded their packs in order to make the attack, they were also without tents or blankets. Even so, those not on picket duty were soon asleep, comforted perhaps by the knowledge that they had bested the enemy at every opportunity. For most of ten hours, from sunrise to nearly sunset, they had fought their way through an entire Federal corps. Five times they had broken a Yankee defensive line. Though their assault had stopped short of complete victory, many of those in Cleburne's front line who lay down on their arms that New Year's Eve knew that they had whipped the Yanks—and whipped them badly. Surely the enemy would appreciate that and withdraw. As Cleburne's men slept, midnight passed unmarked, and 1862 turned to 1863.

At first light, Cleburne called for his horse and accompanied by his staff rode the length of his line end to end to inspect his position by daylight. The Federals threw occasional artillery rounds into the trees at intervals but otherwise demonstrated no offensive intention. Cleburne noted that there were a large number of abandoned shoulder arms in the no-man's-land between the two lines, and to the alarm of his staff officers he rode out into the open to recover them. The group of mounted officers attracted the attention of Federal sharpshooters, who opened fire. Buck recalled that though "the bullets were flying within a few inches of us," Cleburne seemed not to notice. For his part, Buck "felt very uncomfortable," but of course he could not leave until Cleburne did. He later confided to his sister that this particular exploit reminded him of the goat that tried to knock a train engine off the track: "I admired his spunk, but had a very poor opinion of his judgement."[29]

Soon after Cleburne returned to the relative safety of his lines in the cedar break, a courier from Bragg arrived with orders to "push forward [and] feel the enemy." Bragg hoped, and probably expected, that the enemy had retreated after his drubbing the day before. Cleburne sent Liddell's Brigade forward to reconnoiter. Soon he could hear the sound of heavy firing to the front, and not long afterward a courier arrived from Liddell to report that he had found the enemy present in strength and that he needed support urgently. Cleburne sent Wood's Brigade to cover Liddell's flank, with orders to press the enemy hard enough "to develop his lines and ascertain his force." Approximately half of Cleburne's available strength was now committed to the reconnaissance. Worse, by the time Wood's Brigade moved forward, Liddell had been forced to fall back, so that Wood's men found themselves badly outgunned. They, too, had to fall back to the cover of the cedar break, leaving some 100 casualties in enemy hands.[30]

Cleburne reported the results of the skirmish to Bragg: Not only was the enemy still there, he was there in evident strength. For the rest of the day, Cleburne's men remained largely inactive, watching the front from the shelter of the line of cedars west of the Nashville Turnpike. Cleburne did not have the strength to renew the fight, and the Federals apparently did not have any interest in doing so. After dark, the men settled down for what one described as another uncomfortable "night's sleep on the freezing battle field without fires."[31]

That night, and more particularly the next morning, Cleburne's pickets heard the sound of scores of axes ringing in the woods near the turnpike—the Federals were apparently fortifying their lines against another attack. Cleburne reported the activity at once, hoping to forestall another order to advance. He knew that if his depleted command tried to reclaim the Nashville Pike by storming a fortified enemy line, "the result would prove disastrous." No such order arrived, however, because Bragg had decided instead to attack the other Federal flank east of Stones River. That afternoon the men of Breckinridge's Division charged forward in an attempt to seize a piece of high ground to their front. Cleburne could hear the sound of the fight from his position in the cedar break west of the river. The noise crescendoed about 5:00 o'clock, but Cleburne did not learn until later that the assault had proved fruitless, serving only to increase the number of killed and wounded.[32]

That night, an hour before midnight, the Federals on Cleburne's front made a reconnaissance of their own, presumably to ensure themselves that the Rebels were still there. The tentative advance was easily driven back by the division's skirmishers, and not long afterward Cleburne received a message from Hardee to quit his position and fall back quietly to the east bank of Stones River. Once again, as at Perryville, the men of Cleburne's Division were ordered to withdraw from ground that they had conquered at great cost. Through another "cold and drenching rain," they marched back over the rough terrain they had crossed the day before, back across the fords over Stones River, back to the same bivouac north of Murfreesboro they had left forty-eight hours earlier. After a promising start, the situation at Murfreesboro had assumed an ominous character. Despite "winning" the battle on 31 December, the Confederates had no tangible gains to show for it, the Federal army remained unbroken north of town, apparently still game for the fight, while Bragg's army was much the worse for wear.[33]

The next morning, Cleburne attended a meeting in Bragg's headquarters. The army commander's mood was decidedly gloomy. He had received pessimistic reports overnight from both Withers and Cheatham, whose divisions remained west of the river, and the cavalry reported that Federal reinforcements were moving toward Murfreesboro. Bragg talked openly of retreat. Both Polk and Hardee agreed, and the discussion focused on the logistics of the move. The wagons and the walking wounded would start that afternoon; the rest of the army would leave after nightfall. Cleburne returned to his command to prepare his division for the march south, but after the wagons had been sent off, he was called back to Bragg's headquarters for yet another command conference.[34]

The precise nature of this meeting became the subject of much subsequent controversy. It was held at dusk, around 4:30 or 5:00 on a winter's afternoon. Bragg, who called the meeting, explained that he now had second thoughts about conducting a retreat that night. He noted that a hasty evacuation would necessitate the abandonment of some 1,700 men who were too badly wounded to walk. Could the army stay another twenty-four hours at Murfreesboro until these men could also be safely evacuated? Cleburne responded in the affirmative; of course his men could stay and hold off the enemy for twenty-four hours. But both Polk and Hardee pointed out that the army's wagons, with its reserve ammunition, had already gone south. They averred that Cleburne's was the only division in the army that "could be depended upon." If the army had to fight a battle under such circumstances, it was inviting disaster. One by one the other commanders endorsed this view, and Cleburne changed his mind. He announced that since the wagons had already left, it was best to go ahead with the retreat as originally scheduled. At that, Bragg terminated the meeting and Cleburne returned to his division.[35]

The men of Cleburne's Division began marching southward at 11:00 o'clock, and they marched all night with only brief rest stops. Nor did they stop at dawn, continuing to march all day as well, the whole time under gray skies and intermittent sleet and rain. In a letter to his wife, one of Cleburne's officers remarked, "How any set of men can stand such hardships I can't imagine." After dark on 4 January, Cleburne finally called a halt to give his exhausted men a night's rest but they were on the road again by 8:00 the next morning. Straggling was widespread. The army finally halted on 6 January near Tullahoma behind the protection of the Duck River. Morale was terrible. In addition to the physical discomfort of a forced march in midwinter, many in the ranks saw in this retreat a parallel with their arduous withdrawal from Kentucky two months earlier. Once again, they muttered, they had won a victory in the field at great cost only to have that victory discarded by the army commander.[36]

These sentiments reignited the army's latent bitterness against Bragg. As Buck expressed it, "the troops felt that they had won a victory, the fruits of which had been lost from no fault of theirs." He wrote his sister from Tullahoma that "the feeling against General Bragg is very strong." His own view was that Bragg was well-meaning and worked hard, but the job was simply beyond him. His was one of the more benign reactions. Others in the army openly cursed the commanding general; Frank Cheatham told Tennessee governor Isham Harris that he would never serve under Bragg again.[37]

The retreat also renewed the criticism of Bragg in the southern press. The army commander was particularly outraged by an editorial that appeared in the Chattanooga *Rebel* only a week after the battle which declared that Bragg had blundered at Murfreesboro, that he had retreated against the advice of his generals, that he had lost their good opinion as a result, and that he would surely be replaced soon. Bragg felt compelled to respond, and he began by soliciting his officers for their support. On 11 January, he circulated a letter to his corps and division commanders that was both a complaint and a plea. Cleburne received a copy of this curious letter that same day. In it, Bragg noted that he was being "assailed" by "the press" and by both "officers and citizens" for his retreat from Murfreesboro. He asserted that this was unfair since he had "resisted" a withdrawal even "after advised by my corps and division commanders" and that he had agreed to it only "after hearing of the enemy's reinforcements." Now he asked each of his generals to verify this interpretation of events—in writing—in order to salvage his good name. "I desire that you will consult your subordinate commanders," Bragg wrote, "and be candid with me. . . . If I have misunderstood your advice . . . let me know. . . . If, on the contrary, I am the victim of unjust accusations, say so." Then Bragg added what amounted to a direct plea for support: "General [Kirby] Smith has been called to Richmond, it is supposed, with a view to supersede me. I shall retire without a regret if I find I have lost the good opinion of my generals, upon whom I have ever relied as upon a foundation of rock."[38]

What was Cleburne to make of this curious epistle? While he was still puzzling over it, Hardee showed up at his headquarters with his own copy of the letter. Since Bragg had asked his generals to "consult your subordinate commanders," Hardee had come to do exactly that. Indeed, Bragg had all but invited them to collaborate on their replies. He had also asked them to be "candid" and implied that if he had lost the "good opinion" of his officers, he would resign. Unquestionably, Hardee at least had come to believe that such an outcome was much to be desired, and Cleburne was probably inclined to agree. In addition to his own disappointment with Bragg's leadership, Cleburne was sensitive enough to the mood of the army to be aware that Bragg was almost universally disliked. Was it possible that a "candid" statement from the division and corps commanders would result in Bragg's resignation?

Hardee and Breckinridge both replied the next day, and their responses were no doubt far more candid than Bragg had anticipated. "I have consulted with Major General Breckinridge and Major General Cleburne," Hardee wrote, "and I feel that frankness compels me to say that the general officers . . . are unanimous in their opinion that a change in the command of this army is necessary. In this opinion I concur." For his part, Breckinridge noted that he had consulted his brigadiers and that "they request me to say that while they entertain the highest respect for your patriotism, it is their opinion that you do not possess the confidence of the army to an extent which will enable you to be useful as its commander. In this opinion I feel bound to concur."[39]

Cleburne's reply was written the next day, and it is at least possible that he had copies of Hardee's and Breckinridge's letters at hand to guide him. To the first of Bragg's questions (whether Bragg had resisted the notion of a retreat at the 3 January meeting) Cleburne wrote that a retreat had already been agreed upon and indeed was already under way before the generals met that evening. He noted that the only question Bragg had asked at the time was whether the army could suspend the movement for twenty-four hours. "I offered advice on no other point," he wrote. As to the question of whether Bragg retained the confidence of the army, Cleburne's reply echoed that of the others: "I have consulted with all my brigade commanders . . . and they unite with me in personal regard for yourself, in a high appreciation of your patriotism and gallantry, and in a conviction for your great capacity for organization, but at the same time they see, with regret, and it has also met my observation, that you do not possess the confidence of the army in other respects in that degree necessary to ensure success."[40]

The vote in Hardee's Corps was apparently unanimous. But what of the 1st Corps' officers? In Polk's Corps, Cheatham admitted freely that he had been "one of the first" to suggest a retreat and ignored the question of the army's confidence in Bragg's leadership. This response infuriated many of the other general officers in the army, who were outraged that Cheatham was willing to criticize Bragg behind his back but was apparently unwilling to do so to his face. Ten months later, Cleburne gently teased Cheatham about his response by telling him a fable: "The report had been circulated among the beasts of the forest that the lion had a bad breath, whereupon, as king, the lion summoned all to appear, and admitted them to his presence one by one. As each would answer upon smelling his breath that it was bad, the lion would devour him. When at length the fox was brought in, he replied to the question that he had a bad cold, and escaped."[41]

As for Polk himself, no one in the army disliked Bragg more than "the fighting bishop" who commanded the 1st Corps. But Polk was not in camp on 11 January when Bragg issued his letter; he was in Richmond complaining about Bragg to Jefferson Davis. When he returned on 17 January, he asked Bragg what it was he really wanted to know: whether his generals had counseled retreat at Murfreesboro or whether Bragg retained the confidence of the army. Having already heard as much as he wanted about his generals' lack of confidence in him, Bragg told Polk to confine himself to the first question. As a result, Polk returned a vague reply that did not address the question of Bragg's fitness for command.[42]

It hardly mattered. Bragg was in no doubt about how Polk and Cheatham felt. Cheatham's verbal criticisms had been reported to him, and Polk made no secret of his animosity. Indeed, Polk wrote the president to volunteer the information that if Bragg *had* asked him to respond to the issue of the army's confidence, his reply "would have coincided with those of the officers of the other corps." Thus the result of Bragg's request for a vote of confidence from his generals was all but unanimous. Only Jones Withers, whose health made further field service problematical, was willing to give Bragg his unqualified support. Despite his promise, however, Bragg did not resign. Instead he convinced President Davis that he was the victim of a cabal and prepared to purge the army of his most public enemies. Cleburne had not sought a confrontation with his commanding general, but having been asked for his views, he had felt compelled to respond honestly. It remained to be seen if in consequence the lion would devour him.

Cleburne wrote his lengthy report on the Battle of Murfreesboro during the last week of January. He worked in the relative comfort of his headquarters at Tullahoma, warmed by a roaring fire while snow lay in a thick blanket on the ground outside and occasional snowball fights broke out between the regiments. In his report he took the time and effort to mention by name all those who had been reported to him by subordinates as having behaved gallantly during the battle. Unlike most battle reports, particularly from senior officers, this one was filled with page after page of names, enlisted men as well as officers, of those who had fought well. Here was one who had "remained fighting after he was wounded," here was another who had "volunteered to carry the colors after the color-bearer had been shot down," still others had been "ever in the forefront in leading their men." Many of them, according to Cleburne, "ought to be promoted."[43]

For Patrick R. Cleburne, the winter campaign of 1862–1863 should have been a chronicle of personal triumphs. He had been promoted to major general and to the command of a division over the heads of officers senior to him. Within days, he had justified that promotion by performing brilliantly in the battle at Murfreesboro where, as one officer wrote home, "Genl. Cleburne . . . fought, as usual, like a lion." However, those winter months had also embroiled him in a distasteful personal and political squabble between Bragg and the army's senior officers, which he could have avoided only by ignoring a direct question from his commander. If Hardee had taken such a line, Cleburne might have been persuaded to follow his lead, but when Hardee made it clear that his own reply would be ruthlessly candid, Cleburne felt both honesty and loyalty pulling him in the same direction. With Bragg clinging determinedly to command despite the statements of no confidence from his corps and division commanders, the ability of the army to defend the Confederate heartland would be seriously tested.[44]

WAR AND POLITICS

For Pat Cleburne, as for every other general officer in the Army of Tennessee, the issue of army politics was never very far away during the spring and summer of 1863. The frequently bitter squabbling within the high command undermined the army's readiness and morale. Ironically, Braxton Bragg was both its principal cause and its chief victim. His cold and inflexible personality alienated both of his corps commanders and most of his division commanders. Despite a veneer of official courtesy, the confrontation became increasingly divisive and acrimonious. It carried to Richmond as well, where it became entangled in national politics. There the president's critics openly assailed the western army commander in order to embarrass the administration. They pushed hard for Bragg's removal, and the harder they pushed, the more it seemed to Davis that Bragg was the victim of an organized cabal, a conclusion that provoked the president's instant sympathy and determined support. In Richmond as in Tennessee, the sides became increasingly polarized. Throughout much of the winter and spring, the feud absorbed far too much of the energy of the high-ranking officers in the Army of Tennessee. Assailed by his own generals and suffering from poor health, Bragg became increasingly ineffective, simultaneously uncertain and dogmatic, a state of affairs that left the initiative in the spring campaign to the real enemy: the Federal army.

It helped not at all that the army's winter campsite was at Tullahoma. With its dirt streets and few dozen small buildings, Tullahoma was little more than a rail stop on the Nashville and Chattanooga line. Buck complained to his sister that it was a "Godforsaken" place and that during his daily rides with Cleburne, they could travel five miles in any direction and never see "a comfortable house." Neither did the weather contribute to troop morale, as winter rains alternated with occasional snow flurries and turned the roads, churned up by hundreds of wagons, into mud sloughs. One of Hardee's aides quipped that the town's name came from two Greek words: "Tulla" meaning mud and "Homa" meaning more mud.[1]

On 27 January, Joseph E. Johnston arrived in Tullahoma amid speculation that he had come to replace Bragg in command of the army. Buck wrote his sister that "we all hail his appearance with pleasure and think perhaps there will be some change for the better." But after meeting with Bragg and the two corps commanders, Johnston reported to Davis that while there was indeed unrest in the army, his own view was that Bragg had performed extremely well at Murfreesboro. He concluded, "It would be very unfortunate to remove him at this juncture, when he has just earned, if not won, the gratitude of the country."[2]

Bolstered by this support, Bragg composed his report on the Battle of Murfreesboro soon after Johnston departed. To his credit, he did not use the opportunity to assail his detractors; indeed, he especially commended Polk, Hardee, and Cleburne for their "valor, skill, and ability displayed . . . throughout the engagement." He did, however, criticize others. He asserted that Cheatham had allowed Cleburne's advance to outpace his own thereby exposing Cleburne's flank to enfilading fire, and he charged that Breckinridge had been tardy in supplying the reinforcements that might have provided the final margin of victory. As for McCown, Bragg found his conduct so indefensible that he ordered him under arrest for disobedience of orders. Much of Bragg's criticism was justified. Several witnesses later claimed that Cheatham had been drunk on the day of the battle, and unquestionably Breckinridge had dithered fatally on the morning of 31 January. Nevertheless, Bragg's report angered both of those officers, as well as their supporters in the army. Even some of those who had reason to believe that Bragg's criticisms were on target—Hardee, for example—found it useful that Bragg's report further undermined the army commander's support within the officer corps.[3]

Cleburne did not record his own views about the dissension in the high command. Despite his "candid" response to Bragg's query in January, Cleburne was not prone to asserting his opinions even on ordinary issues unless circumstances made it necessary for him to do so. All around him, however, the animosity toward Bragg was both evident and growing. Within his own divisional headquarters, his chief of artillery wrote home to complain of the "half way victories of Bragg," and Buck wrote his sister of his desire to "see some one else at the head of our men." Cleburne could not have been unaware of such sentiments within his own staff. Then, too, because of his continued close association with Hardee, he was almost certainly subject to Hardee's frequent, off-the-record criticisms. Cleburne was an ambitious and determined man who had repeatedly and successfully adapted himself to the culture that surrounded him; he was unlikely to resist the tide of popular feeling against Bragg in the spring of 1863.[4]

As yet, however, Bragg did not count Cleburne among his enemies. He appointed Cleburne and Jones Withers, his only remaining ally among the high command, as the two major generals who, along with five brigadier generals would try McCown on the charge of "disobedience of orders." It was somewhat awkward for Cleburne to sit in judgment on this case, for he was not only the senior officer on the court, he was also the one man, along with Liddell, who could testify firsthand to McCown's errors at the Battle of Murfreesboro. He was, in effect, the chief witness, judge, and jury. Moreover, while it could not be denied that McCown had erred in allowing his division to charge off to the west rather than wheel to the right as ordered, he had been tasked with a complicated maneuver over difficult terrain and unlike Cleburne had not had the advantage of Hardee's close supervision. Still, Cleburne could not find McCown innocent of the charge without implying that Hardee's report was inaccurate. The court met on 16 March (Cleburne's thirty-fifth birthday) and concluded its deliberations the same week. Cleburne and his fellow generals found McCown guilty and recommended that he be suspended from the service for six months with loss of pay and privileges. He never held an important command again.[5]

That same week General Joseph E. Johnston returned to Tullahoma, and on 19 March Cleburne's Division turned out in his honor to participate in a review of Hardee's Corps. It was "a grand review," witnessed not only by Johnston and Bragg but also by scores of ladies dressed in bright silks who had been escorted from Shelbyville for the occasion. Johnston's visit revived the rumor that he had come to replace Bragg in command of the army, a rumor based this time on more than speculation. Capitulating to the tidal wave of hostility, Davis had ordered Johnston to take command at Tullahoma and send Bragg to Richmond. Johnston was loath to do it. Sympathetic to Bragg's situation and morbidly sensitive to the charge of self-promotion, he used the excuse that Mrs. Bragg was ill with typhoid fever to induce Davis to postpone the order. Johnston stayed in Tullahoma, but so did Bragg, and while Johnston was technically in command, he declined to assert personal control of the army. The result was a vacuum of authority at the top. Even after Mrs. Bragg's health improved, the curious lack of direction continued, for then Johnston became ill and declared that he could not spare Bragg in case the enemy attacked.[6]

In April, the publication of Leonidas Polk's report on Murfreesboro re-ignited the generals' feud. It infuriated Bragg that Polk directly contradicted Bragg's own report by complimenting Cheatham's performance in the battle.

As far as Bragg was concerned, the only explanation for such an absurd claim was that Polk and Cheatham were allied in a conspiracy against him. He decided to expose Polk by dragging up an event from several months earlier. Prior to the Battle of Perryville, Polk had declined to obey Bragg's initial order to attack the advancing Federals and had instead withdrawn to Harrodsburg and Perryville. Now Bragg wrote to all of Polk's subordinates asking them "to what extent you sustained the general in his acknowledged disobedience."[7]

Cleburne was perhaps surprised to receive a copy of the letter. He had not been present when Polk had petitioned his generals for their support and had merely obeyed Polk's order to fall back to Harrodsburg. Hardee suspected at once that Bragg was attempting to gather evidence for a court-martial, and he advised Cleburne not to respond. Then he wrote to warn Polk of what was afoot. "The paper has been sent to Cleburne and Wood," Hardee wrote to Polk, "and I suppose to all the general officers who were under your command. If you choose to rip up the Kentucky campaign you can tear Bragg into tatters." Cleburne did not reply to Bragg's letter, but Hardee did, and a colder reply would be hard to imagine: "I do not consider it proper . . . to enter into details of what occurred on the occasions referred to." For his part, Polk thanked Hardee "for the prompt indication of what was brewing."[8]

If, as Hardee suspected, Bragg was seeking evidence for a court-martial, his gambit failed. However, the episode did reveal in even sharper detail the deep schism within the army, and it further polarized the officer corps into hostile camps. The breach was now apparently beyond healing. It seemed that either Bragg would have to go as army commander, or both Hardee and Polk would have to be replaced. President Davis was unwilling to choose between these hateful alternatives, and Johnston was equally unwilling to make the decision for him. As a result, the feud simmered on through the spring and into the summer, paralyzing the Army of Tennessee at a time when it ought to have been preparing for the spring campaign. For all practical purposes, the army was leaderless.[9]

Good weather returned in April when a spell of springlike temperatures promised an end to the winter doldrums. Cleburne increased the frequency of his formal inspections, and wagon loads of ladies were regularly escorted in from Shelbyville to provide an audience for the reviews. Cleburne took a rare break from the routine of camp life to visit Shelbyville himself and returned much refreshed. Buck wrote home suspiciously that the general was in "a heavenly mood." Spring fever was also responsible for Cleburne's unexpected proposal that his staff join him in a ride out to visit a local waterfall some three miles from camp. Two of his young aides accepted the invitation and, though the rain returned during the ride, they persevered and in a short time arrived at the falls, a stepped cascade some fifty feet from top to bottom called Ovoca Falls. Cleburne proposed that they take a shower bath in the falls, and unwilling to be thought unadventurous by their commanding officer, the two young staffers agreed. They peeled off their uniforms and stepped gingerly into the falls. After a short and vigorous dousing, they were soon back on the bank of the stream putting on their clothes. Cleburne could not pull his boots on over his wet socks and ended up jamming his bare feet into his boots for the short ride back to camp. The staffers rode home barefoot carrying their boots over their saddles.[10]

Although the weather gradually improved, it remained cold enough to require a fire most nights in the small house that Cleburne shared with several of his staff officers. In the third week of April, the occupants were awakened by billowing smoke and cries of "Fire! Fire!" They hastened from the house and organized a bucket brigade, but the fire was well-established and they soon shifted their efforts to saving the divisional records and their personal effects. The house, however, was entirely consumed.[11]

The improving weather also signaled the onset of the spring campaign. A thousand miles to the west Federal gunboats ran past the Vicksburg batteries and succeeded in transporting Ulysses S. Grant's Federal army across the river to the eastern bank of the Mississippi thus threatening Vicksburg's back door. At about the same time, Federal troops sortied from Murfreesboro as well, advancing toward Tullahoma on a broad front. They reached the ridge of high ground about halfway between the two armies, then retreated almost as quickly as they had come. In response, Bragg ordered Hardee's Corps to move north, cross the Duck River, and occupy the passes through the ridge. On 26 April, three days after the fire that had consumed his headquarters, Cleburne and his division climbed aboard railcars at Tullahoma for the twenty-mile journey north to Wartrace just south of Liberty Gap.[12]

The two months that Cleburne spent at Wartrace proved to be an escape not only from the political machinations that swirled around army headquarters in Tullahoma but from the war itself. Deriving its name from its location astride an old Creek Indian warpath, Wartrace was picturesquely located along a small branch of the Duck River. Buck noted rhapsodically that "we are in the midst of field, forests, and rivers, all of which we enjoy to their full extent." Cleburne set up his headquarters in a small frame house in town opposite the depot. He shared these quarters with his friend Dr. John M. Johnson and the ever-present Captain Buck, while the rest of the staff bivouacked in tents near a small grove of trees a quarter mile away. Food was plentiful, and dinners at Cleburne's new headquarters featured not only beef or mutton, but fish, eggs, rolls and butter—even real coffee and fresh strawberries.[13]

Hardee established his headquarters nearby at "Beechwood," a lovely plantation home owned by Colonel Andrew Erwin. The colonel's wife, Mary Erwin, was a sympathetic and conscientious hostess, and Beechwood soon became the social as well as the command center for the corps. Mary Erwin's sister, Rowena Webster, remembered how almost every evening, after tea, the officers would gather there "in a most homelike and social manner, the ladies refreshing them with charming music, both instrumental and vocal." She noted that "frequently the soldiers joined in the music."[14]

Cleburne was a regular participant in these social evenings. He could hardly have avoided it; Beechwood was, after all, the corps headquarters as well as its social center. Still, like the romantic he was, Cleburne found social evenings with society ladies a bit of a strain. He idealized women so thoroughly that he suspected they must find him coarse and vulgar. Five years earlier he might have found these evenings almost intolerable; it was a measure of his growing self-assurance that now he could actually enjoy them. He was still relatively reserved, particularly compared with Hardee who was energized by social activities and who was an outrageous flirt. Rowena Webster remembered Cleburne as being "a little awkward" at their social evenings, though she was also aware of his "dreamy hazel eyes" and noted that his conversation was "very agreeable, and cultured."[15]

Even so, he often felt out of place. On one occasion, when he and Hardee were on their way to inspect one of Cleburne's brigades, they encountered a group of ladies on the road and, characteristically, Hardee stopped to chat. Cleburne, who was wearing his working uniform—soiled shirt, no neckcloth —stood apart from the conversation, and when it seemed likely to be prolonged, he excused himself and rode back to his headquarters to change. St. John Liddell happened to be there, and he was surprised to see Cleburne come in muttering to himself. "He came in grumbling about Hardee's tardiness and running after women," Liddell recalled. Soon afterward, Hardee reined up outside and called out, "Have you seen anything of my wild Irish general?" Assured that Cleburne was there, Hardee dismounted and entered. Noticing Liddell, Hardee asked him somewhat archly, "Is it not proper for a subordinate officer invited to ride with his commander to come properly dressed?"

Adopting his tone, Liddell answered in mock seriousness, "Yes. That is the military rule, I believe, everywhere."

"Now here is Cleburne," Hardee continued, "coming out so badly dressed as to be frightened home at the sight of ladies whom we happen to meet on the road."

Cleburne, smiling his characteristic tight-lipped smile, claimed that he had drawn away only to allow Hardee to flirt more effectively. Dr. Johnson thereupon offered the view, "This may all be owing to where Cleburne was raised. I don't know whether Ireland or Arkansas."

"Stop!" Hardee interrupted. "Allow me to correct you, Doctor. Men are reared; horses, hogs, cattle, and sheep are raised."

"I thank you General," said Dr. Johnson bowing, "for the correction. I don't know which category you choose to place Cleburne in. I know he is pretty rough with his staff." At that point, Hardee discarded his mock solemnity and burst into laughter.[16]

Cleburne obtained some measure of revenge for Hardee's gibes about his attire and sophistication. Not long afterward, when most of the high-ranking officers were gathered at Beechwood for one of Mrs. Erwin's social evenings, Cleburne claimed the floor in order to make a presentation to Hardee. He told the assembled crowd that because General Hardee did not dress neatly enough, he had ordered him a new uniform, which he then presented with great fanfare. Since Hardee had a well-established reputation as a dandy, and since Cleburne was frequently to be seen looking more like a private than an officer, the joke was well received. Hardee accepted the new uniform with a graceful speech of his own, and Rowena Webster noted that Hardee "appreciated the joke."[17]

Occasionally Hardee would order a review of the troops. Cleburne's Division always made a good show at these events, but they sometimes caused him a moment or two of personal anxiety, for he was not a particularly good horseman. In Ireland he had never ridden despite his status as a member of the gentry. In Helena he did not own a horse, and on at least one occasion when he had borrowed a horse from Dr. Nash, he had come back on foot much chagrined. He had perforce learned to ride in the army, but he was still rather tentative about it. He deliberately chose slow, plodding, animals rather than the blooded chargers favored by others and as a result often had trouble keeping up. An Arkansas soldier recalled, "On one occasion he almost upset the gravity of us all in the ranks in spite of our discipline and our respect for him, by lumbering along far in the wake of the rest of the dashing cavalcade, on his clumsy old plough horse of an animal."[18]

It was not all social events and parades. Cleburne continued with his normal routine of morning and evening drill, visiting each of his brigades in turn to conduct personal inspections. An Arkansas soldier recorded a typical day: "Roll call at sun-rise, after a fine night's rest. Four hours drill each day will give us some recreation." Two days later he noted, "Regimental inspection by Gen. Cleburne." At one review of Liddell's Brigade at Bellbuckle near Liberty Gap, Cleburne invited Colonel Arthur Fremantle of the British Coldstream Guards to review the troops. Fremantle was mildly surprised to note the varied and rather casual attire of the soldiers who paraded past him, though he admitted that "they drilled tolerably well, and an advance in line was remarkably good."[19]

In addition to his regular routine of drill and inspection, Cleburne renewed his personal interest in sharpshooting when his division was allocated five Whitworth Rifles imported from England. These specialty weapons, credited with being able to bring down a foe at distances as great as three-quarters of a mile, were in short supply, and as at Corinth the year before, Cleburne sponsored shooting contests in camp to select those who would be entrusted with them. Because the Whitworths would be used at unprecedented distances, he contrived a training program wherein he placed men at varying distances from 500 to 1,000 yards apart, then required them to estimate the range to one another. After extracting their guess, he made them pace it off. Repeated drilling eventually enabled his sharpshooters to determine range with remarkable accuracy. As a result, one officer wrote that Cleburne "had the finest and most effective body of sharpshooters in the army." Throughout the ensuing campaign, he continued to take a personal interest in the performance of his sharpshooting teams and was often at the front observing the results of their activity.[20]

As the days lengthened and April turned into May, neither Bragg nor Rosecrans evidenced any particular eagerness to renew the war in Tennessee. In Mississippi, however, events were nearing a crisis. In the second week of May, Grant's army neared the Mississippi state capital at Jackson, threatening to cut the rail line to Vicksburg, and in response the government ordered Johnston to quit Tennessee and take 3,000 soldiers to Mississippi to bolster Pemberton's army. Once at Jackson, Johnston found himself cut off from Pemberton by Grant's army and sent out an urgent call for reinforcements. Bragg saw an opportunity to rid himself of one of his more intractable enemies, so he sent Breckinridge with two of his three brigades to join Johnston in Mississippi. Of course Breckinridge's departure left Hardee with only Cleburne's Division in his "corps." Bragg then took Bushrod Johnson's Tennessee brigade away from Cleburne and added it to Breckinridge's remaining brigade to create a second, small division, which he entrusted to Major General Alexander P. Stewart.[21]

Cleburne was no doubt sorry to lose Johnson's crack brigade, but within days he recouped the loss when Thomas W. Churchill's Arkansas Brigade arrived in Wartrace. As recently exchanged prisoners of war, these men were the objects of much curiosity and some derision, for they had been captured at Arkansas Post on the Red River, which had surrendered without firing a shot. The veterans of the Army of Tennessee claimed not to want such soldiers in their outfit. Even as the new arrivals set up camp, other soldiers wandered in to ask them bluntly why they had not fought for the fort. The Arkansas soldiers were therefore grateful to be welcomed to the army by Cleburne himself, who made it clear that they would be judged not on what had passed but how they behaved in the future. One junior officer in the brigade recorded in his diary, "There was but one General that would have us—Pat. Cleburne said he was not afraid to try us."[22]

Cleburne's reorganized division occupied the advanced salient of Bragg's defensive line that stretched seventy miles across south-central Tennessee from Shelbyville to Hoover's Gap. Polk's Corps held Shelbyville on the left flank. Cleburne, in the center, guarded both the wagon road through Liberty Gap and the railroad through New Fosterville. Stewart's small division had responsibility for Hoover's Gap four miles to the east, and beyond that Bragg had only the weak reed of his cavalry force. Concerned about these dispositions, Hardee wrote Bragg an unsolicited letter in early June warning him that his "command is much too scattered for easy concentration." He predicted that "an enterprising enemy could force a passage through Liberty Gap and cut my command in two."[23]

By accepting the static defensive in Tennessee, Bragg voluntarily surrendered the initiative to the enemy. His general plan was that Hardee's Corps would block any Federal advance from Murfreesboro long enough to allow Polk's Corps at Shelbyville to strike the enemy in the flank or rear. It was not a particularly realistic plan to begin with, and Bragg's chilly relations with his own corps commanders meant that he never made them full partners to his thoughts anyway.

Moreover, Bragg was so badly served by his cavalry that he never knew much about enemy strength or movements until after the fact. His best cavalry officer, Nathan Bedford Forrest, had been wounded in a fight with a fellow officer, and another, Earl Van Dorn, had been shot dead by a jealous husband. John Hunt Morgan was apparently more interested in capturing headlines than providing intelligence and had set off on an extended raid into Kentucky. That left only twenty-six-year-old Joe Wheeler, a sycophantic Bragg supporter, whose infrequent reports were often only marginally useful.[24]

In the hope of obtaining better information, Bragg ordered Polk and

Hardee to push an advance toward Murfreesboro. In the last week of May, Cleburne led his division north through Liberty Gap, encountering only a few Federal pickets who quickly fell back after light skirmishing. He advanced to within five miles of Murfreesboro before returning to Wartrace. It was good exercise for the troops and Buck exulted to his sister that they had given the Federals "a terrible scare," but this minioffensive did little to clarify the strategic picture.[25]

If and when the Federals did advance, Cleburne's job would be to hold them at the passes long enough to allow Polk to get in position to attack in flank and rear. The key point was Liberty Gap from which Cleburne could look past the "beautiful and slightly undulating plain of woodland and fields several hundred feet below, extending even beyond Murfreesborough [*sic*], some 11 miles northward." He entrusted the defense of the gap to Liddell's Brigade, instructing Liddell to put two regiments and an artillery battery in the gap itself and to hold two more regiments as a ready reserve at Bellbuckle only a few miles away. With such a force, Cleburne calculated that Liddell could hold the pass long enough to allow Cleburne to bring up reinforcements as necessary.[26]

When it did come, the Federal attack was a lightning stroke. With no warning from the Rebel cavalry, the Federals appeared suddenly and in force on the afternoon of 24 June, driving Liddell's two regiments out of Liberty Gap in a quick coup de main. They then held off Liddell's efforts to reclaim it. Cleburne, at Wartrace, found out about the Federal attack after dark and ordered Wood's Brigade to prepare to march at dawn. The next morning he rode to Liberty Gap and found Liddell holding onto two wooded hills that commanded the southern exit from the narrow pass. Liddell explained that the Federals had seized the gap from his pickets before he could get his reserves into position, but by holding the two hills south of the pass he could prevent them from exploiting their gains. Indeed, he strongly suspected that the Federals were already in the act of retiring; he had spotted a line of their wagons heading north. With Cleburne's approval, he launched a tentative advance in an attempt to reclaim the pass, but after a lengthy exchange of fire, he was forced back. Cleburne judged that the Federals were in divisional strength at least. He reinforced Liddell with three regiments of infantry and another artillery battery from Wood's Brigade, but decided not to force his way back into the pass itself.[27]

Desultory firing continued the next day as the skies opened and rain fell in torrents. Cleburne limited the shooting to his sharpshooters, including those equipped with the long-range Whitworth rifles. Supervising this firing with some interest, he noted that the Whitworths struck down enemy soldiers at ranges up to 1,700 yards. He did not order an advance. As long as he held the southern exit from Liberty Gap, the Federals would be unable to exploit their advantage and would be held in place for Polk's possible counterstroke. Then that night, well after dark, he received a message from Hardee that a large enemy force had brushed past Stewart's small division at Hoover's Gap four miles to the east and was moving rapidly on Cleburne's flank and rear. Reluctantly but emphatically, Hardee ordered Cleburne to fall back.[28]

It was another unhappy retreat and the continuing heavy rain did not help. But mainly it was the whole idea of abandoning more territory to the enemy without having put up a real fight. "Oh God," one soldier wrote in his diary, "must we leave our homes and our loved ones to the mercy of the ruthless foe again and that, too, without an effort to prevent it?" The swift retreat also meant that the men had to march south without even the minimal comforts that generally attended a change of base. Cleburne noted, "The men had no changes of clothing, no tents, and could not even light fires to dry themselves." Many of his men had no shoes; those who did often lost them in mud so deep it literally sucked the shoes off their feet. Inevitably, there was more muttering in the ranks about Bragg's leadership. "One thing is certain," a soldier wrote in his diary, "if Bragg cannot whip Rosencranz [*sic*] he can OUT-RUN him badly. We are all nearly used up and some have given out entirely and laid down by the road side."[29]

Cleburne was not one of those who either gave up or gave out. His inexhaustible supply of energy sprang from his conviction that the cause for which he fought was not only noble, it was a crusade of good against evil, of right against wrong. His romanticized vision of the issue at hand and his own sense of obligation energized him to hold the division together by sheer will. He had previously investigated possible lines of retreat to Tullahoma, and now he directed his rain-soaked veterans to march for the Schoefner Bridge over the Duck River. When the head of his column arrived at the bridgehead early on the afternoon of 27 June, he found Cheatham's Division there too. Polk ordered Cleburne to halt and let Cheatham pass ahead of him. Cleburne's division thus became the army's rear guard and engaged in some sharp skirmishing with the enemy to protect the bridgehead. Typically, Cleburne commanded in person during this skirmishing, again assessing for himself the deadly effectiveness of the Whitworth rifles.[30]

His men crossed the Duck River that afternoon. Then only a few miles beyond the bridge, they staggered to a halt when they found the road blocked by the wagons of Polk's Corps. Cleburne rode ahead to investigate the problem and found a broken-down wagon in the road. Rather than simply push it out of the way, Colonel D. M. Donnell was having it repaired. Cleburne ordered him to "shove all wagons which were broken down out of the road and push on." But Donnell was unwilling to do so without orders from his own commander, who, he said, had told him "to leave none of the wagons behind."

Angered by Donnell's unwillingness to do what was to him the obvious thing, Cleburne not only sent an aide riding hard to Polk to obtain the necessary orders, he also penned an angry note to Hardee. Hardee passed the complaint on to Bragg, whose chief of staff peremptorily ordered Polk "to see that your baggage wagons move on, and that those that break down [are] removed instantly, as is the custom." Then he added a barb that was particularly aggravating considering the state of relations between Bragg and Polk: "His [Cleburne's] safety is now endangered by this unjustifiable course of your officers." Later it occurred to Cleburne that he had provided Bragg with an opportunity to upbraid Polk; indeed, it may be that the bishop-general pointed this out to Cleburne. In any case, Cleburne subsequently sent a letter of explanation asserting that he had not meant to imply that Polk was in any way to blame for Donnell's mistake. For Cleburne, the incident illustrated pointedly how almost any written message could be used by others as a weapon in the feud within the army high command. He would have to be more careful.[31]

Cleburne's Division arrived at the outskirts of Tullahoma on 29 June "completely worn out and covered with mud." It was still raining "like a mill trail" (as one soldier wrote), and the proximity of the Federals meant that Cleburne had to order his men to "sleep in line of battle." Bragg announced his determination to fight for the city now that his two corps were reunited. Both Hardee and especially Polk argued that this was foolish, asserting that the Federals could outflank them easier here at Tullahoma than they had on the Duck River line. Better, they argued, to fall back behind the Elk River. Bragg wavered, then capitulated, and the retreat continued.[32]

Once again, Cleburne was assigned to hold the bridgehead as the Army of Tennessee crossed the Elk. The army dug in for a defense of the river, but Bragg's spirit was broken. In a state of confusion and indecision bordering on panic, he fired off a series of messages expressing concern about the fordability of the Elk River, then ordered a further retreat. He even failed to order destruction of the railroad tunnel at Cowan, which might have impeded a Federal pursuit. The troops trudged southward, up onto the heights of the Cumberland Plateau, manhandling the wagons over the rough spots, to bivouac in the open air of the Cumberland Plateau on the fourth of July. For the first time in weeks, the men could light fires and cook a warm meal without concern for either the rain or the proximity of the enemy. That same afternoon, though no one in Cleburne's Division or the Army of Tennessee knew it, Pemberton's ragged garrison marched out of Vicksburg to stack arms in surrender, and in Pennsylvania, Lee's army began its retreat from the battlefield at Gettysburg.[33]

The next day, Cleburne's Division led the Army of Tennessee southward off the Cumberland Plateau down to the north bank of the Tennessee River where it went into bivouac. Hardee turned temporary command of the corps over to Cleburne and left for Chattanooga to talk with Bragg. It was Cleburne, therefore, who coordinated the crossing of the river on the pontoon bridge at Kelley's Ford. Over the next week, the corps moved in stages by rail from Loudon to Chattanooga, then to Tyner's Station east of the city; one brigade (Wood's) moved even further east to Harrison's Landing a dozen miles upriver. These dispositions reflected Bragg's conviction that the pursuing Federals intended to cross the Tennessee upriver from the city, and he deliberately placed Cleburne's command in the position of greatest danger and responsibility. Charged to cover the various crossings northeast of the city, Cleburne set his men to work building fortifications and blockhouses at the crossing points.[34]

In command now of over 15,000 men, he found his tasks increasingly administrative as he coordinated the movements of three divisions and nine brigades. This new burden did not improve his mood in the aftermath of the long and depressing retreat from middle Tennessee. Buck recognized his commander's "fearful humor" and avoided approaching him with new paperwork. Even the surgeon, Dr. Erskine, avoided him, telling a friend "he would as soon attack a lion in its lair."[35]

One evening when Cleburne was lying in his cot reading, a young captain pulled aside the tent flap and walked in, taking off his hat and saluting. It was Captain Hampton J. Cheney, the assistant adjutant general in John C. Brown's Division. Cleburne looked up at him without comment, and the captain stepped forward, dropped to one knee, and placed an application for leave between Cleburne's face and the book he was reading. Cleburne smacked the paper away with his hand, knocking it onto the floor halfway across the tent. The captain stood up angrily but then he calmed, and drawing a stool across the tent floor, sat down. Impatiently, Cleburne told him, "Do you know, sir, that your command sends more of these communications to these headquarters than any other command in the army?" Far from being shamefaced, the captain challenged this assertion: "I do not, sir, neither do you . . . because it is not so. . . . I know this is the first communication which has reached these headquarters since you have been corps commander."

"Well, sir," Cleburne rejoined, "you know that you are now violating orders by not sending your application by courier?"

"Yes, General," the captain averred. "I admit all that you say; but if you will read my application, you will see that there are extenuating circumstances which render my action somewhat pardonable, and I will also say that if I am not a good soldier it is your fault and you are to blame."

At that confrontational statement, Cleburne sat up and faced his visitor. "How, sir?" he demanded.

"Well, General, I belonged to your old brigade; you trained me, and I received my first baptism of fire by your side at Shiloh. . . . I was so close to you through it all that I could have placed my hand on your shoulder."

Cleburne got to his feet and began pacing. "Was it not a hard-fought but magnificent and glorious battle?" he exclaimed, almost to himself. "Were there ever such soldiers as fought that day? No country but ours ever produced such. It was a battle gallantly won and as stupidly lost." He stopped pacing and, looking down, noticed the discarded application for leave on the floor. He picked it up and read it. It requested three days leave for the captain so that he might visit his three-year-old daughter who was dying. Sitting at a small desk, Cleburne wrote his approval at the bottom and handed it to the captain. The young officer left with the precious document in his hand, but he recalled later, "I felt that I had just fought a harder battle than Shiloh." [36]

Hardee did not return to the corps. After a week in Chattanooga, he left for Mississippi with orders to give whatever aid he could to Joe Johnston's scratch force there. Now that Vicksburg had fallen, Johnston's small army of 23,000 faced the full power of Grant and Sherman whose force had swollen to over 70,000. Cleburne was sorry to lose the companionship of his friend and patron, and he was under no illusions that his own temporary command of the corps would be made permanent. For one thing, Cheatham was senior to him by date of rank and could easily be transferred from Polk's Corps (though given Bragg's opinion of Cheatham, that was no sure bet). For another, Cleburne was aware that he owed his last promotion to Hardee's sponsorship, and Hardee's transfer to Mississippi suggested that his patronage no longer carried the weight it once did. Finally, the same factors that had made President Davis hesitate about Cleburne's last promotion were still in place: his foreign birth and the fact that he had not attended West Point. Those factors were compounded now that Davis had become convinced that new blood was necessary in the Army of Tennessee.[37]

That new blood was already on its way in the form of Daniel Harvey Hill, an 1842 West Point graduate who had been serving in Virginia. As a major general, Hill was nine months senior to Cleburne, and Davis promoted him to lieutenant general effective 11 July to assume the command of what had been Hardee's Corps. Hill arrived in Chattanooga by rail on 19 July, though he did not report to his new command for a week, remaining in Chattanooga to talk with Bragg. Almost certainly Bragg hoped that with the departure of Breckinridge and Hardee—two of the three who had sent him no-confidence letters in January—he had purged the army of his most prominent detractors. Unquestionably he hoped that Hill would become if not an ally, then at least a loyal subordinate. He was to be disappointed. Hill had known Bragg years ago in the "old army" and was stunned to see him now so "gloomy and despondent," aged and beaten down by his trials. His first interview with Bragg doused Hill's enthusiasm like a bucket of cold water. As their conversation progressed, Hill found himself increasingly repulsed. Bragg probably only made it worse when he invited Hill to suggest strategies for the army, allowing Hill to conclude that Bragg did not plan to exercise effective command himself.[38]

Hill assumed command of Hardee's former corps from Cleburne on 24 July. If Cleburne was disappointed to find this stranger placed over him in a job he might have had himself, he gave no sign of it. The two men got along well, Hill appreciating Cleburne's quiet efficiency and no-nonsense approach, and Cleburne according Hill the same obedience and commitment he had given Hardee. Hill came to rely on Cleburne both for advice and to exercise command on those occasions when Hill had to return to Chattanooga. Bragg encouraged this dependency. During the Federal advance on Chattanooga, Bragg frequently queried Hill for his views, writing him on one occasion: "Consult Cleburne. He is cool, full of resources, and ever alive to a success."[39]

Bragg remained convinced that Rosecrans would cross the Tennessee in Cleburne's sector. For one thing, the terrain east of the city was much more amenable to a crossing than the rough countryside downriver, and for another, such a move would allow the two Federal armies in Tennessee— Rosecrans's and Burnside's—to cooperate. Bragg based his deployments on these suppositions since the intelligence reports from his cavalry were no better now than they had been during the campaign for Tullahoma. The truth was that he did not know where the Yankees might appear. He ordered Hill to watch the crossings, and that officer took the order literally, charging Cleburne to guard "every ford and ferry from the mouth of the Chickamauga to the mouth of the Hiwasee," a distance of over thirty miles. "Rumors fly thick and fast here about the movements of the Yanks," a junior officer in Cleburne's Division recorded in his diary, "but we keep on drilling morning and evening."[40]

While he drilled his troops, watched the river, and waited, Cleburne renewed his association with the Masonic Lodge. He attended a number of meetings at Lodge No. 199 in Tyner's Station, and the experience inspired him to think about creating a fraternal organization for Confederate officers and soldiers—a brotherhood of comrades in arms. He talked with several of his subordinates about it, all of whom expressed interest or encouragement, though some may simply have been unwilling to dampen their commander's enthusiasm. At any rate, Cleburne took their responses at face value, and the result was the Comrades of the Southern Cross. According to the organization's constitution, which Cleburne helped to write, membership would be open to any "commissioned officer or enlisted soldier in the Confederate States service, a free white male over eighteen years of age, intelligent in his military duties and of known patriotism and integrity." Members would pay monthly dues from their pay and contribute as well to a charity fund for the support of wounded veterans, widows, and orphans.

In Cleburne's conception, the Comrades of the Southern Cross was more than a patriotic organization, it was an affirmation of faith. Members obligated themselves to stand together; they took an oath never to desert their comrades in arms or the cause of their country. He believed that such an affirmation was a moral force worth several divisions on the battlefield. He later told a fellow officer, "Had this order been disseminated throughout the Southern army, they could [have] march[ed] to the Ohio river without a check." Like a medieval crusader, Cleburne believed that the moral superiority of his cause could be translated into military strength. More prosaically, he anticipated the childlike faith of Horatio Alger (who published his first book at about the same time) that if you simply tried hard enough, you could not lose. God was not always on the side of the strongest battalions, He was on the side of those with the greatest commitment. The organization Cleburne founded did not remain active once the campaign heated up again in September, but his sponsorship of it is testimony to both his patriotic sentimentality and his naive faith in the power of the human spirit.[41]

Rosecrans moved against Chattanooga in mid-August. One element of the Federal army appeared on the north bank of the Tennessee River directly opposite the city on 21 August and began lobbing shells into the town. Other elements appeared upriver across from Cleburne's position. Cleburne was watching the Federal dispositions through his field glasses on 28 August when by chance or by skill a Federal artillery shell landed three feet in front of him. It did not explode. Cleburne's reputation for coolness under fire was greatly enhanced when he returned to his observations without comment. Perhaps it seemed to his men that he was immortal. In a letter home, Buck exulted that the Yankees had bragged about having killed General Cleburne in the skirmish near Liberty Gap. "The Yankees are determined if they cannot kill him in reality they will in imagination, on paper. But he is alive and will worry them yet before he 'gives up.'"[42]

Cleburne expected a battle any day. Scouts reported that the Federals were concentrating for a crossing near the mouth of the Hiwassee. Buck wrote his sister that "they will certainly attempt to cross the Tennessee and if so we will just as certainly pitch into them." Unquestionably the troops across the river were busy at some mischief. All day Cleburne's pickets could hear the sound of felling trees, sawing boards, and hammering; those on the riverbank saw scraps of lumber and the rough ends of boards floating downriver, suggesting that the Yankees were constructing barges and rafts for a crossing. But though Cleburne did not know it, the enemy had already crossed the Tennessee. Rosecrans had never intended to cross east of the city; all that sawing and hammering was an elaborate ruse. Instead he crossed downstream, west of the city, with the first troops coming over on 26 August. By the time Bragg heard about it five days later—from a civilian visitor to camp who had watched them cross—three full Federal divisions were moving against Bragg's communications. Even then, Bragg was frozen in indecision by his suspicions that the move downstream was a feint, and he kept Cleburne watching the upper fords for what he was sure would be the real Federal effort.[43]

By 1 September a full Federal corps of 40,000 men—more than Bragg had in his whole army—was across the river and south of Chattanooga threatening the Confederate line of retreat. Bragg seemed paralyzed, unwilling to admit he had been wrong to assume that the Federals would cross upriver. Finally, on 5 September he obtained a recent copy of the Chicago *Times,* which revealed Rosecrans's plan in some detail and which convinced him that he would have to evacuate the city. That night, ironically, Cleburne urged Hill to attack across the river and "crush" the Federal division on his front. Whatever Hill thought of the suggestion, Bragg was in no mood to consider it; instead he issued orders to retreat the next day. Then thinking better of it, he canceled the order. Two days later, he held another council of war where he announced his determination to stay; almost immediately afterward, he sent out new orders to evacuate the city. This time the orders stood.[44]

Cleburne started his division marching southward late on the afternoon of 7 September. His men tramped down the LaFayette Road into Georgia, leading the Army of Tennessee as it abandoned the state for which it was named. There seemed little prospect for optimism as the army high command continued to be riven by internal quarrels. Lacking the support of his senior commanders, Bragg had grown irresolute and tentative; sensing his self-doubts, his senior commanders lost even more confidence in his leadership.

Cleburne, too, had become frustrated by the spring and summer campaign. Twice he had been charged to hold the line against an enemy assault only to be ordered to fall back when the enemy advanced elsewhere. Now all of Tennessee had been lost. The culprit was not hard to identify. Even if Bragg had been resolute and assertive, the fact that his senior officers lacked confidence in him made an effective campaign unlikely. Cleburne was not a political schemer by nature. His own worldview was an uncomplicated one: strict discipline, constant drill, and a fierce personal commitment to the cause would result in victory. Men such as those whom he led could not fail to win if only they were given an opportunity to face the enemy on anything like equal terms. But time after time, they—and he—were denied that opportunity. It had become evident that Bragg could not inspire the kind of loyalty or enthusiasm that bred victories. Cleburne did what he could to sustain the fighting edge that he believed necessary to military success. His continued devotion to strict discipline and constant drill plus his sponsorship of the Comrades of the Southern Cross were all efforts to strengthen that inner core of commitment which could hold the army together amidst the squabbling and posturing of the political battles. In spite of these efforts, however, he must have begun to fear that the poisonous influence of the political bickering was likely to bear bitter fruit.

8

BARREN VICTORY: THE BATTLE OF CHICKAMAUGA

The Army of Tennessee was ailing. If the disease was not yet terminal, it was severely debilitating. Nine months of retreat and internal bickering had bred self-doubt about its character and ability. Bragg's leadership was so problematic that his senior generals wondered if his poor health and uncertain state of mind had not rendered him wholly unfit for further service. He had become alternately vacillating and dogmatic—at one point reaching out for advice and support, then spurning any suggestion that did not match his preconceived vision. Physically he was broken down; mentally he was under siege.

As for Cleburne, whatever doubts he may have had about the competence of the army commander, he had none about his own division. As he led it southward down the LaFayette Road at the head of the army, his faith in the indomitability of the men he commanded was undiminished. His division had been restructured yet again. St. John Liddell's Brigade was no longer in the division, for Bragg had promoted Liddell to divisional responsibilities of his own. Churchill, too, was gone, transferred back to the trans-Mississippi Department, though his small brigade of Arkansas infantry and dismounted Texas cavalry remained in the division under the command of Alabama native James Deshler, the only West Point graduate among the general officers in the division. The change was popular because Churchill had never won the hearts of his men, whereas (as one Texan wrote) "everybody in the brigade liked" Deshler. The other two brigades remained intact. Lucius Polk continued to be Cleburne's strong right arm. A comrade since the days of the Yell Rifles, Polk had served nearly a year in the ranks before being elected colonel of the 15th Arkansas in the reorganization after Shiloh. Since then he had advanced in tandem with Cleburne, moving up to command Cleburne's Brigade when "Old Pat," as the men now called him, became division commander. One soldier who admired both men, claimed that "Polk was to Cleburne what

138

Murat or the old guard was to Napoleon." Sterling Wood led the other brigade, composed of Alabama and Mississippi troops. At forty years of age, he was exactly five years older than Cleburne (born on St. Patrick's Day, 1823). Wood was a former lawyer, newspaper editor, and state legislator who had fought bravely at Shiloh and Murfreesboro. He was not a particularly inspirational or imaginative leader, but so far he had proved entirely reliable. With a total of just over 5,000 men, Cleburne's Division retained its esprit de corps despite the discord in the upper echelons of command.[1]

As the men marched southward toward LaFayette, Georgia, the view to their right was dominated by the looming bulk of Lookout Mountain, which ran north-south like an enormous molehill and which separated the retreating Confederates from the advancing Federals. Everyone in the Rebel army knew that at some point the Yankees would have to emerge through one or more of the passes in that imposing ridge line, but because of the poor performance of the Confederate cavalry, none of the gray-clad officers knew precisely where. Thirty miles south of Chattanooga, just opposite LaFayette where Cleburne's Division bivouacked on 8 September, the molehill threw off a spur, Pigeon Mountain, which angled away from Lookout Mountain to the northeast. The cleft formed by their juncture was McLemore's Cove, birthplace of the west branch of Chickamauga Creek. Like the larger ridge line, Pigeon Mountain was dissected by several passes—Catlett's, Dug Gap—and Blue Bird Gap, and Cleburne sent elements of Wood's Brigade into each of them to keep an eye on activity in the cove.

It seemed illogical that Rosecrans would send a portion of his force into the cul-de-sac of McLemore's Cove, but the Federal commander was convinced that the Confederate army was in headlong retreat, and he flung his three corps in pursuit on widely separated roads. As a result, the Federal division of Major General James S. Negley, from George Thomas's XIV Corps, ventured through Stevens Gap into McLemore's Cove that same day unaware that several Confederate divisions were within easy marching distance of his position. For all his illness and confusion, Bragg recognized this opportunity for the golden chance it was, and at midnight on 9–10 September, he ordered Hindman to march south into the cove to attack Negley from the north. Bragg sent a copy of these orders to Hill, directing him to order Cleburne to join in the attack as soon as Hindman struck. Between them, the former Helena law partners would annihilate Negley's force.[2]

Hill received Bragg's order an hour before dawn on the 10th. Rather than galvanize him to action, however, it elicited instead a list of reasons why the

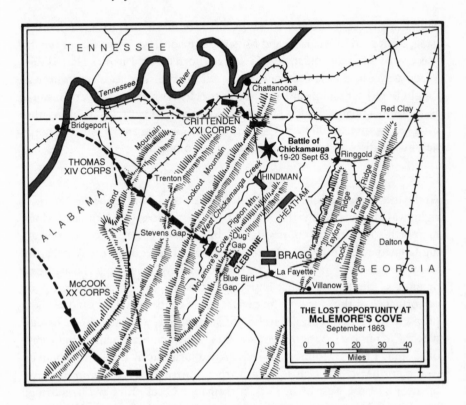

move was impossible. Hill wrote Bragg that the road through Dug Gap was blocked, that Cleburne's command was widely scattered, and that Cleburne could not be sent into the cove in any case because he was ill ("in bed all day yesterday"). Hill informed Bragg that his orders could not be executed and suggested that "either Hindman should be stopped or the movement postponed." In part, Hill's response was a product of his assumption that Bragg wanted Cleburne to attack that same morning, which indeed would have been impossible. But in addition, Hill's reply was conditioned by the fact that Bragg's subordinates had come to regard his orders almost as arguments, inviting contradiction or refutation. After the war, Hill wrote that "Bragg's want of definite and precise information had led him more than once to issue 'impossible' orders, and therefore those intrusted [*sic*] with their execution got in the way [habit] of disregarding them." If Hill did not quite disregard them on this occasion, neither did he take any extraordinary measures to co-operate.[3]

If Cleburne was ill, it did not stop him from riding up into Dug Gap himself that afternoon. From the top of the pass, he could see the road winding downward off Pigeon Mountain, across the flat plain of McLemore's Cove through the small community of Davis's Cross Roads, then up the other side into Stevens Gap through Lookout Mountain. He could see as well long trails of dust, proving that some Federals at least had emerged through Stevens Gap and entered the cove. It was impossible, however, to tell how many Federals there were, and it was not clear whether this was the advance of the Federal main army or only a portion of it. To Hill he reported, "I cannot pretend to state in what force [they are] or any thing else about them." The pass was indeed blocked by fallen timber. If he was expected to hold it against an attack, he would leave the barrier in place and bring up Polk and Deshler. If he was to prepare an attack of his own, he would set the men to work removing the obstructions. He asked Hill for "definite instructions."[4]

Hill ordered Cleburne to clear away the barricade in Dug Gap and "hold himself ready to strike Thomas [Negley] in his rear when he should be engaged with Hindman," who had not yet made an appearance. The gap was cleared in an hour or two, and Polk's and Deshler's Brigades marched up just at nightfall. The horses had difficulty pulling the artillery up the steep incline, so the men laid hold of long ropes and hauled the guns up by hand. Cleburne sent Wood and Deshler through the pass to deploy within the cove on the lower slope of Pigeon Mountain so that they would waste no time in joining the assault when it did come. Well before dawn, all three brigades were in position.[5]

But where was Hindman? He had started off well enough, marching his division southward an hour past midnight. Then soon after sunrise, still four miles short of Davis's Cross Roads, he had stopped to write to Hill that he did not plan to move any further until he heard that Cleburne's Division was in motion. Bragg sent him a series of dispatches "to finish the movement now going on" and "to move vigorously," but like Hill, Hindman behaved as if Bragg's orders were discretionary. Even after Bragg reinforced him with Buckner's Division, Hindman feared that if he entered the cove, he might be trapped there by other Federals who could cut off his line of retreat. That night, as Cleburne's men hauled their artillery up and over Dug Gap and prepared for a morning assault, Hindman sent a staff officer to Bragg to explain his reluctance to advance further. Bragg ordered Hindman's emissary to tell the reluctant commander to carry out his orders.[6]

At Dug Gap, Cleburne was up well before dawn. Hill also arrived before sunrise and soon afterward Bragg appeared as well, eager to witness the springing of his trap. Cleburne sent couriers down the valley in the direction of Hindman's expected arrival to listen for the earliest possible sound of an attack. The light grew slowly, and soon the sun was fairly up, revealing that the Federals were still there "in plain view in the valley." Indeed, there were now even more of them—perhaps two divisions and a total of 10,000 men—though still only half as many as Bragg was bringing against them. As the day lengthened, the waiting became excruciating. If Cleburne was anxious, he did not show it; his demeanor was stoic as ever. Bragg's restlessness, however, was clearly evident. He paced back and forth in an agitated state, stopping periodically to drive his boot spur violently into the ground in obvious frustration. He later wrote in his report of his "great anxiety" while waiting for "the attack by Hindman's column."[7]

Of course Cleburne might have attacked first in anticipation of Hindman's arrival. Though his own forces totaled only about half the number of Federals now in the cove, his assault would hold the Federals in position and would presumably attract Hindman's support. With both Hill and Bragg at his shoulder, however, it was not his decision to make. Finally, just before noon Bragg could stand it no longer and ordered Cleburne forward. "Old Pat" hurried down the gap to begin the attack. His skirmishers were already engaged when a courier from Bragg galloped up to tell him to halt. In one of those abrupt reversals that had so undermined his credibility with Hill, Hindman, and others, Bragg had changed his mind again. A half mile from the Federal bivouac, Cleburne's three brigades stopped, grounded arms, and resumed their wait.[8]

Finally at half past four, with the sun low in the sky, the sounds of skirmishing could be heard from the north. Hill ordered Cleburne's Division forward in support, and he even advanced with it, but it was soon evident that the quarry had flown. Appreciating at last the precariousness of his situation, Thomas had withdrawn his two divisions back to the relative safety of Stevens Gap. Cleburne pursued, and his men engaged in a long-range firefight near the foot of Lookout Mountain, taking a handful of prisoners, but the opportunity to achieve a decisive victory was irretrievably lost. The escape of the enemy sent the troops of Cleburne's command into "ecstasies of grief." "Men and officers swore, some were almost in tears, many were in despair." Cleburne shared in the general disappointment, but given his natural reserve he showed little outward sign. Bragg did not bother to disguise his feelings. When he met Hindman at Davis's Cross Roads, he chastised him loudly and publicly.[9]

Without question Hindman deserved his tongue-lashing. On the other hand, Bragg had not exercised the kind of strong leadership that might easily have led to a successful outcome. For one thing, his orders to both Hill and Hindman had been phrased so that the recipients might reasonably conclude they were invited to exercise their discretion. Given Bragg's habit of holding his subordinates strictly to account for the consequences of every action, his officers had become chary of assuming any initiative in executing orders. Neither did Bragg exercise personal command where it was most needed. When he learned of Hindman's hesitancy from that officer's emissary the night before, he ought to have ridden personally to Hindman's bivouac where he could have exercised direct command over the divisions of Hindman and Buckner. Instead he rode to Dug Gap where, especially with Hill already at hand, he was mainly a supernumerary.[10]

Finally, Bragg's tendency to vacillate also weakened the chances for success. At 11:00 A.M., even as he waited impatiently with Cleburne at Dug Gap for the sound of an attack, Bragg dispatched a note cautioning Hindman that if he believed himself outnumbered, he could retreat through Catlett's Gap. What was Hindman to make of such a note? *Was* he outnumbered? *Should* he retreat? If he advanced after receiving such a note and met a reverse, he could be sure of being arrested and court-martialed. Another example of Bragg's uncertainty occurred barely an hour later when he ordered Cleburne forward, only to recall him minutes later. Once again, boldness might have saved him. The sound of a full-scale attack by Cleburne on the Federal force at Davis's Cross Roads would almost surely have provoked Hindman's immediate support and Bragg might yet have had his victory. Instead the episode ended in an all-too-familiar pattern: the officers engaged in heated self-justifying conversation, the soldiers frustrated, and the enemy escaped.[11]

For a week Cleburne and his three brigades remained in the gaps through Pigeon Mountain watching McLemore's Cove. Cleburne slept on the ground wrapped only in a thin blanket. One morning when he woke at dawn, he stood, stretched, shook his blanket, and was startled to see a large rattlesnake drop out of it. It had evidently spent the night seeking warmth by coiling itself about his feet. He had little time to speculate about his near escape, however, for he had more dangerous foes to consider. The cove was again filled with Federal soldiers; evidently Rosecrans had brought most of his army east of the ridge line. On the other hand, Cleburne almost certainly had learned from Hill that substantial Confederate reinforcements were expected daily from Lee's army in Virginia. With such reinforcements at hand, the Army of Tennessee might yet find an opportunity to inflict a decisive defeat on its enemy.[12]

On the afternoon of 19 September, Cleburne received orders to leave Pigeon Mountain and march his division northward at once. Bragg had conceived of a plan to attack the Federal army on its left flank, cut it off from

Chattanooga, and drive it southward into McLemore's Cove where it could be destroyed in detail. He was concentrating his army and wanted Hill's Corps, with Cleburne's Division, to spearhead the attack. Cleburne set out at once on a six-mile march along a road "much obstructed by trains and artillery." He rode ahead of his marching columns and arrived at Bragg's headquarters near Thedford's Ford over the Chickamauga at around 4:00. Already he could hear the sound of artillery in the east. He met briefly with Bragg, who ordered him to continue northward where his division would join the right wing of the army under Leonidas Polk.[13]

The sun was beginning to set as Cleburne's men pulled off their boots (those who had them), many removing their trousers as well, in the expectation of crossing the river. Having been impressed by Bragg with a sense of urgency, Cleburne called out to them, "Boys, go through that river, we can't wait." The men splashed into the chilly water and, holding their rifles and shot pouches over their heads, breasted the stream in water up to their armpits. Then they hastened up the far side and prepared to light fires to warm themselves. Instead Cleburne ordered them to take up their arms and resume the march. Having marched six miles to the ford, they marched two more after crossing the Chickamauga and arrived near the extreme right of the Confederate position just at sunset.[14]

Cleburne reported his arrival to Polk, and the bishop-general ordered him "to form as a second line" behind the men of Liddell's Division, who were lying prone in a long skirmish line. The acrid smell of gunpowder was heavy in the air, mixed with wood smoke from fires in the undergrowth that had been started by the flash of powder. Liddell rode up to Cleburne to urge him to "attack at once" and assured him that the enemy "must be greatly exhausted from our constant fighting." Liddell's suggestions sounded very much like orders, which may have grated a bit on Cleburne's ear since Liddell had been one of his own brigadiers until two weeks ago. Liddell pressed his case with some passion. If the attack were delayed until morning, he insisted, "the enemy would be found entrenched and fully prepared." Excitedly, he declared that "no time should be lost." Not about to take orders from Liddell, Cleburne was noncommittal. He was not eager in any case to begin an attack at sunset in heavy woods against an unknown foe over ground he had not had a chance to reconnoiter. He told Liddell he would wait for orders from Hill or Polk. When Hill rode up, Liddell turned his attentions to that officer and convinced him that an opportunity was fast slipping away. Hill acceded and ordered Cleburne to get ready. Satisfied, Liddell told Cleburne, "General, I hope you will be quick, for a minute now will be worth an hour tomorrow."[15]

Cleburne personally deployed his brigades in line, taking more time than

Liddell thought necessary. He placed Wood's Brigade in the center with Polk on the right and Deshler on the left. Finally at about 6:00 P.M., he issued the order to advance. His troops passed through the prone ranks of Liddell's men, who gave them a cheer, and moved forward in a single rank through the smoke-filled woods in twilight darkness. Cleburne took up a position just behind the file closers in Wood's Brigade. Within minutes, muzzle flashes and the increasingly frequent "pop, pop" of musket fire indicated that they had made contact with the enemy. Polk on the right and Deshler on the left advanced through thick woods, but in the center a cleared field lay directly in front of Wood's men, and as they stepped into the open ground, the firing rose to a crescendo. "For half an hour the fire was the heaviest I had ever heard," Cleburne later reported. In the dark and smoke, it was also mostly inaccurate. Men on both sides aimed at the muzzle flashes in the evening gloom; one officer later wrote that the fight "took on the bewildering aspect of some enchanted forest." A captain in Deshler's Brigade claimed it was "so dark you can't see anything," and the attackers could hear the Yankees calling out, "What command is that?" as they attempted to determine friend from foe.[16]

If Cleburne had been less than eager to initiate this twilight attack, he was enthusiasm personified once it began. According to Calhoun Benham, he rode "like a fury" from brigade to brigade to encourage the men forward. "I never saw Cleburne before or afterward so demonstrative," Benham recalled. "I suppose, knowing it was indispensable [that] the charge should be successful, and reflecting that his men had not seen a regular battle for nine months, he deemed it necessary to encourage them as much as possible." Hill later claimed, "I have never seen troops behave more gallantly than did this noble division."[17]

In the general confusion, two Federal regiments on the Confederate right fired into each other, and when Polk's Brigade struck them, they turned and fled. In the center, however, Wood's Brigade failed to press the attack and even began to give way. In the dark, regimental commanders were reluctant to push ahead of the units on either flank, and they called periodic halts to ensure that they maintained proper alignment. A few even fell back when it was evident they had lost contact with their supports. Disappointed by this hesitancy, Cleburne ordered Major Hotchkiss to bring up his artillery. The artillerists ran their guns up to within sixty yards of the enemy line and opened fire with double canister. An artillery lieutenant later bragged that he "moved up at a trot and let fly the dogs of war into the Yankee ranks." That, combined with the pressure from Polk's Brigade on the right, forced the enemy to flee.[18]

Cleburne's men pursued. Taking up the Rebel yell, which echoed eerily through the dark, they clambered over the improvised Federal fieldworks and occupied the enemy camp, where they captured three artillery pieces and two regimental standards. Further pursuit was impossible in the growing darkness. Attempting to deliver one of Cleburne's orders, Lieutenant Hanley rode up to a group of officers and was about to speak when he heard the commander call out an order to an Indiana regiment. Wordlessly, Hanley wheeled about and rode off before he could be recognized. Sometime after 9:00 o'clock, Cleburne halted his brigades, set out pickets, and ordered the men into bivouac.[19]

Despite the victory, it was not a comfortable night for the troops. The men were still damp from crossing the Chickamauga and had to bivouac on the ground they had conquered without the benefit of camp fires. A few ignored the order and lit small fires which immediately attracted the attention of enemy marksmen and necessitated a quick dive for cover. With the moon in its first quarter and in the thick woods, it was extremely dark. One veteran later recalled that "the faint moonlight, almost wholly shut out by dense foliage, added to the weird spell of the sombre scene." Several of the men, seeking a place to lay their heads, discovered that many of the prone forms on the ground around them were not sleeping men but dead Federal soldiers. "We had slept with dead Federals thick amongst us," a veteran recalled, "some of our men actually sleeping with their heads resting on the dead." To add to their misery, they could hear "the noise of axe blows and falling trees along the Union lines," sure evidence that any renewal of their attack in the morning would necessitate assailing prepared enemy defenses.[20]

Several hundred yards behind the front line, screened from enemy sharpshooters by the thick foliage, Cleburne authorized a small fire at division headquarters, and he was sitting beside it with a few of his officers when a group of soldiers ushered a captured Federal lieutenant into his presence. Cleburne began asking him about the disposition of the Federal army, but the lieutenant proved silent or evasive, and Cleburne dismissed him, telling a staff officer to take charge of him. The staffer asked the prisoner if he had had anything to eat. When the Federal assured him that he had, the staff officer sighed and admitted he had not. The prisoner remarked that he had some hardtack and coffee in his saddlebag. The staff officer hastened to claim the prize, but the soldiers who had made the capture argued that any spoils should go to them. The argument attracted Cleburne's attention, and he got up from the fire to investigate. After listening to both sides, he declared that the disposition of private property was at the discretion of the prisoner. All eyes turned to the captured lieutenant who thereupon announced that he guessed he would keep the food himself. With a small smile, Cleburne congratulated him on his very sensible decision and returned to the fire. The lieutenant later recalled that Cleburne "was very polite."[21]

The sun rose at 5:47 on 20 September. It was cold with a heavy frost on the ground and wisps of winter fog amongst the trees. Cleburne rose, pulled on his boots, and ordered that rations be issued and the men told to cook their breakfast. He was at breakfast himself only minutes later when Hill reined up and joined him. Soon afterward, Breckinridge also arrived. The three generals were gathered together in conversation at about 6:30 when a young staff officer rode up and dismounted. He announced that he had orders from General Polk. Hill put out his hand to receive them, but the courier snatched them back and announced, "These orders are for Generals Cleburne and Breckinridge." Hill demanded to know why he was being bypassed in the chain of command, and the courier, Captain J. F. Wheliss, declared somewhat smugly that it was because orders had been issued to him the night before and no one had been able to find him. On his own he added that those orders had called for a dawn attack.[22]

While this conversation was going on, Cleburne read the new orders, which were dated 5:30 that morning and which ordered him to "move upon and attack the enemy so soon as you are in position." There was no mention of a dawn assault, which was impossible now in any case. He handed the orders to Hill and declared that his men could not go into battle until they had had their rations. Hill agreed, and he sat down with a notebook to write a response to Polk. The courier stood by impatiently while Hill composed his letter. As he wrote, the sound of Federal axmen felling trees could be heard in the near distance. Cleburne mentioned that they had been at work all night, and Hill added that information to his note: "General Cleburne reports that the Yankees were felling trees all night, and consequently now occupy a position too strong to be taken by assault." He handed the note to the courier who galloped off.[23]

Only minutes later Leonidas Polk arrived in person. He saw Cleburne first and asked him why he had not yet attacked. Cleburne told him that his men were drawing rations and that the attack would begin after they had eaten. Hill confirmed Cleburne's report, and Polk acknowledged the response without indicating that there was any greater urgency. Soon after Polk left, Bragg arrived. He had met Captain Wheliss en route and his mood had not been improved by that officer's report. Bluntly, he asked Hill why he had not attacked at dawn. Somewhat ingenuously, Hill replied that this was the first he had heard of a dawn attack. The orders to Cleburne and Breckinridge had only stated that an attack should begin as soon as they were in position. Clearly unsatisfied, Bragg made some comment about Polk's lack of energy, declared that the attack should begin as soon as possible, then rode off to find Polk. It was 8:00 A.M., two and a quarter hours after daybreak.[24]

Bragg's original conception for the morning assault was for Breckinridge, on the extreme right, to attack first, followed soon thereafter by Cleburne, and then by the divisions of Cheatham's Corps on Cleburne's left. As he visualized it, the attack would fold the Federal left back across the LaFayette Road and cut the enemy's line of retreat to Chattanooga. In the hasty rearrangement of the morning, however, the goal now was simply to attack and as soon as possible. Bragg believed that the Federal left flank did not extend much further north than Lee and Gordon's Mills, and that his assault would encounter little resistance. He did not know that Rosecrans had recognized the threat to his left and had shifted most of his strength there. Ironically, Hill's entire corps had marched eight miles past the front of the weak Federal right the day before in order to attack the reinforced Federal left. Now, Cleburne's three brigades fronted what was by far the strongest part of the Federal position.

Breckinridge departed to position his troops for the assault, and Cleburne again deployed his three brigades for battle. Once again he placed Lucius Polk on the right with orders to maintain contact with Breckinridge; the center he entrusted to Wood's Brigade despite his qualms about its performance the evening before, and he placed Deshler on the left. With the benefit of daylight, he reconnoitered the ground in front of his division and talked with each of the brigade commanders. He had barely completed these arrangements at about 9:30 when the sound of Breckinridge's assault reached him. One veteran remembered "the clear ring of Pat Cleburne's 'Forward!'" as the division advanced.[25]

Almost at once, his men encountered a fierce enemy fire from behind a line of concealed breastworks. Federal Major General George Thomas, the Virginia native who was to earn his nickname as "the Rock of Chickamauga" this day, had concentrated his forces in a semicircular salient that by a cruel fate jutted out squarely across Cleburne's designated line of advance. Shooting from behind a log breastwork, the Federals had a 4 to 1 numerical advantage over the milewide section of front assigned to Cleburne's Division. Their fire was a perfect storm of lead, and Cleburne's men struggled forward as if facing a strong wind.

The brigades of Polk and Wood became separated almost at once. Polk's men veered off to the right, forced to break into double-time in their effort to maintain contact with Breckinridge. Cleburne went with them. The attack made little progress against the withering enemy fire. "Polk's brigade and the right of Wood's encountered the heaviest artillery fire I have ever experienced," Cleburne wrote in his official report. "I was now within short canister range of a line of log breastworks and a hurricane of shot and shell swept the woods from the unseen enemy in my front." He estimated that "five hundred men were killed and wounded by this fire in a few minutes." The attackers moved to within 175 yards of the Federal position, marked by the line of musket flashes, but they could go no further. Almost by instinct, they took cover, lying prone behind a small rise of ground.[26]

Hoping that a success by Wood on Polk's left might allow a renewal of the advance, Cleburne galloped toward the left and found the men of Wood's Brigade halted and clinging to a low rise about 400 yards from the Federal line. He asked Wood why his men were not advancing, and Wood replied that he had lost contact with Polk's Brigade on the right and that Deshler was blocked by Stewart's Division on his left, so that both of his flanks were exposed. Cleburne told him that he would see to it that Deshler advanced on his left and ordered him to get on with the attack. He rode further to the left to find Deshler and soon had him disentangled from Stewart. Indeed, Stewart agreed to attack in conjunction with Cleburne, and the men of both divisions went forward in a renewed assault. One small band advanced to within forty yards of the Federal line before breaking. Wood's Brigade renewed its attempt to advance but was repelled with horrific losses. Two of Wood's regiments, the 16th and 33d Alabama, lost 60 percent of their number. Though Cleburne was instinctively inclined to force the attack until the enemy fled or until his own command was annihilated, he could see that it was "a useless sacrifice of life" to continue to press the issue under these circumstances. At about 11:00 A.M., he ordered Wood and Polk to fall back, and he ordered Deshler to cover their withdrawal.[27]

The men of Deshler's Brigade remembered being chivied about their surrender of Arkansas Post and were determined to show what they could do in this, their first battle as part of Cleburne's Division. "Old Pat Cleburn orders us in to stay and we stay," one veteran wrote in his diary. "But we are too close to the Yanks who have made works in the night out of logs and are protected. . . . We are so flat on the ground that we don't make much show. They shoot at us, but we do not return it . . . the Yankees are blazing away at us like fury. Bullets fly like the wind, you can hear them zip zip—zip but you can't see them." Deshler walked along the front line encouraging his men to hold on against the withering Federal fire, and as he did so he was cut nearly in half by an artillery shell. Even so, his three regiments were still holding their position three hours later at 2:00 P.M. when they finally withdrew, under orders, after losing 50 percent of their number. The Federal line remained intact.[28]

The heroism and sacrifice of the men in the ranks had been entirely in vain. Cleburne passed along the line to offer solace and encouragement to the troops. Years later, the colonel of the 45th and 32d (consolidated) Mississippi regiment remembered proudly that "General Cleburne complimented me personally." But however glorious, the gallantry had been wasted. Or so it seemed. What Cleburne did not know was that while his division had been all but broken against the powerful salient on the Federal left, Lieutenant General James Longstreet, who had arrived only the night before, was carefully massing his troops for at attack on the weak Federal right. Longstreet was a careful planner—some said he was overly careful. As the morning passed, he meticulously pieced together an attacking force five brigades deep on a front less than half a mile wide. By contrast, Cleburne's attack had been a single brigade deep on a front twice as wide and against a far stronger position. Not until an hour past noon did Longstreet feel that his forces were ready. At just that moment, Rosecrans, concerned by the ferociousness of Cleburne's attack on his left, issued orders to send even more troops from the right to the left. As Longstreet prepared to launch his massed assault, the Federal defenders in his front were pulling out of the line to march north.[29]

Longstreet's attack burst through the weakened Federal line like a storm-fed river smashing through a dam of twigs. His massed brigades drove a deep wedge into the Federal rear area. Within two hours, Rosecrans and two of his three corps commanders decided that the battle was lost and fled the field. A stream of soldiers in blue headed west, away from the fight, seeking safety through the passes in Lookout Mountain. Only George Thomas, still commanding the forces on Cleburne's front, remained in place. His unbroken salient along the LaFayette Road plus several thousand more Federals on Horseshoe Ridge backed by most of the Yankee artillery still held the field.

Cleburne could only guess at what might be happening on Longstreet's front. He could hear the sound of battle—one of his soldiers wrote later that "it seemed that ten thousand earthquakes had been turned loose"—but he had no certain knowledge of what it meant. He was still holding his position with his battered division in front of Thomas's salient at 3:30 in the afternoon when a staff officer from Leonidas Polk arrived with orders for him to move to the right, consolidate his front line, and renew the advance. His assignment now was to draw the attention of the Federal defenders while Breckinridge worked his way around their flank. Determined this time to conduct a personal survey of the ground over which his men would have to pass, Cleburne ordered the young captain who brought him the orders to accompany him on the reconnaissance and started off on horseback. He wanted the staffer to point out precisely where he was to join his own command to the forces on his right. Cleburne rode forward in what the staff officer thought was a "slow inpurturbable [*sic*] fashion" when the captain noticed that they were getting uncomfortably close to the enemy front line. He ventured to express that opinion, but Cleburne only grunted noncommittally and rode onward. Suddenly there was a flurry of minié balls singing past them with a high-pitched thwip, thwip. Startled from his reverie, Cleburne quickly turned away and galloped out of range with the relieved staff officer hard on his heels.[30]

Back with his command, Cleburne arrayed what remained of his three brigades to cover the sector assigned to him. Just before 5:00 P.M. he ordered his command forward again, and this time the fates were kinder. Appreciating that his were the only Federal forces still holding the field, Thomas had ordered a staged withdrawal, and Lucius Polk's Brigade hit the left of his salient just as the Yankees were falling back. Cleburne ordered the battery of Captain James P. Douglas to advance in close support of the infantry. Since horses could not be expected to survive the heavy fire, the guns had to be maneuvered forward by hand. Calling on volunteers, Cleburne led the guns forward personally through the thick timber to a point only eighty yards from the enemy line. Then they unlimbered and opened fire on the Federal defenses. "Gen'l Pat Clebourn planted two batteries as to enfilade the enemies strongest position," a veteran wrote in his diary, and those guns "scatter[ed] death and destruction into the ranks of the Federals."[31]

The Federal evacuation turned into a stampede. Cleburne's men clambered over three lines of the hated breastworks and took hundreds of prisoners and captured three more guns. They stopped in the middle of the Yankee camp, surprised perhaps still to be alive. There was "a death-like stillness for a second," as if the men could hardly imagine that they had achieved their objective. "My God!" one wrote in his diary, "Listen! Those shouts . . . we have gained the victory!" A few of Polk's men marched a short distance up the LaFayette Road, but Hill ordered Cleburne to halt the advance. Hill claimed later that further pursuit in the growing dark would have been useless and even dangerous. They had gained the LaFayette Road for which they had fought for two days. Exhausted, "the troops bivouacked where night found them."[32]

Like Shiloh, Chickamauga was a soldier's battle. Fought over a wide front in heavy woods and partly at night, the generals at the top had little clear conception of what was happening. Casualties were appalling. A total of 34,000 men fell in the two-day fight, half again as many as at Shiloh. Over 18,000 of them were Confederates who had assumed the burden of the offensive. They had attacked in the direction they were pointed and behaved bravely but often to little avail. For most of the morning, Cleburne's Division had battered itself against the unyielding lines of Thomas's Corps; it broke through in the late afternoon only as the Federals withdrew. Although on the one hand it might be argued that the sacrifice of his division had contributed to the eventual victory by drawing strength away from Longstreet's front at the critical moment, the results had been more a product of luck than strategy.[33]

Bragg's management of the battle had been poor. His initial error was a nearly unworkable organizational structure. On the very eve of battle he had reorganized the army into two "wings," assigning Longstreet to the left and Leonidas Polk to the right, which put Hill (with Cleburne and Breckinridge) under Polk's command. This change in structure not only contributed to the confusion about the stillborn dawn assault on 20 September, but it also made Hill dependent for his support on Walker and Liddell who were not under his command. As a result, when Cleburne and Breckinridge did attack later that day, their assault was a single brigade deep, and there were no reserve forces to fill the gaps or to exploit a breakthrough.

Even worse was Bragg's apparent inability to adjust to changing circumstances. Having conceived of an attack on the Federal left, he could not abandon the concept even after events demonstrated that his conception of the battlefield was flawed. As a result, he failed to recognize that he had won a victory when it was bequeathed to him. When Polk congratulated him on his victory at about 9:00 P.M., Bragg dismissed such comments as premature. Because the battle had not unfolded as he had envisioned, it could not be a victory. Unable or unwilling to adjust to circumstances he had not foreseen, Bragg could think of nothing more productive to do than brood about how he had been thwarted by his enemies, particularly Hindman and Polk.[34]

This inaction contributed to his greatest error: the failure to pursue the defeated Federals early on 21 September. Cleburne's men were exhausted to be sure, but there were other elements of the army that were not. Cheatham or Walker might have been sent up the LaFayette Road to Chattanooga. At the very least they could have harried the Federal retreat. Instead Bragg refused to believe that his army had been victorious. For the third time in the war, Cleburne's men had poured their blood out to achieve a tactical victory, and for the third time they saw the fruits of that victory uncollected as the army failed to follow up its success.

The day after the battle, the men of Cleburne's Division got a welcome day's rest, cooking newly issued rations in the morning, then conducting the lugubrious task of adding up the casualties in the afternoon. Of just over 5,000 men in the division, a total of 1,743 were officially listed as killed or wounded—one out of every three. Amazingly, though Cleburne's chief of staff was wounded and Buck had a horse shot out from under him, Cleburne himself emerged unscathed. Almost as remarkable is the fact that of the 5,115 men of Cleburne's Division who fought over two days, partly at night and in thick woods, only six were listed as "missing."[35]

Late that afternoon Cleburne received verbal orders to march his division toward Chattanooga. His men covered half the distance before nightfall, and he had them back on the road by 7:00 A.M. on 22 September. That same afternoon he arrived on Missionary Ridge overlooking the city. Bragg had hoped and expected that the Federals would abandon Chattanooga after their defeat. Nathan Bedford Forrest had reported the day before that they were already in the process of evacuating. By the time the Rebel infantry arrived, however, the Federals were fortifying the city. Bragg ordered a reconnaissance in force to test the seriousness of the defenses, and on 24 September Cleburne pushed his skirmishers forward "to within two hundred yards" of the Federal earthworks. He was perfectly willing to turn the advance into a full-scale assault, but the divisions on either side of him fell back and he had little choice but to do likewise. He reported to Hill that "heavy working details of the Enemy seemed to be actively engaged in or about Chattanooga." Having thrown away the chance to outflank the city by his leisurely pursuit, Bragg determined that he had no alternative now but to settle down to a siege.[36]

If Bragg had no energy for a pursuit of the Federals, he had no shortage of it for assailing his enemies within the army. He spent most of his time during the weeks that followed the battle preparing charges against those who had defied him. It was a long list. He started with Cleburne's former law partner Thomas Hindman, suspending him from his command for disobedience of orders in McLemore's Cove. Then Bragg demanded an explanation from Leonidas Polk for the late start of the attack on the morning of 20 September. Polk blamed the delay on Hill, and although Bragg instantly dubbed Polk's response as "unsatisfactory," he also added Hill's name to the list of guilty officers. Bragg suspended Polk from his command, but President Davis, hoping to discourage him, told Bragg he would have to file official charges for a court-martial. Bragg thereupon ordered Polk under arrest.

None of Bragg's targets was willing to take his assault lying down. Instead, the flurry of official charges acted once again to crystallize the opposition within the high command and even provoked what amounted to a petition for Bragg's removal. Written by Simon Buckner and addressed to President Davis, it was carefully worded to avoid any direct criticism of the army commander. It requested that the president relieve Bragg of his command solely because of his continued poor health. At the very least the circulation of such a petition constituted a conspiracy; at worst it might easily be construed as a mutiny. A dozen general officers signed it, and the order of the signatures on the document suggests its history. It was signed first by Buckner and two of his division commanders (William Preston and Archibald Gracie). Apparently, it was then carried to Hill's headquarters, for he was the next to sign, followed by John C. Brown, the third of Buckner's brigade commanders who may have ridden over to Hill's headquarters for the purpose.[37]

The petition sat in Hill's headquarters for several days. Hill presumably invited Breckinridge to sign it. He declined, though two of his three brigade commanders did sign. Cheatham also declined. Breckinridge and Cheatham, of course, were the two general officers who had returned evasive replies in response to Bragg's query about the army's confidence in him after Murfreesboro. Both men were willing to criticize Bragg privately, but neither wished to put his name to a petition for removal. Others were less cautious. Lucius Polk could hardly wait to sign—Bragg's arrest of his uncle may have been an important factor for him—and he even brought one of his regimental commanders along to sign as well. Polk tried to convince Liddell to add his signature, but though Liddell admitted that Bragg was an indifferent commander and frequently irritating, he insisted that there was no one else. Polk dismissed such arguments, claiming that "anybody would do better." Cleburne was in the room during their discussion and Liddell thought that "Cleburne was of Polk's opinion," but typically, Cleburne "was very reticent of expression." Quiet warrior that he was, Cleburne did not engage in public criticism of Bragg, nor did he debate the issue with others. But he *did* sign. He may have felt that a refusal to do so would have been moral cowardice. Bragg was unquestionably ill, and whatever his attributes as a general, his removal from command would undoubtedly raise the morale and efficiency of the army. Cleburne's was the last signature on the list, at the very bottom of the page where there was barely enough room for him to write his name. From Hill's headquarters, the petition then made its way to Longstreet, and he and Bushrod Johnson, whose division had broken Rosecrans's front at Chickamauga, signed as well.[38]

Far from convincing the president to relieve his beleaguered army commander, the petition served instead to provide Davis and Bragg with a convenient list of Bragg's enemies. When Liddell visited Bragg to warn him of the unrest among the officers and to urge him to offer some conciliatory gesture, he found the army commander unrelenting and unforgiving. "I want to get rid of all such generals," Bragg told him bluntly. "I have better men now in subordinate stations to fill their places. Let them send in their resignations. I shall accept every one without hesitation." [39]

Hoping to calm the storm, President Davis arrived in Marietta, Georgia, a few days later on 9 October. The next night he met with Bragg and his corps commanders—Longstreet, Hill, Buckner, and Cheatham (who was temporarily commanding Polk's Corps). In a positively surreal conference, and with Bragg present, they declared one by one that Bragg was unfit for command. Davis listened but was unconvinced. The next day he told Bragg that he still had confidence in him and encouraged him to do whatever was necessary to restore harmony and unity among the high command. Bragg believed that the president had given him carte blanche to purge the army of his personal enemies. [40]

Leonidas Polk got a reprieve of sorts. At Davis's request, Bragg agreed to drop his charges against Polk if Davis sent him to another command. Hindman, too, received a pardon. It was Hill who now emerged as the chief scapegoat. Bragg insisted that Hill be relieved of his command, claiming that "he weakens the *morale,* and military tone of his command," and Davis approved the request two days later. Determined to have his day in court, Hill began to assemble testimonials and collect written orders as evidence. He asked Cleburne to write him a letter for the record defending his decision not to comply with Bragg's 10 September order to advance into McLemore's Cove. Cleburne loyally confirmed Hill's interpretation of the events. He wrote that he remembered the morning "very distinctly" and claimed that any attempt to concentrate his division at Dug Gap "would have taken several hours," which was the reason that "General Bragg's order could not have been carried out." It was, Cleburne concluded, Hill's "duty to postpone the movement." Cleburne's loyal attempt to support his commander was unavailing. Davis insisted that Hill's removal was purely administrative and that he had no grounds for a court-martial. Hill never got his day in court, and Cleburne's support served mainly to identify him even more closely with what were now openly referred to as the anti-Bragg men. [41]

Under the shadow of these maneuverings, which might have done justice to the Roman Senate, Cleburne sat down to write his report on the Chickamauga campaign. He made no mention of the misunderstandings and frustrations of McLemore's Cove, nor did he engage in a discussion about the errors and confusion surrounding the order to attack on the morning of 20 September. Instead he devoted his report to describing the combat on 19 and 20 September. He was full of praise for "the gallant conduct of Brigadier-General Polk," whose "intrepidity and stern determination of purpose . . . drove the enemy from his breastworks and gave us the battle." Likewise he praised the martyred Deshler, whom he called a "brave and efficient" officer who "brought always to the discharge of his duty a warm zeal and a high conscientiousness." He even had accolades for the "gallantry and intelligence" of Colonel R. Q. Mills, who had briefly commanded the brigade after Deshler's death. About Sterling Wood, however, he made no comment at all. The day before Cleburne wrote his report, Wood had submitted his resignation.[42]

Wood's Brigade had performed less effectively at Chickamauga than Polk's, though in fairness it should be noted that it faced a more difficult assignment. Several months after the battle, Cleburne's chief of staff wrote a friend that Wood's Brigade "was badly broken" during the twilight attack on 19 September. In his report, Wood admitted that there had been some confusion in his brigade that night, but he attributed it to "some unauthorized person giving a command to retreat." Somewhat defensively, he claimed, "In no action has this command ever displayed more eagerness to engage the enemy." Cleburne, apparently, was not satisfied. He did not criticize Wood publicly, but neither was he willing to offer praise where he believed it had not been earned. It is tempting to speculate that Cleburne's sense of fair play led him to show Wood a draft of his report before he submitted it; perhaps he even suggested that Wood should consider resigning. Or perhaps the initiative came from Wood who, when confronted with Cleburne's expressed disappointment, offered his resignation in contrition. None but the two principals knew, and they never said.[43]

For Cleburne, Chickamauga was a particularly barren victory. Despite the loss of a third of his command, he had failed to break the enemy's defensive line. Even when the Federals were finally routed, it had not led to real victory. Moreover, instead of gaining new laurels for himself or his command, the campaign had rekindled the officers' feud. Although Cleburne was never a prime mover in the conspiracy against the army commander, he was the only one of all the general officers who was on record twice for advocating Bragg's removal. Of the three officers who had replied to Bragg's request for their "candid" views after Murfreesboro, Cleburne was the only one who also signed the petition for his removal after Chickamauga. He did not seek a leading role in army politics, but his sense of personal responsibility had compelled him to identify himself publicly with the opposition. His aide and former law partner Learned Mangum wrote later that "Cleburne had too little of the political general in him to conceal his views." His ambition continued to burn brightly—Liddell thought him "exceedingly ambitious"—but with Bragg firmly in command, his chances for further recognition or promotion flickered to a tiny spark.[44]

STONEWALL OF THE WEST

Bragg's siege of Chattanooga was a disaster. Although his plan was to starve Rosecrans's army out of the city, food was nearly as scarce in the Rebel camp as it was in town. Cleburne's troops subsisted on a small "pone" of corn bread and a cup of corn coffee twice a day. In addition, the Yankees in the city had better accommodations. Cleburne's men had no tents, and had to bivouac outdoors either on the boulder-strewn heights of Missionary Ridge or in the swampy bottom lands nearby. There the mud was so deep one unit placed a sign in the middle of the road reading "Mule Under Here" to mark the spot where a mule had supposedly disappeared into the bottomless muck. Moreover, the lack of activity during the siege sapped the army's energy and enthusiasm. "Soldiers that have been marching and fighting as long as we have must be kept on the move," a captain in Cleburne's Division noted in his diary. "They want to march or drill every day, and here we can do neither." Instead they spent the days gambling, trading, and arguing. Morale fell so low that hundreds of men simply walked away from their posts and deserted to the Federals. Finally, the internecine bickering in the officer corps continued, soon reaching a point where Bragg and Longstreet could barely tolerate one another. Such conditions contributed significantly to the disastrous Confederate defeat on Missionary Ridge in November 1863 and a humiliating retreat into Georgia.[1]

Yet amid the gloom of these disasters, Pat Cleburne's own star shone brighter than ever—like "a meteor shining from a clouded sky" in the words of Robert E. Lee. Twice during this crisis, fate placed Cleburne at the vortex of battle where circumstances gave him the opportunity to demonstrate his greatest strength as a field commander: his coolness and reliability in a crisis. Amid the disasters of the late fall, Cleburne's steadfast performance in the field was a rare bright spot for the Confederacy and provoked Jefferson Davis to christen him the "Stonewall of the West," granting him a status coequal with that of the martyred Stonewall Jackson who had fallen at Chancellorsville in May.[2]

As his men settled into their new positions overlooking Chattanooga, Cleburne faced yet another reorganization of his division. Deshler's death and Wood's resignation made Lucius Polk the only returning brigade commander. To replace Wood, Cleburne recommended Mark P. Lowrey, the son of immigrants and, like himself, an Irish Protestant. Lowrey had wrestled with an "almost unconquerable resolution to become rich" in his youth but instead had "yielded to the call" to become a Baptist minister. When the war broke out, Lowrey had been elected captain of a company of volunteers and like Cleburne had risen to command the regiment. At Chickamauga Cleburne had noted Lowrey's steadfastness and had made a point of complementing him personally. Now he tapped the fighting preacher for brigade command. For the Texas Brigade, Cleburne recommended a Tennessean, James A. Smith, an 1853 graduate of West Point. Smith had compiled a solid command record as colonel of the 5th Confederate regiment (a predominantly Irish unit), and he, too, had performed particularly well at Chickamauga. A fourth brigade joined Cleburne's Division with the return of St. John Liddell, though Liddell was not particularly happy about it. Before Chickamauga, he had petitioned Bragg repeatedly for orders to the trans-Mississippi Department. Unwilling to let him go, Bragg had instead awarded him a divisional command. Now, still without his transfer, he reverted to a brigade command under Cleburne.[3]

The rest of the army also underwent reorganization. The departure of D. H. Hill, a victim of Bragg's purge, left a vacancy for a corps commander. Almost certainly Cleburne nursed a hope, perhaps even an expectation, that he would be elevated to the position himself. After all, he had commanded the corps successfully in Hardee's absence prior to Hill's arrival and was now poised to assume the command in his own right. Instead, Bragg gave the job to Breckinridge, naming Cheatham and Longstreet to head the other two corps. Longstreet was an unavoidable choice despite his contrariness, though Bragg limited his command to the two divisions he had brought with him from Virginia. The other two appointments were more problematic. It is hard to avoid the conclusion that Bragg may have been inclined toward Breckinridge and Cheatham at least in part because they were the two most senior officers who had refused to sign the round-robin letter urging Davis to replace him.

It was not in Cleburne's character to complain about specific high command decisions. Even on this occasion, he did not protest Bragg's appointments officially, but he did express private disappointment. He told Liddell that Breckinridge was an unfortunate choice to command the corps, claiming that he was "an unlucky man and inspired no confidence," an assessment that might also have been applied to Bragg. Liddell did not disagree with Cleburne's analysis but suggested that there was no one else to whom the job could be entrusted. Cleburne demurred. Surely there were other candidates for command, he insisted pointedly, even telling Liddell, "I would rather the command were given to you." Very likely he was inviting Liddell to reciprocate, to suggest that Cleburne would also make a good corps commander. He may even have hoped that Liddell would carry the suggestion to Bragg with whom Liddell was on good terms. But either Liddell refused to rise to the bait, or the gambit passed over him completely. He did not tell Cleburne that he would make a good corps commander, nor did he suggest it to Bragg. Increasingly thereafter Cleburne and Liddell shared fewer confidences as Cleburne relied more and more on Lucius Polk, his old comrade from Arkansas. This situation, at least, Liddell noted and resented. In his postwar memoirs, he wrote, "Cleburne was resentful, exceedingly ambitious, friendly to those useful to him, until they stood in the way of his advancement. Then he did not hesitate to shake them off."[4]

Bragg's purges and subsequent reorganization did not eliminate the antagonism toward him in the army. Longstreet, in particular, carried on a surly guerrilla campaign, undermining Bragg in subtle and some not so subtle ways until the two men were barely on speaking terms. Disappointed that Bragg had managed to cling to command, Longstreet virtually lost interest in the campaign. He failed to exercise initiative—or even simple responsibility—in superintending his portion of the siege lines around Chattanooga. As a result, the Federals seized Brown's Ferry on 27 October and occupied Lookout Valley the next day, effectively breaking the siege. Bragg was furious. His strategy now ruined by these reversals, his only realistic alternative was to withdraw. But unwilling or unable to admit failure, he continued to occupy Lookout Mountain and Missionary Ridge as if nothing had changed.[5]

There was some good news that week, at least it was good news as far as Cleburne was concerned: Hardee returned to the army. Recalled from Alabama, Hardee assumed command of Cheatham's Corps with Cheatham reverting to a divisional command. Probably at Hardee's request, Cleburne's Division was then transferred from Breckinridge's Corps to Hardee's. Cleburne was delighted; serving under Hardee was almost as good as getting the corps command himself. Hardee's return had other consequences as well—it provided Bragg with an additional rationale to rid himself of Longstreet.

He got the chance to do exactly that when Davis suggested that Bragg might send Longstreet to East Tennessee to confront a Federal army under Major General Ambrose Burnside near Knoxville. The official justification for such a move was that it would prevent Burnside from outflanking Bragg's "siege" of Chattanooga, but it also meant that Bragg and Longstreet would no longer have to serve together. Bragg seized upon the suggestion and even promised to send additional forces to Longstreet within a fortnight. Longstreet left on 4 November, and even though it left the army with only two corps and no more than 37,000 men, Bragg wrote Davis that his departure was "a great relief."[6]

To a casual observer, the Confederate position on Lookout Mountain and Missionary Ridge seemed nearly impregnable, but a number of factors made it more insecure in fact that it appeared. First, Bragg's much reduced army occupied lines that were far too extended for his depleted forces. Second, the difficult terrain that Bragg counted on to deter the enemy also meant that he could not easily shuttle his own forces from one point to another. Each division would have to rely largely on its own assets to beat off an enemy assault in its sector. Third, no defensive position is any stronger than its flanks, and if the Federals could seize either Lookout Mountain on his left or Tunnel Hill on his right, there was no way Bragg could hold Missionary Ridge. Unable or unwilling to perceive these weaknesses, however, Bragg merely stretched his remaining manpower to cover that portion of the front previously held by Longstreet and continued to behave as if the Federals in Chattanooga were still under siege.

Cleburne did not record his views of the unraveling situation. He may have been surprised, however, when a courier arrived near midnight on 22 November with orders from Bragg for Cleburne to evacuate his position on Missionary Ridge and march his division to Chickamauga Station. There he was to take command of Buckner's Division (temporarily under the command of Bushrod Johnson) as well as his own—a total of some 11,000 men—and supervise the transfer of both divisions to eastern Tennessee as a reinforcement for Longstreet. Bragg's remarkable order had been provoked by a request from Longstreet for another division, which, he claimed, would "shorten the work here very much." Even though Bragg had wired Davis the day before that "the enemy is at least double our strength," he agreed to send Longstreet not one division, but two. Perhaps he hoped that with Cleburne on hand, Longstreet could whip Burnside quickly and return to Chattanooga before the storm broke on his own front. More likely, he simply underestimated the precariousness of his own position. Good subordinate that he was, Cleburne did not enquire as to Bragg's rationale, but it may have occurred to him that he and Buckner were the last two divisional commanders still in the army who had signed the petition for Bragg's recall.[7]

Cleburne broke camp early the next morning (23 November) and marched his division down off the ridge line to Chickamauga Station where he set up temporary headquarters while he supervised the transfer of troops to Knoxville. All morning, trains shuttled in and out of the station to pick up carloads of soldiers—Johnson's first—one brigade at a time. All but one of Johnson's brigades had departed by midmorning when a courier arrived from Bragg with orders not to embark any more units. There was no particular sense of urgency in the orders; they specified that if any part of a unit had already entrained, the rest of the troops of that unit could follow as far as Charleston, but Cleburne was not to start any new units pending further orders. Not long afterward, a second courier arrived with orders that were a bit more ominous: the troops who had already left should return "at once." Cleburne sent a telegram down the line to order the men of Johnson's Division to return to Chickamauga Station. He had barely done so when a third courier arrived. This time the orders were blunt: "We are heavily engaged. Move up rapidly to these headquarters." Cleburne turned temporary command of his division over to Lucius Polk with orders to follow as quickly as possible and galloped ahead to Bragg's headquarters. From there, Cleburne could see with his own eyes that the Federals in Chattanooga had advanced across the open plain below and chased the Rebel skirmishers from Orchard Knob. Bragg had concluded that despite the daunting height of Missionary Ridge, the Federals were about to assault his lines. He ordered Cleburne to place his two divisions "immediately behind Missionary Ridge" and rest there for the night. Cleburne's force would constitute the army's principal reserve and would report directly to Bragg.[8]

Cleburne was up early the next day. It was cold on Missionary Ridge; there was a heavy ground fog and it was raining a light drizzle. When he reported to Bragg at army headquarters, he found the commanding general even more lugubrious than usual. He looked "dejected and despondent," his face deeply creased with worry. One officer thought he had "a wild abstracted look" as if he were under unbearable stress. Bragg told Cleburne to send a brigade and a battery to the railroad bridge over Chickamauga Creek and to guard it "at all hazards" to ensure a secure line of retreat if necessary. Cleburne sent the best he had: Polk's Brigade with Semple's Battery. The other three brigades of his division—Lowrey's, Smith's, and Liddell's (under the command of Colonel Daniel Govan since Liddell was on leave)—remained on the reverse slope of Missionary Ridge near Bragg's headquarters.[9]

When the blow fell, it was not on the center, but the left. At midmorning the sound of battle from Lookout Mountain reached Bragg's headquarters. From his vantage point, Cleburne could just make out the summit, though the lower slopes of the mountain were "obscured by a thick mist, from which the enemy's shells emerged in graceful curves, bursting high above this veil, and throwing out white puffs of smoke against the dark background of the mountain." Buck thought the tableau constituted "a battle piece so grand and magnificent that anxiety as to the result was lost in admiration and the spectacle." The spectacle lasted all morning; then about an hour past noon, the sound and fury began to die down. Soon afterward news arrived at Bragg's headquarters that the Federals had captured the summit. This outcome effectively turned Bragg's left. Worse, the Federal divisions on the right also began to move forward threatening that flank as well. Bragg ordered Cleburne to move his division there at once; a courier from Hardee informed him that he would find Major D. H. Poole near Tunnel Hill and that Poole would show him the position he was to occupy. After starting his troops en route, Cleburne galloped ahead of them along the ridge line toward Tunnel Hill.[10]

At the northern end of the extended Rebel line, Missionary Ridge descended gradually to accommodate the course of South Chickamauga Creek. A mile south of the creek, the Chattanooga and Cleveland Railroad passed through a tunnel in the ridge line before linking up with the Western and Atlantic. The knoblike eminence above the tunnel was known as Tunnel Hill, and it was as critical to the security of the Confederate right as Lookout Mountain was to the Confederate left. When Cleburne arrived there at about 2:30, he found Major Poole waiting for him. The major pointed out a detached hill— subsequently identified as Billy Goat Hill—a half mile or so northwest of the main ridge, and he told Cleburne that Hardee wanted him to place one of his brigades there. The rest he was to deploy on Tunnel Hill itself and on the ridge line extending southward until they connected with the forces on his left. Cleburne saw at once that he could not possibly cover such an extended front with only three brigades. (Polk was still guarding the railroad bridge over the Chickamauga.) He sent Poole to tell Hardee so. There was no time to await a response, however, for even as his own forces began to arrive, with Smith's Texans in the lead, a private in the divisional signal team rushed up excitedly to tell him that the Federals were advancing. Cleburne ordered Smith "to move his brigade rapidly and try to get possession" of the detached hill that Major Poole had pointed out to him. Smith's men gamely started up the hill, but they were halted by a Yankee infantry line and forced to fall back. The Yankees were already on the summit, and they cheered lustily as Smith's men hastily withdrew.[11]

The Texans rallied on Missionary Ridge, and Cleburne placed them atop the end of the main ridge, about 500 yards north of the tunnel, deploying them so that they wrapped around the promontory of high ground in a horseshoe formation with one regiment facing west, one north, and one to the northeast. They had barely occupied these positions when the Federals attacked. Had they advanced in strength, Smith's three regiments might easily have been overwhelmed, but the attack was undermanned and halfhearted, and Smith's Texans successfully repelled it. What neither they nor Cleburne knew at the time was that the Federal commander, Major General William T. Sherman, had a confused understanding of the terrain. He believed that the detached hill that his troops had already occupied *was* Missionary Ridge (hence the loud cheering when Smith's tentative advance was driven back). Not for some hours did he appreciate his error, and meanwhile the rest of Cleburne's Division was marching up onto Tunnel Hill. With the late afternoon repulse of his reconnaissance in front of Smith's position, Sherman decided to wait until the next day before sweeping over the ridge.[12]

The reprieve gave Cleburne a chance to deploy his three brigades with some care. He placed Lowrey's Brigade on Smith's left and sent Govan with Liddell's Brigade to the right, directing it to occupy a lower ridge running almost due east just north of the railroad. The result was that his line resembled a hairpin with the right arm bent out at an angle: Lowrey's Brigade constituted the straight arm of the pin, Smith's salient made up the sharp bend, and Govan's force the bent arm.[13]

Hardee arrived in Cleburne's sector about 4:00 P.M. just after the repulse of Sherman's first halfhearted assault. He looked over Cleburne's arrangements and tinkered a bit with his dispositions, sending two of Lowrey's four regiments from the left to the right to occupy another detached hill further north. This bolstered Cleburne's right flank which was in the air, but it left Lowrey with only two regiments to defend nearly a mile of front. Hardee promised to send Cleburne reinforcements for this weak point, then he left to supervise his other division commanders.[14]

The sun set at about 6:30 and soon it was dark, though a full moon cast a silver sheen over the ridge line. Cleburne doubted that his men would be asked to defend their positions the next day. It seemed to him that with the fall of Lookout Mountain, Bragg would be compelled to order a retreat. He rode back to the Chickamauga Creek Bridge to satisfy himself that Polk's Brigade still held open the line of retreat. On his own authority, he sent all but

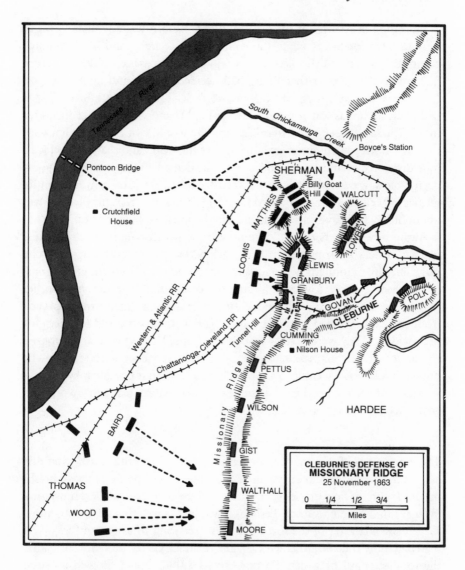

**CLEBURNE'S DEFENSE OF
MISSIONARY RIDGE**
25 November 1863

0   1/4   1/2   3/4   1

Miles

two guns of the divisional artillery to the rear, and though he ordered the men to prepare breastworks, he left the supervision of them to Major Dixon, who rode from unit to unit "fussing around," as one soldier recalled, "on a little white mule." As the night wore on and no orders from Bragg arrived, Cleburne began to worry. He decided to send Captain Buck to Bragg's headquarters to find out what was happening. "Go at once," Cleburne told him, "ask what has been determined upon, and say that if it is decided to fight it is necessary that I should get my artillery into position."[15]

Buck did not return until almost midnight. He had waited outside Bragg's headquarters for hours while the commanding general and his two corps commanders debated the alternatives. Finally, well past ten o'clock, Hardee had emerged to report that Bragg had decided to stay and fight it out on Missionary Ridge. Bragg had planned to order a retreat, but Breckinridge had made an impassioned plea to stay and fight, and Bragg had changed his mind. The new orders were that Breckinridge would command the left with three divisions spread out over two-thirds of the front, and that Hardee, with four divisions, including Cleburne's, would defend the right where the expected blow was most likely to fall. Hardee asked Buck to deliver a private message: "Tell Cleburne we are to fight," Hardee said, "that his division will undoubtedly be heavily attacked, and that he must do his very best." [16]

Aware now that there would be no evacuation that night, Cleburne dispatched orders to bring his artillery back across the river and up onto the ridge line. By moonlight he personally supervised the placement of the guns, putting one battery (Swett's) in support of Smith's Brigade and another (Key's) on the knob directly above Tunnel Hill to command the approach from the west. He had axes distributed so that the men could fell trees for breastworks. They were hard at work a few hours later when Hardee arrived to conduct a personal reconnaissance. As the two generals rode along the lines, the full moon went into a total eclipse and soon it became inky black— so dark that the men had to suspend their work. More than a few wondered what such an omen portended. [17]

The morning of 25 November dawned clear but cold, with a north wind that carried the promise of an early winter. There was some perfunctory skirmishing, and with his field glasses Cleburne could see blue-clad soldiers mustering in large numbers on his front. Perhaps it was just as well that he did not know the precise character of the force that was preparing to assail him, for Sherman had more than 30,000 men available to attack Cleburne's three brigades, the total strength of which did not exceed 4,000. Bragg showed up soon after daybreak, made a quick inspection of Cleburne's lines, then returned to his headquarters. Hardee, too, made a short visit, and soon afterward Brigadier General Joseph Lewis and his Kentucky (Orphan) Brigade reported to Cleburne, bringing the division's strength back up to four brigades. Cleburne placed the new arrivals in rear of his main line as a divisional reserve. [18]

The skirmishing grew heavier as the morning wore on, and at about 11:00 A.M. the Federals began a general attack. From Cleburne's vantage point atop the ridge it was a stirring sight: "The enemy was now in sight, advancing in two long lines of battle, his right stretching far beyond my left, his left stretching beyond Smith's right." Cleburne ordered his artillery to open fire as soon as the attackers were within range. The twelve-pound Napoleons of Swett's and Key's batteries fired round after round into the blue ranks, but despite serious losses, the Yankee infantry came determinedly onward, driving in the Rebel skirmishers and aiming at the three regiments of Smith's Brigade holding the northernmost salient of Cleburne's line. Captain Samuel Foster, commanding a company in the Texas brigade, recalled the assault with some vividness: "They are now coming in a run, stooping low to the ground, but when they get in [close], about 50 yards of us, they halt [and] commence wavering, some keep coming, others hang back, some are killed in 20 ft. of our works." At Chickamauga, Cleburne's men had been the attackers, charging through the trees against an entrenched enemy. Now the shoe was on the other foot, and Foster reveled in it. "See how they do fall," he wrote, "like leaves in the fall of the year. Oh this is fun to lie here and shoot them down and we not get hurt."[19]

With grim determination, the Yankees pressed the attack, advancing to within fifty yards of the Confederate lines before they finally broke. Caught up in the excitement of the moment, Smith sought approval from Cleburne to launch a counterattack to speed them on their way, and Cleburne quickly gave his assent. The counterattack was successful, driving the Federals back to their starting point at the base of the hill, but Smith was badly wounded, and Cleburne had to turn the brigade over to the senior colonel, Hiram Granbury of the 7th Texas.[20]

It was not over. The Federals rallied, regrouped, and tried again. This time a few of them succeeded in making it over the Confederate breastworks, though they were shot or taken prisoner almost at once. The rest, instead of falling back, took whatever cover was available and maintained a steady fire-fight. They concentrated on picking off the Rebel gunners, hoping to take the artillery out of the fight. The losses among the artillerymen were so severe that Granbury had to delegate some of his infantry to keep the guns firing. Cleburne moved two guns of Swett's Battery to support Douglas's Battery on Granbury's right in order to enfilade the Yankee firing line. Unable to hold their position in the face of this crossfire, the Federals fell back again.[21]

Only a half hour later, near one o'clock, the Federals struck again. This time they hit both the right and the left simultaneously; Sherman had four divisions to commit to the attack, and his greatest advantage was sheer numerical superiority. On the left, in front of Tunnel Hill where Cleburne commanded personally, Key's six-gun battery "fired rapidly into the charging line," tearing huge holes in the blue ranks, but the enemy continued to advance with a determination that drew the admiration of friend and foe alike. When the attacking infantry reached the foot of the ridge line, the Rebel gunners could not sufficiently depress their guns to hit them, and the Yankees "rushed up the hill in the direction of the batteries." They scrambled hand over hand up the slope and halted just below the crest, aware that once they topped the ridge they would face the full fury of the infantry and artillery fire. They "lay down behind trees, logs, and projecting rocks" only about twenty-five yards from Cleburne's lines and opened a steady fire, again targeting the artillerists, now fully exposed. The air was filled with whining minié balls. It seemed, Cleburne said later, "like one continuous sheet of hissing, flying lead." As their comrades fell one after another, the artillerists abandoned their guns and sought cover. Cleburne reinforced the threatened position with the 2d/15th/24th Arkansas, his old regiment from Govan's Brigade. Terrain was as much of a problem as numbers; unable to fire downhill at their tormentors without exposing themselves, the Rebels took to rolling heavy stones down the slope. Federals lying under cover in relative safety got up and ran to avoid the cascading stones and thus came under musket fire. Even so, without the artillery, it was entirely likely that the press of superior numbers would soon drive Cleburne's division off the ridge altogether.[22]

Cleburne called for reinforcements from Alfred Cumming's brigade of Georgia troops holding the ridge line south of Tunnel Hill. Cumming sent one regiment, then another, and finally reported to Cleburne in person with a third. Cleburne threw all three into line behind Granbury where the stubborn Federals still occupied a shallow depression only two dozen yards from the Rebel main line. Noting the arrival of the Georgia troops, the commander of the 2d/15th/24th Arkansas, Lieutenant Colonel Warfield, suggested a counterattack, and Cumming volunteered to lead it. Cleburne immediately consented and galloped quickly to the right to ensure the cooperation of the 6th/10th/15th Texas from Granbury's Brigade.[23]

Cumming arranged the four regiments that Cleburne committed to the assault one behind the other and gave orders for them to dash quickly through a gap in the front lines and "engage the enemy with the bayonet." With Cleburne's order to attack, Cumming gave the signal, and at about 3:30 P.M. the men charged forward. Only a relative few could fit through the gap in the breastworks; the rest had to scramble over the top, and while doing so they were hit by renewed fire from the Federals. The attack stalled, but they regrouped and tried again. They clambered over their own works "shrieking like fiends." So surprising was their rush down the hill that some of the startled Federals thought the Rebels had charged out of the mouth of the railroad tunnel. Those Federals who could, ran, while others surrendered and were escorted to the rear. (Cleburne was observing the fight from horseback atop the ridge line when a breathless scout rode up to him to report excitedly that he had just seen a column of Federal soldiers marching across their rear. Ever the stoic, Cleburne quietly explained that it was a column of Federal prisoners.) The men of the 6th/10th/15th Texas pursued the enemy to the foot of the hill, then retreated slowly back to their own lines with four captured battle flags. Cleburne suspected that the success of this counterattack would compel the Federals to give up their assault altogether. At five o'clock, in the twilight darkness, he organized a reconnaissance to find out, and again his men charged down the hill. The enemy was gone.[24]

For seven hours against odds of greater than four to one, Cleburne had used advantageous terrain, interior lines, and effective artillery fire to bolster first one threatened position then another, repelling three separate assaults by a determined foe. As night fell, he could begin to feel confident that for this day at least, the enemy would not drive him from the ridge. He had little time for self-congratulation, however, for even as his men returned from their twilight reconnaissance, a courier from Hardee rode up with an urgent message: Cleburne was to send all the troops he could spare to the center. Obediently, he ordered Cumming's and Maney's Brigades to follow him and was leading them personally when he met a second courier who brought astonishing news: the Rebel center had given way and the enemy was atop Missionary Ridge.

Amazingly, while Cleburne with a single reinforced division had held off the main Federal attack, Yankees mounting a diversionary assault on Breckinridge's front exceeded their orders, pushed on up the ridge line on their own initiative, and broke through the thinly manned Confederate lines on the crest. Hardee now ordered Cleburne to take personal command of the three divisions still left atop the ridge (his own, Stevenson's and Walker's) and "form a line across the ridge" to prevent the Federals from rolling up the whole Rebel line.[25]

Cleburne placed Walker's Division (temporarily under Brigadier General S. R. Gist) athwart the ridge as a blocking force and ordered that all vehicles be moved at once toward the bridge over the Chickamauga still being held by Lucius Polk's Brigade. It was full dark by now as Cleburne rode to each command to ensure that his orders were understood. As he approached one cluster of fires surrounded by a group of officers he called out, "What brigade is this?" Identifying Colonel James C. Nisbet commanding a regiment in Gist's Brigade, he addressed him quietly "Colonel Nisbet, what about these fires?" The colonel admitted that he had authorized cooking fires since his men had not eaten all day. Cleburne explained to him the disaster that had occurred in the center and the necessity of an immediate retirement. He wondered why the colonel seemed to be on his own. "Have you no orders?" he asked. "Where's General Gist?"

"I have no orders," the colonel told him. "I don't know where General Gist is."

"Well, said Cleburne, "the whole army is in retreat. I give you orders to withdraw your brigade and battery to Chickamauga Station, Western and Atlantic Railroad; there you will find rations in the depot." With that, he spurred off to find the next unit.[26]

As ever, Cleburne's Division served as the army's rear guard during the retreat. He ordered Lowrey, whose brigade was the least battered from the all-day fight, to launch a counterattack to clear the enemy pickets from in front of the ridge. Then, under the cover of that assault, the rest of his command fell back to the bridge. In the dark, with news of the disaster running through the ranks like electricity, not all commands maintained their discipline or unity. Cleburne later noted ruefully that there were "a few stragglers lingering here and there under the shadow of the trees for the purpose of being captured, faint-hearted patriots succumbing to the hardships of the war and the imagined hopelessness of the hour."[27]

With the exception of these stragglers, Cleburne shepherded the army off the ridge and back across the river. The precipitous retreat meant that huge stockpiles of supplies, especially food, would have to be abandoned. Reluctantly but without qualms, Cleburne ordered them burned. Soldiers who had been on short rations for two months were reluctant to obey. Cleburne's men helped themselves to all they could carry before lighting the bonfires. They emptied out the grain sacks and filled them with hardtack; a few slung sides of bacon over their shoulders. Then they set fire to the rest and started south.[28]

Cleburne rode alongside his troops on the march south. Only a few miles down the road, a young staff officer reined up with more verbal orders from Hardee. Cleburne was to abandon the rear guard, the young staffer explained, and march toward Graysville to fend off an expected Federal flank attack. Cleburne was skeptical. He did not know the staff officer personally and he questioned him sharply. Under this intense cross-examination, the officer admitted that he had not slept for two days and may have misunderstood the orders. Knowing that obedience to these curious and unexpected orders would leave the army's wagons entirely unprotected, Cleburne decided to ignore them. As events proved, the aide *had* misunderstood Hardee's instructions. Cleburne's decision to ignore them may have saved Bragg's army from destruction, and it also demonstrated both Cleburne's growing self-confidence and his willingness to make hard decisions.[29]

At about ten o'clock, nearly twelve hours after the first Federal assault that morning, Cleburne's Division arrived on the northern bank of the East Chickamauga Creek. Once across, his command would be relatively secure from the pursuing Federals. The bridge, however, had been burned and the river would have to be forded. One of Bragg's staff officers was waiting there and told Cleburne that Bragg wanted his men to wade through the river and then go into bivouac on the southern bank. He was to resume the march toward Ringgold Gap through Taylor's Ridge at 4:00 A.M. Again Cleburne was skeptical. He knew that if his men waded the freezing water of the East Chickamauga River and then spent the night sleeping on the ground without benefit of tents they would all become sick and some might even die. For the second time that afternoon, he ignored orders from the high command. He directed his men to go into bivouac where they were despite the chance that an aggressive Federal pursuit might catch them with their backs to the river and no viable line of retreat.[30]

A few hours after midnight, Cleburne was roused by a courier who brought new orders from Bragg: he was to position his command in Ringgold Gap and hold it "at all costs" until he was notified that the army's wagons had gotten safely away. The courier emphasized that these were "positive orders." Apparently Bragg was willing to purchase the security of the army's wagon train at the price of Cleburne's Division. Aware that these instructions could well result in the loss of his command, Cleburne asked the courier to put them in writing, and he sent Buck galloping ahead in the dark to find Bragg's headquarters for both confirmation and further instructions. Buck returned after midnight and reported that he had found an emotional Bragg in his command tent only half a dozen miles to the south. Bragg had been uncharacteristically demonstrative, grasping Buck's hand in both of his own and telling him that the salvation of the army depended on Cleburne and his division.[31]

Cleburne ordered reveille for 2:30 A.M. As the cold and groggy men assembled, they could see their commander, already mounted, contemplating the day's work. "Something is going to happen," one soldier muttered to another. "Why?" came the response. "Look at General Cleburne, don't you see war in his eyes?" Despite the cold—one soldier thought it was "the coldest night our thinly clad men had ever experienced"—Cleburne passed the order for the men to strip off their uniforms. As they prepared for the crossing, Cleburne sent volunteers across to the far side to build fires on the opposite bank. Then the men were herded across the river. The waist-deep water was bitterly cold, "thin sheets and crystals of ice were dancing over the water," recalled one veteran. "But thoughtful old Pat had big fires on the south side and [we] warmed some but dried little."[32]

His division safely across, Cleburne rode ahead to reconnoiter the pass that Bragg had ordered him to hold "at all hazards." It was still dark when he left the camp, and the sun was not fully up when he arrived at the small north Georgia town of Ringgold at the foot of Taylor's Ridge. He studied the terrain with considerable interest. On the one hand, the pass itself—Ringgold Gap—was a virtual Thermopylae: it was a steep, narrow passage barely wide enough to accommodate a small stream, the line of the Western and Atlantic Railroad, and a wagon road. In front of its western end, which he would have to defend, his troops would have an open field of fire. On the other hand, the ground to his rear, on the eastern side of the pass, was cut three times by a meandering stream so that in the event of a reversal his men would have to cross several bridges to make good an escape. He was as confident as ever that his own command could hold the pass, but several times previously, most recently on Missionary Ridge, he had held his own position only to be outflanked when the enemy advanced elsewhere. If it happened again, it occurred to him that his division would be in "a most dangerous position."[33]

The first of Cleburne's infantry to arrive was Liddell's Brigade, commanded by Govan since Liddell was still on leave. Cleburne personally supervised the deployment of the 5th/13th Arkansas, led by Colonel John E. Murray, across the entrance to the gap. Since Murray's single regiment literally filled the gap from side to side, Cleburne placed Govan's other three regiments behind it in support. Murray's men occupied a shallow ravine that provided both cover and concealment, and Cleburne put two Napoleon guns of Semple's Battery in their midst, again personally choosing the positions and ordering the gunners to erect a screen of bushes and shrubs to conceal their presence. A soldier in Murray's regiment recalled, "There was no fuss, no cheering or anything of that sort. Silence reigned, for Cleburne wanted to lay a trap."[34]

Granbury's Texans were the next to arrive, and Cleburne again deployed the regiments personally. He ordered two of them into a fringe of young trees to the right (north) of the gap, sending the 7th Texas onto the high ground to their rear with orders "to keep out of view but watch well the right flank." Polk's Brigade he sent marching through Govan's troops in the gap to guard the roads to the south, but he also told Polk to communicate with the 7th Texas in case of a Federal attempt to turn the right.[35]

The last to arrive was Lowrey's Brigade with the Federal advanced guard close on its heels. Cleburne sent three of Lowrey's regiments into the gap behind Govan's men, and the last, the 16th Alabama, he sent to the high ground on his left (south of the gap) with orders "to conceal itself and guard well the left flank." By this time, the Federals were already in the town of Ringgold and had deployed skirmishers to test the strength of the Confederate forces in the gap. Barely half an hour had transpired between the time the first Confederate troops arrived and the appearance of the Federals.[36]

Only minutes after giving these orders, and with most of his troops not yet in position, Cleburne watched as the Federals deployed in front of Ringgold for an attack. At about eight o'clock they advanced, a strong line of skirmishers in front and heavy lines of infantry behind. Cleburne, watching with the 5th/13th Arkansas from the mouth of the gap, noted that "they moved with the utmost decision and celerity." An artillery officer thought they advanced "with the beautiful order and precision characteristic of well-drilled troops." Closer and closer they came, breaking now into two wings, one heading for the gap itself and the other for the high ground to the north of it. To the soldiers in the ravine, the tension was unbearable. One recalled: "Seconds seemed like hours. We felt they would be on us before Cleburne ever gave the signal. Would he never give it?" Finally, with the enemy only 150 yards away, Cleburne shouted, "NOW, Lieutenant, give it to 'em!" The gunners pulled aside the brush in front of their two Napoleons and opened fire with shell and canister. The effect was galvanic. Colonel Murray noted that "the cannister seemed to strike about the center of the line, and scattered them like chaff before the wind." A private in the 6th/7th Arkansas was so excited by the spectacle that he jumped to his feet and exclaimed, "By Jove, boys, it killed them all!" Cleburne smiled and remarked calmly, "If you don't get down, young man, you are liable to find that there are enough left for you to get the top of your head shot off." The gunners got off "five or six rapid discharges" with the Napoleons, and Cleburne watched as the Federal right wing was broken to pieces, the survivors fleeing for the protection of the railroad embankment.[37]

If the Federal right wing was shattered, the left continued to advance, and soon the Yankees began to climb the high ground north of the gap where Cleburne had placed the 7th Texas. Cleburne sent a courier galloping down the gap to order Lucius Polk to reinforce that regiment. Polk ordered the 1st Arkansas to follow him and immediately set out on horseback. En route he encountered a straggler who told him that the Federals were already near the top. Polk ordered the 1st Arkansas to hurry and spurred up to the crest of the ridge. The Federal infantry was only twenty yards away and advancing. The men of the 1st Arkansas, puffing up the hill behind Polk, began firing even as they deployed. Polk ordered up a second regiment, and the fighting welled up into a full-scale battle.[38]

Cleburne, meanwhile, decided to send Lowrey to the right as well. As Lowrey recalled it, Cleburne told him, "Go upon that hill and see that the enemy don't turn my right!" Like Polk, Lowrey rode ahead of his troops to the crest of the ridge to find the 1st Arkansas "standing alone against a large force of the enemy." He saw they were about to give way under the pressure of the Federal attack and called out to them that his brigade was just behind him and would arrive soon. Thus reassured, they fought with renewed determination and managed to hold their ground until Lowrey's three regiments arrived. The tide of battle then shifted, and it was the Federals who gave way. "The enemy," Cleburne noted in his report, "went down the ridge in great confusion." Polk rushed up to Lowrey and gripped his hand in silent thanks for his timely arrival while all around them their troops cheered and tossed their caps. Lowrey thought it was "the most glorious triumph I ever witnessed on a battlefield."[39]

But the Federals were not through. They were soon back again, swinging further to the north trying to find a way around the Confederate flank. Polk and Lowrey merely shifted further to the right to meet them. The Yankees advanced through the woods in what one soldier called "a rollicking sort of way . . . whooping and yelling." As they closed to within range, the front line of Confederates fired a volley and then lay down to load while the second line fired. "Time after time, line after line of Federals charged up that ridge against Cleburne's lines," a soldier recalled, "only to be shattered and hurled back in[to] the valley."[40]

By midmorning the enemy had been repelled on all fronts, but they were not yet ready to give up. They attacked again at about eleven o'clock, this time on the left, assailing the ridgeline south of the pass where Cleburne had positioned the 16th Alabama. With much of his reserve employed on the right, Cleburne had few forces available to send to the left. Even so, this advance was also beaten back, the attackers fleeing down the hill. One of the Federal regiments left a stand of colors lying near a scrub apple tree a tantalizing sixty yards in front of the Confederate lines. Captain McGehee of the 2d Alabama pleaded for permission to dash out and retrieve the colors, but Cleburne would not allow it. "As it promised no solid advantage to compensate for the loss of brave soldiers," he wrote in his report, "I would not permit it." His decision in this case, as well as his actions throughout the day, proved how much he had matured from the reckless brigadier who had led his brigade to its near destruction at Shiloh.[41]

By noon, Cleburne's division had been in action almost continuously for four hours against a force that was perhaps three times its size. As he waited to see what the Federals might try next, he received a dispatch from Hardee.

It stated that the wagon trains were now well beyond any immediate danger and that he might safely withdraw. Before he made any decision about it, he consulted with Breckinridge who was present as an observer. Breckinridge advised a withdrawal as did General Wheeler the cavalry commander. Accepting their guidance, Cleburne decided to execute a staged withdrawal to a new position about a mile in the rear.[42]

To disguise his withdrawal, Cleburne ordered that the brush screen be re-erected in front of the artillery at the mouth of the gap, then he had the two Napoleon guns hauled away. The infantry followed, leaving only the skirmishers in place. This was the critical moment. If the Federals attacked now, they could easily overrun his position and perhaps inflict a decisive defeat on his division. The Federals did open an artillery barrage, but there was no infantry attack, and at two o'clock Cleburne recalled the skirmishers. As soon as his rear guard had crossed the bridges behind the gap, he ordered them burned.[43]

He was sitting his horse on the south bank of the river watching the last bridge burn when a pair of Confederate stragglers appeared on the far shore. They halted at the sight of the burning bridge that cut them off from their comrades, and Cleburne shouted across to them to use a ford a hundred yards upstream. One of them decided to risk the fire and dashed over the burning bridge, emerging with charred clothing and patting out his smoking hair. The other chose the ford and disappeared upriver, returning in a few minutes wet from the waist down. He turned out to be the Arkansan whom Cleburne had cautioned to lie down earlier that day. As he passed, he remarked, "General, that battery didn't kill quite all of them this morning, but what was left have been taught a lesson in good manners." Recognizing the man, Cleburne smiled and replied, "You are quite right, young man. I am proud of what you boys have done to-day, and I don't think they will bother us any more this evening." Noticing that the soldier was limping, he asked how badly he was hurt. Assured that he was only bruised by a spent bullet, Cleburne congratulated him on his escape.[44]

Cleburne was right; the Federals "showed no further inclination to attack." His men bivouacked two miles to the rear of Ringgold Gap, and he ordered them to build large fires. "Ah," thought one soldier in the 6th/10th Arkansas, "Old Pat wants us to be comfortable after our good day's work." But Cleburne ordered that fires be built well out beyond both flanks where there were no troops, and it became evident that the fires were for the benefit of the enemy. At about 9:00 P.M., he ordered the men to leave the fires burning and march southward to winter quarters just north of Dalton, Georgia. It was the last stage of the fall campaign. As at Missionary Ridge, Cleburne's Division at Ringgold Gap had held off forces three or four times their number and yet suffered relatively light casualties: 20 killed and 190 wounded. The men in the ranks knew that they had accomplished something special. One recalled with pride that "we knew we [had] won a signal victory." Another, more prosaically, wrote home that they had given the Yankees "a decent whippin.'"45

Cleburne and his division went into winter camp at another "Tunnel Hill," this one halfway between Ringgold Gap and Dalton, Georgia, where the rest of Bragg's army was quartered. Despite the achievements of Cleburne's Division, Bragg could not disguise the fact that his army had suffered an appalling defeat, and on 27 November he sent Davis his formal resignation. The president accepted it at once and placed Hardee in temporary command of the army. Despite his resignation, Bragg was not inclined to accept the responsibility and characteristically blamed the defeat on his enemies within the army. To a friend, Bragg wrote, "The whole clamor against me was by a few individuals of rank and their immediate partisans who were actuated by one of two motives—*Ambition* and *Revenge.*" As for Cleburne, not only was he delighted by the change in command, he was the recipient of a flood of congratulations. Bragg specially commended him in his report to Davis; Congress passed a resolution of thanks; even the Federals offered a tribute of sorts when one Union commander explained the reversal at Ringgold Gap by reporting that, after all, Cleburne's Division "was reputed as the best in Bragg's army."46

Basking in such praise, Cleburne sat down in the second week of December to write his own report on the fall campaign. As usual he praised his subordinates, especially his brigade commanders—Polk, Lowrey, Govan and Granbury—claiming that "four better officers are not to be found in the service of the Confederacy." In addition, however, he allowed himself a few literary flourishes. About Ringgold Gap, for example, he wrote that when the enemy attacked, "our immense [wagon] train was still in view, struggling through the fords of the creek . . . and my division, silent, but cool and ready, was the only barrier between it and the flushed and eager advance of the pursuing Federal army." He was so proud of his report that he invited passing officers to come into his tent to listen to him read portions of it aloud.47

Not only had Cleburne emerged from this campaign as the "Stonewall of the West," he was also emerging from the shell of enigmatic reserve that had marked his personality from the moment of his arrival in Helena. He was as intense as ever and continued to take his responsibilities with uncompromising seriousness, but in addition he was now capable of unbending once in a while. Liddell returned from leave and reported his arrival at headquarters, where he found Cleburne raging about the impertinence of a local farmer who had agreed to sell forage to the army but was now demanding more money. Cleburne told Liddell, "I threatened to blow a hole thro' the fellow as big as a Barn Door." Liddell laughed aloud, and Cleburne was provoked to insist, "D——d if I would not have done it!" Liddell then explained that he did not doubt Cleburne's resolve, he merely wondered at the sheer size of a man who could accommodate a hole the size of a barn door. Liddell wrote that Cleburne "saw at once the bull he had made and relaxing the sternness of his features, joined in the laugh, fully restored to good humor."[48]

PART THREE

AN HONEST HEART
AND A STRONG ARM

10

"A PLAN WHICH WE BELIEVE WILL SAVE OUR COUNTRY"

Patrick Cleburne was a true believer. In the summer of 1861, when he took up arms alongside his friends and neighbors and went to war, he had acted in the sincere conviction that a resort to military force was necessary to preserve his society from the tyranny of a hostile government. Lincoln's election to the presidency, in spite of nearly universal southern disapproval, had proved that the South had lost its ability to control, or possibly even to influence, the policies of that government. Even then, it was the administration's decision to use force to compel the southern states to remain in the Union that had convinced him to take up the cause of the South lest Arkansas become little more than a subject province. To his brother in Cincinnati, Cleburne had professed his belief that "the North is about to wage a brutal and unholy war on a people who have done them no wrong. . . . They [northerners] no longer acknowledge that all government derives its validity from the consent of the governed." The extent to which he was swept up by the rhetoric of the day was evident in his passionate insistence that "they are about to invade our peaceful homes, destroy our property, and inaugurate a servile insurrection, murder our men and dishonor our women."[1]

Two and a half years of war did not diminish his passion or his resolve. If anything, he was more committed to the war in the winter of 1863–1864 than he had been in the crisis summer of 1861. Moreover, the intensity of his commitment had gradually recentered his frame of reference. Just as he had wedded himself to the values and ideals of frontier Helena in the 1850s, so too did he absorb and reflect the values of the martial community of which he was now a part. If his commitment to Arkansas had made him a soldier, the experience of soldiering had made him a Confederate. His effort to organize the Comrades of the Southern Cross was evidence of his faith in the indomitability of a righteous cause. As far as he was concerned, the object of the war was the defense of self-government; it was a struggle for liberty, independence, and, in his own words, the right of men "to live under laws of their own making." He spoke with the voice of a conservative Whig rather than a radical revolutionary when he insisted that the real issue was Lincoln's apparent determination "to subjugate and enslave the whole Southern people and divide their property among his vulgar unprincipled mob." It was more than rhetoric to him; he accepted at face value the claim that the issue of the war was the right of every person to govern himself. He had taken up arms in support of that principle; he would not lay them down again until the goal had been achieved. "An honest heart and a strong arm," he wrote, "should never succumb."[2]

Of course he was aware that the political *issue* that had provoked the break—and the war—was slavery. But for him, at least, that was not the *principle* that was at stake. "I never owned a Negro," he wrote to his brother, "and care nothing for them." Almost certainly, he viewed Lincoln's Emancipation Proclamation with a cynic's eye. Here was one more grotesque effort by the tyrant to "inaugurate a servile insurrection" in order to further his goal of subjugation. For Pat Cleburne, slavery was incidental to the conflict, a transparent justification put forward by Republicans to promote their war of conquest. If southerners ever had to choose between securing their own freedom and maintaining their system of slavery, he had no doubt that his friends and neighbors, indeed the entire South, would willingly let slavery expire in order to ensure their own political independence.[3]

He was wrong. Indeed, his misunderstanding of the South's emotional and psychological commitment to the peculiar institution marked him unmistakably as an outsider. For all his effort to become fully integrated into the culture of his adopted land, he never fully grasped the complicated role of slavery in southern society. It proved to be a fatal error.

Bragg left the Army of Tennessee on the second of December. Though some in the rank and file made a show of regret at his departure, Cleburne did not. Indeed, his optimism soared, partly because he had implicit confidence in Hardee, who now assumed temporary command of the army. In addition, he was the recipient of continued official and unofficial congratulations for the performance of his division on the battlefield. Even so, his staffers were surprised to note that Cleburne was "unusually communicative," willing, even eager, to discuss the recent campaign and commenting freely on what he called Bragg's "military mis-management." Indeed, for him, Cleburne was downright garrulous. As officers passed by his headquarters, he invited certain of them in to sit and listen to an idea he had been working on to address the army's other great problem—its apparently insurmountable numerical inferiority to the Union armies.[4]

Increasingly since the first summer of the war, the conflict had become a numbers game. Confederate armies routinely confronted much larger Union armies, and even when they overcame the odds to win battles, the casualties were often more than the southern army or, indeed southern society, could sustain. The previous May, for example, Lee's Army of Northern Virginia had routed Hooker's Army of the Potomac and inflicted 11,116 casualties while suffering "only" 10,746 of its own. But as a percentage of the available forces, Federal losses came to just over 11 percent, while Confederate losses represented 18.7 percent: In a long war, this was a numbers game the South could not win. The root of the problem was a simple matter of demographics: The eleven states that seceded to form the Confederacy had a total population of just over 9 million; the population of the loyal states was 22 million. Even worse from the southern point of view was that over a third of the Confederacy's population (3.52 million) consisted of black slaves. That left the Union States with a 4 to 1 superiority in available military manpower. In addition, German and (to Cleburne's disgust) Irish immigrants were being inducted into the Union armies quite literally at the water's edge as they arrived in America.[5]

In an effort to keep up with the expanding war, the Confederacy had found it necessary to initiate a conscription program as early as the spring of 1862. Although philosophically at odds with the South's veneration of states' rights, the move was unavoidable if the new government were to survive the second summer of the war. The original conscription act had obligated all males ages eighteen to thirty-five to serve in the army; since then the government had raised the upper age limit to forty-five. There were few left now who could be called to arms, and the Confederate armies were dwindling to a fraction of their former strength. Morale was down; desertion was up. The Army of Tennessee was reduced to no more than 35,000 effectives. Although Cleburne still believed in the moral ascendancy of right over might, he was enough of a realist to recognize that the South might soon be literally overwhelmed by armies in blue. It was hardly an original insight. Several weeks earlier, a junior officer in Cleburne's command had noted in his diary, "The Confederacy wants more men. Lee wants men. Bragg wants men. They are wanted everywhere; but where are they to come from?" To Cleburne the answer was self-evident—the only realistic option was to mobilize the South's black population.[6]

Cleburne did not come to this conclusion suddenly or without serious consideration. He had been mulling it over at least since the previous spring. At Wartrace in April 1863 he had been engaged in conversation with St. John Liddell when he suddenly asked, "Would you be willing to give up slavery for the independence and recognition of the South?" Liddell replied at once, "Willingly!" Cleburne told Liddell that he had been giving the subject a great deal of thought and wondered what support there would be for arming slaves and putting black regiments in the field. At the time he had kept the idea largely to himself. Now, however, it seemed to him that it was time to address the question openly. That very month, Cleburne's old political ally Tom Hindman wrote to the Memphis *Appeal* (publishing out of Atlanta since Memphis was occupied) to argue that the Confederacy should arm some of the South's most courageous slaves and grant them their freedom in exchange. After all, the Yankees were using black troops, adding even more to their numerical superiority—some twenty black Union regiments had been organized in the western theater alone. Surely, Cleburne thought, slaves bred in the South would fight better under the leadership of southern officers—men to whom they were accustomed to giving both deference and obedience—than they did under Yankee officers. The image of half a million fresh troops committed to the war blinded him to a full appreciation of the impact that such a proposal would have on the southern Confederacy. It was not only a social, political, and cultural revolution; to many, it was treason.[7]

In the second week of December, as the troops set to work constructing winter quarters near Tunnel Hill seven miles north of the main army encampment at Dalton, Captain Buck noticed that Cleburne was spending many hours alone in his tent "preoccupied and engaged in writing." Eventually, Cleburne invited Buck to read the document he had been working on and asked for his opinions. It was nothing less than a proposal that the South immediately recruit black slaves into the army and grant them their freedom in exchange. Buck was cautiously skeptical, remarking that the slaveholding class might not be willing to give up its slaves. In any event, he said, the proposal was certain to be extremely controversial and was likely to jeopardize Cleburne's possible promotion to corps command. If Buck hoped that such an argument would deter his commander, he misread his man. Cleburne declared that "a crisis was on the South" and that it was "his duty" to do whatever he could to avert it "irrespective of any result to himself." Trying another tack, Buck suggested that it seemed improbable that slaves would make good soldiers. Again Cleburne disagreed, insisting that "with reasonable and carefull drilling" he had "no doubt" they could be made into efficient soldiers. If no other officer was willing to command them, he declared, he would gladly assume command of "a Negro division" himself. If Buck was skeptical, Cleburne's chief of staff, Calhoun Benham, was positively appalled. When Benham failed to convince Cleburne that he should shelve the proposal, he asked for a copy of it so he could prepare a rebuttal. Since Cleburne's purpose was to encourage a full and open consideration of his proposal, he readily consented and asked Buck to make a copy for Benham's use.[8]

Two days after Christmas—"a very *sober,* quiet Christmas," according to Buck—Hardee turned command of the army over to Joseph E. Johnston, with Hardee reverting to corps command. The trim, dapper new commander announced himself to the troops in a formal address that same day, and almost at once the Army of Tennessee seemed to find new confidence. Despite a decidedly mixed record as a field commander, Johnston exuded a calm confidence and professionalism that went a long way toward restoring morale. Cleburne thought that perhaps the time had come to make his proposal formally.

The very next day, he was in his tent fine-tuning his written proposal when Captain Thomas Key stopped by for a visit. In addition to commanding a battery of Cleburne's divisional artillery, Key was also an acquaintance from Helena where he had edited a newspaper. Key had scarcely seated himself when Cleburne asked him what he thought about the idea of drilling and arming as many as 300,000 black slaves and putting them in the army. Key was taken aback both by the idea and by Cleburne's evident enthusiasm for it. He suggested that slaves might not be willing to put their lives on the line for the Confederacy, for they had nothing to gain by doing so. To be sure, Cleburne responded, which was why slaves who volunteered to serve would be granted their immediate freedom. Not only that, he declared, but freedom would have to be granted to their wives and children as well, for no man could be expected to fight for a government that kept his family enslaved. "Would the Negroes fight?" Key asked. Cleburne insisted that they "could be induced to fight as gallantly as the Yankees." Besides, he argued, such a step would completely undercut the Republican claim that the war was being fought to free the slaves, and it would attract diplomatic support from Europe. Key had other objections. Would not such a scheme mean the virtual end of slavery in the South? Probably, Cleburne admitted, but was not independence worth the sacrifice? Key listened respectfully but secretly thought the notion a pipe dream. He later noted in his diary that while many in the army agreed that peace and liberty were "paramount," the principal motivation for southern soldiers "whose veins throb with the proud blood of Anglo Saxons" was the fear that "if the Yankee subjugate his country, his sister, wife, and mother are to be given up to the embraces of their present 'dusky male servitors.'"[9]

Cleburne was completely undeterred by the skepticism he encountered from Buck, Benham, and Key. He continued to polish the arguments in his formal proposal, which had grown by now to more than two dozen pages, and he decided to try it out on his brigade and regimental commanders. Their reaction was much more positive; indeed, many endorsed the idea with enthusiasm, though it is likely that at least some of that enthusiasm was a product of the respect and loyalty they felt for their commander. Cleburne asked Buck to write out a fair copy of the document and invited as many of his own officers to sign it as wished to do so. Both Govan and Lowrey signed, as did their regimental commanders. So did Brigadier General John H. Kelly, who commanded a division of cavalry and who at age twenty-three was the youngest general officer in the army. Polk and Granbury were not at hand when the clean copy was ready or they would also have signed, but both men gave Cleburne their permission to express their support. Thus armed, Cleburne asked Hardee to request a meeting of the army's general officers to present his petition. Hardee sent memos to all corps and division commanders on 2 January asking them to "meet him at General Johnston's headquarters" that evening at 7:00 P.M.[10]

Quite likely, Cleburne and Benham rode the seven miles from Tunnel Hill to Dalton together. Before going to Johnston's headquarters, they met up with Hindman, and the three arrived together a few minutes before the appointed hour. A half dozen other officers were already there. They talked casually for a few minutes while still more arrived, and then, once everyone was settled, Johnston asked Hardee to explain the purpose of the meeting. Hardee stated simply that Cleburne had prepared a paper "on an important subject" and had requested the meeting in order to present it. All eyes turned to the Irishman from Arkansas. Without formal preamble, Cleburne read his prepared script. He read slowly and emphatically, perhaps stopping periodically to assess the reaction of his listeners. He spoke in the first person plural, assuming the role of spokesman for the fourteen officers who had attached their names to the document.[11]

"The subject is grave," he declared, "and our views so new, we feel it a duty both to you and the cause that before going further we should submit them for your judgement and receive your suggestions in regard to them." Hardee, Hindman, and a few others in the room were aware of what was coming, but the rest were not. "We have now been fighting for nearly three years," Cleburne noted, yet the enemy occupies a third of our country and "menacingly confronts us at every point with superior forces." The conclusion was inescapable: "If this state continues much longer we must be subjugated." Although the Confederacy had only its own white population to call upon, the northern tyrant had three sources of manpower: "his own motley population; secondly, our slaves; and thirdly, Europeans whose hearts are fired into a crusade against us by fictitious pictures of the atrocities of slavery." Slavery, Cleburne insisted, had become a handicap—"our most vulnerable point, a continued embarrassment, and in some respects an insideous [*sic*] weakness."[12]

By now, everyone in the room must have guessed the direction of Cleburne's argument. But how far would he take it? Cleburne did not rush to his conclusion. He first listed all the other sources from which the South might gain additional manpower: putting wagon drivers, nurses, and cooks into the ranks; rounding up malingerers; and forbidding the practice of substitution. The draft might be extended to include those from seventeen to fifty. But even all of these measures, Cleburne argued, would be insufficient to halt the Federal juggernaut and would at best be "a temporary expedient" that would cripple the southern economy by stripping it of its skilled labor. There was no viable alternative; therefore, "we propose that we immediately commence training a large reserve of the most courageous of our slaves, and further that we guarantee freedom within a reasonable time to every slave in the South who shall remain true to the Confederacy in this war." Challengingly he declared, "As between the loss of independence and the loss of slavery, we assume that every patriot will freely give up the latter—give up the negro slave rather than be a slave himself."

If his audience reacted to the revelation of his proposal, it is not recorded. In any event, Cleburne was not finished. Like the lawyer he was, he had compiled not merely a proposal but a brief. He talked for another twenty minutes, outlining both the compelling reasons for adopting such a course and the many benefits that would result: the sympathy and possible friendship of England and France; the elimination of a motive for southern Negroes to fight for the Union armies; the exposure as a sham of the northern crusade to eliminate slavery in the South. In addition to giving the South numerical superiority on the battlefield, Cleburne declared, "The measure will at one blow strip the enemy of foreign sympathy and assistance and transfer them to the South; it will dry up two of his three sources of recruiting; it will take from his negro army the only motive it could have to fight against the South, and will probably cause much of it to desert over to us; [and] it will deprive his cause of the powerful stimulus of fanaticism."

Some of these arguments stretched credulity, but Cleburne was only getting started. In an effort to demonstrate how much the South had to gain by freeing its slaves and putting them in the army, he offered up a portrait of slavery itself that was more compatible with Lincoln's vision than it was with that of any slaveholder. "For many years," he declared, "ever since the agitation of the subject of slavery commenced, the negro has been dreaming of freedom, and his vivid imagination has surrounded that condition with so many gratifications that it has become the paradise of his hopes. To attain it he will tempt dangers and difficulties not exceeded by the bravest soldier in the field." Such assertions were not likely to win the sympathy of skeptical officers, many of whom were themselves slaveholders. Plantation masters asserted as a matter of course that slavery was the natural condition of the black race, that Negroes were happy in that condition and wanted no other. Their acceptance of slavery as their natural status was the reason cited for the rarity of slave rebellions in the Old South—and the reason why John Brown could not incite blacks to rebel in 1859. As one South Carolina planter had put it years earlier, slaves were "a peaceful, kind-hearted, and affectionate race; satisfied with their lot, happy in their comforts, and devoted to their masters."[13] Slaves, southerners insisted, preferred being slaves. Moreover, Cleburne's notion that a black man could be "the bravest soldier in the field" was to impute to blacks not only martial skills but the status of manhood, a condition that most slaveowners were unwilling to concede.

Cleburne's logic led him step by step to an unavoidable conclusion. To arm the slaves was dangerous to be sure; "therefore when we make soldiers of them we must make free men of them beyond all question." The South must free the slaves' wives and children, must sanctify marriages, and must give legal status to their paternity. Although such measures would undercut the institution of slavery itself, Cleburne did not hesitate to propose the final step: "If, then, we touch the institution at all, we would do best to make the most of it . . . by emancipating the whole race." Anticipating the argument that without slavery the agricultural economy of the South would collapse, Cleburne argued that it was not true that only blacks could perform agricultural labor in the South. Just look at the accomplishments of the Army of Tennessee. These white soldiers had marched dozens of miles a day and fought bravely and tenaciously in the heat of the summer, thus proving that they could labor in the worst of conditions. Again, this was an argument more likely to inflame than convince, since few southerners were cheered to hear that white men could do the work of slaves. The more Cleburne talked and the more he pressed his case, the more he challenged the fundamental assumptions and values of his audience.

After speaking for over half an hour, Cleburne arrived at his peroration: "It is said [that] slavery is all we are fighting for, and if we give it up we give up all. Even if this were true, which we deny, slavery is not all our enemies are fighting for. It is merely the pretense to establish sectional superiority and a more centralized form of government, and to deprive us of our rights and liberties. We have now briefly proposed a plan which we believe will save our country. It may be imperfect, but in all human probability it would give us our independence. No objection ought to outweigh it which is not weightier than independence." Having finished, Cleburne sat down.

By prearrangement, Hindman was the first to respond. He argued that the only alternative to Cleburne's proposal was to enlist boys and old men, and he suggested that at the very least blacks should be employed as cooks, wagon drivers, and laborers to free up more white men for the front lines. Next Cleburne's chief of staff, Calhoun Benham, read the rebuttal he had prepared. As befitted a junior officer, his criticism was respectful, though he asserted that Cleburne's proposal challenged the most fundamental assumptions of southern society.

If Cleburne was disappointed by the lack of enthusiastic support, he soon heard much worse. William Bate, Patton Anderson, and especially W. H. T. Walker all made emotional attacks on Cleburne's proposal. Their exact comments at the meeting went unrecorded, but in subsequent correspondence they were scathing. Bate declared that Cleburne's proposals were "hideous and objectionable," and he branded them as nothing less than "the serpent of Abolitionism." He predicted that the army would mutiny at the very suggestion of such a scheme. Anderson called it a "monstrous proposition" that was "revolting to Southern sentiment, Southern pride, and Southern honor." He also predicted that if black troops were enlisted, the white troops would all quit in disgust. He was shocked that such a proposal came from a man whom he considered "one of our bravest and most accomplished officers" and feared that it would bring down on Cleburne "the universal indignation of the Southern people and Southern soldiers." Walker was the most offended, asserting that the proposal was nothing less than treason, and that any officer advocating it should be held fully accountable.[14]

Cleburne did not argue his case further. He was disappointed by the reaction his proposal had evoked and surprised by its intensity and hostility. The army commander, General Johnston, declared that Cleburne's "Memorial" would not be forwarded to Richmond. Indeed, no one was even to discuss it beyond that room. Whatever personal views Johnston may have had about Cleburne's proposals, he was enough of a realist to see that pushing such a proposal was likely to provoke at least as many problems as it solved, and he ordered everyone to keep it secret.

That was not good enough for Walker. Known as "Old Shot Pouch" for the many wounds he had taken in the Mexican War, Walker was a pedantic and literal-minded stickler for detail. Liddell described him as "a crackbrained fire-eater, always captious or cavilling about something." Declaring that it was his duty as a patriot to bring this outrageous document to the attention of the president, he asked Cleburne for a copy of it, telling him candidly that he planned to forward it to Richmond to expose Cleburne's seditious views. Cleburne instantly agreed. To his friends, Cleburne explained that this way he could be sure his proposal would be heard in the highest councils of the government. In addition, he would have considered it dishonorable not to accept full responsibility for any of his words or deeds. Given the reaction to his proposal by the army's high-ranking officers, he must have suspected that it was not likely to be particularly welcome in Richmond, and that there might be many more who, like Anderson, Bate, and Walker, viewed it as seditious. Still, he had written it, and he would stand by it. He had Buck prepare yet another copy and signed his name at the bottom. He deliberately omitted the names of the others who had signed the earlier version because he was unwilling that they should share the burden of the government's retribution if it came to that.[15]

Walker still was not satisfied and wrote to every officer who had attended the 2 January meeting demanding that each man declare "whether you favor the proposition and sentiments of the document in any form." Though Hardee, Hindman and others did favor at least some aspects of Cleburne's proposal, none would admit to it in writing. Clearly irritated by Walker's sanctimonious assumption of responsibility as the South's cultural guardian, Hindman replied, "I do not choose to admit any inquisitorial rights in you." Then he penned a quick note to Johnston warning the army commander of Walker's evident determination to disobey his order to keep the document a secret. When Walker asked Johnston for permission to send a copy of Cleburne's "Memorial" to the president, Johnston turned him down. Walker sent it anyway, entrusting it to Congressman Herschel V. Johnson of Georgia who promised to hand-carry it to Richmond. Walker's excuse for violating the chain of command was "the gravity of the subject" and his conviction that "further agitation on such sentiments" would "involve our cause in ruin and disgrace."[16]

Within the army, secrecy was maintained. Only now and again did rumor of the meeting seep out. After securing a pledge of confidentiality from Colonel James Nisbet, Brigadier General Clement H. Stevens told him the secret of Cleburne's astonishing proposal. Stevens suggested that although Cleburne was "a skilled army officer, and true to the Southern cause," he did not have "a proper conception of the Negro, he being foreign born and reared." When Nisbet responded that he thought arming slaves was a good idea, Stevens exploded. Slavery, he declared, was the cause of the war and the reason why the South was fighting. "If slavery is to be abolished then I take no more interest in our fight. The justification of slavery in the South is the inferiority of the negro. If we make him a soldier, we concede the whole question." Stevens's outburst was evidence of how badly Cleburne had misread the society he called his own. Cleburne's assumption that "every patriot will freely give up . . . the negro slave rather than be a slave himself" failed to take into consideration the fact that many southerners viewed the loss of slavery as virtually synonymous with the loss of their own liberty. As James McPherson has asserted in *What They Fought For,* "most Confederate soldiers believed that they were fighting for liberty *and* slavery, one and inseparable." [17]

While Walker's package—like a ticking bomb—made its way to Richmond in the care of Congressman Johnson, Cleburne embarked on quite a different journey, one that was to have an equally profound impact on his life. Several months earlier, Hardee had confided to him that while on detached duty in Alabama he had fallen in love and become engaged. Now that the army was safely ensconced in winter camp, he intended to travel to Mobile and marry his fiancée. He asked Cleburne to travel with him and act as his best man. Cleburne agreed at once.

Cleburne took two weeks' leave—his first since the war began—and he and Hardee departed in the second week of January, boarding the dilapidated cars of the Western and Atlantic Railroad in Dalton for the slow, jolting trip to Atlanta. There they shifted to the Atlanta and West Point Railroad, traveling southwest through West Point and Opelika to Montgomery, where the Confederate government had been born in the hopeful spring of 1861. At Montgomery, where the railroad ran out, they boarded a river steamer, cruising down the Alabama River to Selma, where they stopped at the home of Dr. Charles Nash, Cleburne's former partner in the Drugstore of Nash and Cleburne. Nash hosted a dinner for his distinguished visitors to which he also invited the officers of a Confederate naval ship under construction at the Basset Shipworks in Selma. Hardee was in a jovial mood and told a number of stories that kept the guests entertained. Then he turned to Nash. "Doctor," he asked, "can't you give us one on Cleburne, as he says you were young men together and particular friends?"

"Yes, sir," Nash replied. "I can give you a good horse joke on him." Knowing what was coming, Cleburne protested: "Doctor, don't tell that." But, of course, he did.

It seems that one fall day during Cleburne's first year in Helena, he was invited to go riding, and he had asked Nash if he could borrow his horse. Nash told him that his horse was "a wild and unruly animal" and hard to control. Cleburne assumed that Nash was merely putting him off. "Doctor, if you don't want to lend me your horse, say so, but don't say I cannot ride him." Nash capitulated, and soon afterward Cleburne left on his ride. Outside Helena, however, Cleburne's companion kicked his horse into a gallop, and Cleburne's borrowed mount took the bit in his teeth and answered with a burst of speed as if engaged in a race. Cleburne could not control his mount, and he hung on for dear life as they dashed cross-country over fences and streams. Cleburne lost his hat and feared losing his seat. Finally, he leaned forward, took hold of the horse's nose, and turned him toward a nearby lake, hoping to "mire him up, and jump off." The plan succeeded, but in leaping from the horse's back, Cleburne landed in mud up to his waist. He returned, hatless and muddy, leading the horse. As he passed the reins to Nash, he remarked: "I can't tell which got the best of it, he or I. I shall part company with him, he wants his way and I mine. I am satisfied to let him have it in the future." As Nash finished the story, the guests gave way to general laughter, and Nash recalled that "no one enjoyed it more than Cleburne." [18]

The next morning, Hardee and Cleburne continued their journey, coasting downriver until they arrived at the small landing for Bleak House plantation, the home of Major Ivey Lewis, his wife, and his sister Mary, the thin, dark-haired young woman of twenty-six who was to become Mrs. William J. Hardee. Despite its isolated location, Bleak House was a center of culture that would rival many of the salons of Boston. Mary Lewis had studied in both France and Germany and had returned just before the outbreak of war with an extensive art collection. At Bleak House, there were carpets on the floors, a piano in the parlor, and servants with lighted lamps to help the visitors negotiate the path from the river landing to the big house. [19]

The wedding, held on the evening of 13 January, was an elegant affair despite a cold winter rain that ruined the slippers and hems of many of the female guests. Cleburne was dazzled; it was such a dramatic contrast to the dreary winter quarters at Tunnel Hill. He was dazzled, too, by the beauty, refinement, and self-possession of the young women in attendance—especially the maid of honor, twenty-four-year-old Susan Tarleton of Mobile, who stood across from him during the ceremony. In addition to the charms of the young woman herself, Cleburne could not help but be affected by the romance of the occasion: the candle-lit surroundings and the example being set by Hardee. He was instantly and hopelessly smitten. He was attentive to Miss Tarleton throughout the evening, and before the celebration wound down late that night and the guests retired to their rooms, he begged permission to call upon her. Sue Tarleton was nearly as shy as her suitor and somewhat flustered to be the object of such unfeigned adoration by a celebrated Confederate hero who was dressed impeccably in his best full dress uniform. Nevertheless, she consented.[20]

The next day, the entire wedding party traveled downriver to Mobile and stayed at the Battle House Hotel. Almost as if the spirit of the ceremony at Bleak House had been transported with them, the weather cleared, the sun came out, and the mud dried up. "We are authorized to declare that winter has broken," exulted the editor of the Mobile paper. In Mobile, the Hardees were hosted at several dinners attended by the wedding party. This included both Cleburne and Sue Tarleton as well as Sue's older brother Robert and her younger sister Grace. Those four, plus Sallie Lightfoot (a friend of Sue's) and Henry Goldthwaite (a friend of Robert's) became a nearly inseparable social group. Robert Tarleton, as it turned out, had attended Princeton at the same time as Cleburne's former law partner and current aide-de-camp Learned Mangum, and Henry Goldthwaite was first cousin to an officer in Cleburne's Division whom Cleburne had cited for gallantry at Chickamauga. While Cleburne paid fond attention to Sue Tarleton, Robert was equally dutiful to Sallie Lightfoot, and Henry Goldthwaite waited on Grace Tarleton. At the Tarleton home on the corner of St. Louis and Claiborne Streets, the six of them talked, went for walks, or sang while Sue played the piano in the parlor. As the oldest and most celebrated, Cleburne may have been more at ease on these occasions than he was in most social circumstances. It did not hurt his campaign to impress Miss Tarleton that the Mobile *Daily Advertiser and Register* ran a story about the "gallant Irishman" who was "now in our city." The paper noted that it was Cleburne who "seems to have been the real hero in the late fight at Chattanooga."[21]

Cleburne's celebrity status was confirmed on Sunday, 23 January, when the Mobile garrison held a formal review of the troops in his honor. Riding alongside the garrison commander, Major General Dabney Maury, Cleburne again wore his best uniform. Reporting on the occasion for its readers, the local paper described the guest of honor as "a tall and rather slender officer, with erect form but slightly bowed shoulders, a finely shaped head, with features prominent and striking—the firm set lip, betokening resolution and will." All too soon, however, Cleburne's two weeks were up, and he had to return to Dalton. Before he left, he asked Sue to marry him. She would not give him an immediate answer, but she did give him permission to write to her and promised that she would write him too. On the trip back, Cleburne stopped again at Nash's home in Selma and confessed to Nash that "he fell in love with Miss Sue on first sight" and that he intended to marry her.[22]

Cleburne arrived back in Dalton in the last days of January in wet and cold weather and received a friendly welcome from his staff. Buck had written home just the day before that he was eager for Cleburne's return. "Gen'l [Lucius] Polk is in command during his absence," Buck wrote, "and is a nice gentleman & good soldier, but still he is not 'old Pat.' " Within days of his return, "Old Pat" proved that he had not forgotten his plan to arm the South's slaves. Indeed, even while in Mobile he had found time to discuss the idea with "the wealthy men of Alabama" (probably Major Lewis) and was satisfied that "many advocated the measure and believed that it would redound to the advantage of the South." Back in Dalton, he wrote an admirer that "once our people . . . sincerely value independence above *every other earthly consideration,* then I will regard our success as an accomplished fact." He told Congressman A. S. Colyar of Tennessee that the arming of the South's slave population was not only a military necessity but a social imperative as well. Colyar wrote his cousin that Cleburne's "great argument is that if the Yankees succeed in abolishing slavery, equality and amalgamation will finally take place." But if the southern states took the action themselves, some semblance of the old relationship between the races could be maintained.[23]

That same week, Walker's copy of Cleburne's "Memorial" arrived on Jefferson Davis's desk in Richmond. Davis saw at once that this was a potential bombshell for his administration. He had just received a letter from his estranged vice president, Alexander Stephens, in which the Georgian asserted that the real crisis in the Confederacy was not a shortage of manpower, but Davis's wartime policies that undercut traditional southern values. Privately, Davis thought Stephens a crank, but he knew that the vice president represented a widely held view. Even the slightest hint that his administration was considering arming slaves was certain to provoke a firestorm of protest that could rip the Confederacy apart. Davis therefore directed "the suppression, not only of the memorial itself, but any discussion or controversy growing out of it." Seddon wrote the order and in it praised Walker's "zeal and patriotism" for bringing the issue to the attention of the executive. As for Cleburne, Seddon declared that "no doubt or mistrust is for a moment entertained of the patriotic intents of the gallant author of the memorial," but he also noted that the issue was not one that was appropriate for military officers to consider.[24]

Johnston dutifully passed the word to his corps and division commanders, quoting liberally from Seddon's letter. He added a postscript for Cleburne asking him to communicate the president's views to those brigade and regimental officers in his division who had signed the memorial, and Cleburne did so, making sure to include those junior officers, like Buck and Key, to whom he had confided his plan. Once all had been pledged to secrecy, the issue disappeared—as did the document. Only a single copy (the one Buck had made for Calhoun Benham) survived, and for the rest of the war and for a quarter century afterward, the very existence of Cleburne's proposal was a closely held secret.[25]

It did contribute to a few minor changes. Johnston approved a general order that authorized commanders to use slaves as teamsters and cooks and to transfer the white soldiers who had been doing those duties to the front lines. But none of the slaves so engaged would receive his freedom, and certainly none of them was to be armed.

There was at least one more long-term consequence. Davis and Seddon were no doubt sincere when they declared that "no doubt or mistrust" should adhere to the author, but it soon became evident that not everyone agreed. When Bragg heard about Cleburne's proposal he was "jubilant," for he was still chafing at what he considered his own bad treatment by his "enemies" in the Army of Tennessee, and he saw that this proposal of Cleburne's would discredit them. To an ally he wrote: "A great sensation is being produced by the Emancipation project of Hardee, Cheatham, Cleburne & Co. It will kill them." That same month, Davis named Bragg as his official military adviser, charging him "with the conduct of military operations in the armies of the Confederacy" and granting to him many of the powers formerly exercised by the secretary of war. It was a position of tremendous influence, particularly in terms of officer promotions. Ten days after assuming these new duties, Bragg wrote privately that Cleburne and those who supported him were "agitators, and should be watched." To ensure that his point was unmistakable, he added ominously, "We must mark the men."[26]

Hardee returned to Dalton from his honeymoon in the first week of February bringing his new bride with him. Cleburne visited the happy couple the morning after their arrival and had breakfast with them. Buck, who accompanied Cleburne on his visit, decided that General Hardee "has shown his usual good sense in his selection of a wife." To Cleburne the Hardees' example of domestic bliss was further proof, if any were needed, that marriage was a condition much to be desired, and his delight at the prospect of a marital union with Sue Tarleton balanced his disappointment at the failure of his proposal to arm the South's black population. Indeed, Buck reported to his sister that his boss was in "a heavenly mood." Rumors were already afoot at headquarters that Cleburne had "lost his heart with a young lady in Mobile," and his staff officers looked at one another knowingly as he talked offhandedly about the possibility of taking another leave soon.[27]

Meanwhile, however, the manpower problems remained unresolved. If the Army of Tennessee had to fight the war with white soldiers only, it must have all of them. Enlistments were expiring, and the army's commanders had to convince the cold, underfed veterans of the Army of Tennessee to reenlist. Buck wrote home, "The subject of reenlistment is making some stir in this army, but I believe our Division will all go in again for the war, cheerfully." There was a note of fatalism, however, in his declaration that "I am for hold- ing out to the last." Apparently, Cleburne's men felt the same. Though cut off from their homes in Arkansas and Texas due to Union control of the Mississippi, the men signed up for the duration of the war in overwhelming numbers. "The greater part of the Division has re-enlisted," Buck reported, and he, at least, attributed it to the fact that "the troops are as much devoted to General Cleburne as Stonewall Jackson's men were to him."[28]

That winter, Cleburne also initiated an educational program for his offi- cers. Among the log huts of the winter encampment at Tunnel Hill, he had one built especially for use as a school—or what today might grandly be called a staff college. He conducted the classes himself, hosting discussions on "the art of war" with his brigade commanders—Polk, Lowrey, Govan, and Granbury—and then encouraging them to do the same with their regi- mental commanders.

In late February there was a flurry of activity when it appeared that a strong Yankee force was moving from Mississippi into Alabama. A large portion of Sherman's army of some 35,000 men that had been holding Vicksburg ven- tured out of that river city and marched east to the Mississippi state capital at Jackson. Then, crossing the Pearl River, they continued east, leaving unprece- dented destruction in their wake, arriving finally at Meridian astride the rail line south to Mobile. Leonidas Polk's small Army of the Mississippi (some 10,000 infantry plus another 6,000 cavalry) was insufficient to stop the ma- rauding Sherman, and he called on Johnston for help. Johnston demurred, arguing that he could not spare the troops, and that in any case this Federal initiative was most likely only a feint intended to draw attention away from the more important confrontation at Dalton. In Richmond, Davis saw it dif- ferently. He worried that Sherman might march right through the Confeder- ate heartland, and he ordered Johnston to send Hardee's Corps to Alabama.[29]

As a result of these events, Cleburne's men left their log huts at Tunnel Hill on the morning of 20 February and marched south to Dalton. There they scrambled aboard boxcars and flatcars for the train ride south to Atlanta. Cheatham's Division had gone ahead of them and Walker's was to follow, so that a total of some 16,000 men, arguably the best in the army, were heading to Alabama. They followed the same route Cleburne and Hardee had taken six weeks before: south to Atlanta, then west to Montgomery. For Cleburne, it almost certainly conjured up memories of his recent trip to Mobile and of Sue Tarleton. Before he had traveled as far as Montgomery, however, the scenario changed abruptly. Even as Cleburne's Division left Dalton, Sherman had begun to evacuate Meridian and retreat westward. Meanwhile, in Georgia the Federals at Ringgold lunged southward, sweeping past the log huts that Cleburne's men had abandoned when they left Tunnel Hill and assailing the Confederate defenses on Rocky Face Ridge north and west of Dalton.

Cleburne's Division was at a rail siding in Alabama awaiting a change of trains when news arrived of this newest Federal initiative. Johnston's orders to return to Dalton conveyed a sense of urgency: "The enemy is advancing; is now in force at Tunnel Hill. Lose no time." Thus prodded, Cleburne ordered his men to reboard the trains and return to Dalton. The first to arrive—Granbury's Brigade of Texans—reached Dalton on 25 February, and the men marched immediately to the foot of Rocky Face Ridge below Dug Gap. With the first light of dawn, they charged up the pass and drove a regiment of mounted infantry out of the gap. That night, the Federals fell back, leading Johnston to conclude that it had only been a reconnaissance in force after all. Within days, life slipped back into the winter routine.[30]

All through this minor crisis in February Cleburne continued to write to Sue Tarleton whenever he could. The evidence suggests that he wrote frequently, perhaps even daily, though of the six young people who had shared the romantic week in Mobile—Cleburne and Sue Tarleton, Robert Tarleton and Sallie Lightfoot, and Henry Goldthwaite and Grace Tarleton—only the letters to "Dear Miss Sallie" survived. From them, however, it is possible to piece together the unsteady course of Pat Cleburne's long-distance courtship. Characteristically, he labored over his letters, striving to find just the right balance between declarations of affection and gentlemanly restraint. Sue also worried about striking the right note and agonized over her letters as well. Her brother confided to Sallie that her first letter to "the general" was especially difficult for her, and "it cost her an immense deal of trouble to write it." Later, when he was rummaging through her desk in search of some writing paper, he found it "filled with rough drafts in pencil of her letters to the Gen'l." A thousand miles away, Cleburne pressed his suit with some force. Having decided that Sue was the woman for him, he pursued her with the same single-minded intensity that marked all his actions. She found it somewhat wearing. Her brother wrote that "poor Sue is like 'the last rose of summer'" and suggested that Sallie should come for a visit to comfort her (an invitation that was partly self-serving). "You would be an inestimable boon to her," Robert wrote, "& besides she needs you to advise her about Gen'l C. She is in some perplexity."[31]

Cleburne was determined to bring matters to a head. The same day that Robert Tarleton wrote of his sister's "perplexity," Cleburne was packing for another trip to Mobile. After three years without taking leave, he was now taking his second within six weeks. Though he had not confided his purpose to any save Hardee, the officers at headquarters found it amusing. "General Cleburne expects to start on a twelve day leave this evening to visit his sweetheart," Buck wrote to his sister. "He has scarcely been back a month, this is very suggestive is it not? Would not be surprised at another wedding soon."[32]

For the third time, Cleburne rode the train to Atlanta, then to Montgomery, and downriver to Mobile. Apparently he did not stop to visit Nash this time—his errand was too urgent. He arrived in Mobile on Sunday, 6 March, and visited Sue that same afternoon. "Gen'l Patrick is in town," Robert reported to Sallie Lightfoot on Thursday. "He has been there several days & has been pressing his suit with complete success." Under the eager and relentless urgings of her suitor, Sue agreed to accept him. Cleburne was both relieved and elated; he wrote to Sallie himself to share the good news. "After keeping me in cruel suspense for six weeks," he wrote, "she has at length consented to be mine and we are engaged." His enthusiasm led him to heights of giddiness reflected in uncharacteristically florid prose as he described "the feelings of an accepted lover . . . when the fair one has relented, when the heartless little conqueror shows that she is all heart by descending from her triumphal car lifting her wounded captive from the mud and placing him palpitating with a thousand new emotions by her side."[33]

In such a mood, he left Mobile the next day (12 March) for the three-day trip back to Dalton and the war. There everything looked the same: the log huts, the camp fires, the men drilling. But at the same time everything was different. A genuine romantic, Cleburne endowed his status as an engaged man with supernatural importance and devoted many hours a day to penning long letters of devotion. The arrival of a letter from Mobile was the high point of his day. He complained to Sue, and even to Robert, about the brevity of her letters, objecting that she wrote too large and left large spaces between the lines. One suspects that even had she written in tiny script in letters of Dickensian length they still would not have been long enough to satisfy him.[34]

While Cleburne was preoccupied with thoughts of love and matrimony, there had been an important organizational change in the army. In late February, newly promoted Lieutenant General John Bell Hood had arrived in Dalton to supersede Hindman in permanent command of what had been Breckinridge's Corps, thus assuming the job that Buck had expected Cleburne to get. Hood was a large man with a thick mane of light brown hair and a golden beard flecked with gray. One soldier described him as "a gigantic old Saxon chieftain come to life." He was, moreover, a proven combat veteran whose reputation as a battlefield leader was not unlike Cleburne's. In most other ways, however, Hood was very different. Whereas Cleburne was so quiet and self-effacing as to be often mistaken for a private, Hood was flamboyant and not averse to self-promotion. After losing a leg at Chickamauga, he had spent the winter recuperating in Richmond where, like Cleburne, he had fallen in love, fervently pursuing Sally Buchanan Preston despite his physical handicap. When not thus engaged, he had spent much of the rest of his time currying favor with Jefferson Davis. Whether or not his sycophancy had been the direct cause of his promotion, he nevertheless felt a personal loyalty to Davis that would manifest itself in unfortunate ways during the spring campaign.[35]

Meanwhile camp life resumed its orderly routine. Reveille was at daylight, followed by roll call and breakfast. Cleburne supervised drill from 10:00 to 11:30, when the troops had their lunch, or what was then called dinner. Then it was more drill from 2:30 to 4:00, often followed by a dress parade at sunset. Tattoo was at 8:00, taps at 9:00. Meals were dominated by corn bread, often seasoned with red peppers and supplemented by beef when it was available, and potatoes. Occasionally the men were issued bacon, which was especially welcome. At night, the companies often engaged in singing while gathered about the fires. They preferred maudlin and sentimental tunes like "Annie Laurie" and "Do They Miss Me at Home." Another favorite was "Silence, Silence, Make No More Noise nor Stir."[36]

Occasionally the unpredictable March weather broke the routine of camp life and interrupted the training schedule. On rare occasions it snowed and, like children released from school, the troops treated any snowfall as an occasion for play. On 22 March dawn revealed a fresh five inches of new snow, and spontaneous snowball fights broke out all across the camp. The men threw themselves into the fracas with enthusiasm. One Arkansas soldier recalled, "Such pounding and thumping, and rolling over in the snow, and washing of faces and cramming snow in mouth and ears and mixing up in great wriggling piles together."[37]

In Cleburne's Division, Lucius Polk's Brigade attacked Govan's Brigade, pitting Arkansan against Arkansan, and Cleburne could not resist getting involved. He placed himself at the head of his old brigade and led the attack on Govan's campsite. The snowballs flew thick and fast, and Govan's men were getting the worst of it when they decided to launch a counterattack. They charged forward, no doubt yelling for all they were worth, and Cleburne suddenly found himself a prisoner of war. After some tongue-in-cheek deliberation, his captors decided to parole their commander, and Cleburne was released. The snowball fight continued. Polk's men were now getting the worst of it, and Cleburne once again entered the fray. Alas, he was captured a second time, and this time his captors confronted him with mock solemnity about his violation of parole. According to one veteran, "Some called for a drumhead court martial; others demanded a sound ducking in the nearby creek. Still others, mindful of Cleburne's reputation as a stern disciplinarian, insisted that the general be meted out his own customary punishment. The idea caught on, and soon the whole brigade took up the familiar order: 'Arrest that soldier and make him carry a fence rail!'" Cooler heads prevailed, with Cleburne's defenders arguing that after all this was the first occasion on which he had been known to break his word, and once again his captors granted him parole. When it was all over, Cleburne authorized a ration of whiskey to the troops, and they stood around great bonfires singing and yelling "at the top of their lungs."[38]

More snow fell on 23 March, provoking yet another snowball fight, and rain and snow continued through the rest of the month. On 31 March a more serious sham battle occurred when Johnston organized a mock engagement involving Hardee's entire corps. Cleburne's and Bate's Divisions squared off against those of Cheatham and Walker. It was fine weather for a change, and the troops entered the spirit of the drill, firing off a half dozen blank cartridges each, thrilling the small audience of ladies who had driven out from Dalton to watch. One veteran recalled, "The noise was terrific and the excitement intense, but nobody was hurt. . . . except perhaps one of the cavalry men who was dismounted while charging a square of infantry." That night, back in camp, it was peaches and corn bread again for dinner.[39]

Springlike weather returned in the first week of April, and on the 19th Johnston ordered a review of the whole army. "Boots and saddles" sounded at 8:00 A.M., and the sprawling campsite around Dalton became a beehive of activity as 40,000 men prepared for the grand parade. Again there were a number of observers on hand, including hundreds of ladies in crinolines who stood in a gusting wind to admire the martial display. The troops formed up in two long lines, and General Johnston, trailed by his staff, rode slowly past before taking his position with the observers. Then the divisions passed in review. Riding at the head of more than 7,000 men, Cleburne could be proud of his command. In spite of the weather, the indifferent rations, and the long winter of inaction, the men of his division had reenlisted for the duration.

His command was a dangerous instrument of war, proud of its reputation and its unique blue battle flag. Buck thought the men were "in better fighting trim now than I have ever seen them."[40]

It was just as well, for less than twenty miles away the Federal army, too, was a dangerous instrument of war. At Ringgold, the armies of William T. Sherman, whom Cleburne had bested on Missionary Ridge in November, were completing their preparations for the spring campaign.

11
FROM DALTON TO THE CHATTAHOOCHEE

Spring returned to Georgia in May. That month, too, the Federal armies began to advance, both in Georgia and in Virginia, inaugurating the twin campaigns that would decide the outcome of the war. In both theaters, the numerical superiority of Union forces eventually compelled the Confederates to accept the strategic defensive. Johnston had resisted repeated urgings from Richmond to initiate a winter offensive, arguing that it would be better to repel the first Federal offensive of the spring and then counterattack. Now spring was here, but if Johnston ever had any serious intention of mounting an offensive, he was compelled to abandon it almost at once. As Cleburne had foretold, the reason was manpower.

The Army of Tennessee contained a grand total of perhaps 55,000 men, some 42,000 of whom were "effectives," or frontline troops. Polk's Army of Mississippi, which joined Johnston in mid-May, brought the number of effectives up to more than 60,000, but Sherman had nearly double that number under his command, well in excess of 100,000. That numerical advantage allowed him to use part of his force to hold the Confederates in place with a frontal assault while he sent a strong column to find the Confederate flank or to threaten the Rebel line of supply. As a result, he was able to seize and hold the initiative. For his part, Johnston accepted the role of defender: blocking Sherman's frontal assaults, then scurrying back to guard his line of supply. Each time, however, he had to give ground, and throughout May and June the Army of Tennessee retreated slowly but inexorably southward, deeper and deeper into Georgia.[1]

For Cleburne, the spring campaign began on 8 May when three Federal divisions assailed the center of the Rebel line at Mill Creek Gap just west of

Dalton, while another enemy division advanced toward Dug Gap four miles to the south. Since he could hear the sound of the fighting from his headquarters near the Spring Place Road, he could not have been surprised when he received orders to move at once with two of his four brigades to reinforce Dug Gap, the same defile where in February Granbury's Brigade had arrived in the nick of time to repel an earlier Federal probe. This time Cleburne ordered Granbury and Lowrey to follow him as quickly as they could, and he and Hardee galloped south to assess the situation.[2]

Perspiring heavily in the heat, the two generals spurred their mounts up the steep slope of the ridge line and arrived at Dug Gap in midafternoon to find a fierce battle raging. Approximately 1,000 Confederate troops (250 infantry and about 800 dismounted cavalry) were holding their ground, but they were being hard-pressed by forces more than four times their number. Hardee was concerned lest the defenders give way before Cleburne's infantry arrived, and he sent a courier dashing back to order Granbury's men to come at the double-quick. Throwing off their knapsacks and blankets, they lurched into a trot. When they reached the base of the ridge, a few of them appropriated the horses of the dismounted cavalry and rode up to the ridge line. At the crest, one young private galloped up to the two generals, jumped off his borrowed mount, and asked, "Where am I most needed?" The notion that this lone private was ready to hold the line against the entire Yankee army broke the tension, and both Hardee and Cleburne burst into laughter. Soon afterward, the rest of Granbury's Texans came huffing and puffing up the steep incline in time to hold the pass, and Cleburne personally placed them in position.[3]

Satisfied that the situation was now well in hand, Hardee left at sundown to look after the rest of his corps. Cleburne stayed in the gap and bedded down with the men of Granbury's Brigade. Though it had been a hot day, the night was cool, and since they had shed their knapsacks en route to the pass, Granbury's men had no blankets or food. Cleburne, too, made do with what he had, stretching out on the ground with only his saddle blanket.

Soon after dawn, Cleburne received a query from Johnston's headquarters asking if the Federals were still in force on his front. He sent pickets out as far as Mill Creek, but the only Yankees they encountered were the dead and a few wounded from Joe Hooker's Federal corps, whom they brought in as prisoners. In his report to Johnston, Cleburne was unwilling to state with certainty whether the Federals were present in strength. He could not say if the attack on Dug Gap had been a Federal reconnaissance in force, a precursor to a general assault, or a feint designed to distract attention from elsewhere. These were questions that could be answered only by energetic and intelligent cavalry patrols. But the army's cavalry commander, twenty-seven-year-old Joe Wheeler, who was a Bragg protégé, seemed to be more interested in seeking battle with his Federal counterpart in Crow Valley, half a dozen miles to the north. Johnston's desperate thirst for intelligence was evident in the unusual request from headquarters that Cleburne lend the army commander five mounted men from his personal escort for additional scouting duty west of Rocky Face Ridge.[4]

Lacking hard evidence, Johnston was reduced to guessing Sherman's intentions. It seemed to him that the open terrain of Crow Valley offered the most logical line of approach for a superior army. He did know that a Federal column was moving through the mountains well to the west of Rocky Face Ridge, which he interpreted as a Federal thrust toward Rome, Georgia, and he assumed Leonidas Polk's Army of Mississippi could handle that probe. Then that afternoon, the Kentucky cavalry that Cleburne's two brigades had relieved in Dug Gap reported that another strong Federal column was moving through Snake Creek Gap toward Resaca on the Western and Atlantic Railroad. This news was more serious, for if the Federals seized the railroad, the army's line of supply and support would be cut. This evidence of a Federal move toward Resaca forced Johnston to react: he ordered Hood to go there personally to assess the situation and report, and he decided to send reinforcements there as well.[5]

As a result of these circumstances, Cleburne was awakened just after midnight on 9–10 May by a courier who bore orders for him to evacuate Dug Gap, leaving it in the care of two small Arkansas regiments, and take three brigades south to Resaca. (Govan's Brigade was still in Crow Valley.) Cleburne ordered Granbury to draw in his pickets "as quietly and promptly as possible" and prepare to march. At the foot of the ridge, the Texans discovered to their disgust that the Kentucky cavalry they had relieved two days before had pilfered their knapsacks, taking most of the food and all of the coffee. Cleburne ordered the men to fire off the charges in their guns, wet from the evening dew; then, reunited with the brigades of Polk and Lowrey, he headed all three brigades southward as the sun rose. They arrived at Resaca after a five-hour march and stood at ease for several hours until new orders arrived from Hardee for them to turn around and march back. After another five-hour march, they arrived about sundown at the foot of Dug Gap where they had started.[6]

All this fruitless marching to and fro was a reflection of the continued uncertainty at army headquarters about Sherman's intentions. The Federals were still mounting what appeared to be a major effort against the Confederate lines on Rocky Face Ridge, and another substantial Federal force was massing in Crow Valley north of Dalton. There Wheeler found the confrontation he had been seeking with the Federal cavalry, fighting and winning what became known as the Battle of Varnell's Station. But however satisfying this small triumph was to Wheeler's vanity, it did little to reveal the meaning behind Federal movements. Hood, meanwhile, reported that things were secure at Resaca: "R[esaca] all right," he had telegraphed at 8:00 A.M. "Hold onto Dalton." As a result, Johnston had ordered Cleburne back to Dug Gap.⁷

But Hood was wrong; Resaca was not all right. The Federal move through Snake Creek Gap was, in fact, Sherman's main effort, a fact that became evident that afternoon when the commander at Resaca, Major General James Cantey, sent an urgent call for help: "Enemy advancing on this place in force!" For the second time in twenty-four hours, Cleburne received orders to march his command to Resaca. Hood ordered him "to move at sunrise" on 11 May, "to threaten the enemy and under certain circumstances to attack him." By now Cleburne must have begun to recognize a familiar pattern: at Liberty Gap near Wartrace, again on Missionary Ridge near Chattanooga, and now on Rocky Face Ridge, his division had held a critical position against long odds only to be informed afterward that the line had been breached elsewhere. While Granbury's Texans had defended Dug Gap, a substantial Federal force had marched unopposed through Snake Creek Gap to threaten the army's communications. Cleburne found this lapse inexplicable. At the first opportunity he asked Johnston's chief of staff, William Whann Mackall, how such a thing could have happened. Mackall told him that "it was the result of a flagrant disobedience of orders, by whom he did not say." But Cleburne could guess. Almost certainly Mackall's enigmatic reference was to Wheeler, the flamboyant but unreliable Bragg protégé.⁸

Joined by Govan's Brigade, Cleburne started his reunited division southward a few hours after dawn on 11 May. Because his troops were tired from their march and countermarch the day before, he did not start until 7:00 A.M., and he ordered frequent rest stops. Riding considerably ahead of his troops, he narrowly escaped capture when a Federal patrol passed between his mounted escort and the column of infantry. By late afternoon, his men had covered ten miles, and Cleburne ordered them to bivouac in line of battle northwest of Resaca where the Sugar Valley Road intersected a new military road. He wired Hood that "the enemy seem to be moving everything in this direction . . . but whether their destination is Resaca, I am unable to say."⁹

His division was still there at seven o'clock the next morning when his pickets were driven in by advancing Yankees. The pickets reported that the enemy force was a strong one, division strength at least. He could hear distant bugles blowing, apparently summoning even more forces. He made a few last-minute adjustments to his dispositions and ordered the men to throw up breastworks. But the enemy did not attack. Though Cleburne did not know it, the Federal force was the cavalry division of Major General Hugh Judson Kilpatrick, who was fulfilling orders to push out "on the Resaca Road feeling as far up on the crossroads toward Dalton as practicable." Finding Cleburne in his path, Kilpatrick halted, then fell back as instructed. He reported Cleburne's presence to the Federal commander, Major General James B. McPherson, who decided to wait until Sherman arrived before testing the strength of the force in his front.[10]

Meanwhile the Rebel army was concentrating at Resaca. Johnston kept up a bold front on Rocky Face Ridge while he arranged for the Army of Tennessee to move southward; at the same time, he welcomed the news that Leonidas Polk was bringing his entire Army of Mississippi—some 10,000 infantry and another 6,000 cavalry—to Resaca as well. While all these units were in motion, Cleburne attempted to keep track of the enemy through the reports of his scouts and the handful of prisoners they brought in. He interviewed the prisoners personally and found them not only unchastened by their capture but full of confidence. When Cleburne asked them where the Federal army was going, they answered with undisguised candor that they were "going to Resaca, Calhoun, and Atlanta." He reported their remarks to Leonidas Polk and noted as well that the Yankees had fortified Villanow during the night and were massing forces near the mouth of Snake Creek Gap.[11]

By the next day, virtually all of Johnston's Army of Tennessee and Polk's Army of Mississippi was concentrated west of Resaca. Polk's arrival boosted Johnston's total strength to over 60,000 men, and the combined armies took up defensive positions west of town. Hardee's Corps occupied the center with Hood on the right and Polk on the left. Cleburne's Division held the center of Hardee's Corps so that it marked the exact center of the Confederate position. As usual when he expected a battle to be fought, Cleburne conducted a personal reconnaissance of the ground to his front. He scouted the terrain on foot as far as Camp Creek, a quarter mile in front of the lines.[12]

The Battle for Resaca began in earnest at daylight the next day (14 May) when the Federals opened "a heavy fusillade" and began to advance. For once, however, the heaviest fighting was not on Cleburne's front. The Yankees seemed disposed to leave the center largely unmolested and concentrate on the flanks. They achieved their greatest success on the left, adjacent to the Oostanaula River crossings, where they gained a piece of high ground and forced the men of Polk's Army of Mississippi to fall back a half mile. Gradually toward nightfall, the firing sputtered out until it was limited to the sharpshooters on both sides.[13]

The battle continued the next day with similar results; this time the fighting was heaviest on the Confederate right. There, two divisions of Federals furiously attacked Hood's Corps, and soon thereafter Hood undertook a counterattack that was recalled at the last minute because of news that the Federals had crossed the Oostanaula River downstream from Resaca. Once again the army would have to fall back. In an ominously familiar scenario, Cleburne left his skirmishers in place, pulled his men out of their works with orders "not to speak above a whisper," and sent them marching silently southward through the dark toward Calhoun, Georgia. An hour before sunrise they noted a glow in the northern sky signifying that the high command had quite literally burned the bridges behind them.[14]

The loss of Dalton and Resaca set a pattern for the campaign. Both times Sherman feinted with a convincing frontal assault, freezing the Rebels in place, then sent a strong column to threaten the army's critical supply line to Atlanta, compelling Johnston to order a retreat. It was a pattern that would become all too familiar over the next two months, months characterized by virtually continuous combat. As the days lengthened and the temperature rose in the pine forests of northern Georgia, the men of Cleburne's Division fought their opponent almost daily in a series of large and small face-to-face encounters; the skirmishing between the two armies never ceased. In each of these confrontations, the troops in butternut more than held their own, defending their ground and punishing the Federal attackers, but following each engagement, they received orders to evacuate their lines quietly and fall back southward. They were not defeated—not once were they driven from a position they were ordered to defend, but they fell back nonetheless.

The Army of Tennessee did not make a stand at Calhoun, for the terrain there offered no particular advantage to a defending army. Cleburne and Walker, ideological enemies but partners in war, launched a successful counterattack west of Calhoun to stall the Federal advance, then Cleburne's Division acted as the army's rear guard on the march south. Cleburne himself arrived at Adairsville at daylight on 17 May, halting his division two miles north of town where his men collapsed into bivouac. Plaintively, he reported to Hardee, "My men are very tired and need much rest."[15]

Johnston had hoped to make a stand at Adairsville where mountains to the east and west narrowed the fighting front, thus protecting the army's flanks and minimizing Sherman's numerical advantage. But after looking over the position, he decided that it was not as advantageous as he had assumed and ordered another withdrawal. This time, however, he hoped to lay a trap for his pursuer. South of Adairsville, the roads forked. Hardee's Corps, with Cleburne's Division again acting as rear guard, marched due south along the line of the Western and Atlantic Railroad toward Kingston, while the other two corps (Hood's and Leonidas Polk's) took a secondary road that angled off to the southeast toward the small town of Cassville. As Johnston had hoped, Sherman divided his forces in pursuit, and the Confederate army commander prepared to spring his trap by pouncing on those forces headed toward Cassville. He even issued a ringing call to battle on 19 May. But confusion over orders, and the untimely appearance of Federal cavalry on Hood's flank, scuppered the scheme, and the army fell back once again. By 20 May, less than two weeks after the initial Federal attack on Rocky Face Ridge, the Army of Tennessee was encamped in the Allatoona Mountains south of the Etowah River, more than halfway to Atlanta.[16]

For three days (20–23 May), Cleburne's men and the remainder of the army rested south of the Etowah near Allatoona. There the men could sleep without being awakened for another night withdrawal. They ate hot meals and wrote letters home. Many stripped to the skin and enjoyed the luxury of an alfresco bath in a nearby mill pond. Despite the repeated retrograde movements, Cleburne remained outwardly confident. In part this was due to a certain fatalism that was inherent in his character; the darker the prospects, the more he felt compelled to embrace his duty. But in addition, he maintained an unshakable trust in Hardee, and since Hardee continued to voice confidence in Johnston, that was good enough for him. Although Cleburne had felt compelled to acknowledge his dissatisfaction with Bragg, he never uttered any criticism of Johnston.[17]

Others did. In Richmond, the government was nearly frantic that Johnston had given up so much territory to the invader. In the privacy of his headquarters tent, Johnston, too, was frustrated, confessing in a letter to his wife, "I have never been so little satisfied with myself. . . . I have seen so much beautiful country given up." He described his circumstances as "distressing" and "humiliating." During the three days in the Allatoona hills, however, he began to envision the campaign differently. After all, Sherman had never defeated him. Indeed, it was virtually certain that the Yankees had suffered far more casualties than his own forces. A member of Johnston's staff estimated that Sherman had lost as many as 25,000 men to all causes since the campaign had begun. Moreover, as the two armies moved south, Johnston's own supply lines to Atlanta became shorter, and Sherman's grew longer. To secure his communications, Sherman would have to detach troops to guard the railroad lest it become vulnerable to cavalry raids. Johnston began to construct the outlines of a new strategy. Rather than pin his hopes on a counteroffensive into Tennessee, he would trade space for time and conserve his forces, fighting from cover whenever possible, until he had negated Sherman's numerical advantage. Then he would strike.[18]

Years later, when survivors of the war engaged in a long-running dispute about the wisdom of Johnston's strategy in this campaign, Cleburne's adjutant general, Irving Buck, cast his lot with those who defended Johnston's "Fabian" tactics. Buck wrote: "Notwithstanding the fact that the army had retired before General Sherman's from Dalton, there was no demoralization or depression. The troops were in splendid spirits and fighting trim. The intelligent soldiers felt that though under seeming defeat they were actual victors." If Buck's views, committed to paper a half century later, reflected those of his idolized commander, Cleburne presumably accepted the notion that Johnston knew what he was doing and that it would all work out in the end. Under Braxton Bragg, Cleburne had been part of the perceived opposition, allying himself with Buckner, Cheatham, and Hardee. Now with Johnston in command, Cleburne remained allied with Cheatham and Hardee in support of the new commander. Of course in Bragg's view, that only confirmed his status as an enemy of the administration.[19]

Perhaps, too, Cleburne remained buoyant because he now had Sue Tarleton to think about, he took advantage of the respite at Allatoona to write to her. Though no letters have survived, he occasionally read parts of them aloud to his aide and friend Learned Mangum. Mangum, who knew Cleburne as a quietly efficient and reserved individual, was surprised by the obvious "depth of his feelings" evident in his commander's letters. Cleburne's letters to Sue were not sentimental fluff. "Devoid of all approach to sentimentality," Mangum wrote, "they were full of a most sweet and tender passion." Cleburne offered his intended glimpses of his "thoughts and fancies" in a style "that was exquisite in its pathos and tenderness." Although Cleburne was willing to share some passages from his letters to Sue with Mangum, he kept the letters *from* her entirely to himself. She wrote him twice a week, though the irregular mail service meant that they often arrived at odd intervals—sometimes a week went by with no letters, then he would receive two or more the same day. In any event, whether it was due to his fatalism, his confidence in Johnston's strategy, or his cherished vision of postwar wedded bliss, Cleburne remained quietly efficient and publicly confident in the pursuit of his professional obligations.[20]

There was some bad news, however. It was probably during the three-day halt at Allatoona that Cleburne learned of the death of his youngest half brother, Kit, at the age of twenty-three. A lieutenant in the 5th Kentucky Cavalry (Confederate), a part of John Hunt Morgan's command, Christopher Cleburne had been killed in a skirmish at Dublin, Kentucky, on 10 May.

Morgan had recently promoted the young officer to acting captain, and despite his youth his peers considered him "one of the most promising young officers in the army." It was perhaps some comfort to Cleburne to learn that his brother had fallen "while gallantly leading his men in a charge on the enemy." It was, after all, a fate any soldier could be proud of.[21]

The campaign resumed on 23 May. It would require a detailed history of each of the ensuing fifty-six days to illustrate the unremitting nature of the warfare that took place between the Etowah and the Chattahoochee as the two armies maneuvered in what Shelby Foote has dubbed a "red clay minuet." There were, however, two occasions when Cleburne found himself at the exact center of the maelstrom of violence. Both times fate placed him at precisely the point chosen by the enemy to attempt a decisive breakthrough: at Pickett's Mill in the thick woods around Dallas on 27 May and on the shoulder of Kennesaw Mountain exactly a month later. Both times Cleburne again demonstrated his determination and efficiency in the management of a division and validated his reputation as the Stonewall of the West.[22]

The respite at Allatoona was all too brief. At midmorning on 23 May, the order came to break camp and resume the march: not south this time but west, the soldiers tramping through a light spring rain that was, as one veteran recalled, "just enough to lay the dust." Sherman was flanking again. Unwilling to force his way across the Etowah in the face of Johnston's defenses, he was making a wide swing to the west through the wilderness of north Georgia. Johnston was rushing west to interpose his army. Neither knew with any precision where the other was—the terrain and thick woods made that impossible—but Sherman was determined to get around Johnston, and Johnston was just as determined that he should not.[23]

Tramping along on narrow dirt roads through dense woodlands, the two armies groped blindly toward one another. Cleburne's Division marched and countermarched along the narrow tracks in response to verbal instructions from staff officers who were themselves unsure of the local geography. On 24 May, Cleburne set up temporary headquarters in the farmhouse of one George Darby. All around him for a radius of three miles in any direction, units from both armies moved uncertainly toward one another. That afternoon, they met. Joe Hooker's XX Federal Corps collided with Hood's Corps near a small crossroads chapel called New Hope Church. At dusk Cleburne received orders to march to Hood's support, though by the time he got his men ready, it was full dark and the scouts could not find the road. He appealed for orders to Hardee, who told him to wait until morning. Cleburne ordered his men to hold themselves in readiness to move "at a moment's notice," but their sleep was not interrupted.[24]

Cleburne woke his troops in the predawn darkness, issued rations of hard-tack and bacon, and started his division north at 4:00 A.M. The sound of skirmishing grew louder and louder as he advanced. Occasionally a minié ball whistled past "like it was on the hunt of some one." He arrived at the front at about 6:30 and deployed his brigades behind the firing line as a reserve. The uneven terrain and dense woods made visibility poor, and some of the Texans in Granbury's Brigade wondered just who it was they were supporting. A few ventured forward and found the Georgia troops of Walker's Division. Untrusting of any but Arkansas troops, they warned the Georgians that if they ran, they would shoot them down.[25]

The sound of intermittent skirmishing continued throughout the morning, but Cleburne received no further orders until midafternoon when he got word to move to the east where the Yankees were apparently again attempting an end run, this time around the right flank held by Tom Hindman's Division. After marching several miles up the Mt. Tabor Road, Cleburne arrived on the extreme right of the extended Confederate line at about 3:00 and spoke with Hindman. The sound of the battle had faded as he rode, but headquarters claimed that the Federals were moving in this direction. Cleburne therefore deployed three of his brigades behind Hindman's front and sent Polk's Brigade even farther to the right, deployed in echelon by regiments, to secure the right flank. There, too, he placed the twelve guns commanded by T. R. Hotchkiss. As a final precaution, he put one of Govan's regiments a quarter mile beyond the right flank to provide warning of a wider Federal flanking movement. Although ordinarily he would have ordered the troops to cut a clear field of fire by felling trees, the woods and undergrowth were so thick that he decided to leave them in place both to screen his own line and to impede the advance of the enemy. He did, however, order the troops to dig rifle pits and to cut rude trails behind the front, parallel to it, so that he could shuttle troops from point to point along the line should that become necessary. After completing these tasks, the men slept on their arms in line of battle.[26]

Dawn on 27 May brought no sign of enemy activity, but Cleburne worried that the enemy might be moving in the dense forest to the east, beyond his own flank, where there was nothing to stop them but Wheeler's cavalry. He ordered Govan to lead a reconnaissance in force in that direction. Govan's thousand or so men spread out in a long skirmish line and moved forward. One soldier later recalled "vividly the feeling of surprise and loneliness I felt when our skirmish line continued to advance . . . for quite a distance." Govan reported that as Cleburne had suspected, the Yankees were present in large numbers and moving to the right. Cleburne recalled Govan and placed him on Polk's right, thus extending the army's front by another brigade. It was soon evident, however, that the Yankees would overlap even this line. Granbury's scouts reported that the Yankees were "massing their troops on the right of our army and would flank us before night if we did not stop them some way." Cleburne therefore ordered Granbury, too, to move to the right beyond Govan's flank. Instead of a second line behind Hindman, therefore, Cleburne's Division had become the front line of the army, holding its extreme right flank with only Lowrey's Brigade as a reserve.[27]

The men of Granbury's Brigade had barely taken their positions "in a heavy timbered section with chinquapin bushes as an undergrowth," when Wheeler's dismounted cavalry skirmishers came running back through the woods calling to the Texans to run for it because the Yankees were coming "by the thousand." With no time to dig in, Granbury's men piled up "a few disconnected heaps of stones loosely piled together" and awaited the enemy attack. On their left, Govan's skirmishers also came running back to the main line. They leaped over the makeshift breastworks and took up positions alongside their companions. Within minutes, the sound of a ragged volley and the crash of brushwork signaled the initiation of what became known as the Battle of Pickett's Mill. Through the woods the Federals advanced "several lines deep" cheering the deep-throated "hurrah" of Union troops. Had Cleburne not placed Govan and Granbury beyond Polk's right, this Federal assault would have overlapped the army's flank and possibly rolled up the Rebel line. Instead, the Federals encountered the veterans of Missionary Ridge and Ringgold Gap.[28]

In front of Govan's position, the Federals encountered a daunting natural obstacle as well: a thirty-foot-deep circular sinkhole filled with fallen trees, thick underbrush, and chinquapin bushes. At this barrier, they stopped, threw down their knapsacks and crouched behind them to open a steady wasting fire on the Rebels. The men of Govan's and Granbury's Brigades knelt or stood behind rocks and trees and returned the fire. The Yankees were delighted to find their enemy unentrenched. Cleburne could hear some of them cry out, "Ah, damn you, we have caught you without your logs now!" After twenty minutes or so, the Federals renewed their advance, some of them trying to fight their way through the brambles in the sink hole, others moving further to the right seeking the Rebel flank. Granbury lifted his voice above the din to call out, "Cease firing!" In the relative silence that followed, he hollered again, "Fix bayonets!" Then, "Commence firing!" and the din welled up again. It was going to be close quarters.[29]

On the right, where the Federals continued to probe for the open flank, Granbury felt compelled to call for support. Govan sent him the 8th/19th Arkansas, and Cleburne detached two guns from Key's Battery to go with it. There was no time to limber up, so the artillerists rolled the guns forward by hand. En route to the flank, the Arkansans met their former commander, the baby-faced brigadier John H. Kelly. He waved them into action, and they responded with "lusty cheers." Their impetuous charge turned back the Federal advance, but the bluecoated soldiers continued to press forward searching for the Confederate flank. Cleburne had to commit Lowrey's Brigade, his only reserve, sending it to extend the right. He met Lowrey as his regiments advanced at the quick-step along the narrow forest paths that Cleburne had ordered cut the day before. Lowrey later recalled: "General Cleburne met me on the way, and with his usual calmness told me that it was necessary to move rapidly. He then explained to me the situation and as he left he said, 'Secure Granbury's right!'" Lowrey's men came into line regiment by regiment, firing as they deployed. In his subsequent report, Cleburne noted laconically that Lowrey's arrival was "most opportune"; indeed, it was near miraculous.[30]

Cleburne's line held, but virtually every soldier in his division was now in the front line; there were no more troops available to extend the right. If the enemy broke through here or managed to get around the flank, it could be Missionary Ridge all over again. The fight continued for several hours. Cleburne was impressed by the determination of the attackers. In his official report, he offered a grudging tribute that they "displayed a courage worthy of an honorable cause, pressing in steady throngs within a few paces of our men."[31]

The crisis of the battle came at dusk. Lowrey's lead regiment (the 33d Alabama) and Colonel George Bausam's 8/19th Arkansas decided that their position was untenable, and they determined to pull back a few dozen yards to straighten the line. When they began the move, Cleburne's staff officers concluded that the right wing was giving way. They ordered two more of Lowrey's regiments to rush to the spot, and the flurry of conflicting orders nearly led to disaster. As Lowrey expressed it, "victory trembled in the scale." Calm as always, Cleburne recognized the error and countermanded the orders of his staff, preserving the integrity of the line.[32]

Sporadic firing lasted until well past sundown and then slowly dwindled away, with random muzzle flashes punctuating the darkness. Then it stopped. It was very dark, for clouds obscured the moon and stars. After the din of battle it was also eerily quiet—so still, claimed one officer, "that the chirp of a cricket could be heard 100 feet away." Soldiers could hear rustling in the thick underbrush as the Yankees removed their dead and wounded from between the lines. In the pitch-dark their "footsteps could be distinctly heard." A captain in Granbury's Brigade thought it sounded "like hogs rooting for acorns." Uncertain as to whether the enemy was still present in strength, Cleburne ordered Granbury to send out pickets. Granbury suggested that he send his whole brigade instead, and Cleburne gave his approval. At 10:00 P.M. the Texans fixed bayonets and charged into the darkness. One soldier recalled, "To make that charge in the dark . . . knowing that the enemy were just in front of us, was the most trying time I experienced in the whole war." The Yankees had not withdrawn—the flash of their guns revealed the location of their firing line. But when Granbury's men charged into their midst, "yelling like all the devils from the lower regions," the enemy fled. The Texans returned to their own lines herding more than 200 prisoners.[33]

When the sun came up the next day, Cleburne's men looked out on a tangle of wilderness filled with hundreds of dead and dying Union soldiers. "The battle field looked as though a great blue carpet had been spread on the ground," a Texas soldier recalled. "Dead men were everywhere." One Rebel counted the bodies of thirty-two Federals all of whom had tried to hide behind the same tree; another found the body of a Federal soldier who had been struck by forty-seven bullets. Many of those who escaped had left their knapsacks behind. One of Cleburne's officers venturing into no-man's-land found that more than one of the knapsacks contained "surenough coffee." "Oh, I am rich," he exclaimed, "crackers; bacon; and coffee." Cleburne estimated that Federal losses could not have been fewer than 3,000 men, the figure that Johnston reported to Richmond. The Federals claimed they lost "only 1,600," but either way it was another clear victory for Cleburne's Division, which had lost 85 killed and 363 wounded and which was developing a reputation in both armies for invincibility.[34]

At Pickett's Mill, as on Missionary Ridge, Cleburne had exploited advantageous terrain and interior lines to defeat a much larger enemy force. He had selected the division's position, prepared for the battle by ordering parallel trails to be cut for rapid reinforcement, and maintained effective control of the battlefield during the fight. To be sure, his subordinates contributed as well, not only with prompt obedience to his orders but in the exercise of individual initiative. It was Govan who sent the 9th/18th Arkansas to Lowrey's aid, and it was Granbury who suggested the late-night charge that drove the Yankees from the field. Their actions demonstrated that Cleburne had successfully established and maintained a spirit of comradeship and partnership among his subordinate officers. Throughout the afternoon, he had maintained his legendary stoic calm amidst the fury of battle. When two regiments had pulled back to straighten his line, provoking near panic among his staff, he had quietly intervened and restored stability. Finally, he had been aided by the mistakes of the enemy. As on Missionary Ridge, the Yankee commander, in this case Major General Oliver O. Howard, had committed his forces piecemeal rather than en masse. Cleburne's success at Pickett's Mill proved that Missionary Ridge and Ringgold Gap had not been flukes. For a third time, his command had decisively repelled an attack by a much larger force, and for a third time he had saved the army from potential disaster.

The day after the Battle of Pickett's Mill, other elements of the Rebel army tried a probing attack near Dallas at the opposite end of the extended battle line. Finding the Yankees well placed, the Confederates did not press the issue. After that, during a week of nearly constant rain, both armies moved crablike back to the line of the railroad. By the first week of June, the Army of Tennessee was entrenched on a series of low hills athwart the railroad, again blocking Sherman's path. Cleburne's Division anchored the army's left near Gilgal Church where the Sandtown Road intersected the Due West Road. It was not a happy week for Cleburne. The incessant rain made marching a physical trial, and Cleburne fought a severe cold accompanied by diarrhea that incapacitated him for several days. There were no great battles, though daily skirmishing and occasional long-range cannon fire continued and no day passed without its share of casualties. For the most part, these casualties went largely unremarked in the army save by the friends and family of the victims. But in the second week of June, two casualties in particular affected Cleburne and the entire army on a personal level.[35]

On 14 June an enemy artillery shell aimed at a cluster of Confederate officers just east of Cleburne's position struck and killed Lucius Polk's uncle, the bishop-general Leonidas Polk. That Yankee gunners had apparently deliberately targeted high-ranking officers and had killed a man of the cloth, general or not, seemed to many Rebels irrefutable evidence of Yankee perfidy. Polk was not a great general, but he had been well liked and his death was widely mourned. Johnston appointed Major General William L. Loring, the senior division commander in Polk's Corps, as temporary commander. There is no evidence that he seriously considered Cleburne for the job. Loring was ten years older than Cleburne, ten months senior in rank, and being from Polk's command, he was more likely to retain the confidence of the corps. More curious was the elevation of Alexander P. Stewart to the permanent command of the corps a week later. Stewart was from Hood's Corps, he was six months junior to Cleburne as a major general, and though he had compiled a solid record as a division commander, it was not as glittering as Cleburne's. But he *was* a West Point graduate (class of 1842) and untainted either by participation in anti-Bragg conspiracies or the advocacy of arming slaves. There is no evidence, however, that Cleburne was either surprised or disturbed by the appointment.[36]

It was not a good week for the Polk family. The day after the death of General Polk, Cleburne's position near Gilgal Church came under heavy artillery fire, and he received orders to pull back and take up new positions behind Mud Creek. While establishing his new line, the enemy unleashed another artillery barrage. A Tennessee private recalled that "a bomb, loaded with shrapnel and grapeshot, came ripping and tearing through our ranks." It exploded near Lucius Polk, killing his horse and severely mangling the general's legs, tearing away a large portion of his left calf. Officers nearby called for litter bearers who carefully loaded the general on a stretcher and carried him gingerly to the rear. Just as he had at Perryville, Cleburne rushed to Polk's side to enquire about his friend's condition. He asked Polk if he was badly wounded, and recalling Cleburne's notorious stinginess with furloughs, Polk remarked smilingly, "Well, I think I will be able to get a furlough now." Polk got his furlough, but he never did recover, at least not so that he could resume his duties. He retired from the army in July, and Cleburne was deprived of his closest friend in the army. Polk's retirement ended the brigade as well. The regiments in his command were so reduced from long service and heavy casualties that rather than appoint them a new commander, they were broken up and distributed throughout the army.[37]

Cleburne's men skirmished for a week along the aptly named Mud River. The Yankees pressed them hard, urged on by their officers who called out, "Charge them boys, it's nothing but cavalry." Overhearing this, an Alabama soldier jumped up and yelled back, "Yes, come on up here. This is *Cleburne's* cavalry." Cleburne's "cavalry" held the line, but within a week they moved again, this time onto the slopes of Kennesaw Mountain two miles west of Marietta. Loring's (formerly Polk's) Corps occupied the heights of Kennesaw itself, rising an imposing 700 feet above the forested plain. Hood's Corps held the left near Kolb's Farm where on 22 June he launched a fierce but profitless attack on Hooker's Corps. Hardee's Corps held the center. There the men of Cleburne's and Cheatham's Divisions dug in side by side on a modest rise two and a half miles south of Kennesaw Mountain. If Sherman employed his usual tactics of feint and flank, Cleburne's men should have been in the quietest part of the line. As fate would have it, however, Sherman had become frustrated by his inability to inflict a decisive defeat on the Rebel army and had decided to launch a major frontal assault on the precise center of the Confederate line. Once again, Cleburne's Division stood at the fulcrum of the war.[38]

The day of 27 June dawned hot. Even before the sun was fully up, the men could feel the heat of the coming day. Troops sought shade under trees or draped blankets over the cross posts in the trenches to create their own shade. A few minutes past 8:00 A.M. the sound of heavy firing could be heard from Kennesaw Mountain to the north. It crescendoed within a half hour, then died down again. Apparently the Federal assault there had been unsuccessful. Soon afterward the Yankees opened a concentrated artillery barrage on the low rise occupied by Cheatham and Cleburne. At approximately ten o'clock, the men in Cleburne's Division noted what one called "quite a commotion across on the Yankee side," and 8,000 Federal soldiers emerged from the tree line in front of them to form up for an attack. Sherman had ordered Thomas to ignore traditional light infantry tactics that called for troops to assault enemy positions in two ranks. Instead, he was to concentrate five brigades across a front only a thousand yards wide thus creating, Sherman hoped, an irresistible mass. Indeed, the Yankee soldiers were ordered to remove the firing caps from their rifles and to storm the Confederate positions with bayonets. It made a grand martial display: the massed columns of blue shimmered in the muggy summer heat, their 8,000 bayonets "gleaming in the bright sun."[39]

The circumstances posed few tactical problems. Cleburne's men were entrenched on good ground with a clear field of fire; it was simply a matter of urging them to hold their positions and shoot low. As always, Cleburne had prepared his lines with some care. An attacking enemy would first encounter a chest-high barrier of felled tree limbs called "tanglefoot," the name providing an adequate explanation of its purpose; then they would hit a row of thick wooden spikes driven into the ground and pointed toward the enemy; finally there was a row of chevaux-de-frise, the barbed wire of the nineteenth century, made by inserting sharpened stakes into logs. If the Yankees managed to fight their way through all that, they would then encounter Cleburne's main line, a deep trench filled with armed and determined men who were protected by cross poles and head logs.[40]

Cleburne passed orders to his brigadiers for the men to withhold their fire until they were sure of their target. The massed blue ranks advanced steadily. No doubt more than a few of the waiting Rebels were tempted to squeeze the trigger but discipline held. The Federals were only sixty yards away from the breastworks when the line of leveled muskets exploded in a near simultaneous volley, the billowing smoke from the black powder temporarily obscuring the defenders' view of the battlefield. Men bit off their cartridges and reloaded quickly, firing at will. The attackers fell in windrows; those in the rear pressed forward, while others stopped and knelt to return fire. A few reached the Rebel line. On Cheatham's Front, a Union color-bearer ran forward and placed his regimental colors on the breastworks, where a fierce hand-to-hand struggle over them ensued. On Cleburne's front, one Union sergeant made it to the head logs only to be grabbed and pulled over the top by two men in butternut.

The Federals demonstrated astonishing bravery. Cleburne's men could not believe they could face death so coolly; to one they seemed like wooden men. But bravery was not enough. Eventually, after several hours of fierce combat in the sweltering heat, the Federals began to fall back, and Cleburne's men let them go. If Cleburne considered a counterattack, he never gave the order. Indeed, it would have been a severe test of discipline if he had, for his men were exhausted. Fighting in the heat and humidity of midsummer, breathing smoke for more than four hours, they were near collapse. A few began to convulse with the dry heaves of dehydration.[41]

The Yankees had been severely punished, and the bodies of their dead and wounded covered the field. Worse, the flash of powder had ignited the dry grass, and flames were spreading toward the wounded who cried out they did not want to be burned alive. Major William H. Martin of the 1st Arkansas in Govan's Brigade sized up the situation and acted quickly. "Boys, this is butchery," he said to his troops. Then, tying a white handkerchief to a ramrod and using it as a flag of truce, he jumped up onto the breastworks to call for the Federals to come rescue their wounded. "Cease firing and help get out those men," he called. "They are burning to death; we won't fire a gun till you get them away. Be quick." Men from both sides worked together to pull the wounded to safety. Then the truce ended and they became enemies again.[42]

The Battle of Kennesaw Mountain was an unquestioned Confederate victory, proving finally and decisively what the soldiers knew instinctively. As General Howard phrased it, "We realized now, as never before, the futility of direct assault upon intrenched lines." Sherman tried to minimize the significance of his setback, reporting losses of 2,500, a figure he later revised upward to 3,000. More astonishing were the paltry losses among the defenders. In front of Cleburne's Division, the Federals had lost some 300 killed and more than 500 wounded, whereas his own division lost 2 killed and 9 wounded. Johnston reported these nearly incredible figures to Richmond: "The loss of

Cleburne's Division, 11; that of the enemy in his front, 1,000." Cheatham's Division, which had borne at least an equal share of the fight, suffered 195 casualties.[43]

The relatively light casualties within Cleburne's command during its engagements with the enemy were in one sense deceptive. The wasting effect of an uninterrupted campaign over ten weeks could not be disguised. When the spring campaign had begun, Cleburne reported a total of 5,218 effectives in his command; two months of constant skirmishing had reduced it to 3,855. Notwithstanding these losses, and the particularly painful loss of Lucius Polk, morale in Cleburne's Division remained high. Buck later claimed that "the *morale* of the army was better when it reached the Chattahoochee than when it left Dalton."[44]

The Confederate victories at Pickett's Mill and Kennesaw Mountain notwithstanding, the Army of Tennessee was soon in retreat again. Sherman slid past Johnston's left and raced for the Chattahoochee River crossings. Johnston stalled him there with an elaborate fortification system composed of dozens of small, self-contained forts supported by artillery batteries strategically placed to sweep their front—the brainchild of Brigadier General Francis A. Shoup. The army veterans never fully trusted these little forts, but they effectively deterred Sherman, who sought another way around, crossing the Chattahoochee several miles upstream and threatening the army's communications with Atlanta. Johnston evacuated his string of small forts and retired across the river. For President Davis, it was the last straw.[45]

Late on 17 July, Cleburne learned from Hardee that Johnston had received a telegram from Richmond dismissing him from command and ordering him to turn the army over to Hood. This was astonishing news. For one thing, Cleburne did not believe the crisis was as critical as these orders implied; to change commanders in the midst of a campaign, and on the eve of what was likely to be the decisive battle for Atlanta, was truly desperate. In addition, the elevation of Hood to command was a slap in the face to Hardee, the senior corps commander and the man who had led the army before Johnston had arrived. By jumping Hood over Hardee, the administration was signaling its dissatisfaction with Cleburne's mentor. Cleburne was not alone in his astonishment. Even Hood, whose secret letters to Richmond had undermined Johnston and promoted his own candidacy, was taken aback now that his backstairs maneuvers had won him the job. He agreed to join Hardee and Stewart (commanding Polk's Corps) in urging Johnston to postpone the execution of the order until the fate of Atlanta was decided. Johnston turned them down. He was a soldier, he said, and he would obey orders. For better or for worse, the Army of Tennessee, and the fate of Atlanta, was now in the hands of thirty-year-old John Bell Hood. It was a fateful move. For Pat Cleburne, it would prove to be a fatal one.

12
THE BATTLES FOR ATLANTA

Hood fought four battles for Atlanta, and Cleburne played a central role in two of them. In the Battle of Bald Hill (also known as the Battle of Atlanta) on 22 July and the two-day battle at Jonesboro on 31 August–1 September, he was again at the center of the whirlwind. At Jonesboro, he commanded a corps in a major battle for the first and only time in his career. The campaign brought him little satisfaction, however, for despite some local success on the battlefield, none of his efforts managed to reverse the deteriorating military situation, and his performance as a corps commander at Jonesboro was both frustrating and disappointing. In addition, the battles near Atlanta devastated his command: two-thirds of the men who had filled the ranks of his three brigades in mid-July were killed, wounded, or captured by the end of August. Finally, despite all his efforts—and the blood of his men—the Army of Tennessee failed to hold Atlanta against Sherman's unrelenting pressure. The city's fall on 2 September was the first tone sounding the death knell of the Confederacy.

News of Johnston's dismissal began circulating through the ranks at mid-morning on 18 July. It sent a shock wave through the army; in Cleburne's Division, men gathered spontaneously in small groups to discuss it. Buck wrote that the news "was received with depression by the Confederate troops"; Captain Key claimed that "every man looked sad and disheartened." Some "wept like children," others were moved to anger and shouted, "Hurrah for Joe Johnson [*sic*] and God D——n Jeff Davis." A captain in Granbury's Brigade wrote, "For the first time we hear men openly talk about going home." Although the anger was genuine, it soon passed. By now the men in the ranks were bound less to a particular army commander than they were to each other. They were disappointed, even angry, but their disappointment did not lead to a mass exodus.[1]

Cleburne, too, was dismayed. Characteristically, he kept his thoughts to himself, though his closest friends later testified to his state of mind. Mangum claimed that Cleburne believed the dismissal of Johnston was "a great disaster," and Cleburne's old friend Dr. Nash wrote, "Cleburne believed that the death warrant of the Confederacy had been sealed when Gen. Joseph E. Johnson [*sic*] was removed to give place to a leader who had nothing but courage to recommend him." Indeed, it was the appointment of Hood that Cleburne found most appalling. Hardee was significantly senior to Hood, more experienced, and the man, above all, whom Cleburne trusted to command. Hood was without doubt personally brave, but he had been with the army for less than six months and was badly crippled. Moreover, he was three years younger than Cleburne and only two months senior as a major general. Like the men in the ranks, however, and like the fatalist that he was, Cleburne perceived it his duty, quite literally, to soldier on.[2]

Ironically, Johnston's dismissal created a potential opportunity for Cleburne since Hood's old corps now needed a new commander. By near-universal acclaim, Cleburne had compiled the best record in the army as a division commander, and even if he did not seek or expect his own promotion, he was certainly a logical candidate for it. Ordinarily the post would be given, at least temporarily, to the senior division commander in Hood's Corps, but Hood did not believe that any of his major generals was suited for the job so he approached Hardee to ask him which of his division commanders was best qualified. Hardee named Frank Cheatham.[3]

In the years since, students of the Civil War have suggested a variety of reasons to explain why Cleburne was not promoted to lieutenant-general and a corps command: He was foreign-born; he was not a West Point graduate; he had participated in the cabal against Bragg; and he had proposed arming the slaves. But none of these explanations fit the circumstances in July 1864. Cheatham, who *was* promoted, was not a West Point graduate; he too had been a vocal opponent of Bragg's leadership; and though he had failed to sign Cleburne's Memorial about arming the slaves, Bragg and others counted him among those who had supported the idea. If anything, Bragg hated Cheatham more than he distrusted Cleburne. And in any case, Cleburne's name was never submitted up the chain of command where Bragg's presumed malevolent influence could bear on the question. It was Hardee, Cleburne's friend and mentor, who nominated Cheatham to command Hood's old corps. To be sure, Cheatham outranked Cleburne as a major general by nine months. But in the fall of 1862, Hardee had urged Cleburne's promotion over the heads of others who were senior to him. This time he did not.[4]

Perhaps Hardee was loath to lose Cleburne as his principal lieutenant. But perhaps, too, Hardee had come to believe that while Cleburne was unquestionably a superb division commander, he lacked that spark of independent initiative necessary to be effective in the command of a corps. Hardee relied heavily on Cleburne's diligence and conscientiousness. In many ways he was the ideal subordinate: he did not quail at the most difficult assignments; he was straightforward and direct in his reports; he had no subterfuge or hidden agenda. But in addition, Cleburne seldom initiated new plans of action. At meetings of corps and division commanders, he listened attentively and gave his opinions if asked, but he almost never claimed the floor to present an alternate proposal, the single and dramatic exception being his notorious proposal to arm the slaves. Sensitive to this aspect of Cleburne's character, Hardee had kept his headquarters close to Cleburne's during most of their campaigns. In part this derived from their personal friendship and a sense of partnership, but perhaps, too, Hardee wanted to be near Cleburne to provide oversight and supervision. It may be that Hardee had come to believe that for all his virtues, Cleburne had reached his proper rank as a major general.

As for Hood, he knew precisely what Davis now expected of him. Johnston had been sent packing because he had allowed Sherman to advance deep into Georgia without once launching a serious counteroffensive. Hood had a reputation as an aggressive commander, but in addition he had sent a series of secret and self-promotional letters to Davis, Seddon, and Bragg urging a more aggressive strategy. Now he would have to act. On 19 July he called his corps commanders to his headquarters to issue orders for battle. He told them that while Wheeler's cavalry fended off Federal forces approaching from the east, Hardee and Stewart would pile into Thomas's Army of the Cumberland after it crossed Peachtree Creek and drive it along the south back of the creek into the cul-de-sac it formed with the Chattahoochee River. Hardee was to initiate the attack, striking Thomas on his left flank. It would begin, Hood told them, at one o'clock the next day.

Cleburne's designated role in this attack was as the corps reserve. Rather than lead the attack, he would hold his three brigades in readiness to reinforce and exploit the breakthrough. The morning passed quietly as the forces moved to their designated positions. Cleburne deployed his division behind Walker's, moving his artillery to the front where it could fire over the heads of the attackers into the Federal lines. At noon, only an hour before the attack was to begin, he received orders to shift his position a mile to the right. Out of concern for his right flank, where Wheeler was calling for help, Hood had ordered Cheatham to move in that direction, and to avoid opening a gap in the line, he also ordered Hardee to sidestep to the right to maintain contact. This change provoked some confusion and inevitable delays, and as a result the attack along Peachtree Creek was not only late, it took place over ground that the unit commanders had had no opportunity to examine. Bate, commanding Hardee's right-hand division, never found the enemy at all. Walker, directly in front of Cleburne, found that the delay had given the Federals an opportunity to prepare breastworks, and he was driven back. Though some other units enjoyed local success, particularly Loring's Division in Stewart's Crops, the attack on Hardee's front was stillborn.[5]

Cleburne was sitting his horse alongside Hardee in a small grove of trees adjacent to the Atlanta Road when a courier from Walker reported that his attack had been repulsed. Hardee ordered Cleburne to commit his division. At that moment, a courier from Hood reined up, saluted, and declared that the enemy was turning the army's right; Hardee was to send a division there at once. Hardee thereupon revoked Cleburne's orders and told him to take his division to the right instead. Of course that also meant the attack along Peachtree Creek would lose what little momentum it had. Bate's men were lost, thrashing about somewhere in the undergrowth, and Walker's men were (in Hardee's word) "beaten." Without Cleburne's fresh troops, the attack had little chance.[6]

As the fighting along Peachtree Creek sputtered out in the twilight darkness, Cleburne faced his men away from the battle and marched them southward into Atlanta. They passed through town and out the Decatur Road, arriving at the designated point east of the city at an hour past midnight. The men of Wheeler's dismounted cavalry were ecstatic to see them. Wheeler had been sending Hood increasingly frantic messages all day, claiming that he was fending off two full enemy corps. Now that the infantry had arrived, even if it was only a single division, he was ready to turn the assignment over to Cleburne. As the cavalry moved off, several of them whispered to Cleburne's men that the enemy was very close and would open fire at the least noise.[7]

It was pitch-dark as Cleburne's men filed into line. There were no earthworks—only a line of shallow rifle pits the cavalrymen had scraped out of the soil. Cleburne ordered his men to prepare proper fieldworks as quietly as possible. The clay soil was hard as bricks, and the men jabbed at it with their bayonets. Almost at once, the sound of their work alerted the Yankee gunners, and the Federal artillery opened fire. One enemy battery in particular was sited so as to enfilade Cleburne's line, and forty men were blown apart by an unseen foe even as the rest scrambled to build breastworks.[8]

Dawn revealed how exposed Cleburne's position was, but there was no possibility of choosing better ground now. Once the sun was up, the Yankee gunners redoubled their fire, and soon the sharpshooters opened up as well. Just past eight o'clock, the Federals launched an infantry assault. But for the presence of Cleburne's Division, that assault would have overrun Wheeler's cavalry pickets and been into Atlanta within an hour. As it was, the few cavalrymen who had been left behind to guard Cleburne's right flank fired off one volley, then broke and ran, advising the infantry to do the same. Their flight left Cleburne's right exposed, and he ordered James A. Smith, again commanding the Texas Brigade, to counterattack and regain the lost ground. At the same time, he sent to Hood for support. Hood sent him Cheatham's old division, commanded now by George Maney, and Cleburne used it to extend his right flank. Thus reinforced, he fought off a series of determined Federal attacks that lasted virtually all day. This time, the terrain was no help to the defenders who were caught in a crossfire: the men simply had to stand to the work, loading and firing as fast as possible. It was, one soldier recalled, "a dreadful fight." Cleburne later told Hardee that it was the bitterest fight of his life.[9]

Night could not come fast enough. Cleburne's hard-pressed soldiers prayed for it, and when at last the sun set, they slumped back in their shallow trench and fell into oblivion. After all, they had been marching and fighting continuously since the morning of the previous day. But the day was not over yet. At eight o'clock, new orders arrived from Hardee for Cleburne quietly to abandon his line and fall back into the city—not for a rest but to participate in another attack. Cleburne could not leave at once, however. If the enemy were to be deceived, he could not begin his move until well past dark, and in late July the twilight lingered for hours. Finally, after full dark, he ordered his pickets to remain in place while the rest of his force stole quietly from their lines and crept back toward Atlanta, some of them quite literally on their hands and knees. The last of them did not leave the line until after ten o'clock.[10]

Once inside the city, Cleburne's men had a short rest while he met with Hardee. Cleburne was probably present when Hardee received his final orders from Hood. In conscious imitation of Robert E. Lee, Hood planned for Hardee (playing the role of Stonewall Jackson) to lead his corps on a lengthy and circuitous march to strike the flank and rear of the Federal army that was approaching from Decatur. As Hood envisioned it, Hardee's dawn strike would roll up the Federal line from the south. Then Hood would unleash Cheatham's Corps—his own former command—to administer the coup de grace. The plan was a good one, but it failed to account for what Clausewitz had called "friction." Even as the generals talked it was already approaching midnight, and though Hood later described Hardee's Corps as "fresh," most of the men had not slept for two days. For such men to cover the required fifteen miles, marching at night, before launching a dawn attack was simply unrealistic. Another factor was that the soldiers' progress through the city would be slowed by crowds of panicked civilians who feared that Hood was evacuating Atlanta. Under the press of Hardee's objections, Hood agreed that instead of striking the Federal rear, he could turn north at a moment of his choosing and hit the enemy flank.[11]

At midnight, Cleburne rode southward out of the city at the head of his division. Hardee, as usual, rode alongside. They rode all night under a full moon that made it nearly as light as day: south on the McDonough Road, then southeast, and finally northeast toward Decatur. About an hour before dawn, they halted near Cobb's Mill, and the men fell out by the side of the road for a few hours sleep. There was no sleep for Cleburne. He and Hardee met with Walker and Wheeler in Cobb's home to discuss details of the attack. Though Wheeler reported that the road ahead was clear of enemy forces, Hardee knew he could not delay much longer. The sun was already well up, and from his headquarters west of Atlanta, Hood was no doubt waiting impatiently for the sound of the attack. Hardee decided that the troops would march only another two miles: Bate and Walker would continue northwestward to Sugar Creek, then face left and move against the presumed Federal flank; Cleburne and Maney would move northward along Flat Shoals Road and deploy on Walker's left. That decided, Cleburne left the meeting and awakened his sleeping troops for the last leg of the march. With the exception of that two-hour nap by the side of the road, his men had now marched or fought continuously for forty-eight hours.[12]

The troops were not in position until the sun was nearly overhead; "It was awfull hot," an Arkansas soldier recalled. Cleburne deployed his three brigades just to the west of the Flat Shoals (or McDonough) Road, with Govan on the left and the Texas Brigade (under Smith) on the right. He placed Lowrey 500 yards behind in a second line as a reserve. At approximately 12:45, he gave the command, and the men moved forward. Cleburne disliked advancing over ground he had not had an opportunity to reconnoiter, and very soon the thick underbrush and tangle of blackberry bushes broke up the attack formation. After thrashing forward for nearly a mile, Cleburne called a halt and ordered his brigadiers to correct their alignment. Alas, this consumed valuable time, and though Cleburne was still not satisfied, he ordered the advance resumed.[13]

Finally, Govan's Arkansans encountered a score of Yankee skirmishers who scampered quickly back to a line of light breastworks. Two of Govan's regiments assailed the works with such fury that the defenders ceased firing and

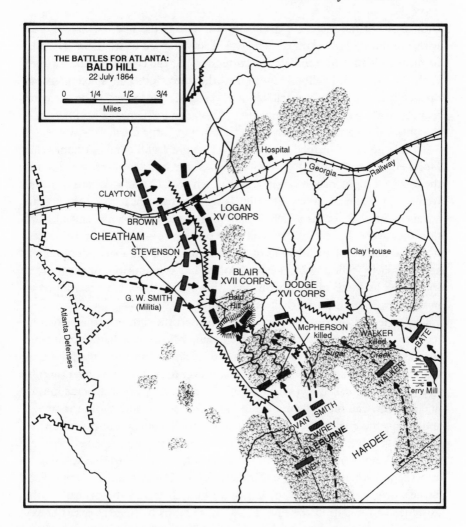

THE BATTLES FOR ATLANTA:
BALD HILL
22 July 1864

0   1/4   1/2   3/4
Miles

Hospital

Georgia   Railway

CLAYTON

LOGAN
XV CORPS

BROWN

CHEATHAM

Clay House

STEVENSON

BLAIR
XVII CORPS

DODGE
XVI CORPS

G. W. SMITH
(Militia)

Bald
Hill

McPHERSON
killed

WALKER
killed

BATE

Atlanta Defenses

Sugar   Creek

WALKER

Terry Mill

GOVAN   SMITH

LOWREY
CLEBURNE

HARDEE

MANEY

called out that they surrendered. When Govan's two regiments approached to take possession of the works, however, the Federals realized how few of them there were and opened fire again. Only when Govan's other two regiments came up on their flank did they lay down their arms.[14]

On Govan's right, Smith's Texans had even better luck, finding an unguarded gap in the Federal defenses. Here were abandoned caissons, ordnance and tool wagons, even ambulances, parked randomly in apparent unconcern. Tired as they were, this evidence that they had caught the enemy by surprise was a tonic to the soldiers, and they pursued the surprised and fleeing bluecoats with enthusiasm. (Smith later complained of the "ungovernable enthusiasm of the men.") A group from the 33d Alabama met face to face with a mounted Yankee officer who was clearly startled to see them. The Alabamians called for him to halt and surrender, but the officer instead touched his hat in salute and galloped off in the other direction. The Alabama troops opened fire, and the officer fell. Upon investigation it proved to be the commander of the Army of the Tennessee, Major General James B. McPherson—the only Union army commander to be killed in battle during the war.[15]

To this point, it seemed that the attack might fulfill the high hopes that Hood entertained for it. But by two o'clock, the heat, the lack of sleep, and the long, all-night march began to take their toll. Govan's Arkansas troops were gasping for air; a few literally passed out from heatstroke during the advance. Smith's Texans suffered many of the same problems, and in addition they were slowed by the need to gather up prisoners and take possession of a number of artillery pieces. Others ransacked the abandoned wagons and knapsacks, claiming blankets, oilcloths, and ammunition for themselves. Inevitably, as some stopped to harvest this booty, those who continued to pursue the Federals found their ranks thinned.[16]

Cleburne was only a few dozen yards behind the fighting front when he received a request for support from Govan, whose men had encountered another line of Yankee breastworks, this one more formidable than the first. Govan declared that he needed more manpower to fight his way over this obstacle. Cleburne called a young staff officer to his side and instructed him to find Lowrey. Tell him to come up in Govan's rear, Cleburne told the staffer, and storm the enemy breastworks. The young lieutenant rode rearward to find Lowrey, but en route he noted that a huge gap had opened between Cleburne's right and Walker's left. An enemy force sent into that gap would imperil both divisions. The staff officer found Lowrey and delivered Cleburne's orders, but he also took it upon himself to tell the general of the existence of the gap in the line. He went so far as to suggest that Lowrey ignore Cleburne's orders and take his brigade into the gap instead. Lowrey "unhesitatingly" accepted the responsibility of doing exactly that, marching his troops eastward and coming into the fight on Govan's right. He wrote later that he was positive that if Cleburne had known of the gap, he would have ordered Lowrey to fill it, and, indeed, when he learned of Lowrey's actions, Cleburne instantly approved them. It speaks volumes about Cleburne's command style, and his relationship with his subordinates, that Lowrey felt not the least hesitation in behaving as he did. Cleburne's subordinates knew their commander well enough to understand his mind. He was a stickler for discipline, but he was no pettifog; blind obedience to orders was not a virtue if the military objective was imperiled. Cleburne's relationship with his subordinates was as much a partnership as a hierarchy.[17]

Meanwhile the fight on Govan's front continued. Always an advocate of the use of artillery on the attack, Cleburne had ordered his field guns to advance with the infantry, and now he ordered Captain Key to bring his battery up to within 200 yards of the Federal line and open fire. The Federals wavered. When Granbury's Texans came in on their left, they broke. Key galloped back to where Cleburne and Govan were watching the fight and reported that the Yanks were running. "Generals to the front!" he called out, a remark that "caused a smile to play upon Cleburne's face." Cleburne put the spurs to his mount and cantered forward with Key to the base of a round-topped hill known as Bald Hill, which was crowned by a third line of Federal breastworks and which was the pivot of the Federal line. One Tennessee soldier later claimed to remember his arrival as a dramatic moment. "Cleburne himself was leading us in person," wrote Sam Watkins of the 1st Tennessee. "His sword was drawn. I heard him say 'Follow me, boys!' He ran forward, and amid the blazing fires of the Yankee guns was soon on top of the enemy's works." The decisive breakthrough seemed at hand.[18]

But the Yanks were not running. The night before, they had built defensive breastworks facing Atlanta, and now that they were assailed from the south and east, they clambered over to the other side of their works and fought off the renewed attack by Cleburne's Division. Lowrey's Brigade added its impetus to the struggle, and Maney's Division came into the fight on Cleburne's left. Despite their exhaustion, the Rebels charged with impetuosity. Furiously, the Yankees hurled them back. For three-quarters of an hour, the soldiers fought each other across the entrenchments with color-bearers from both sides striving to plant their flags atop the works. Though some of the Rebels gained a temporary lodgement, night closed with the Yankees still in possession of Bald Hill. Cleburne's men fell back to the second line of Federal entrenchments they had captured earlier and dug in.[19]

Incomplete as it was, the partial success of Cleburne's Division on Bald Hill was the high point of the Confederate assault. On his right, Bate and Walker had been slowed by difficult terrain and suffered a repulse; Walker had been shot dead before the attack was fairly under way. As for Cheatham's Corps, it did not get into the fight until late in the day, after Cleburne's attack was losing momentum. Hood had delayed ordering Cheatham forward in the hope that Hardee's assault would drive the Federals north of the Decatur Road, in which event Cheatham's attack would prove decisive. Despairing of such an outcome, he finally unleashed Cheatham at three o'clock.

Cheatham's men fought furiously, but except for a temporary breakthrough by some troops in John C. Brown's Division, the attack was disappointing.

That night, the men of Cleburne's Division improved the lines they had captured and prepared to defend the ground they had won. Almost by mutual agreement—or perhaps by mutual exhaustion—there was little firing during the night. For the first time in forty-eight hours, Cleburne's men slept; even the proximity of the enemy proved no impediment to their consuming exhaustion. When the sun came up on 23 July, both armies remained in place, unwilling to renew the slaughter, and at midmorning, they agreed on an armistice to remove the dead and wounded from between the lines.[20]

Hood reported the action as a victory. He wrote Seddon that his forces had captured 22 artillery pieces, 5 stand of colors, and 2,000 prisoners, noting that "our troops fought with great gallantry." Ominously, he added that his own losses were "not fully ascertained." Indeed, Confederate losses were heavy, though the precise numbers became a point of contention. Hardee reported losses of 3,299 in his corps, 40 percent of whom (1,388) were from Cleburne's Division. That exceeded the combined losses in all the division's previous battles in the campaign. The carnage was particularly evident at the top of the command hierarchy. Even though Cleburne himself survived unscathed, thirty of forty field grade officers in his division had fallen. Eight of the fifteen regimental commanders in the division were killed or wounded; among the dead was John E. Murray, the boy colonel of the 5th/13th Arkansas who had defended Ringgold Gap. James A. Smith, commanding the Texas Brigade, was badly wounded and had to turn command back to Granbury. Lowrey lost 578 out of just over a thousand men and reported simply that his brigade was "cut to pieces."[21]

The fight on 22 July was, in Hardee's phrase, a "desperate and bloody battle." But desperate as it was, it was also indecisive. It failed to halt, or even appreciably slow, Sherman's tightening noose on the city. More than that, it had cost far more than the Army of Tennessee could afford. Total Confederate casualties (including those in Cheatham's Corps) numbered between 5,500 and 8,000. By contrast, the Federals lost about 3,800 men. Many more such "victories" would destroy the army.[22]

After three nearly sleepless days of fury, Cleburne and his men enjoyed a respite of sorts. Sherman's army disappeared from their front, and Hood recalled Hardee's Corps back into the defenses of the city. As usual after a bloody fight, some reorganization was necessary. First, Stephen Dill Lee arrived to take permanent command of Hood's former corps, with Cheatham reverting to divisional command. There was some skepticism in the ranks about Lee's promotion, which at least one soldier thought was "above his deserts." A distant cousin of Robert E. Lee, this much younger Lee (age thirty) had graduated from West Point a year behind Hood.

A second organizational change that affected Cleburne was the breakup of Walker's Division. Rather than find another division commander to replace Walker, who had been killed in the recent fight, his brigades were parceled out among the other divisions. Cleburne drew Mercer's Brigade, which was composed of three Georgia regiments and commanded by Colonel Charles Olmstead. Until recently, the Georgians had enjoyed easy duty as part of the garrison of Savannah, but in the Confederacy's crisis they had been added to Walker's Division just prior to the battles for Atlanta. Cleburne was no doubt glad of the additional manpower, but their presence in his command greatly affected the chemistry of the division. Not only did the Georgians lack the shared history that bound the rest of the division together, but they also were largely untested in battle and thus significantly outnumbered the veteran brigades. One Alabama soldier noted sourly that Mercer's Brigade "contained nearly as many men as all the old brigade together." Cleburne was also disappointed by his newest brigade commander, warning Hardee that if he expected Mercer's brigade "to do any good, a brigade commander is immediately necessary. Its present commander [Olmstead] is not efficient."[23]

Cleburne set his men to work improving their entrenchments. The Georgians had to be taught how to do it properly, so he ordered them to dig deep ditches with an elevated ledge against the forward wall on which the men could stand to fire, then step down to reload. He ordered the preparation of a brush abatis and the placement of spiked sticks in front of the lines, and he supervised the work personally, riding daily along the line, often accompanied by Hardee. Cleburne's experience had convinced him that strong fieldworks were essential, particularly to a numerically inferior army. Hood agreed only to a point; he could not shake off the notion of the moral superiority of the offensive. On 25 July, even as Cleburne supervised the improvement of the lines on his sector of the front, the army commander issued a General Field Order that was intended to restore the soldiers' enthusiasm for the attack, but which may have struck many as singularly inappropriate coming so soon after the heavy losses at Bald Hill. Victory, Hood asserted, was largely a matter of will: "You have but to will it," he declared, "and God will grant us victory." Cleburne was not one to discount the importance of moral factors in combat; he, too, believed that commitment and determination could overcome matériel superiority. But the timing of Hood's General Order seemed to imply that such a will had been lacking in the battles of the previous week, an implication that many saw as a slur on the army, and particularly on Hardee's Corps.[24]

Two days later, Cleburne's pickets reported that once again the enemy had disappeared from his front. He mounted up and rode out to examine their abandoned works. A newspaper found in their camp confirmed the death of General McPherson. But what did it mean that the Federals had decamped? Though a few grasped at the hope that they were retreating, it was more probable that Sherman was once again searching for a weak flank. If he had abandoned the approach from the east, his legions were very likely marching even then for the roads into Atlanta from the west. Accordingly, the whole Confederate army rotated its defensive axis ninety degrees. Cleburne occupied the lines north of the Augusta Railroad, where he was assigned to cover a mile and a half of trenches with fewer than 3,000 men—approximately one man per yard.[25]

Cleburne established his headquarters in a large stone house on a small knoll. The house was a prominent landmark and therefore a target for Federal artillery, and the headquarters staff got in the habit of dining outside, behind the house, using its substantial bulk to screen their dinner table from enemy gunners. On 27 July, however, the mess cooks set up the table in a new spot, more exposed than before. Approaching the table for lunch, Benham objected that "while he was perfectly willing to take all legitimate risk of battle, he could not see the sense of unnecessary ones." Even so, he sat down and began to eat. Within minutes an enemy shell exploded almost directly overhead. A fragment from the shell cut Benham's face, and he leaped up from the table bleeding profusely. Cursing at the cooks and the Yankees by turn, Benham then turned to Cleburne and pointing to his facial wound insisted, "This is 'not as deep as a well, or wide as a church door,' but is good for thirty days' leave!"[26]

It was soon evident that Sherman was indeed maneuvering his forces to approach Atlanta from the west. The day after Benham's narrow escape from a Yankee artillery shell, the men of S. D. Lee's Corps fought the Battle of Ezra Church, a badly bungled attempt by Hood to block Sherman's new approach. Hood tried to put the best face on it, reporting to Richmond only that "a sharp engagement ensued with no decided advantage to either side." In fact, the Confederates had launched a series of fruitless frontal assaults that netted little besides an additional 5,000 Confederate casualties. Having lost between 12,000 and 15,000 men in ten days, Hood fell back on the strategy that he had dismissed with contempt when Johnston had advocated it: sending Wheeler's cavalry to cut Sherman's supply lines. Meanwhile, Sherman continued to probe from the west, edging southward toward the railroad connecting Atlanta to what remained of the Confederacy.[27]

On 6 August, Cleburne received orders to move once again, and for the rest of the month, his division was on the move almost constantly, extending the Confederate lines toward the southwest, entrenching in front of Sherman as that indefatigable Yankee sought persistently to find a way around them. As one soldier described it, "Every night we would move further to the left in single rank and send out pickets in front in the dark facing west." As always, Cleburne personally supervised the digging of the entrenchments. At first, his men occupied their ditch only during the day, climbing out after dark to lie down on the ground for a night's sleep. Soon, however, the Yankees got into the habit of lobbing artillery shells into the rear area at night, and the men began sleeping and eating in the trenches. "We remained in the ditch night and day," a soldier in Lowrey's Brigade recalled, "and dug traverse trenches at night . . . to protect us in passing to the rear and back carrying water, food, or ammunition, or carrying the wounded or dead out on stretchers." Because fires attracted the attention of enemy sharpshooters, there could be no fires at night, and even in the daytime, the men built fires only in the trenches or well to the rear.[28]

Picket duty was particularly dangerous, but it also provided occasional opportunities. One company from the 6th Texas in Granbury's Brigade was on picket duty when a farmer's cow wandered within range. The seizure of private property was strictly against orders. Hood had declared that soldiers guilty of "the lawless seizure and destruction of private property" were subject to arrest, and he announced that he would hold officers accountable "that their men conduct themselves properly."[29] Still, the prospect of fresh beef was so tempting that the Texans took a chance. They shot the cow and slaughtered it on the spot. Each company took a share back to camp to cook it. One company was busily engaged cutting the beef into chunks and watching it sizzle over the fire and failed to notice Cleburne approaching. "We were all busy working," private T. O. Moore recalled, "when one of the company looked up and saw old Pat coming down the line on a tour of inspection. We had no time to hide the beef, and knew we were in for it." Calculating that he might as well be hanged for a sheep as a lamb (or in this case a cow), one soldier leaped to his feet, walked up to Cleburne, saluted, and said, "General, we have some nice, fat beef cooking, and it is about done; come and eat dinner with us." Cleburne was not so naive that he did not suspect how the soldiers had come by their fresh beef. He looked at the soldier for a long moment and then spoke: "Well," he said, "it does smell good. I believe I will."

Cleburne sat down on a log by the fire, and one of the Texas soldiers handed him a piece of beef, still sizzling. Another handed him a piece of corn bread, and they all set about eating happily. "The General ate quite heartily," Moore remembered, "thanked us for the dinner, took out his cob pipe, filled it, and began to smoke." He chatted pleasantly with the men, asked them what they thought of their current position, and did they think they could whip the Yankees? Then he thanked them for dinner and passed on down the line, the men cheering. In recalling the incident thirty years later, the private mused, "How could we help admiring him?"[30]

By the second week of August, Cleburne had extended the Confederate left as far as East Point, five miles south of Atlanta where the Atlanta and West Point Railroad met the Macon and Western. This was the critical point; Hood wrote Davis, "To hold Atlanta, I have to hold East Point." On 11 August, Hood showed up personally at Cleburne's headquarters, and the two generals rode together along the line. Despite his prosthetic leg and crippled arm, Hood rode easily enough and seemed to be in a good mood. He was "sociable and affable," Captain Key recalled, speaking "in a friendly way" to the men as he passed, conversing "freely upon the condition of the army, and appeared in hopeful anticipation of ultimate victory."[31]

But Hood's confident demeanor was at least partly an act designed to boost the morale of the troops. Because he had sent most of the army's cavalry north in what proved a futile effort to cut Sherman's supply lines, he was not sure where Sherman was or what he was doing. In modern military jargon, he had lost the bubble. To compensate for his lack of cavalry, he urged increased vigilance along the picket line and warned the soldiers against fraternization across no-man's-land. Throughout the campaign, the pickets on both sides had frequently traded gossip and even newspapers during brief, self-declared cease-fires. Now Hood declared that any soldier attempting to communicate with the enemy would be shot. As a further precaution, he directed Cleburne to keep one regiment from each brigade out of the trenches as a ready reserve. Of course, this meant that the men in the trenches had to stretch themselves even thinner. The next day, Captain Foster noted in his diary, "Our brigade are put in one rank and about 3 feet apart, but I believe we can hold our position." Indeed, Hood urged them to hold on "to the very last." "Let every man remember that he is individually responsible for his few feet of line," Hood declared in a circular intended for the entire army, "and that the destiny of Atlanta hangs upon the issue."[32]

The month of August was filled with constant alarms. Hardee reminded

Cleburne to be ready to move at a moment's notice. For a while Hood suspected that Sherman was preparing to attack his right between East Point and Atlanta, and he ordered Cleburne to send two of his brigades northward. By the next day it was evident that the enemy activity there had been only a feint, and that the blow was likely to fall further south below East Point on the left flank of the Confederate lines. Cleburne readied his division for a rapid movement in either direction and set up his headquarters in the telegraph office at East Point to await developments.[33]

On 20 August, after a week of hot, sultry weather, the rain came pelting down in torrents, filling the trenches and muddying the roads, but it did little to help clarify the unfolding military situation. Hood remained desperate for intelligence. He queried Cleburne about the location of his lines and told him, "Keep your scouts close up to [the] enemy day and night." Cleburne did keep his scouts out, and on 29 August they reported that once again the enemy had decamped. Where was Sherman going this time? Captain Key noted in his diary, "Some believe Sherman to be retreating; others think he is preparing for a flank attack on our corps."[34]

The answer became evident the next day when the lead elements of a strong Federal column appeared some fourteen miles south of East Point opposite Jonesboro on the Macon and Western Railroad. Hood ordered Hardee to come to Atlanta immediately to discuss the Confederate response; he even sent a special engine down to pick him up. Hardee left Cleburne in temporary command of the corps with orders to march south to Jonesboro overnight. Though the railroad nearly paralleled the road, there was not enough rolling stock to transport the men by train; they would have to march. The first of them left their lines around East Point around four o'clock. Cleburne sent a scout ahead to reconnoiter the road, but impatient for news, he rode forward himself with a small escort. He overtook the scout a few miles ahead and at almost the same moment discovered a strong enemy force that was holding a bridge on his line of march. The Yankee skirmishers at the bridge fired a volley at the mounted group in the road, and Cleburne rode out of range to contemplate his alternatives. He might be able to force his way over the bridge, but to do so he would have to stop the column and deploy. It was already full dark, and Hardee had instructed him to have his division in Jonesboro by dawn. Even if his troops could secure the bridge, it would take time he could not spare. He decided to seek an alternate route.

He rode back to his marching column and found a side road leading southward. Cleburne was impatient. The night was passing quickly and Jonesboro was still a dozen miles away. Generally imperturbable even in the midst of battle, this delay caused him visible anxiety. His state of mind was not improved by the discovery that only a narrow wooded ridge separated his marching column from "a large body of Sherman's army," which was holding the main road south. Under such circumstances, the march seemed to take forever. The side road was narrow, and in the dark there were numberless stumblings and wrong turns. Cleburne's chief of staff thought it was "the slowest march I ever saw; the men dragged themselves along, constantly recurring halts protracted it." During the short rest breaks, the men simply tumbled down in the road and went to sleep where they were. Aware that Sherman's main force might discover them at any moment, Benham wrote later, "I trembled for the division." [35]

As Cleburne marched the corps south, Hardee was heading north for his conference with Hood in Atlanta. There, the army commander instructed Hardee to assume command of Lee's Corps as well as his own and to drive the Federals back at all costs. Hardee arrived at Jonesboro a few hours before daylight to discover that the troops were still en route. The first units of Cleburne's Corps began to arrive only after sunrise, "worn out by the march," and the men of Lee's Corps were two more hours behind them. Meanwhile, Hardee received a series of increasingly urgent messages from Hood to get on with it. The first arrived a few minutes after 3:00 A.M.: "As soon as you can get your troops in position . . . you must attack and drive the enemy." Ten minutes later there came another: "You must not fail to attack the enemy so soon as you can get your troops up." And ten minutes later, another: "The necessity is imperative. The enemy must be driven into and across the river." [36]

The Federal force that Hood expected Hardee to drive across the Flint River consisted of three divisions of Major General John A. (Black Jack) Logan's XV Corps plus most of two more divisions from supporting units, altogether a force of perhaps 20,000 men, approximately the same number of soldiers that Hardee had to send against it. The Federals, moreover, were well rested and entrenched in a semicircle with both flanks anchored on the river. To attack such a position with no better than even numbers bordered on desperation, but if the enemy were *not* driven back, Hood would have to evacuate Atlanta.

Hardee met with Cleburne and Lee that morning and outlined his plan for the attack. Cleburne, Hardee explained, would initiate it. Retaining the command of Hardee's Corps, he would advance its three divisions in echelon formation against the southern flank of the Federal bridgehead and roll up the line south to north. To achieve this, Cleburne's Corps would attack in a sweeping right wheel movement. Lee would join in only after Cleburne's attack was well developed, and he was to judge the proper moment from the sound of Cleburne's gunfire. [37]

Cleburne left Hardee's headquarters and met with his division commanders. Though it was his first experience directing a corps in combat, the ravages of war had so reduced the army that managing a "corps" of 10,000 men posed little greater tactical complexity than directing the division of 6,000 he had led at Murfreesboro. Indeed, Cleburne may have remembered his experience at Murfreesboro in making his dispositions at Jonesboro. In that earlier battle, the left-hand division in the attack (McCown's) had failed to execute the sharp right wheel that was the key to the plan, and as a result Cleburne's own division had been forced to carry the burden of the fight. Perhaps to ensure that such a thing did not happen again, Cleburne directed that this time his own division, now under the former Baptist minister Mark Lowrey, deploy on the left and initiate the attack. Lowrey understood that his own left-hand brigade, Granbury's Texans, would be "the battalion of direction," and that the rest of the division, and hence the rest of the corps, would adjust the direction and speed of its advance to Granbury's movements. Accordingly, Lowrey ordered all his regimental commanders "to guide to the *left*." Major General George Maney, meanwhile, understood just the opposite: that the front line was to advance "swinging to the right, dressing on the *right* and touching the left or wheeling flank." Compounding this misunderstanding, Cleburne may well have erred when, with the best of intentions, he emphasized the imperative tone of Hood's multiple telegrams to Hardee to drive the enemy over the Flint River. Lowrey forwarded these orders to his brigadiers, telling them that "General Hood expected them to go at the enemy with fixed bayonets and drive them across the river." Some of them may have reasonably concluded that getting to the river was the object of the attack.[38]

The battle began about 3:30 when Lowrey's brigades charged forward. The first enemy troops they encountered were some dismounted cavalry who fired at them from behind a low breastwork of rails. Though only in brigade strength, the cavalrymen had four artillery pieces and were armed with breech-loading Spencer rifles and six-shooters so that they put out a surprising volume of fire. "They just fairly made it rain bullets as long as they had any," Captain Foster wrote in his diary, "but as soon as they gave out, and we were getting closer to them every moment, they couldn't stand it but broke and ran like good fellows." Instead of swerving to the right to assail the Federal infantry, however, Granbury's Texans set out in pursuit of the fleeing cavalry, chasing them all the way to the river. Granbury later reported, "My orders were to drive all opposing forces beyond Flint River," and that is exactly what he did. Lowrey claimed that Granbury's men were "too full of impetuosity" and that they had pursued the Federals "contrary to instructions." Perhaps so, but following Lowrey's own orders to "guide left," the

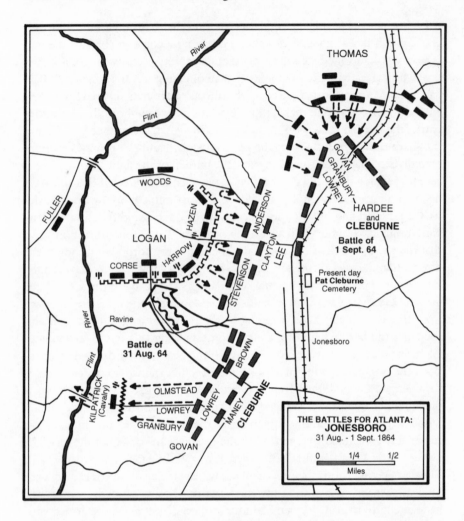

THE BATTLES FOR ATLANTA:
JONESBORO
31 Aug. - 1 Sept. 1864

next two brigades in his division followed Granbury's route, pursuing the dismounted Federal cavalry across Flint River but ignoring the entrenched infantry to the north.[39]

To Lowrey's right, Brown's Division with Maney's behind it swung to the right as instructed. But lacking the support of Lowrey's Division and with their left flank now open, the attack on the Federal breastworks lost much of its impact. Cleburne could see for himself that the planned right wheel was falling apart. He sent a courier off to find Lowrey and get his division back on track, and he rode forward personally to direct Maney's Division into the fight. When he reined up in front of Maney, that officer told him he had ordered two of his four brigades into the widening gap between Lowrey and Brown. Cleburne approved the move and told Maney "to take personal supervision" of those two brigades to ensure that Brown was supported. Maney saluted and wheeled off to obey. Even with those two additional brigades, however, it was evident that Brown's assault against an entrenched and superior enemy was all but hopeless. Only a moment after Maney left, Cleburne sent an orderly galloping after him with revised orders to take his whole division to the right and to attack alongside Brown.[40]

Cleburne watched Maney's brigades move to the right to close with Brown. Soon afterward, however, a Captain Locke galloped up to report that Maney's men had barely started forward when they encountered most of Brown's command streaming back toward the rear. Another courier brought word from Maney that he was suspending his attack until he could gather all of his brigades together. General Maney was willing to renew the assault, the courier explained, but he wanted to ensure that supporting forces were available either to prevent disaster in case of a repulse or to exploit a breakthrough. It was a discreet way of asking if Cleburne expected him to assail the enemy entrenchments unassisted.[41]

It had all come unglued. Lowrey's men had taken themselves out of the fight; Brown's men were repulsed and demoralized; Maney's attack was "suspended." Though Cleburne's instinct was to regroup and attack again, Hardee told him to "make no further attempt upon the enemy's works." Cleburne ordered a courier to ride quickly to Maney and tell him "not to assault the enemy in his works and to hold [his] division intact." Hardee's decision was based less on the disorganization evident on Cleburne's front than on the utter failure of Lee's attack on the right. Lee had not waited for Cleburne's attack to be "well developed" but instead had ordered his corps into the fight an hour *before* Cleburne. His men had overrun the Yankee picket line, but then, reluctant to attack an entrenched enemy, they had taken cover and engaged in a profitless but bloody firefight. They would not go forward, and Lee would not order them to fall back. In resignation, Hardee decided to cancel the attack.[42]

Cleburne's brief tenure as a corps commander did not enhance his reputation as the Confederacy's best combat leader. In the past he had been able to wring victories from improbable situations by relying on his intense commitment to training, single-minded determination, and cool self-possession in a crisis. On this occasion, however, he had demonstrated an inability to communicate a clear understanding of the battle plan to his division commanders. To be sure, some of the blame belonged to the division commanders themselves, particularly Lowrey. But Lowrey's failures must inevitably be laid at Cleburne's feet as well, for of the three division commanders under his orders that day Lowrey had the longest and closest association with Cleburne. Perhaps this time Cleburne had counted too much on Lowrey's ability to intuit his intentions.

That night, Hardee ordered Cleburne to pull back closer to Jonesboro. Two Confederate corps had failed to drive away elements of four Federal corps. Worse was to come. At 6:00 P.M. Hardee received orders from Hood to send Lee's corps back to Atlanta. Learning that a Federal force was across the Macon and Western Railroad at Rough and Ready, Hood recalled Lee to deal with this new threat. That, of course, left Hardee with only his own corps, under Cleburne, to face two full Federal corps and elements of two more.[43]

Cleburne could have been under no illusions about what to expect when the sun came up on 1 September. Still in nominal command of Hardee's Corps, his force occupied a makeshift line of fieldworks that wrapped around Jonesboro in a fishhook configuration. From first light it was evident that the enemy was moving in overwhelming numbers to attack his position. Cleburne did not need his field glasses to assess their strength and movement. Indeed, the men in the ranks could see it for themselves. "All the forenoon we can see the Yankees passing to our right," the diarist Captain Foster wrote, "Regt after Regt of the blue coats going to the right." Along the Confederate battle line, there were only enough men for a single line of defenders, about one man per yard—"not quite touching elbows" as one soldier put it. It was evident to all that if they were attacked, they must surely be overwhelmed. The *best* scenario was that instead of attacking, the Yankees would be satisfied merely to interpose themselves between Jonesboro and Atlanta. Even that would only postpone the inevitable, for it would cut Hardee and Cleburne off from the rest of the army. There was nothing to do but wait and see which fate Sherman had in store for them. As Major Benham wrote, "Our position was a sorry one."[44]

Sherman decided to attack. At three o'clock in the afternoon, the Yankees charged toward the hinge of Cleburne's line, focusing their assault precisely on that portion of the defenses held by Govan's Brigade of Arkansans. As at Kennesaw Mountain, the Federals attacked in mass formation, six ranks deep; and as at Kennesaw Mountain hundreds of them were gunned down by the butternut-clad men in the breastworks. But this time the disparity of numbers was too great. "Death had no appreciable effect upon these exhaustless masses," Major Benham wrote. "Moving with volume and power, like succeeding waves, the masses of blue come on." Cleburne rushed support to bolster Govan's position. Captain Buck was directing reinforcements into the line when he was struck in the leg by a minié ball. Nevertheless, he stayed in the saddle long enough to report to Cleburne that the line was breaking. Overhearing the report, Hardee asked Cleburne if he had another officer who could guide the last of the reserves, A. T. Vaughn's Tennessee Brigade, into the breach. Cleburne responded, "Yes! All of us will go." Ordering Buck to the rear, he led Vaughn's Brigade toward the fight.[45]

Even as Cleburne rode toward the line, the Yankees burst through. Govan's men swung their muskets like clubs; the artillerists plied their ramrods. Swett's Battery continued to fire even as the Yankees swarmed over the works. A survivor recalled, "The Union soldiers had to bayonet the gunners where they stood to prevent them from firing again." A soldier in the First Arkansas wrote, "We were surrounded and fought in front and in the rear. Fought as General Cleburne always fought." The Arkansas soldiers stood their ground and continued to load and fire until the Yankees literally took their guns away. It was useless. Govan and nearly 600 of his men—virtually every member of his brigade who was still standing—were taken prisoner. On both sides of the break, the adjoining units changed fronts and continued the fight. This was the situation Cleburne found when he arrived on the scene just at dusk. He deployed Vaughan's Brigade across the breach and, in Benham's words, he "welded the line together." Miraculously, it held.[46]

If Sherman had pressed his advantage and continued the fight into the evening, he might have destroyed Cleburne's entire corps. He did not. With the coming of full dark, the Federals disengaged, taking their prisoners with them, and near midnight Hardee directed Cleburne to conduct a cautious retreat southward. With the Yankees in possession of the railroad to Jonesboro, Atlanta was no longer tenable; that very night, Hood ordered the evacuation of the city. As what was left of Cleburne's command marched southward in yet another night march, the men could hear the sound of muffled explosions in the distance as Hood destroyed the munitions he could not carry away.

13

THE LAST CRUSADE

September 1864 was a difficult month for Cleburne. The capture of most of Govan's Brigade—the Arkansas troops who had been with him longest—was a hard blow. He lost as well the loyal and ubiquitous Captain Buck, who had been wounded at Jonesboro and was taken to a military hospital in Americus, Georgia, and his chief of staff Major Benham, who resigned in despair and left for Mexico. Of course there were the thousands of others who had been killed or wounded in the six-week struggle to hold Atlanta, and the unavoidable fact that the city had been lost nevertheless. What was almost equally unbearable was the news that Hood apparently blamed its loss on Hardee and, by implication at least, on Cleburne. Hood wrote to Bragg that the attack at Jonesboro had been "a disgraceful effort," which was evident, he said, by the paltry number of casualties suffered. Hardee found the charge insulting as well as unjustified and renewed his request for a transfer, unwilling to serve under Hood any longer than necessary. Cleburne thus faced the prospect of losing Hardee, too. Finally, he heard from Mobile that Sue was suffering from an attack of "neuralgia," the all-purpose malady of the nineteenth century, and that she would not be able to write to him again until she improved.[1]

In short, Cleburne's personal and professional prospects were as grim in that first week of September 1864 as they had been at any time in all the three years of war. They would not improve. Perhaps it is just as well that he did not know this, though in a larger sense it would not have mattered if he had, for Cleburne did not measure his duty by assessing the prospects for success. Indeed, his commitment to duty became more intense as the outlook grew darker. Had he known all that fate had in store for him during the next three months—his last—he would have behaved no differently.

After their defeat at Jonesboro, Cleburne and Hardee fell back southward to Lovejoy's Station. There the men enjoyed "the first unmolested rest" they had experienced "in one hundred and twenty days." When only a few days later Sherman abandoned Jonesboro to occupy Atlanta, the Rebels cautiously returned. Along the road, the stench from the smell of "dead horses, decaying men, and the debris of the battlefield" was all but overwhelming. They found Jonesboro not only empty but virtually destroyed. Within days, Hood arrived there with the rest of the army.[2]

Hood was belligerently uncontrite. Though he offered to resign, his offer was pro forma, and he wired President Davis that he could have saved Atlanta "had the officers and men of the army done what was expected of them." He was particularly disappointed in Hardee. As far as Hood was concerned, Hardee's halfhearted assault along Peachtree Creek, his failure to roll up the Union line in the Battle of Bald Hill, and most of all, his failure to drive the bluecoats over the Flint River at Jonesboro were evidence of his inability or unwillingness to conduct offensive operations. He asked Davis to transfer Hardee elsewhere. In his search for a scapegoat, Hood ignored the fact that the outcome of the fight at Jonesboro was largely irrelevant. Even as Cleburne and his command fought against long odds to hold that railside village, the Federals had interposed a large force between Jonesboro and Atlanta. Even if Hardee and Cleburne had won an unqualified victory at Jonesboro, Hood could not have held Atlanta for more than a day without driving away these troops, too. The simple truth was that the Army of Tennessee lacked sufficient force to hold both Atlanta and its rail lines against Sherman's vastly superior army.[3]

The army stayed in Jonesboro for ten days during a period of relatively benign weather. Cleburne turned command of the corps back over to Hardee, and the men drew fresh rations of beef and cornmeal, though the daily ration was reduced to three-quarters of a pound per man. The good news was that Govan returned with his 600 men, the beneficiaries of an unusually prompt prisoner exchange, which raised Cleburne's divisional strength back up to 3,290 "effectives." There was no hostile action, just the "usual picket firing" that had become a constant background noise to every waking hour. After Sherman's troops withdrew northward, Cleburne rode out to investigate the abandoned enemy camp. There was the usual detritus of war, though the discovery of eleven boxes of unopened ammunition demonstrated how well supplied the enemy was that he could be so profligate with such valuable goods.[4]

On 15 September, Governor Brown of Georgia declared a day of prayer and fasting. Cleburne's Division held a religious service in a "grove of gigantic poplars and oaks where seats made of logs covered almost half an acre." Lowrey, the erstwhile Baptist minister, presided over the meeting and delivered a sermon based on the Psalms: "Call upon me in the day of trouble:

I will deliver thee and thou shalt glorify me." With his long, flowing beard and piercing blue eyes, Lowrey was the very personification of the warrior-evangelist. "He teacheth my hands to war, so that a bow of steel is broken by mine arms. . . . I have pursued mine enemies, and overtaken them: neither did I turn again till they were consumed."[5]

The day after this camp meeting in the woods, the army left Jonesboro and marched westward. The men marched all night, stopped and rested briefly at daylight, then set out again at midmorning, arriving at Palmetto on the Atlanta and West Point Railroad late on 20 September. There President Davis visited the army, arriving late in the afternoon five days later. The president visited most of the units in turn, presenting to the troops several variations of the same talk: he offered the country's thanks for their sacrifices, ensured them of eventual victory, and challenged them to sustain their efforts until that victory was won. Hood's chief of staff recorded in his journal that the speeches were "enthusiastically received by the troops." But the enthusiasm was considerably muted. Some of those in Govan's Brigade, only recently repatriated from captivity, shouted "Johnston!" when Hood and Davis rode past. That night, staff officers came to Govan's campsite and warned the men not to shout "Johnston!" because it hurt Hood's feelings.[6]

Hardee took advantage of Davis's visit to confront the president about Hood's command of the army. Twice previously Hardee had asked to be relieved from service under Hood—once when Hood was first appointed over him and again after the Battle of Atlanta (Bald Hill). Both times, the president had appealed to his patriotism and asked him to swallow his pride for the sake of the country. Hardee had done so. This time he was adamant. Either Hood had to go as army commander, or Hardee would insist on a transfer to some other command, any command. Hood was as eager to rid himself of Hardee as Hardee was to go. Like Bragg before him, Hood wanted to purge the army of those who either did not or could not support him fully. Davis recognized that Hood was nearly as unpopular in the army as Bragg had been, but he was determined not to bring back Johnston, and the only other possibility he could imagine was Beauregard. Forced in the end to choose between Hood and Hardee, he chose Hood and granted Hardee his transfer. Cleburne was devastated and was tempted to submit his own papers as well. He told his staff that he would rather serve as a volunteer aide under Hardee than as a division commander under Hood. It was only his loyalty to the division, he said, that kept him from resigning.[7]

Hardee left the army on 27 September and once again Frank Cheatham assumed command of the corps. The next day, after Davis had also departed, Cleburne went to Hood's headquarters and applied for a furlough. Now that the campaign for Atlanta had ended, he wanted two weeks leave to return to Mobile to be married. Hood listened, then shook his head. He told Cleburne that the campaign season was not over. He planned to take the army across the Chattahoochee and assail Sherman's flank and rear, break up his communications, and force him to fight or flee. He could not spare any of his generals, least of all Cleburne. Cleburne saluted and returned to his tent to write the bad news to Sue. His letter arrived in Mobile only five days later—this time, at least, bad news did indeed travel fast—and after reading it she shut herself in her room and cried all day. "I don't know how I am to get through it," she wrote to her friend Sallie. The news meant "another long and arduous campaign," and the energy required to keep up her good spirits was wearing her down. Worrying about Patrick during the battles for Atlanta had been a trying experience and "nearly used me up." Her friends told her she looked thin and stretched. "I believe," she wrote, "I have had a regular fit of 'the blues.'" [8]

The same day that Sue shut herself in her room for "a good cry," Cleburne's Division was marching northward from Palmetto through a cold, merciless rain. "Rain, Rain, Mud, Mud, March, March" was Captain Foster's gloomy diary entry for 3 October. It was a grim trek, and not solely because of the rain. The army's route carried it past old battlefields where the victims of earlier fights had been hastily buried. The summer rains had uncovered many of those shallow graves so that here and there an arm or leg stuck out of the ground. A few of the more jaded veterans made light of it; one group began playing soccer with a human skull. Most of the men, however, were deeply troubled by this macabre sight, and hundreds of them voluntarily set to work shoveling dirt over the exposed bodies, partly out of respect and partly to spare themselves the view. [9]

While Stewart's Corps turned off to strike the railroad near Allatoona where a determined Federal garrison beat off an attack by French's Division, Cleburne and the rest of the army continued northward. Rations were scarce, and inevitably some of the men were tempted to scavenge on the countryside as they passed, though Hood's warnings about the respect for private property were regularly repeated. Cleburne was riding ahead of his command with a few members of his staff when he came across a half dozen "hard-looking" soldiers who had all but stripped an apple orchard of its fruit. Six bushels of red apples lay in profusion at their feet. Cleburne sized up the situation at once and with a grim expression ordered the men to move the apples over to the roadside. Then he sat on the rail fence, loaded his pipe, and calmly began to smoke. The apple thieves eyed him nervously. Finally, up the road came the head of Granbury's column, which had the point that day. As Granbury rode up, Cleburne addressed him, "General Granbury, I am peddling apples today."

Adopting his mood, Granbury replied, "How are you selling them, General?"

"These gentlemen," Cleburne said, gesturing to the guilty-looking soldiers shuffling their feet behind him, "have been very kind. They have gathered the apples for me and charged nothing. I will give them to you and your men. Now, you get down and take an apple, and have each of your men pass by and take one—only one, mind—until they are all gone."

Smiling, Granbury selected his apple. Then he sat his horse munching happily as his entire brigade marched by in single file, each man picking up an apple as he passed. Many of the Texans flashed a grin at the guilty foragers as they passed, and a few offered a hurrah for "Old Pat." Cleburne continued to sit quietly and smoke his pipe until all the apples were gone. Then he rose from the fence and ordered the scavengers each to carry a rail for a mile before rejoining their unit.[10]

The army struck the Western and Atlantic just south of Dalton in the second week of October. Hood gave orders to break up the railroad, but the men did not have proper tools for this task. Their small axes, used for building breastworks, made little impression on the heavy ties. Cleburne ordered the men of his division to line up in a single rank along the tracks. "Attention men!" he called out. "When I say ready, let every man stoop down, take hold of the rails, and when I say 'heave ho!' let every man lift all he can and turn the rails and crossties over." Several thousand men poised themselves for the task. Cleburne called out "Heave!" and with a great yell, they lifted the Atlantic and Western Railroad from its track bed and flipped it over. After that it came apart much easier.[11]

The men pried the ties loose from the rails, stacked them in great piles, and set them afire. Then they heated the rails over the blaze and bent them around the nearby telegraph poles. They made great play of the work, calling the twisted rails "Mrs. Lincoln's hair pins" and "making a great frolic of it." Captain Foster, at least, began to think that this gambit was worth a try. Busting up railroads, he wrote, "beats fighting all hollow."[12]

It was only a short march up the line of the wrecked railroad to Dalton. There, Cleburne deployed his division in front of the town, directly opposite the small Federal fort. Hood sent a flag of truce in to the commander of the garrison, telling him that he was surrounded and that it was his duty to surrender and thus save lives. The hapless Federal commander, Colonel L. Johnson, had only about 750 men, more than two-thirds of them black troops with no combat experience. He was realistic enough to recognize that he had no hope, but he sought assurance from Hood that his black soldiers would be treated fairly as prisoners of war. Hood declined to offer any such promise, saying only that the Confederate War Department would have to make that decision. The parley took place between the lines directly in front of Cleburne's position, and Granbury's Texans were in no mood to grant concessions. "Kill every damn one of them!" several called out. Colonel Johnson later wrote that Cleburne's men made a great show of being eager for a fight. He declared that they "were over anxious to move upon the 'niggers' and constantly violated the flag of truce by skirmishing near it."

Still, Johnson was in no position to haggle and surrendered his garrison. He later claimed to be horrified when after stacking arms, the black soldiers were set upon by their captors and robbed of their shoes and various other items. A few threatened to kill the black soldiers and enjoyed making them beg for their lives. "The poor negroes, with eyes popped out nearly two inches, begged, prayed, and made all sorts of promises," recalled one Arkansas soldier. Cleburne did not interfere with this torment, but he did turn the prisoners over to the engineers who organized them into gangs and set them to work busting up the railroad. The Texans agreed, perhaps reluctantly, that "this was better than killing them."[13]

The army left Dalton at night, passing through the gaps in Rocky Face Ridge that they had defended only five months (and a seeming eternity) earlier. They marched west now, toward Lafayette, and Cleburne's Division bivouacked on the same campground it had occupied the night before the Battle of Chickamauga. From Lafayette, the army marched to Alpine on the Georgia-Alabama border, then across Sand Mountain into Alabama. It rained most of the way. "The road was full of water and mud," Captain Foster wrote, "some places knee deep."[14]

The army arrived at Decatur on 28 October. In accordance with Hood's orders, Cleburne deployed his division and engaged in some long-range skirmishing with the Federal garrison, but Hood did not want to lose time trying to compel the city to surrender. He bypassed it and moved further west, arriving at Tuscumbia on the last day of October. There, Hood ordered a pontoon bridge built over the Tennessee River. The engineers constructed a bridge to an island in midstream, then another to the far bank—more than a mile long all told. Cleburne's Division began crossing on 13 November, the bands playing and the soldiers marching in a column of fours. The bridge floated only inches above the water, so that from a distance it looked like the men were marching on the surface of the river itself. Once across, Cleburne bivouacked his division in Florence, and the next day Nathan Bedford Forrest came galloping into camp at the head of his command. He and his men immediately became the objects of much curiosity. Several of the brigade bands got together to serenade the famous "Wizard of the Saddle," and it turned into an impromptu outdoor concert.[15]

Now that his army was across the river and unified with Forrest's command, Hood unveiled his grand scheme: He would march the army north into central Tennessee and retake Nashville. He believed that there were few Federal soldiers in Tennessee so that the campaign should not require much of a fight if he could move fast enough. Hood convinced the new Confederate theater commander, P. G. T. Beauregard, of the soundness of his plan and assured him that he would move "at the earliest possible moment." Instead, continued rains forced repeated postponements, but on 20 November Hood issued another General Order to inform the troops of his plan and called upon them to accept a period of short rations with "a cheerful manly spirit."[16]

Cleburne's opinion of this scheme is unrecorded. In the postwar years, after Cleburne had become a symbol of the martyrdom of the army, various individuals claimed that he had been skeptical of Hood's strategy all along, and that he had obeyed in a "cheerful manly spirit" only because it was his duty to do so. Nash claimed that he saw Cleburne at Selma, Alabama, and Cleburne had told him, "We are going to carry the war into Africa, but I fear we will not be as successful as Scipio was." But if Nash saw Cleburne at Selma, it could only have been during one of the general's earlier trips to Mobile before Cleburne knew of Hood's scheme. On the other hand, that same week Cleburne made at least two public addresses to the troops: fervent patriotic speeches in which he repeated several times his determination to die rather than surrender. Did such behavior suggest that he was optimistic about the forthcoming campaign; or was it a manifestation of a determined fatalism? He was by nature quietly intense, and it would have been perfectly consistent with his fatalist view of the world that as the prospects grew darker, he would feel compelled to assert his commitment more passionately.[17]

Hood directed his army northward from the Tennessee River by three different roads. Cheatham's Corps, with Cleburne in the lead, was assigned the westernmost road through Waynesboro. Mercer's Brigade of Georgians was left behind to guard the river crossings, and on 20 November Cleburne's other three brigades—Govan's, Lowrey's, and Granbury's—set out northward in the middle of a sleet storm. The rain soon stopped, but the sun melted the snow and left the roads a perfect mess. One soldier noted that the mud seemed to be exactly "shoe mouth deep." That same night the head of the column crossed the Tennessee state line, where someone posted a large sign: "A free home or a soldiers grave."[18]

Pleased to be advancing and convinced that they were stealing a march on the enemy, the army's morale was generally good, though it began to deflate due to poor weather, short rations, and bad roads. The horses, themselves on short rations, could not pull the guns through the mud, and frequently the infantry had to be detailed to haul them along by hand. In spite of these difficulties, Cleburne's Division marched through Waynesboro on 22 November and two days later arrived at Ashwood, the home of the martyred Bishop-General Leonidas Polk. Hood set up his headquarters in the home of Andrew J. Polk, who lived across the road from "Hamilton Place," Lucius Polk's plantation home. Cleburne was happy to see Polk again and was very taken with the peacefulness and grandeur of the estate, especially the charm of the little chapel. Idly he remarked to his staff, "It is almost worth dying to rest in so sweet a spot."[19]

The next day the army arrived on the south bank of the Duck River and occupied Columbia. Across the river two Federal corps under Major General John M. Schofield blocked further advance. It was rainy and cold, and the army went into bivouac to await the arrival of the supply wagons. Hood had no intention of forcing a way across the river in the teeth of the Federal defenses. He planned to leave two divisions of Lee's Corps, and most of the army's artillery, in Columbia to freeze Schofield in place, then cross the Duck River upstream with the other two corps and race northward to cut off the Federal line of retreat. If all went well, he would completely surround and destroy this force.[20]

Early on the morning of 29 November, Cleburne roused his division before dawn and set the men marching toward Davis Ford, five miles upriver. Lowrey's Brigade crossed first just after 7:00 A.M., followed by Govan, and then Granbury. Cleburne rode with the advance accompanied by both Hood and Tennessee governor Isham Harris. Hood was in a hurry. He repeatedly emphasized the importance of speed and told Lowrey to attack the enemy wherever he found him "without regard to numbers or position." Northward from Davis Ford the narrow road twisted and bent back on itself so much that Hood wondered if he had made a wrong turn. He stopped the column to consult with a local scout who told him that although the road was a winding one, it did indeed lead to the Franklin and Columbia turnpike. The scout drew a rough sketch in the dirt, which Cleburne carefully copied into his notebook. What was supposed to have been a twelve-mile march, however, was instead a seventeen-mile march. Hood restarted the column and the men settled down to the work, striding northward at a steady gait toward the small crossroads town of Spring Hill.[21]

Lowrey's vanguard crossed Rutherford Creek just south of Spring Hill at three o'clock. The sun was already low in the sky. Ahead on the Davis Ford Road, Forrest's cavalry was skirmishing with a Federal infantry force the strength of which could not be ascertained at once, but which seemed to be drawn up in a semicircle around the town. Hood told Cleburne "to form line of battle to the left of the road . . . , then move forward and take the enemy's breastworks that were just over the brow of the hill." He told Cheatham to remain at the stream crossing and feed in other units as they arrived, then he rode ahead to some high ground for a view of the town.[22]

Cleburne accompanied Lowrey's Brigade up the Davis Ford Road for another mile, then he ordered the brigade to face left, cross McCutcheon's Creek, and form up for an attack. Lowrey's men pulled off their shoes and socks, rolled up their trouser legs, and splashed across the creek. Govan's Brigade was coming up the road behind them, and Cleburne was directing those men into line on Lowrey's left when Hood reappeared from his visual reconnaissance of Spring Hill and ordered Cleburne to deploy his brigades in echelon formation with his right-hand brigade (Lowrey's) somewhat advanced. Though the evidence is sketchy, it is likely that after looking over the Federal position in Spring Hill, Hood had decided that the Federal forces there were not a serious threat and that he wanted Cleburne's three brigades to be in position to swing *south* once they hit the turnpike in order to block Schofield's advance from Columbia. If so, Hood never bothered to explain this shift in his plans to Cheatham. Throughout the evening, and indeed for the rest of his life, Cheatham believed it was the *town* of Spring Hill, and not the turnpike south of it, that was the object of Cleburne's advance.[23]

Between 3:30 and 4:00, Cleburne arranged his three brigades for the attack. Forrest rode up and offered to add one of his brigades, the only one that had any ammunition left, to cover Cleburne's right flank. The two generals, both mounted and with swords drawn, were immediately behind Govan's Brigade at about four o'clock, when Cleburne rose up in his stirrups and called out, "Forward echelon!" The men scrambled over the rail fence and moved forward. They advanced almost due west over rolling, open farmland for about a third of a mile before encountering a Federal line of light breastworks off to their right. The Federals were making a great deal of noise, cheering and waving their swords and hats, and Lowrey reported to Cleburne that he believed they were about to charge. Lowrey remembered Cleburne's reaction: "With his right hand raised, as though he held a heavy whip to be brought down upon his horse, and in a tone that manifested unusual excitement, he exclaimed, 'I'll charge them!'" He ordered the Arkansans of

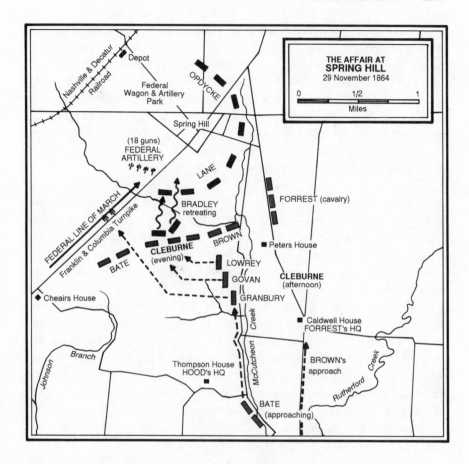

Govan's Brigade to swing to the right, maintaining contact with Lowrey, in order to assail the Federal breastworks in their own right flank.[24]

The target of Cleburne's assault was the Federal Brigade of Luther P. Bradley, composed mostly of Illinois troops. Though Bradley had nearly 2,000 soldiers in his five regiments, they were largely inexperienced. When Govan struck their flank and rear, they lasted only minutes before breaking. Cleburne rode among his cheering men and pursued the Federals to the bed of a small rivulet, a tributary of McCutcheon's Creek. There, however, they found themselves suddenly at the nexus of a crossfire from Federal artillery. The Federal division commander, David S. Stanley, had arrayed eighteen field pieces hub to hub just south of Spring Hill along the Franklin and Columbia turnpike, and these guns opened up as soon as the Rebels cleared the trees along the creek bed. Cleburne's men were also targeted by two Napoleon guns a half mile further south along the turnpike itself. These last two guns did not remain there long, however. Granbury's Texans, who did not participate in the assault on Bradley, charged straight toward them and would have captured them if the artillerists had not been quick to limber up and gallop away. Having disposed of Bradley's force, Cleburne had to order Lowrey and Granbury to fall back to the line of the creek bed. He sent a courier to Cheatham to tell him that "his right brigade had been struck in the flank by the enemy and had suffered severely, and that he had been compelled to fall back and reform his division with a change of front." [25]

In addition, however, Cleburne now faced a new problem: what appeared to be another Federal brigade was marching to Bradley's support. It belonged to Brigadier General John Q. Lane who had been on Bradley's left facing Forrest's troopers, but who had decided that Cleburne was far more dangerous at the moment than Forrest. Lane pulled his men out of the line facing east and sent them marching at the double-quick to face south. To deal with this new threat, Cleburne would need Granbury's Brigade. He called Lieutenant Mangum to his side to give him the orders to recall Granbury. Cleburne pointed out a rail fence parallel to the pike and about 200 yards from it where Granbury was to form his brigade. At just that moment, perhaps at around 4:45, an artillery shell burst almost directly overhead. Cleburne's horse, a chestnut named Red Pepper, was severely wounded in the hip. The horse "reared furiously" and Cleburne, who was not a great horseman, fought for control. Mangum was poised to carry Cleburne's orders to Granbury, but he paused to ensure that his commander was unhurt. "No, no, go on, Mangum," Cleburne called out. "Tell Granbury what I told you." [26]

As Mangum galloped off to deliver Cleburne's orders to Granbury, Cleburne rode to talk to John C. Brown, whose division had followed his own from Davis Ford and who was now on his right. Cleburne was in the midst of a conversation with Brown near five o'clock when Cheatham rode up to tell him that he and Brown were to renew the attack on Spring Hill, which Cheatham still considered the primary objective, "as soon as they could connect their lines." Brown was to initiate the attack, Cheatham said, and Cleburne would pitch in when he heard the sound of Brown's firing to his right. Cheatham would personally ensure that Bate came up on Cleburne's left, noting also that Hood had promised them the support of Stewart's Corps if necessary. Then Cheatham left to direct Bate's Division into line on Cleburne's left. [27]

Cleburne returned to his own command to prepare the renewed attack at about 5:15. The sun had set at 4:26, and although there was sufficient twilight still to see the battlefield, it would not last long. Meanwhile, Cheatham was having trouble with Bate's Division. Though Cheatham did not know it, Hood had ordered Bate to advance west to the Franklin and Columbia Turnpike, then turn *south* and sweep the road from Columbia. But because Cleburne had been forced to swing *north* to repel Bradley's Brigade, a huge gap had opened between Bate's right and Cleburne's left. Just as Bate's Division was approaching the turnpike a few hundred yards north of the Cheairs House, a lieutenant from Cheatham's staff rode up to tell Bate to move to the right and join his division to Cleburne's. Bate therefore ordered his three brigades to sidle sideways to connect with Cleburne. To do so, however, he had to move nearly a quarter mile back from the edge of the turnpike.[28]

At 5:30 both Bate and Granbury had been in virtual contact with the pike, but by 6:00 both forces had been withdrawn in order to present a continuous front to the enemy. Meanwhile, Cleburne was waiting for the sound of Brown's attack on his right, which was to be the signal for him to renew the assault on Spring Hill. He waited in vain. Though he did not know it, Brown had decided not to attack. Instead, he sent a courier to Cheatham to complain that he was outflanked on his right and unable to advance. It was full dark at 6:17 that evening, and at just about that time, Cleburne was sitting his wounded horse behind his three brigades when Cheatham's assistant inspector general, Major Joseph Bostick, rode up with orders for Cleburne "to remain where he was and not move upon the pike until further orders." By that time these were very likely welcome orders. Cleburne disliked fighting at night but especially over unexplored ground. At Chickamauga, he had resisted St. John Liddell's pleas for a night advance, refusing to undertake it until Hill ordered it. Released now from the obligation to make an attack in full dark over unfamiliar ground, he ordered his troops to lay down on their arms in line of battle where they were, a half mile south of Spring Hill and a quarter mile east of the turnpike.[29]

When Cleburne awoke the next morning—the last day of his life—he learned that the enemy was gone. Spring Hill was abandoned; the brigades of Bradley and Lane were no longer in his front. What was worse—far worse—was that the bulk of Schofield's army at Columbia had slipped by in the darkness as well. Certainly Cleburne felt disappointment, and very likely he felt anger; but did he also feel guilt? Stephen Lee, who was not present, claimed after the war that when Cleburne realized the enemy had escaped, he stated, "This is the first time I have ever disobeyed the spirit of my orders and if God will forgive me, it shall be the last." Lee told his correspondent that he had heard this story secondhand and cautioned him, "You must not use this."[30]

Did Cleburne fail to do his full duty that night at Spring Hill? It is quite possible that once he appreciated the enormity of the lost opportunity, he tortured himself with that very question. He may have wondered if he had erred in attacking Bradley rather than advancing directly to the turnpike. But what option did he have? Bradley was in position not only to contest his passing but to assail his flank. Perhaps, then, he ought to have renewed the advance on the turnpike after disposing of Bradley instead of waiting for Brown's attack, which never came. But Cheatham had ordered him to await the sound of Brown's attack before advancing and to ignore that order might have plunged the whole corps into chaos. Should he have questioned or protested Cheatham's order "to remain where he was and not move upon the pike"? No matter how he turned the question around in his mind, it would have been difficult for Cleburne to construct a scenario in which he was to blame for the escape of the enemy.

Even so, Hood's profound disappointment the next day was the talk of the army. Brown, who saw Hood early in the morning, found him "wrathy as a rattlesnake." His disappointment was perhaps justified; his anger, however, was not. He was, after all, the army commander, and he had been within easy riding distance of the front throughout the two critical hours from 4:00 to 6:00. Instead of supervising the action, he had retired to Thompson Mansion for an early dinner and a laudanum-induced sleep. Moreover, there is strong evidence that he knew that night that his troops were not holding the turnpike. Both Cheatham and Stewart wrote later that he was already criticizing the army for its lack of energy, and in particular for its failure to seize the turnpike, before he went to bed.[31]

But Hood's anger was not feigned. Once again his bold stroke had failed to produce the victory that he had felt certain would be his. Three times— at Peachtree Creek, at Bald Hill, and now at Spring Hill—he had contrived a master stroke worthy of Robert E. Lee himself, only to see victory slip through his fingers as the execution of his plan fell sadly short of the imagined results. Bold cavalier that he was, Hood had both the ability and the imagination to envision clearly the sequence of events that he was sure would result from his carefully crafted battle plans. He then judged the performance of his subordinates by how closely subsequent events matched his preconceived vision. When the friction of war disrupted the vision, Hood found fault with the commander on the scene. At both Peachtree Creek and Bald Hill, he had blamed Hardee; this time he blamed Cheatham. Had he not ordered Cheatham to move his divisions forward and seize the turnpike? Had he not *personally* ordered Cleburne to advance westward, in echelon formation, and secure the pike?[32]

The Confederate pursuit of the fleeing Federals from Spring Hill to Franklin was a painful and conflicted experience for Pat Cleburne. When he learned that Hood held him partly responsible for failing to do his full duty, he told Brown that "he could not afford to rest under such an imputation" and that he would demand a full investigation at the earliest opportunity. When Brown asked him who he thought was responsible for the escape of the enemy, Cleburne replied, "Of course the responsibility rests with the Commander-in-Chief as he was upon the field during the afternoon and was fully advised during the night." Cleburne was visibly hurt and angry during their conversation, and as he prepared to leave he told Brown, "We will resume this conversation at the first convenient moment." But, of course, they never did.[33]

After his conversation with Brown, Cleburne rode northward toward the twin hills flanking the turnpike just south of Franklin, Tennessee. At their foot he dismounted and distracted himself by inviting a staff officer to join him in a game of checkers. The game was soon interrupted by orders from Hood for him to report to headquarters. In the parlor of Harrison House, Cleburne listened impassively as Hood outlined his plan for an assault on the Federal lines. Hood was quite emphatic: The attacking force was to "go over the main works at all hazards." A witness recalled Cleburne's last words to Hood: "I will take the enemy's works or fall in the attempt."[34]

Cleburne rode back to his command to pass the attack order on to his brigadiers, instructing them to bring their troops up to the foot of Winstead Hill east of the turnpike. Though he tried to keep any sense of foreboding from his voice, Govan was unsettled to note that instead of the usual excitement that Cleburne exuded when going into battle, he now "seemed to be more despondent than I ever saw him." Sobered by Cleburne's demeanor, Govan sought to engage him in conversation, perhaps seeking reassurance. "Well, General," he said, "there will not be many of us that get back to Arkansas." Unsmiling, Cleburne responded, "Well, Govan, if we are to die, let us die like men."[35]

Leaving his brigadiers to move their men into position, Cleburne rode alone into the open ground in front of Breezy Hill to a small knoll from which he could observe the enemy lines. Dismounting, he walked the few steps to the top of the knoll where some sharpshooters were posted. Having left his field glasses behind, he asked the commander of the sharpshooters, Lieutenant John Ozanne, if he could borrow a telescope. Ozanne detached the scope from his Whitworth rifle and handed it to him. Kneeling by the stump of a tree, Cleburne trained the scope on the enemy works. He could see the city of Franklin clearly, resting prosaically in a bend of the Harpeth River. He saw the evidence of apparent panic as Federal wagons crowded across the narrow bridges over the Harpeth. In front of Franklin, however, the Federal army occupied a long line of mature entrenchments. Cleburne spoke his thoughts out loud, "They have three lines of works." Sweeping his scope across the field left to right, he saw that the lines extended around the city with both flanks anchored on the river. "And they are all completed," he said.[36]

In addition, what looked like a division of Federal infantry was posted about 300 yards in front of their main line. The troops in that advanced position were unentrenched and vulnerable to a direct attack. Still, to get to them his men would have to cross about a mile and a half of open ground broken by few trees or fences and which appeared to be flat as a tabletop. Cleburne knew it would take at least twenty minutes, perhaps longer, for his men to cross that open ground, and all the while they would be exposed to direct fire from both artillery and musketry. He studied the position for a long time. Finally he stood. "They are most formidable," he said to no one in particular. Then without further comment he sat down on the stump and, pulling out a small notebook, he made a few brief entries. He knew that the attack would be costly, maybe even ruinous. Worse yet, he suspected that it was unnecessary. A flanking movement across the river would not only force a Federal evacuation, it might trap a large portion of the enemy army inside the city. But with Hood's as yet unspoken accusations still sharp in his memory, he could not bring himself to protest Hood's desperate orders.[37]

By three o'clock, Cleburne's brigades had moved over the line of hills to deploy on the forward slope in brigade columns. Advancing in columns would expose fewer men to the direct fire of the entrenched foe, and he could deploy them into lines just before the final charge. Having made these dispositions, Cleburne waited for Cheatham's signal that the other units were ready. He visited each of his three brigades. Granbury's Texans plus the 35th Tennessee stood easily on their arms among the trees immediately adjacent to the turnpike; next to them was Govan's brigade of Arkansas troops, a few of whom had come with him from Helena through nearly four years of war; on the right was Mark B. Lowrey's brigade of Alabamians and Mississippians. Lowrey used the lull to inspire his troops with a short sermon. Cleburne passed along the front ranks cautioning the men to save their ammunition and "use the bayonet." Load, he told them, but carry your rifles at right shoulder shift; don't stop to fire a shot but move in quick-time and attack with the bayonet.[38]

It was almost four o'clock. The sun was low in the sky on the last day of November, and a bank of dark clouds in the west made it look and feel like sunset. The sun's rays cast what one soldier called "a crimson light" over the

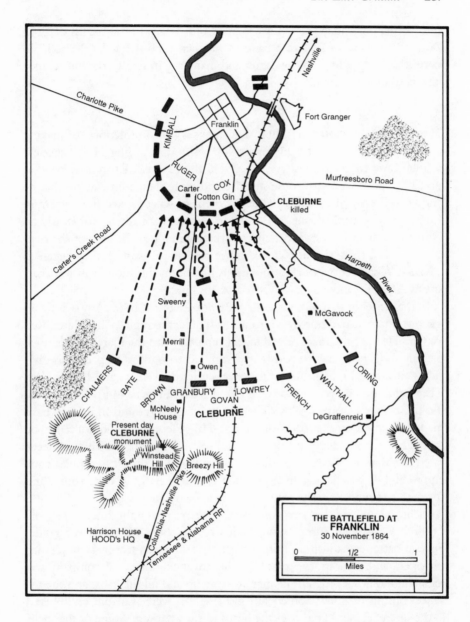

THE BATTLEFIELD AT
FRANKLIN
30 November 1864

0   1/2   1
Miles

prospective battlefield. Cleburne looked back up to Winstead Hill for Cheatham's signal. Near the crest, a flag dropped; Cleburne called out "Forward!" in his rolling brogue and kicked his horse into motion, keeping pace with the line of marching men. The brigade bands struck up a march as if they were going on parade. Never before had the "tooters" carried their instruments into battle, but today the troops stepped out boldly to the strains of "The Bonny Blue Flag": "We are a band of brothers, and native to the soil." In perfect order, guiding on the center and marching in step to the music, they advanced into the open.[39]

Hood was right about one thing. The Yankees had no intention of making a stand at Franklin. After his miraculous escape at Spring Hill, Schofield wanted only to get his army safely across the Harpeth River as quickly as possible, and it was with some surprise and more than a little alarm that he and his officers had watched the deployment of what looked like the entire Confederate army in front of the low ridge south of town. For nearly an hour the Rebel forces had maneuvered threateningly at the base of the tree-covered hills; then at four o'clock, in the first hint of sunset, they began to advance. Whatever Schofield's intentions had been, they now bent to necessity as 20,000 Confederates advanced on his lines.[40]

In the center of that advancing line, Patrick Cleburne rode purposefully on a brown mare he had borrowed from a staff officer to replace the injured Red Pepper. He kept the mare reined in to keep pace with the march of his three brigades. His head turned constantly from left to right as he paced his division's advance to match that of those on either flank: Bate and Brown with Cheatham's other two divisions were on his left; French, Walthall, and Loring of Stewart's Corps on his right. Whatever grim resolution he may have made to himself on the road from Spring Hill, Cleburne could not fail to be stirred by such an awe-inspiring martial display. A hundred battle flags decorated the attacking wave of soldiery, a wave that was almost two miles wide end to end. It was half again larger than Pickett's charge at Gettysburg, and the men had twice as far to go to reach the enemy line.

Cleburne guided his division in an unerring straight line, using the Columbia-Nashville Turnpike on the left of Granbury's Brigade as a guide. Federal batteries had opened fire almost as soon as his troops stepped into the open, and their shot tore holes in his advancing line, but company and regimental officers ordered the men to close up and fill the gaps, and the advance continued. A few Confederate guns, all that were available, unlimbered in the open field and fired over the heads of the attackers. Some of the shells fell among the enemy soldiers now only about 400 yards away.

Cleburne rose up in the stirrups to shout an order to halt. He recalled the skirmishers and deployed his brigades from column into line, all the while under fire. Then the charge began in earnest. Fifty yards from the advanced Federal salient, the Yankees delivered a full volley into the faces of Granbury's

Brigade. The Texans barely paused to reply. Shrieking the Rebel yell, they charged into the enemy advanced line.[41]

The object of this furious assault was the Federal brigade of Colonel Joseph Conrad, about 2,000 midwesterners from Illinois, Indiana, and Ohio. They had watched the advancing storm with mounting disbelief and growing anger that they had been left out in this exposed position to take the brunt of an attack by the whole Confederate army. Now with that enemy upon them, they broke. Men peeled back from the Federal line so quickly that one witness was reminded of a fuse burning down. With little regard for unit integrity, they simply turned and ran. Cleburne's soldiers stopped only long enough to fire a "telling volley" into their backs before running after them. Watching from horseback, Cleburne urged them on. Brown called out to him above the din, "We will go into the works with them!" Cleburne repeated the cry, and it spread through the ranks, "Go into the works with them!"[42]

Now it was a race. Two thousand fleeing Federals pursued by 5,000 Confederates. The slowest of the bluecoats were soon overtaken by the fleetest of the attackers, and the mass of running men became intermingled. Union soldiers watching the race from the main defensive lines about the city withheld their fire for fear of hitting their own men. But they could not wait forever lest they themselves be overwhelmed. Cleburne, still mounted, spurred ahead into the mass of men, charging diagonally across the front of his own brigades toward the center of the Union line. In midcanter, his brown mare went down heavily, nose first, killed by rifle fire. Picking himself up, Cleburne called for another horse. A staff officer, Lieutenant James Brandon, rode up and dismounted quickly, offering the reins to Cleburne. Cleburne had one foot in the stirrup when this horse too fell to the ground, shot dead. Dropping the reins, Cleburne drew his sword and, waving it over his head, charged forward on foot toward the Yankee line where he could see the men of his command clambering over the earthworks. Granbury's Texans and Govan's Arkansans had breached the enemy main line; the blue divisional flag flew atop the parapets. Cleburne ran toward the spot, perhaps adding his own shouts to the general cacophony of noise. He was fifty yards short of his goal when a single enemy bullet hit him in the chest, penetrated to his heart, and killed him instantly.[43]

The fight, of course, went on without him. The men of Granbury's and Govan's brigades seized a battery of Federal guns adjacent to the turnpike and attempted to turn them around, but the Union gunners had taken out the primers and the guns could not be fired. Meanwhile the Yankees organized a counterattack spearheaded by Opdycke's Brigade, known as the Tigers. The Confederates met the attack head-on, and the fighting was furious and hand-to-hand. In the thick of the fight, Granbury was shot just below his right eye, the bullet passing through his brain and exploding out the back of his head. Like Cleburne, he died instantly. Opdycke's charge staunched the breach in the Federal line, but the Rebels did not fall back. They clung tenaciously to the outside of the Federal entrenchments. Those daring enough to resume the attack by clambering over the top either fell back dead or were grabbed and pulled over the works to be made prisoner. Separated only by the width of the earthworks, the two sides fired blindly over the top or through the space below the head logs, their rifles sometimes overlapping each other. "We kept getting over," one Arkansas veteran recalled, "but they would reinforce and drive us out." After a time the Arkansas troops agreed to wait and collect their strength until Cleburne gave them the order to go over the top all at once. "We waited and waited and waited," the veteran remembered, and he wondered why Cleburne did not give the order. "When it didn't come, I knew Pat Cleburne was dead; for if he had been living he would have given us that order."[44]

As twilight turned to full darkness, a darkness punctuated only by frequent muzzle flashes, the two sides fought stubbornly beyond the point of exhaustion. Finally, near ten o'clock the firing died down, and both sides drew back from the berm of blood-soaked earth. Cleburne lay where he had fallen, absolved now of his guilt. This time no one could charge him with having failed to do his full duty. As he lay on the ground—one anonymous corpse among thousands—Schofield's men slipped away in the darkness for the second night in a row and plodded northward.[45]

EPILOGUE

Dawn revealed a grisly scene. The Federals had constructed their defensive lines by scooping dirt from in front of the lines and banking it up against a vertical wall of logs. As a result, the berm of earth was more than ten feet high from the bottom of the ditch to the top of the head logs. The ditch in front of those lines was literally filled with the bodies of the dead piled one on top of another. Cleburne's body lay fifty yards south of this horror. His boots were missing, perhaps taken by some barefoot Confederate who had no idea whose boots he took. Once Cleburne was identified, volunteers lifted his body onto a litter and, stepping gingerly over the bodies of others, they carried him to Carnton, the McGavock plantation house, just over a mile away. There they laid him down gently on the wide planks of the front porch. There, too, were Granbury, the sometime commander of the Texas Brigade, and Granbury's chief of staff, Colonel R. B. Young. Alongside them were Brigadier Generals John Adams, the son of Irish immigrants, and Otto French Strahl, both from Brown's Division. Next to Strahl was his aide, Lieutenant John H. Marsh.[1]

In the afternoon Cleburne's body was loaded onto a wagon and carried southward down the Franklin and Columbia Turnpike, past Spring Hill, to Columbia. There, in a short ceremony presided over by the Reverend Quintard, he was interred in Rose Hill cemetery. Lucius Polk stood graveside and watched as his old commander was committed to the earth, but neither Polk nor Quintard was at ease about Cleburne's resting place. Someone pointed out that it was in the pauper's section of the graveyard. Even more disquieting was the fact that during their occupation of Columbia, the Yankees had also buried their dead at Rose Hill, including some black soldiers. To Quintard, it was entirely inappropriate that Cleburne should spend eternity among paupers, Yankees, and former slaves. Learning from a few of Cleburne's staff officers that the general had commented upon the beauty of the little church at Ashwood on his way to Franklin, Quintard resolved to move him there, and he was soon reburied near St. John's Chapel on Lucius Polk's plantation.[2]

Hood, meanwhile, refused to admit any error in ordering the assault at Franklin. He reported to Richmond that the battle had been a success, if not quite a victory. "We captured several stand of colors and about 1,000 prisoners," he reported. "Our troops fought with great gallantry." That they had. But they also had fought to no useful purpose. Hood's army was ruined, and everyone but Hood recognized it. With barely 18,000 men, he pushed on in worsening weather toward Nashville, where George H. Thomas and 70,000 Federals waited for him. When Thomas sortied from the city two weeks later, the result was the virtual destruction of the Army of Tennessee.[3]

Sue Tarleton learned of the death of her fiancé five days after the Battle of Franklin. She was prostrate with grief. When she gathered the strength to appear again in public, she wore mourning and did so every day for a year. Eventually she did marry. In the fall of 1867, three years after Cleburne's death at Franklin, she married a former Confederate army captain named Hugh Cole, another friend of her brother Robert. She died less than a year later.[4]

In the meantime, Cleburne had become even more of a Confederate hero during the hard years of Reconstruction than he had been in life. His martyrdom at Franklin seemed to many to represent the martyrdom of the Army of Tennessee, if not the entire South. Veterans recalled now with increased clarity his sterling character and uncomplaining devotion to duty. The Ladies Memorial Association of Phillips County raised funds for a suitable monument, and Learned Mangum, once again practicing law in Helena, made arrangements for the third and final movement of Cleburne's body to that city. Lucius Polk, Frank Cheatham, Isham Harris, and even Jefferson Davis walked in the public procession that accompanied Cleburne's coffin down to the docks at Memphis for the trip downriver. He was re-interred in Evergreen Cemetery overlooking Helena on the last day of April 1870, exactly twenty years after he had first arrived so hopefully in that small frontier town. A monument was erected over the site in May 1891, and General George Gordon gave the memorial address:

A truer patriot or knightlier soldier never fought and never died. Valor never lost a braver son or freedom a nobler champion. . . . He was a patriot by instinct and a soldier by nature. He loved his country, its soldiers, its banners, its battleflags, its sovereignty, its independence. For these he fought, for these he fell.[5]

Cleburne lived in America for fifteen years, the last four of them under arms. He arrived filled with hope and determination, and he devoted himself wholly to understanding and internalizing the values and ideals of his adopted land. For all his seriousness of purpose and intensity of commitment, he never fully succeeded. He absorbed the rhetoric of southern nationalism and accepted without question that the rhetoric reflected the full meaning of the struggle for Confederate nationhood. He went to war with his friends and neighbors and joined in their professed outrage at Yankee perfidy. As a soldier he did his full duty and devoted himself faithfully to the cause without feeling the need to agonize overmuch as to its meaning. By the time he proposed his naive and hopeless scheme to arm the South's slaves in the winter of 1863–1864, he had become, in effect, a citizen of the Army of Tennessee, and his disappointment in the failure of his proposal could not diminish his loyalty to that entity.

His love of the Confederacy was as genuine as his love for Sue Tarleton. But both his loves were in part the product of an idealized vision. Despite the fervidness of his commitment, his nationalism was more duty than ideology, his love more adoration than passion. Cleburne was an emotional man who felt the pull of patriotic sentiment and romantic love as well as the burden of duty. In their name, he sought—and found—glory on the battlefield; Gordon was quite correct to assert that Cleburne loved the Confederacy's banners and its battle flags. But he was never fully a part of the society he defended. Hardee, who admired Cleburne greatly even while understanding his limitations, may have sensed this. It was Hardee who wrote what may stand as his epitaph. Cleburne, he said, was "an Irishman by birth, a Southerner by adoption and residence, a lawyer by profession, a soldier in the British army by accident, and a soldier in the Southern armies from patriotism and conviction of duty in his manhood."[6]

NOTES

ABBREVIATIONS

AAG	Assistant Adjutant General
ADAH	Alabama Department of Archives and History
AHQ	*Arkansas Historical Quarterly*
AIGO	Adjutant and Inspector General's Office
B&L	*Battles and Leaders of the Civil War*, ed. Clarence Buell and Robert Johnson
CV	*Confederate Veteran*
CWR	*Civil War Regiments*
CWTI	*Civil War Times Illustrated*
Duke	William R. Perkins Library, Duke University
GHQ	*Georgia Historical Quarterly*
HEH	Henry E. Huntington Library, San Marino, California
MVHR	*Mississippi Valley Historical Review*
NA	National Archives, Washington, D.C.
O.R.	*Official Records of the Union and Confederate Armies in the War of the Rebellion*
PRC	Patrick R. Cleburne
RG	Record Group (National Archives)
SHC	Southern Historical Collection
SHSP	*Southern Historical Society Proceedings*
TSLA	Tennessee State Library and Archives, Nashville
U.Ark	University of Arkansas Library, Fayetteville
UNC	University of North Carolina, Chapel Hill
USAMHI	U.S. Army Military History Institute, U.S. Army War College, Carlisle Barracks, Pennsylvania
VSLA	Virginia State Library and Archives, Richmond
WRHS	Western Reserve Historical Society, Cleveland, Ohio
Yale	Yale University Library, New Haven, Connecticut

PROLOGUE

1. James H. M'Neilly, "Franklin—Incidents of the Battle," *CV* 26 (1918): 117. See also Larry Daniel, *Soldiering in the Army of Tennessee: A Portrait of Life in a Confederate Army* (Chapel Hill: University of North Carolina Press, 1991); Wiley Sword, *Embrace an Angry Wind: The Confederacy's Last Hurrah: Spring Hill, Franklin, and Nashville* (New York: Harper-Collins, 1992); James McDonough and Thomas L. Connelly, *Five Tragic Hours: The Battle of Franklin* (Knoxville: University of Tennessee Press, 1983).

2. Sumner A. Cunningham, "Disastrous Campaign in Tennessee," *CV* 12 (1904): 338–48, and "Events Leading to the Battle," *CV* 18 (1910): 17–20. Several versions of this firsthand memoir appear in *Confederate Veteran*. Cunningham was the manager and editor of the magazine, and he reprinted modified versions of his own account periodically for more than a dozen years. Some errors in the first version are corrected in later versions. See also Joseph Bryce (captain, 1st Missouri), "Missourians in Battle of Franklin," *CV* 24 (1916): 102; Sword, *Embrace an Angry Wind*, 177; Christopher Losson, *Tennessee's Forgotten Warriors: Frank Cheatham and His Confederate Division* (Knoxville: University of Tennessee Press, 1989), 217–18.

3. D. H. Patterson (private, 1st Alabama), "Battle of Franklin," *CV* 9 (1901): 116.

4. Cunningham, "Disastrous Campaign in Tennessee," 339; W. H. Rees, "Cleburne's Men at Franklin," *CV* 15 (1901): 508.

5. Irving Buck, *Cleburne and His Command* (1908; reprint, Dayton, Ohio: Morningside Bookshop, 1992), 280–81; Howell Purdue and Elizabeth Purdue, *Pat Cleburne, Confederate General* (Hillsboro, Texas: Hill Junior College Press, 1973), 414–15; W. J. Hardee, "Maj. Gen. Patrick R. Cleburne," *CV* 12 (1904): 17; W. F. Douglas, "A Sketch of Maj. Gen. P. R. Cleburne," *The Land We Love* 2 (1867): 460.

6. John C. Brown to Cheatham, 24 October 1881, in Benjamin Franklin Cheatham, "The Lost Opportunity at Spring Hill," *SHSP* 9 (1881): 538–39; J. P. Young, "Hood's Failure at Spring Hill," *CV* 16 (1908): 25–41.

7. Buck, *Cleburne and His Command*, 280.

8. Richard M. McMurry, *John Bell Hood and the Southern War for Independence* (Lexington: University Press of Kentucky, 1982), chap. 10. For Hood's belief that Cheatham's Corps was at fault, see Hood to Cooper, 15 February 1865, O.R., I, 46(1):652.

9. Brown to Cheatham in Sumner A. Cunningham, "Spring Hill and the Battle of Franklin," *CV* 12 (1904): 346; Cheatham, "The Lost Opportunity at Spring Hill," 524–41.

10. The objections of Forrest and Cheatham may have been expressed atop Winstead Hill rather than in Harrison House. Buck, *Cleburne and His Command*, is the source most frequently cited for this conversation (p. 280), but Buck was not present at Franklin. Losson, *Tennessee's Forgotten Warriors* (p. 218), relies on Frank Burr, a Philadelphia newsman, who in turn cited a postwar conversation between Cheatham and his aide Major James D. Porter (Frank A. Burr with Talcott Williams, *The Battle of Franklin* [Philadelphia: Philadelphia Press, 1883], 21). Forrest's biographer, John Allan Wyeth, cites a personal letter from the Reverend D. C. Kelley, a lieutenant colonel in Forrest's horse artillery (Wyeth, *That Devil Forrest* [1889; reprint, Baton Rouge: Louisiana State University Press, 1959, 1989], 480).

11. Hood's instructions to Cleburne were overheard by Dr. D. A. Linthicum, Cle-

burne's surgeon, who reported them to Cleburne's aide Learned Mangum, who in turn wrote them into his "Statement . . . Regarding the Death and Burial of General Patrick R. Cleburne," in Thomas A. Head, *Campaigns and Battles of the Sixteenth Regiment Tennessee Volunteers in the War Between the States* (Nashville, Tenn.: Cumberland Presbyterian Publishing House, 1885), 375. The original of this document is in the John R. Peacock Collection, SHC, UNC. Two years later in a longer essay on the same subject, Mangum admitted that "to his most intimate friends these words do not sound like Cleburne." Mangum, "General P. R. Cleburne, A Sketch of His Early Life and His Last Battle," *Kennesaw Gazette,* 15 June 1887, 4. In his memoir *Advance and Retreat* (New York: DaCapo Press, 1993), Hood claimed that Cleburne returned to Harrison House twenty minutes later. Hood asserts that Cleburne reported his division ready, then said, "I have more hope in the final success of our cause than I have had at any time since the first gun was fired" (p. 294). Hood's memoir is the only source for this tale, and many historians doubt that the conversation ever took place. Another possibility is that Cleburne *did* return to Hood's headquarters to assure him, in light of the yet unspoken accusation, that he would do his utmost in the battle. Frank Cheatham later recalled, "It was reported to me that he [Cleburne] had some words with the commander of the army just before going into the battle" (Burr, *The Battle of Franklin,* 24). It is unlikely, however, that the context of their exchange is accurately reflected in Hood's memoir, which was written a dozen years after the fact by a man who was attempting to salvage his place in history and who may have felt that citing the support of the martyred Cleburne would bolster his case. Hood claimed that Cleburne's remarks proved "that I was not the reckless, indiscreet commander the Johnston-Wigfall party represented me [to be]" (*Advance and Retreat,* 297).

CHAPTER ONE. PAT CLEBURNE'S IRELAND

1. Robert Kee, *The Green Flag: The Turbulent History of the Irish National Movement* (New York: Delacorte Press, 1972), 179–92; D. George Boyce, *Nineteenth-Century Ireland: The Search for Stability* (Savage, Md.: Barnes and Noble, 1991), 58–97; Llewellyn Woodward, *The Age of Reform, 1815–1870,* vol. 13 of *The Oxford History of England* (Oxford: Clarendon Press, 1938, 1962), 328–32; Cecil Woodham Smith, *The Great Hunger: Ireland, 1845–1849* (New York: Harper and Row, 1962), 20–29. The visiting Frenchman was one deBeaumont whose views were recorded in *Ireland: Social, Political, and Religious* (1839), 1:268.

2. James A. Reynolds, *The Catholic Emancipation Crisis in Ireland, 1823–1829* (New Haven: Yale University Press, 1954), 8; Kee, *The Green Flag,* 184; Woodham Smith, *The Great Hunger,* 20, 29.

3. Interview with Nora Lynch, Ballincollig, Ireland, 31 August 1994; Cork *Constitution,* 5 and 12 January 1843; Howell Purdue and Elizabeth Purdue, *Pat Cleburne, Confederate General* (Hillsboro, Texas: Hill Junior College Press, 1973), 18n.

4. The house still stands and was memorialized in March 1994 with a bronze plaque erected by "Cleburne's Brigade" of Civil War reenactors. The stepping-stones appear on the 1845 Ordnance Survey Map in Cork County Library.

5. Cork *Constitution,* 10 and 17 January and 25 February 1843.

6. Reynolds, *The Catholic Emancipation Crisis,* 93–95; Brian M. Walker, ed., *Parlia-*

mentary Election Results in Ireland, 1801–1922 (Dublin: Royal Irish Academy, 1978), 205; J. Connor, ed., *A Full Report of the Proceedings at the Election for the City of Cork* (Cork: J. Connor, 1818), 14–29; Ian d'Alton, *Protestant Society and Politics in Cork, 1812–1844* (Cork: Cork University Press, 1980), 133.

7. Connor, ed., *A Full Report,* 29–32; J. Connor, ed., *Lists of Freemen and Freeholders . . . Who Voted at the Cork Election, December 1826* (Cork: J. Connor, 1827), 99; d'Alton, *Protestant Society,* 137.

8. Oliver MacDonagh, "The Age of O'Connell," in W. E. Vaughan, ed., *A New History of Ireland,* vol. 5, *Ireland Under the Union, 1801–1870* (Oxford: Clarendon Press, 1989), 158–68; Reynolds, *The Catholic Emancipation Crisis,* 93–107. In a typical response, the president of the Board of Trade, William V. Fitzgerald, wrote that "no man can contemplate without alarm what is to follow in this wretched country" (Fitzgerald to Peel, 5 July 1828, in Angus MacIntyre, *The Liberator: Daniel O'Connor and the Irish Party, 1830–1847* [London: Hamish Hamilton, 1965], 10).

9. In the nineteenth century, Charles E. Nash claimed that Cleburne had told him that he had "a great horror of a step mother," but Nash's account of Cleburne's life before his arrival in Helena is so full of errors that this statement cannot be accepted at face value; Nash, *Biographical Sketches of Gen. Pat Cleburne and Gen. T. C. Hindman* (1898; reprint, Dayton, Ohio: Morningside Bookshop, 1977), 13–14. See PRC to "Sister Isey" (Isabella Cleburne), 28 June 1849, and PRC to "Mamma" (Isabella Stuart Cleburne), 26 October 1853, both in Cleburne Papers, U.Ark.

10. Cleburne referred to his sister as both "Isey" and "Issy" in private letters. Most likely this nickname was pronounced to suggest the first two syllables of Isabella. See PRC to "Sister Isey" (Isabella Cleburne), 28 June 1849, and PRC to "Mamma" (Isabella Stuart Cleburne), 27 October 1853, both in Cleburne Papers, U.Ark. The birthdates of Cleburne's half siblings are in the Cleburne Family Bible, Cleburne Papers, U.Ark. See also Purdue and Purdue, *Pat Cleburne,* 5–6.

11. J. C. Hawkes to John Reid, 31 July 1869, Nora Lynch Collection, Ballincollig, Ireland; Purdue and Purdue, *Pat Cleburne,* 6.

12. Hawkes to Reid, 31 July 1869, Nora Lynch Collection; Kee, *The Green Flag,* 171; Woodham Smith, *The Great Hunger,* 22; Cork *Examiner,* 20 December 1843; F. W. Knight, "General Patrick Ronayne Cleburne," *Cork Historical and Archeological Society Journal* 21 (1915): 12.

13. Knight, "General . . . Cleburne," 13; interview with Nora Lynch, Ballincollig, 31 August 1994; Kee, *The Green Flag,* 215; Martina Cleary and Olive Driscoll, "Spedding's School and Hospital," *Journal of the Ballincollig Community School* (1985): 5.

14. Cork *Constitution,* 5 January and 3 August 1841.

15. Ibid., 5 January 1841 and 6 April 1843; Cleary and Driscoll, "Spedding's School," 5.

16. Cork *Constitution,* 5 January 1841; George D. Kelleher, "The Gunpowder Mill at Ballincollig," in *Gunpowder to Guided Missiles: Ireland's War Industries, 1361–1986* (Cork: John F. Kelleher, 1992), 56, 75.

17. Cork *Constitution,* 6 April and 18 July 1843; Cleary and Driscoll, "Spedding's School," 5–6.

18. Learned H. Mangum, "General P. R. Cleburne," *Kennesaw Gazette,* 15 June 1887, 2.

19. PRC to "Sister Isey" (Isabella Cleburne), 28 June 1849, Cleburne Papers, U.Ark.

20. I am grateful to Dr. Denis J. Wilson of Cork, Ireland, for information about medical apprentices in nineteenth-century Ireland. PRC to "Mamma" (Isabella Stuart Cleburne), 26 October 1853, Cleburne Papers, U.Ark.

21. Purdue and Purdue, *Pat Cleburne*, 8–9, 19n–20n.

22. Kee, *The Green Flag*, 209–37; Cork *Constitution*, 23 May 1843.

23. Cork *Examiner*, 22 May 1843; Cork *Constitution*, 29 April 1843; *The Nation*, 14 June 1845. Other quotations taken from Kee, *The Green Flag*, 225, 238. Italics added.

24. Woodham Smith, *The Great Hunger;* Woodward, *The Age of Reform*, 329n.

25. Woodham Smith, *The Great Hunger*, 106.

26. Ibid., 137.

27. Notebook of Frank Harrison Smith, Jill Knight Garrett Collection, TSLA; Irving R. Buck, "Cleburne and His Command," *CV* 17 (1909): 475; John F. Maguire, *The Irish in America* (London: Longmans, Green, 1868), 581–82.

28. J. F. Fleetwood, *The History of Medicine in Ireland* (Dublin: Skellig Press, 1983), esp. chap. 8: "The Apothecaries"; Buck, "Cleburne and His Command," 475; Purdue and Purdue, *Pat Cleburne*, 8–9.

29. Kelleher, "The Gunpowder Mill at Ballincollig," 56; Cleary and Driscoll, "Spedding's School," 5–6; Purdue and Purdue, *Pat Cleburne*, 7, 9; Cork *Constitution*, June–July 1843.

30. Purdue and Purdue cite the War Office pay lists and muster rolls of the 41st Regiment in the Public Record Office (*Pat Cleburne*, 9, 20n); PRC to "Sister Isey" (Isabella Cleburne), 28 June 1849, Cleburne Papers, U.Ark.

31. Kee, *The Green Flag*, 256–69; Woodham Smith, *The Great Hunger*, 116–24; Calhoun Benham to P. W. Alexander, 21 December 1863, Peter W. Alexander Collection, Columbia University.

32. PRC to "Sister Isey" (Isabella Cleburne), 28 June 1849, Cleburne Papers, U.Ark.; Calhoun Benham, "Major-Gen. P. R. Cleburne, A Biography," *Kennesaw Gazette*, 1 January 1889, 2.

33. W. F. Douglas, "A Sketch of Maj. Gen. P. R. Cleburne," *The Land We Love* 2 (1867): 461. Mangum wrote in 1887 that Cleburne was busted from corporal because he had allowed a prisoner to escape ("General P. R. Cleburne," *Kennesaw Gazette*, 15 June 1887, 3).

34. See, for example, David Fitzpatrick, *Irish Emigration, 1801–1921* (Dublin: Economic and Social History Society of Ireland, 1984); Robert E. Kennedy, *The Irish: Emigration, Marriage, and Fertility* (Berkeley: University of California Press, 1973); and Arnold Schrier, *Ireland and the American Emigration, 1850–1900* (Minneapolis: University of Minnesota Press, 1958).

35. William Cleburne to Patrick R. Cashman, 8 July 1849, Cashman Family Papers, Ruth Duemler Collection, Fresno, California; James S. Donnelly, Jr., *The Land and the People of Nineteenth Century Cork* (London: Routledge and Kegan Paul, 1975), 103.

36. PRC to "Mamma" (Isabella Stuart Cleburne), 27 October 1853, and PRC to "Sister Isey" (Isabella Cleburne), 28 June 1849, both in Cleburne Papers, U.Ark.

37. Purdue and Purdie, *Pat Cleburne*, 14; Patrick Thompson, "General Patrick

Ronayne Cleburne," *Cork Holly Bough,* December 1976; PRC to "Mamma" (Isabella Stuart Cleburne), 27 October 1853, Cleburne Papers, U.Ark.

38. PRC to "Mamma" (Isabella Stuart Cleburne), 27 October 1853, Cleburne Papers, U.Ark.

CHAPTER TWO. HELENA, ARKANSAS

1. Howell Purdue and Elizabeth Purdue, *Pat Cleburne, Confederate General* (Hillsboro, Texas: Hill Junior College Press, 1973), 23; George Kelleher, "The Gunpowder Mill at Ballincollig," in *Gunpowder to Guided Missiles: Ireland's War Industries, 1361–1986* (Cork: John F. Kelleher, 1992), 46–47. The Carrollton Railroad boasted a total of only six miles of track by 1852; see J. D. B. DeBow, ed., *The Industrial Resources, etc. of the Southern and Western States,* 3 vols. (New Orleans: DeBow's Review, 1852), 1:476. Patrick Ronayne Cashman had emigrated to the United States in 1838 and lived in Lafayette, Indiana, from 1839 to 1842. There is no evidence, however, that he actually met any of the Cleburne siblings after they arrived in the United States. Another source of information about America for the Cleburnes was John Maines, who lived in Wisconsin and wrote regularly to the Ronaynes from 1836 to 1840. Cashman Family Papers, Ruth Duemler Collection, Fresno, California.

2. Cork *Examiner,* 9 February 1853; Purdue and Purdue, *Pat Cleburne,* 23–24.

3. Charles E. Nash, *Biographical Sketches of Gen. Pat Cleburne and Gen. T. C. Hindman* (1898; reprint, Dayton, Ohio: Morningside Bookshop, 1977), 8; Purdue and Purdue, *Pat Cleburne,* 24. Henry Howe, *Historical Collections of Ohio* (Columbus: Henry Howe and Son, 1891), 32–35.

4. Nash, *Biographical Sketches,* 7–8; Learned H. Mangum in Irving A. Buck, *Cleburne and His Command* (Dayton, Ohio: Morningside Bookshop, 1992), 76; Purdue and Purdue, *Pat Cleburne,* 24–25.

5. PRC to "Mamma" (Isabella Stuart Cleburne), 26 October 1853, Cleburne Papers, U.Ark.; Carl H. Moneyhon, "Economic Democracy in Antebellum Arkansas, Phillips County, 1850–1860," *AHQ* 40 (Summer 1981): 158–60; Nash, *Biographical Sketches,* 10.

6. Nash, *Biographical Sketches,* 9; Purdue and Purdue, *Pat Cleburne,* 26–27.

7. Nash uses the term "bedfellow" (p. 15) to describe his relationship with Cleburne. Although the two men may actually have shared a bed, this situation was not uncommon in frontier communities like Helena (or, indeed, in Ireland), where beds were still something of a luxury, and does not imply any physical intimacy.

8. Nash, *Biographical Sketches,* 10–38.

9. Helena *Democratic Star,* 22 March 1854.

10. Nash, *Biographical Sketches,* 12–13.

11. Ibid., 25.

12. Helena *Southern Shield,* weekly from 10 January 1852; Purdue and Purdue, *Pat Cleburne,* 30, 37; Nash, *Biographical Sketches,* 38.

13. PRC to "Mamma" (Isabella Stuart Cleburne), 26 October 1853, Cleburne Papers, U.Ark.

14. Irving Buck, "Cleburne and His Command," *CV* 17 (1909): 475; Rowena Webster, "Memories of a Southern Girl," Jill Knight Garrett Collection, TSLA. The

poem, dated 9 July 1854, is in the Patrick Cleburne Papers, Arkansas History Commission, Little Rock.

15. Nash, *Biographical Sketches,* 35; Purdue and Purdue, *Pat Cleburne,* 30.

16. Nash, *Biographical Sketches,* 28–31.

17. Ibid., 33–34.

18. Helena *Southern Shield,* 25 June 1853.

19. Carl H. Moneyhon, *The Impact of the Civil War and Reconstruction on Arkansas: Persistence in the Midst of Ruin* (Baton Rouge: Louisiana State University Press, 1994), 54–55; Moneyhon, "Economic Democracy," 158–60; Purdue and Purdue, *Pat Cleburne,* 27.

20. Although the average price of land in Phillips County during the 1850s was only about $5 per acre, good cotton land with river access was much more expensive. Even taking the average ($5) figure, a 600-acre plantation, one large enough for economic viability, would cost about $3,000. Labor was even more expensive. A good field hand in 1850 cost about $415; thus twenty slaves, the number most often cited to define a plantation economy, would cost another $8,300. Of course, a prospective plantation owner would not have to put down the full amount all at once, but even the initial investment necessary to become a planter was about $4,000, plus annual payments (at 8–10 percent interest) on another $8,000 to 10,000. Moneyhon, *The Impact of the Civil War and Reconstruction on Arkansas,* 28–29; see also Moneyhon, "Economic Democracy," 154–72.

21. PRC to "Mamma" (Isabella Stuart Cleburne), 26 October 1853, Cleburne Papers, U.Ark.; Orville Taylor, *Negro Slavery in Arkansas* (Durham, N.C.: Duke University Press, 1958), 37.

22. See Robert M. Calhoun, *Evangelicals and Conservatives in the Early South, 1740–1861* (Columbia: University of South Carolina Press, 1988); Anne C. Loveland, *Southern Evangelicals and the Social Order, 1800–1860* (Baton Rouge: Louisiana State University Press, 1980); Donald G. Mathews, *Religion in the Old South* (Chicago: University of Chicago Press, 1977).

23. Nash, *Biographical Sketches,* 36–37; PRC to "Mamma" (Isabella Stuart Cleburne), 26 October 1853, Cleburne Papers, U.Ark.; Purdue and Purdue, *Pat Cleburne,* 43. Cleburne rejoined the Episcopal Church three years later in 1856 and became a vestryman.

24. PRC to "Mamma" (Isabella Stuart Cleburne), 26 October 1853, Cleburne Papers, U.Ark.

25. Ibid.; Calhoun Benham, "Major-Gen. P. R. Cleburne, A Biography," *Kennesaw Gazette,* 1 January 1889, 2; Helena *Democratic Star,* 19 April 1854. Doctors Grant and Nash ran ads throughout 1854–1855 offering their services at "Nash and Cleburne's Drug Store," while a new firm, Lindsley and Brother, advertised their pharmaceuticals "at the old stand of Grant and Nash, Rightor Street" (*Democratic Star,* weekly, 1854–1855).

26. Ted R. Worley, "Helena on the Mississippi," *AHQ* 13 (Spring 1954): 6; PRC to "Mamma" (Isabella Stuart Cleburne), 26 October 1853, Cleburne Papers, U.Ark.; Helena *Democratic Star,* 17 May 1855.

27. Nash, *Biographical Sketches,* 28, 85.

28. See Diane Neal and Thomas W. Kremm, *Lion of the South: General Thomas C. Hindman* (Macon, Ga.: Mercer University Press, 1993), and James M. Woods, *Rebel-*

lion and Realignment: Arkansas's Road to Secession (Fayetteville: University of Arkansas Press, 1987). The quotations are from Michael Dougan, *Confederate Arkansas: The People and the Politics of a Frontier State in Wartime* (University: University of Alabama Press, 1976), 13.

29. Dougan, *Confederate Arkansas,* 13; Woods, *Rebellion and Realignment,* 77; Nash, *Biographical Sketches,* 57–58.

30. Cleburne went to Gideon Pillow, whose prestige as a general in the war against Mexico gave him latitude in these affairs. Pillow appealed to both Hindman and Badham, and the quarrel was resolved. Nash, *Biographical Sketches,* 58–61; Neal and Kremm, *Lion of the South,* 23–24.

31. Colonel Samuel W. Williams, quoted in Nash, *Biographical Sketches,* 150. See also Neal and Kremm, *Lion of the South,* 26; Helena *Democratic Star,* 1 March 1855.

32. Nash, *Biographical Sketches,* 73.

33. David Potter, *The Impending Crisis, 1848–1860* (New York: Harper and Row, 1976), chap. 7.

34. W. Durrell Overdyke, *The Know-Nothing Party in the South* (Baton Rouge: Louisiana State University Press, 1950).

35. Nash, *Biographical Sketches,* 88; Helena *Democratic Star,* 1 March and 19 April 1855; Little Rock *True Democrat,* 8, 15, and 22 April 1855. See also Harold T. Smith, "The Know-Nothings in Arkansas," *AHQ* 34 (Winter 1975): 292–93, 299–300.

36. Nash, *Biographical Sketches,* 89; Helena *Democratic Star,* 16 August 1855. Additional evidence of their early partnership is in a public letter signed by both Hindman and Cleburne in June 1855 inviting Senator Sebastian to speak at the July meeting of the Phillips County Democratic Association. See also the Helena *Democratic Star,* 9 and 30 August and 20 September 1855.

37. Nash, *Biographical Sketches,* 52–56; Helena *Democratic Star,* 4 October 1855; Neal and Kremm, *Lion of the South,* 32.

38. Helena *Democratic Star,* 8 and 29 November 1855.

39. Helena *States Rights Democrat,* 24 April 1856; Helena *Southern Shield,* 6 January 1855 and 1 January 1856; Nash, *Biographical Sketches,* 80–82.

40. The *Democratic Star* became available for purchase after the owner, James Cleveland, died in the yellow fever epidemic in September. Helena *Southern Shield,* 29 December 1855 (reporting the sale); Helena *States Rights Democrat,* 20 March 1856.

41. Neal and Kremm, *Lion of the South,* 34–35; Nash, *Biographical Sketches,* 64–69; Purdue and Purdue, *Pat Cleburne,* 50–52; PRC to Robert Cleburne, [January 1861], Cleburne Papers, U.Ark.

42. Learned H. Mangum, "General P. R. Cleburne," *Kennesaw Gazette,* 15 June 1887, 2.

43. Helena *States Rights Democrat,* 31 July 1856.

44. Nash, *Biographical Sketches,* 96; Little Rock *True Democrat,* 28 October 1858; Woods, *Rebellion and Realignment,* 95–96.

45. Mangum in Buck, *Cleburne and His Command,* 77; Helena *States Rights Democrat,* 28 January 1860; Robert B. Walz, "Migration into Arkansas, 1820–1880: Incentives and Means of Travel," *AHQ* 17 (Winter 1958): 309–24. Evidence of Cleburne's participation in the railroad promotion scheme is in the Little Rock *Old Line Democrat,* 23 September 1859. See also Nash, *Biographical Sketches,* 85–86.

46. The popular vote in Arkansas was 28,783 for Breckinridge, 20,094 for Bell, and 5,227 for Douglas; Woods, *Rebellion and Realignment,* 81–96. See also Lenette S. Taylor, "Polemics and Partisanship: The Arkansas Press in the 1860 Election," *AHQ* 44 (Winter 1985): 314–35.

47. PRC to Robert Cleburne, [January 1861], Cleburne Papers, U.Ark.

48. PRC to Robert Cleburne, [January 1861] and 7 May 1861, both in Cleburne Papers, U.Ark.

CHAPTER THREE. COMMAND

1. Calhoun Benham, "Major-Gen. P. R. Cleburne, A Biography," *Kennesaw Gazette,* 15 January 1889, 2; PRC to Robert Cleburne, 7 May 1861, Cleburne Papers, U.Ark.

2. Charles E. Nash, *Biographical Sketches of Gen. Pat Cleburn and Gen. T. C. Hindman* (Dayton, Ohio: Morningside Bookshop, 1977), 38; "Memoirs of a Southern Girl," Jill Knight Garrett Collection, TSLA; W. F. Douglas, "A Sketch of Maj. Gen. P. R. Cleburne," *The Land We Love* 2 (1867): 460.

3. PRC to Robert Cleburne, January 1861, Cleburne Papers, U.Ark.

4. Michael Dougan, *Confederate Arkansas* (University: University of Alabama Press, 1976); Little Rock *Gazette,* 29 January 1861.

5. Little Rock *Gazette,* 5, 9, and 16 February 1862; Howell Purdue and Elizabeth Purdue, *Pat Cleburne, Confederate General* (Hillsboro, Texas: Hill Junior College Press, 1973), 71–72.

6. Purdue and Purdue, *Pat Cleburne,* 73.

7. PRC to Robert Cleburne, 7 May 1861, Cleburne Papers, U.Ark.; Irving A. Buck, *Cleburne and His Command* (Dayton, Ohio: Morningside Bookshop, 1992), 81; Nash, *Biographical Sketches,* 178.

8. Purdue and Purdue, *Pat Cleburne,* 73–74.

9. PRC to Robert Cleburne, 7 and 8 May 1861, both in Cleburne Papers, U.Ark. The note of 8 May reads, "I have been elected Colonel 1st Regiment today."

10. Dougan, *Confederate Arkansas,* 65, 77.

11. E. H. Fletcher to My Dear Sister, 18 June 1861, in *The Civil War Letters of Captain Elliott H. Fletcher,* ed. J. H. Atkinson, Bulletin no. 5 (Little Rock, Ark.: Pulaski County Historical Society, 1963), 36.

12. Alfred H. Carrigan, "Reminiscences of the Secession Convention," *Publications of the Arkansas Historical Association* 1 (1906): 309; PRC to Judge Hanley, 30 May 1861, and Carlton to "Col. Grace or Gen. Yell," 30 May 1861, both in *Journal of Both Sessions of the Convention of the State of Arkansas* (Little Rock, Ark.: Johnson and Yerkes, 1861), 423–24.

13. Bradley to Walker, 30 May 1861, *Journal of Both Sessions,* 423.

14. Purdue and Purdue, *Pat Cleburne,* 81–82.

15. Dougan, *Confederate Arkansas,* 75; Nathaniel Cheairs Hughes, Jr., *General William J. Hardee: Old Reliable* (Baton Rouge: Louisiana State University Press, 1965).

16. Articles of Transfer, 15 July 1861, O.R., I, 3:609–10; Nash, *Biographical Sketches,* 104–8; Hughes, *General William J. Hardee,* 75.

17. Hughes, *General William J. Hardee,* 75–76; Purdue and Purdue, *Pat Cleburne,* 84–85; Dougan, *Confederate Arkansas,* 78–79.

18. Nash, *Biographical Sketches,* 111; William J. Hardee, "Maj. Gen. Pat Cleburne," *CV* 12 (1904): 17; T. B. Roy, "General Hardee and the Military Operations Around Atlanta," *SHSP* 8 (1880): 381.

19. Hughes, *General William J. Hardee,* 76–77; St. John R. Liddell, *Liddell's Record,* ed. Nathaniel C. Hughes, Jr. (Dayton, Ohio: Morningside House, 1985), 121.

20. Basil W. Duke, *Reminiscences of Basil W. Duke, C.S.A.* (New York: Doubleday, 1911), 68–69; Douglas, "A Sketch of Maj. Gen. P. R. Cleburne," 2:462.

21. Benham, "Major-Gen. P. R. Cleburne," 2; I. W. Avery, "Patrick Ronayne Cleburne," *Kennesaw Gazette,* 15 May 1887, 2; Learned H. Mangum, "Statement of Judge Mangum," *Kennesaw Gazette,* 1 June 1889, 2.

22. Buck, *Cleburne and His Command,* 128–29; Frank H. Smith, *History of Maury County, Tennessee* (N.p.: Maury County Historical Society, 1969), 359; Anonymous, "Severe Discipline," *CV* 1 (1893): 374.

23. J. M. Berry, "The Quiet Humor of Gen. Pat Cleburne," *CV* 12 (1904): 176.

24. PRC to G. W. Randolph, 3 October 1862, Letters Received, AIGO, reel 14, RG 109, NA; Learned H. Mangum, "General P. R. Cleburne," *Kennesaw Gazette,* 15 June 1887, 4; Berry, "The Quiet Humor of Gen. Pat Cleburne," *CV* 12 (1904): 176.

25. Thomas L. Connelly, *Army of the Heartland: The Army of Tennessee, 1861–1862* (Baton Rouge: Louisiana State University Press, 1967), 46–49; Hughes, *General William J. Hardee,* 77–79.

26. Hughes, *General William J. Hardee,* 78.

27. Govan to My Dear Wife, 17 August 1861, folder 1, Govan Papers, SHC, UNC; Calhoun Benham to P. W. Alexander, 21 December 1863, Peter W. Alexander Collection, Columbia University.

28. Hughes, *General William J. Hardee,* 78; Buck, *Cleburne and His Command,* 83–84; Duke, *Reminiscences,* 69–70; Purdue and Purdue, *Pat Cleburne,* 87.

29. Hughes, *General William J. Hardee,* 80.

30. Connelly, *Army of the Heartland,* 65–66; Hughes, *General William J. Hardee,* 80–83.

31. Hardee to Polk, 17 September 1861, and Hardee to A. S. Johnston, 24 September 1861, both in O.R., I, 3:702, 707; PRC to Polk, 27 September 1861, Miscellaneous Papers, RG 109, NA; E. H. Fletcher to My Dear Father, 22 and 26 September 1861, in *The Civil War Letters of Captain Elliott H. Fletcher,* 10, 12; Hughes, *General William J. Hardee,* 81.

32. Govan to My Dear Wife, 15 October 1861, folder 1, Govan Papers, SHC, UNC. Although he did not learn of it for many months, none of Cleburne's siblings or half siblings entered the Union army, even though William's job on the railroad gave him a quasi-military status and a draft exemption.

33. Connelly, *Army of the Heartland,* 65–71.

34. Ibid., 75; Hughes, *General William J. Hardee,* 83; Thomas Robson Hay, "Pat Cleburne: Stonewall Jackson of the West," in Buck, *Cleburne and His Command,* 22, 29–30.

35. PRC to Hardee, 30 October 1861, O.R., I, 52(2):190.

36. Hughes, *General William J. Hardee,* 85; Purdue and Purdue, *Pat Cleburne,* 89.

37. A. S. Johnston to Hardee, 9 November 1861, O.R., I, 4:531; PRC to Hardee, 11 and 13 November 1861, O.R., I, 4:537–38, 545.

38. PRC to Hardee, 11 November 1861, O.R., I, 4:537–38.

39. PRC to Hardee, 13 November 1861, O.R., I, 4:545–48.

40. PRC to Hardee, 11 and 16 November 1861, O.R., I, 4:458–59, 537–38; Mackall to Hardee, 21 December 1861, O.R., I, 7:782.

41. PRC to Hardee, 11 and 13 November 1861, O.R., I, 4:537–38, 545–48.

42. PRC to D. G. White (Hardee's AAG), 22 November 1861, Combined Service Record, RG 109, NA; PRC to J. J. Thornton (colonel, 7th Mississippi), 22 November 1861, Patrick Cleburne Letters, Doug Schanz Collection (private), Roanoke, Virginia; Wiley Sword, *Shiloh: Bloody April* (New York: William Morrow, 1988; reprint, Dayton, Ohio: Morningside Bookshop, 1983), 64; Hughes, *General William J. Hardee*, 89–90.

43. Sword, *Shiloh*, 61–65; Muster Roll of 15th Arkansas Regiment, quoted in Purdue and Purdue, *Pat Cleburne*, 98.

44. James A. Jones, "About the Battle of Shiloh," *CV* 7 (1899): 556; Notes from Company E, 15th Arkansas, quoted in Purdue and Purdue, *Pat Cleburne*, 104n; Connelly, *Army of the Heartland*, 137–38; Hughes, *General William J. Hardee*, 92.

45. Jones, "About the Battle of Shiloh," 556; Bragg to Benjamin, 27 February 1862, Bragg Papers, WRHS.

46. Johnston to Benjamin, 5 March 1862, O.R., I, 10(2):297.

CHAPTER FOUR. FIRST BLOOD: SHILOH

1. Wiley Sword, *Shiloh: Bloody April* (New York: William Morrow, 1974; reprint, Dayton, Ohio: Morningside Bookshop, 1983), 49–92; James Lee McDonough, *Shiloh: In Hell Before Night* (Knoxville: University of Tennessee Press, 1977), 8–26; Thomas L. Connelly, *Army of the Heartland* (Baton Rouge: Louisiana State University Press, 1967), 126–42; Nathaniel Cheairs Hughes, Jr., *General William J. Hardee* (Baton Rouge: Louisiana State University Press, 1965), 96–98.

2. Connelly, *Army of the Heartland*, 147; Hughes, *General William J. Hardee*, 99–101; General Orders, 29 March 1862, O.R., I, 10(2):370–71.

3. The Inspector General's Office ordered that Hill's regiment be redesignated as the 35th Tennessee in November 1861. Nevertheless, it continued to be referred to as "the 5th (Hill's) Tennessee" in official reports. To avoid confusion, it will be referred to as the 5th (35th) Tennessee in this book.

4. Organizational table in O.R., I, 52(1):28.

5. See Bragg to Johnston, 19 March 1862, O.R., I, 10(2):341–42. Also General Orders, 29 March 1862, Bragg to Hardee, 3 April 1862, and General Orders no. 7, 3 April 1862, all in O.R., I, 10(2):370–71, 387, 389.

6. Sword, *Shiloh*, 99–101; Hughes, *General William J. Hardee*, 101–2.

7. Hughes, *General William J. Hardee*, 102–3.

8. James A. Jones (private, 23d Tennessee), "About the Battle of Shiloh," *CV* 7 (1899): 556.

9. Ricker to Taylor, 4 April 1862, O.R., I, 10(1):92; Hughes, *General William J. Hardee*, 102–3. As fate would have it, the skirmish with Federal cavalry failed to alert the enemy. Although the cavalry commander reported the presence of Confederate infantry to his division commander (none other than Major General William T. Sherman), that officer brushed it off. He assumed that his Ohio troopers had chanced upon

a Confederate reconnaissance in force. Jay A. Jorgenson, "Scouting for Ulysses S. Grant: The 5th Ohio Cavalry in the Shiloh Campaign," *Civil War Regiments* 4 (1994): 68–69.

10. Jasper Kelsey (private, 23d Tennessee), "The Battle of Shiloh," *CV* 25 (1917): 71.

11. William Preston Johnston, *The Life of Albert Sidney Johnston* (New York: D. Appleton, 1878), 561; Sword, *Shiloh,* 103–4.

12. Johnston, *General Albert Sidney Johnston,* 569.

13. Kelsey, "The Battle of Shiloh," 71; Jones, "About the Battle of Shiloh," 556; William C. Thompson, "From Shiloh to Port Gibson," *CWTI* 3 (October 1964): 20–21; Hardee to Cooper, 7 February 1863, O.R., I, 10(1):567; Hughes, *General William J. Hardee,* 103.

14. Sword, *Shiloh,* 147; Connelly, *Army of the Heartland,* 161–63.

15. Kelsey, "The Battle of Shiloh," 71.

16. PRC to T. B. Roy, 24 May 1862, O.R., I, 10(1):580–81; I. W. Avery, "Patrick Ronayne Cleburne," *Kennesaw Gazette,* 15 May 1887, 2.

17. Kelsey, "The Battle of Shiloh," 72; William Preston to Thomas Jordan (AAG), 15 July 1862, O.R., I, 10(1):403.

18. PRC to T. B. Roy, 24 May 1862, O.R., I, 10(1):581.

19. J. A. Wheeler, "Cleburne's Brigade at Shiloh," *CV* 2 (1894): 13; PRC to T. B. Roy, 24 May 1862, O.R., I, 10(1):581.

20. PRC to T. B. Roy, 24 May 1862, O.R., I, 10(1):581; Kelsey, "The Battle of Shiloh," 72; Sword, *Shiloh,* 183.

21. PRC to T. B. Roy, 24 May 1862, O.R., I, 10(1):582.

22. Ibid.

23. Ibid.

24. Ibid.

25. Ibid.

26. Ibid., 582–83.

27. Ibid., 583.

28. Ibid.; John H. Kelly to T. B. Roy, 9 April 1862, and I. P. Girardey to J. B. Cummings, 12 April 1862, both in O.R., I, 10(1):565, 600–602.

29. PRC to T. B. Roy, 24 May 1862, O.R., I, 10(1):583.

30. Ibid., 583–84.

31. Ibid.

32. Ibid., 584.

33. Officially, Confederate losses at Shiloh were 10,699 killed, wounded, and missing. With 7.5 percent of the Confederate army, Cleburne's Brigade suffered just over 10 percent of the casualties. Federal losses were 13,047, making the total losses by both armies over the two days 23,746. O.R., I, 10(1):100–108, 395–96, 391.

34. W. F. Douglas, "A Sketch of Maj. Gen. P. R. Cleburne," *The Land We Love* 2 (1867): 461; St. John R. Liddell, *Liddell's Record,* ed. Nathaniel C. Hughes, Jr. (Dayton, Ohio: Morningside House, 1985), 161; William J. Hardee, "Maj. Gen. Patrick R. Cleburne," *CV* 12 (1904): 17.

35. Yeatman Memoirs, Confederate Collection, TSLA. See the thoughtful analysis of these questions by Grady McWhiney and Perry D. Jamieson in *Attack and Die:*

Civil War Military Tactics and the Southern Heritage (University: University of Alabama Press, 1982), and by Gerald Linderman in *Embattled Courage* (New York: Free Press, 1987).

36. Hardee to Cooper, 7 February 1863, O.R., I, 10(1):570.

37. PRC to T. B. Roy, 24 May 1862, O.R., I, 10(1):584.

CHAPTER FIVE. THE KENTUCKY CAMPAIGN

1. I. W. Avery, "Patrick Ronayne Cleburne," *Kennesaw Gazette,* 15 May 1887, 3.

2. Blakemore Diary (29 April 1862), Confederate Collection, TSLA. Worse yet, Federal forces soon advanced into Arkansas and occupied Helena.

3. PRC to Hardee, 2 May 1862, Compiled Service Record, reel 57, RG 109, NA; General Orders no. 122, 24 August 1862, O.R., I, 16(2):778–79.

4. Blakemore Diary (29 April 1862), Confederate Collection, TSLA.

5. Blakemore Diary (4–6 May 1862), Confederate Collection, TSLA; PRC to Hardee, 6 May 1862, Compiled Service Record, reel 57, RG 109, NA.

6. PRC to Hardee, 6 May 1862, Compiled Service Record, reel 57, RG 109, NA; Blakemore Diary, 9 May 1862, Confederate Collection, TSLA; Beauregard to Hardee, 4 May 1862, O.R., I, 10(2):488.

7. Thomas to Cullum, 3 June 1862, O.R., I, 10(1):740; PRC to Hardee, 23 June 1862, O.R., I, 52(1):35.

8. PRC to Hardee, 23 June 1862, O.R., I, 52(1):34–35.

9. Ibid.

10. Yeatman Memoir, Confederate Collection, TSLA; James L. Nichols and Frank Abbott, eds., "Reminiscences of Confederate Service by Wiley A. Washburn," *AHQ* 35 (Spring 1976): 55; Buck to Lucy Buck, 18 June 1862, Buck Papers, SHC, UNC.

11. Buck to Lucy Buck, 18 June 1862, Buck Papers, SHC, UNC; W. P. Johnston Report, 15 July 1862, O.R., I, 10(1):785; Howell Purdue and Elizabeth Purdue, *Pat Cleburne, Confederate General* (Hillsboro, Texas: Hill Junior College Press, 1973), 127–28; Thomas L. Connelly, *Army of the Heartland* (Baton Rouge: Louisiana State University Press, 1967), 176–77.

12. Buck to Lucy Buck, 18 June 1862, Buck Papers, SHC, UNC; Connelly, *Army of the Heartland,* 181.

13. Grady McWhiney, *Braxton Bragg and Confederate Defeat: Field Command,* vol. 1 (Tuscaloosa: University of Alabama Press, 1991), 51; Arthur J. L. Fremantle, *The Fremantle Diary,* ed. Walter Lord (Boston: Little, Brown and Company, 1954), 115; Bragg to Cooper, 29 June 1862, O.R., I, 17(2):627–28, 673.

14. Blakemore Diary, 26 June 1862, and Yeatman Memoir, p. 3, both in Confederate Collection, TSLA; Buck to Lucy Buck, 18 June 1862, Buck Papers, SHC, UNC; Buck to "My dear Dick," 19 July 1862, Buck Papers, William Pettus Buck Collection (private), Birmingham, Alabama; Nathaniel Cheairs Hughes, Jr., *General William J. Hardee* (Baton Rouge: Louisiana State University Press, 1965), 119.

15. Joseph H. Parks, *General Edmund Kirby Smith, C.S.A.* (Baton Rouge: Louisiana State University Press, 1954, 1982); W. P. Johnston Report, 15 July 1862, O.R., I, 10(1):785; Bragg to Davis, 21 July 1862, O.R., I, 52(2):330.

16. Special Orders no. 4, 21 July 1862, O.R., I, 16(2):731.

17. Bragg to Cooper, 20 May 1863, O.R., I, 16:1089; Jordan to PRC and Kirby Smith, 5 August 1862, O.R., I, 16(2):744–45.

18. Connelly, *Army of the Heartland,* 211.

19. Paul Hammond, "General Kirby Smith's Campaign in Kentucky," *SHSP* 9 (1881): 247; Diary of J. G. Law (15 August 1862), *SHSP* 12 (1884): 391.

20. Diary of J. G. Law (18 and 19 August 1862), *SHSP* 12 (1884): 394.

21. Pegram to Scott, 24 August 1862, and Kirby Smith to Cooper, 24 August 1862, both in O.R., I, 16(2):778, 777. See also Hammond, "Kirby Smith's Campaign," 248–49.

22. Hammond, "Kirby Smith's Campaign," 249.

23. PRC to Kirby Smith, 1 September 1862, and Hill to P. Smith, 15 September 1862, both in O.R., I, 16(2):944, 949.

24. Ibid.; Calhoun Benham manuscript, 21 December 1863, Peter W. Alexander Collection, Columbia University; Yeatman Memoir, p. 3, Confederate Collection, TSLA.

25. Hammond, "Kirby Smith's Campaign," 250; Hill to P. Smith, 15 September 1862, and Kirby Smith to Cooper, 16 September 1862, both in O.R., I, 16(2):950, 934. See also Hill's report, 15 September 1862, in O.R., I, 16(1):950.

26. Hammond, "Kirby Smith's Campaign," 250; Yeatman Memoir, p. 3, Confederate Collection, TSLA; PRC to Kirby Smith, 1 September 1862, O.R., I, 16(2):945–46; Charles E. Nash, *Biographical Sketches of Gen. Pat Cleburne and Gen. T. C. Hindman* (Dayton, Ohio: Morningside Bookshop, 1977), 202; Irving A. Buck, *Cleburne and His Command* (Dayton, Ohio: Morningside Bookshop, 1992), 107; Kirby Smith to Cooper, 16 September 1862, O.R., I, 16(2):934.

27. Yeatman Memoir, p. 7, Confederate Collection, TSLA. As usual, the units under Cleburne's immediate command had the highest number of casualties: 243 of the total of 451 killed and wounded were from the five regiments in Hill's (formerly Cleburne's) Brigade. Union casualties were 1,050 plus 4,300 captured.

28. Kirby Smith to Cooper, 16 September 1862, O.R., I, 16(1):934.

29. Buck, *Cleburne and His Command,* 107.

30. Kirby Smith to Cooper, 6 September 1862, O.R., I, 16(1):933; Pegram to Heth, 18 September 1862, O.R., I, 16(2):844, 933; and PRC to Bragg, 23 September 1862, Joseph E. Johnston Collection (JO 317), HEH Library.

31. PRC to Bragg, 26 September 1862, Bragg Papers, WRHS; W. F. Douglas, "A Sketch of Maj. Gen. P. R. Cleburne," *The Land We Love* 2 (1867): 460.

32. Penciled note by Colonel Brand (Bragg's AAG) to PRC in PRC to Bragg, 23 September 1862, Joseph E. Johnston Collection (JO 317), HEH Library; Polk to Bragg, 2 October 1862, O.R., I, 16(2):898; Kirby Smith to Bragg, 23 September 1862, and Kirby Smith to Polk, 3 October 1862, both in O.R., I, 16(2):866, 901.

33. Polk to Bragg, 2 October 1862, Kirby Smith to Polk, 3 October 1862, and Bragg to Polk, 4 October 1862, all in O.R., I, 16(2):898, 901, 905; PRC to Bragg, 30 September 1862, Miscellaneous Papers, RG 109, NA.

34. PRC to Bragg, 1 October 1862 (10:00 P.M.), Bragg Papers, WRHS; Polk to Bragg, 2 October 1862, Bragg Papers, Duke; Bragg to Kirby Smith, 3 October 1862, O.R., I, 16(2):901. Polk's defenders would later argue that Bragg "was persistently blind of his enemy's position and blind to his intentions" (William M. Polk, *Leonidas*

Polk: Bishop and General, 2 vols. [London: Longmans, Green and Company, 1915], 2:144).

35. Polk, *Polk,* 2:139–40.

36. Polk to Bragg, 6 October 1862 (11:00 P.M.), and Polk to Bragg, 7 October 1862 (5:40 P.M.), both in O.R., I, 16(2):1095, 1098. See also Stanley F. Horn, "Perryville," *CWTI* 4 (February 1966): 10. When Hardee received a copy of Bragg's orders to Polk, he took the unusual action of sending unsolicited advice to his commander: "Permit me, from the friendly relations so long existing between us, to write you plainly. Do not scatter your forces. . . . Strike with your whole strength first to the right then to the left" (Hardee to Bragg, 7 October 1862 [7:30 P.M.], O.R., I, 16[2]:1099). Federal cavalry reported incorrectly that during the retreat from Shelbyville, "the rebel General Cleburne was mortally wounded" (Gay to Fry, 21 October 1862, O.R., I, 16[1]:1037).

37. Buckner's Report, 6 November 1862, printed in Kenneth A. Hafendorfer, "Major General Simon B. Buckner's Unpublished After-Action Report on the Battle of Perryville," *CWR* 4 (1995): 55 (original in Huntington Library); PRC to W. F. Mastin (AAG), October 1862, O.R., I, 52(1):51.

38. Yeatman Memoir, p. 4, Confederate Collection, TSLA. The most complete account of the Battle of Perryville is Kenneth A. Hafendorfer, *Perryville: Battle for Kentucky* (Louisville, Ky.: K H Press, 1991). An excellent shorter account is James Lee McDonough, *War in Kentucky: From Shiloh to Perryville* (Knoxville: University of Tennessee Press, 1994).

39. Yeatman Memoir, p. 4, Confederate Collection, TSLA; PRC to W. F. Mastin (AAG), October 1862, O.R., I, 52(1):51; Johnson to Cosby, 23 October 1862, O.R., I, 16(2):1127.

40. PRC to W. F. Mastin (AAG), O.R., I, 52(1):52; Thomas Claiborne, "Battle of Perryville, Ky.," *CV* 16 (1908): 226.

41. Yeatman Memoir, p. 4, Confederate Collection, TSLA; Hardee to Williamson, 1 December 1862, O.R., I, 16(2):1122; PRC to W. F. Mastin, October 1862, O.R., 52(1):53.

42. Claiborne, "Battle of Perryville," 226; PRC to W. F. Mastin (AAG), October 1862, O.R., I, 52(1):52; Hardee to Williamson, 1 December 1862, O.R., I, 16(2):1122.

43. Yeatman Memoir, p. 4, Confederate Collection, TSLA; PRC to W. F. Mastin (AAG), October 1862, O.R., I, 52(1):52; Buck, *Cleburne and His Command,* 114.

44. PRC to W. F. Mastin (AAG), October 1862, O.R., I, 52(1):53; Claiborne, "Battle of Perryville," 22; Buckner's Report, 6 November 1862, in Hafendorfer, "Buckner's Unpublished Report," 59; Christopher Losson, *Tennessee's Forgotten Warriors: Frank Cheatham and His Confederate Division* (Knoxville: University of Tennessee Press, 1989), 66–71; St. John R. Liddell, *Liddell's Record,* ed. Nathaniel C. Hughes, Jr. (Dayton, Ohio: Morningside House, 1985), 90.

45. Bragg to AAG, 12 October 1862, O.R., I, 16(2):1088; Yeatman Memoir, p. 4, Confederate Collection, TSLA.

46. O.R., I, 16(2):943, 949, 951; Buck, *Cleburne and His Command,* 116–17; Purdue and Purdue, *Pat Cleburne,* 154–55.

47. William E. Bevins, *Reminiscences of a Private,* ed. Daniel E. Sutherland (Fayette-

ville: University of Arkansas Press, 1992), 103; Yeatman Memoir, p. 4, Confederate Collection, TSLA.

48. Buckner to Hardee, 28 October 1862, Letters Received, AIGO, reel 25, RG 109, NA; Hardee to Williamson, 1 December 1862, O.R., I, 16(2):1122.

CHAPTER SIX. CLEBURNE'S DIVISION

1. Joseph H. Parks, *General Edmund Kirby Smith* (Baton Rouge: Louisiana State University Press, 1954, 1982), 243–46.

2. Buckner to Hardee, 28 October 1862, Letters Received, AIGO, reel 25, RG 109, NA (italics added); Bragg to Cooper, 22 November 1862, O.R., I, 20(2):417–18, 508–9. See also Nathaniel Cheairs Hughes, Jr., *General William J. Hardee* (Baton Rouge: Louisiana State University Press, 1965), 138. During the discussion of Cleburne's promotion, Davis told Hardee a story about a West Point bugler who strongly recommended another bugler named Barnes for promotion. The best recommendation he could give his protégé was to exclaim, "I made Barnes." The application of this story to Hardee's entreaties for Cleburne was apparent and provoked Hardee to smile and say, "Yes, I made Cleburne" (St. John R. Liddell, *Liddell's Record*, ed. Nathaniel C. Hughes, Jr. [Dayton, Ohio: Morningside House, 1985], 103).

3. Organizational Tables of the Army of Tennessee, O.R., I, 17(2):765, and O.R., I, 20(1):660. Cleburne first recommended Polk for promotion in October. See PRC to G. W. Randolph, Letters Received, AIGO, reel 14, RG 109, NA.

4. Lucy R. Buck Diary, 31 December 1862, in *Sad Earth, Sweet Heaven,* ed. William P. Buck (Birmingham, Ala.: Buck Publishing, 1992), 157–58.

5. Buck to Dear Nellie, 28 January 1863, William Pettus Buck Collection (private), Birmingham, Alabama; Buck to Lucy Buck, 13 January and 8 February 1863, Buck Papers, SHC, UNC.

6. Buck to Dear Nellie, undated, William Pettus Buck Collection.

7. Liddell, *Liddell's Record,* 122.

8. Kirby Smith to his wife, 20 October 1862, Kirby Smith Papers, SHC, UNC; Hardee to W. P. Johnston, quoted in Hughes, *General William J. Hardee,* 134–35.

9. Thomas L. Connelly, *Autumn of Glory* (Baton Rouge: Louisiana State University Press, 1971), 22.

10. Judith L. Hallock, *Braxton Bragg and Confederate Defeat,* vol. 2 (Tuscaloosa: University of Alabama Press, 1991), 7–27; Craig L. Symonds, *Joseph E. Johnston: A Civil War Biography* (New York: W. W. Norton, 1992), 187–203.

11. Wharton to Polk, 12 December 1862, O.R., I, 20(1):77–78.

12. Charles E. Robert, "At Murfreesboro Just Before the Battle," *CV* 16 (1908): 632; Howell Purdue and Elizabeth Purdue, *Pat Cleburne, Confederate General* (Hillsboro, Texas: Hill Junior College Press, 1973), 155.

13. Peter Cozzens, *No Better Place to Die: The Battle of Stones River* (Urbana: University of Illinois Press, 1990), 29–39; James Lee McDonough, *Stones River: Bloody Winter in Tennessee* (Knoxville: University of Tennessee Press, 1980), 73–75.

14. Hardee to Brent, 28 February 1863, and PRC to T. B. Roy, 31 January 1863, both in O.R., I, 20(1):772, 843.

15. W. E. Preston, "Memoirs of the War," 33d Alabama Papers, ADAH; PRC to

T. B. Roy, 31 January 1863, G. W. Brent to Polk, 27 December 1862, and Hardee to Brent, 28 February 1863, all in O.R., I, 20(1):843, 464, 772. See also Connelly, *Autumn of Glory*, 47.

16. Bragg to Cooper, 23 February 1863, O.R., I, 20(1):663–64; Davis Urquhart, "Bragg's Advance and Retreat," *B&L*, 3:606.

17. Hardee to Brent, 28 February 1863, PRC to T. B. Roy, 31 January 1863, both in O.R., I, 20(1):773, 844. Liddell, *Liddell's Record*, 107. See also Connelly, *Autumn of Glory*, 53.

18. PRC to T. B. Roy, 31 Jan 1863, O.R., I, 20(1):844.

19. W. E. Preston, "Memoirs of the War," 33d Alabama Papers, ADAH; M'Dearman, "Private M'Dearman at Murfreesboro," *CV* 9 (1901): 306; Liddell, *Liddell's Record*, 111.

20. Cozzens, *No Better Place to Die*, 89–91; Liddell, *Liddell's Record*, 108; PRC to T. B. Roy, 31 January 1863, O.R., I, 20(1):844.

21. William E. Bevins, *Reminiscences of a Private*, ed. Daniel E. Sutherland (Fayetteville: University of Arkansas Press, 1992), 115; PRC to T. B. Roy, 31 January 1863, O.R., I, 20(1):845.

22. Wood to Buck, 11 January 1863, and Hardee to Brent, 28 February 1863, both in O.R., I, 20(1):899, 776; Larry Daniel, *Cannoneers in Gray: The Field Artillery of the Army of Tennessee, 1861–1865* (University: University of Alabama Press, 1984), 57, 60–63.

23. McCown to T. B. Roy, 20 January 1863, O.R., I, 20(1):911–16; Hardee to Brent, 28 February 1863, O.R., I, 20(1):774. At the Wilkinson Pike, McCown's brigades closed on Cleburne's from the left, and Liddell's Brigade became the extreme left-hand brigade in the advance; Liddell, *Liddell's Record*, 110.

24. PRC to T. B. Roy, 31 January 1863, O.R., I, 20(1):846; Yeatman Memoir, p. 4, Confederate Collection, TSLA. Preston Smith's Brigade was commanded at Murfreesboro by Colonel W. J. Vaughn and many histories refer to it as Vaughn's Brigade.

25. PRC to T. B. Roy, 31 January 1863, O.R., I, 20(1):848.

26. Ibid.

27. Ibid, 849; Johnson to Buck, 15 January 1863, O.R., I, 20(1):880. For his part, St. John Liddell believed that another attack might have been successful, and he tried to convince Hardee to order it (*Liddell's Record*, 113).

28. Hardee to Brent, 28 February 1863, O.R., I, 20(1):777.

29. Buck to Lucy Buck, 8 February 1863, Buck Papers, SHC, UNC.

30. PRC to T. B. Roy, 31 January 1863, Wood to Buck, 11 January 1863, both in O.R., I, 20(1):849, 899. Wood's Brigade lost almost exactly half its force at Murfreesboro (504 of 1,100).

31. Henry Semple to Emily Semple, 8 January 1863, Henry C. Semple Papers, SHC, UNC.

32. PRC to T. B. Roy, 31 January 1863, O.R., I, 20(1):849–50.

33. Hardee to Brent, 28 February 1863, O.R., I, 20(1):778.

34. PRC to Bragg, 13 January 1863, O.R., I, 20(1):684. Bragg's state of mind is evident in Liddell, *Liddell's Record*, 115.

35. Despite all that was subsequently said and written about this meeting, the substance of it is evident from the responses Bragg received to his letter of 11 January inviting officers to put their recollections in writing. Even allowing for the hostility that

by then influenced virtually all of Bragg's generals, those responses, taken together, probably constitute the best record of what happened. See, in particular, Hardee to Bragg, 12 January 1863, Breckinridge to Bragg, 12 January 1863, and PRC to Bragg, 13 January 1863, all in O.R., I, 20(1):682–84. In addition, Bragg gave his version of events in a private letter to Marcus J. Wright; see Bragg to Wright, 6 February 1864, folder 9, Wright Papers, SHC, UNC.

36. PRC to T. B. Roy, 31 January 1863, Hardee to Brent, 28 February 1863, and Johnson to Buck, 15 January 1863, all in O.R., I, 20(1):850, 778, 881; Henry Semple to Emily Semple, 8 January 1863, Henry C. Semple Papers, SHC, UNC.

37. Irving A. Buck, *Cleburne and His Command* (Dayton, Ohio: Morningside Bookshop, 1992), 124; Buck to Lucy Buck, 13 January 1863, Buck Papers, SHC, UNC. See also Christopher Losson, *Tennessee's Forgotten Warriors: Frank Cheatham and His Confederate Division* (Knoxville: University of Tennessee Press, 1989), 94.

38. Symonds, *Joseph E. Johnston*, 196–97; Chattanooga *Rebel*, 6 January 1863; Bragg to Polk, Hardee, Breckinridge, Cleburne, and Cheatham, 11 January 1863, O.R., I, 20(1):699. Apparently, Bragg did not solicit the views of either Withers or McCown, possibly because they did not attend the 3 January meeting.

39. Hardee to Bragg, 12 January 1863, and Breckinridge to Bragg, 12 January 1863, both in O.R., I, 20(1):683, 682.

40. PRC to Bragg, 13 January 1863, O.R., I, 20(1):684.

41. Cheatham to Bragg, 13 January 1863, O.R., I, 20(1):684. The fable is attributed to Cleburne by A. C. Avery, "Memorial Address on the Life and Character of Lieut.-General D. H. Hill," *SHSP* 21 (1893): 144. Versions of this tale very likely were common in the army. Buck attributes it to William Preston (*Cleburne and His Command*, 160).

42. Polk to Davis, 4 February 1863, O.R., I, 20(1):698.

43. "The snow is thick on the ground, but what do we care so long as we keep such roaring fires as we do" (Buck to Dear Nellie, 28 January 1863, William Pettus Buck Collection [private], Birmingham, Alabama). Cleburne's report is PRC to T. B. Roy, 31 January 1863, O.R., I, 20(1):851–52.

44. Alvin Buck to Lucy Buck, 15 January 1863, Buck Papers, SHC, UNC.

CHAPTER SEVEN. WAR AND POLITICS

1. Buck to Lucy Buck, 11 March 1863, Buck Papers, SHC, UNC; Henry Semple Diary, 4, 5, 15, and 22 February 1863, SHC, UNC; Irving A. Buck, *Cleburne and His Command* (Dayton, Ohio: Morningside Bookshop, 1992), 132.

2. Buck to My Dear Nellie, 28 January 1863, William Pettus Buck Collection (private), Birmingham, Alabama; JEJ to Davis, 3 and 12 February 1863, O.R., I, 23(2):624, 632. Johnston was convinced that except for Davis's decision to send Stevenson's Division to Mississippi on the eve of the battle, Bragg would have won a decisive victory at Murfreesboro. In his view, therefore, the blame for the disappointments of that battle belonged not to Bragg but to Davis himself. Another reason Johnston refused to criticize Bragg was that since he was Bragg's most likely replacement, he believed he could not recommend Bragg's dismissal without appearing to

be self-serving. See Craig L. Symonds, *Joseph E. Johnston* (New York: W. W. Norton, 1992), 196–201.

3. Bragg to Cooper, 23 February 1863, O.R., I, 20(1):670; Special Orders no. 46, 22 March 1863, O.R., I, 23(2):722.

4. Henry Semple to Emily Semple, 7 March 1863, Semple Papers, SHC, UNC; Buck to Lucy Buck, 11 March 1863, Buck Papers, SHC, UNC; Coleman Diary, 9 and 16 March 1863, SHC, UNC.

5. Special Order no. 46, 22 March 1863, O.R., I, 23(2):722.

6. Coleman Diary, 19 March 1863, SHC, UNC; Buck to Lucy Buck, 22 March 1863, Buck Papers, SHC, UNC.

7. Bragg to Hardee, Cleburne, et al., 13 April 1863, O.R., I, 16(1):1099–1100.

8. Ibid.; Hardee to Polk, n.d., Hardee to Bragg, 16 April 1863, and Polk to Hardee, 17 April 1863, all in O.R., I, 16(1):1097–1103.

9. For a full discussion of army politics see Thomas L. Connelly and Archer Jones, *The Politics of Command: Factions and Ideas in Confederate Strategy* (Baton Rouge: Louisiana State University Press, 1973). See also Thomas L. Connelly, *Autumn of Glory* (Baton Rouge: Louisiana State University Press, 1972), 69–92, and Steven E. Woodworth, *Jefferson Davis and His Generals* (Lawrence: University Press of Kansas, 1990), 186–99.

10. Henry Semple to Emily Semple, 4 April 1863, Semple Papers, SHC, UNC; Buck to Lucy Buck, 11 April 1863, Buck Papers, SHC, UNC; Buck to My Dear Nellie, n.d., William Pettus Buck Collection. I am indebted to Betty H. Ferrell of the Tullahoma Chamber of Commerce for the identification of Ovoca Falls.

11. Buck to My Dear Lucie, 26 April 1863, Buck Papers, SHC, UNC.

12. Connelly, *Autumn of Glory,* 116.

13. St. John R. Liddell, *Liddell's Record,* ed. Nathaniel C. Hughes, Jr. (Dayton, Ohio: Morningside House, 1985), 118–22; Buck to Lucy Buck, 26 April and 19 May 1863, Buck Papers, SHC, UNC.

14. Buck, *Cleburne and His Command,* 125; Yeatman Memoirs, p. 5, TSLA; Rowena Webster, "Memories of a Southern Girl," Jill Knight Garrett Collection, TSLA.

15. Rowena Webster, "Memories of a Southern Girl," Jill Knight Garrett Collection, TSLA. It may be that Cleburne established a social connection at Beechwood that was strong enough to foster an intermittent correspondence with one of the young ladies he met there. Two months after the army left Wartrace, Captain Buck reported to his sister that his boss was "sitting on the opposite side of the table under a tent fly answering a letter written in a very delicate hand." Buck suspected that "Mars is yielding a little to Venus" (Buck to Lucy Buck, 29 August 1863, Buck Papers, SHC, UNC).

16. Liddell, *Liddell's Record,* 122–23.

17. Rowena Webster, "Memories of a Southern Girl," Jill Knight Garrett Collection, TSLA.

18. Charles E. Nash, *Biographical Sketches of Gen. Pat Cleburne and Gen. T. C. Hindman* (Dayton, Ohio: Morningside Bookshop, 1977), 19–22; P. D. Stephenson, *The Civil War Memoir of Philip Daingerfield Stephenson, D.D.,* ed. Nathaniel C. Hughes (Conway: University of Central Arkansas Press, 1995), 111–12.

19. W.W. Heartsill, *Fourteen Hundred and Ninety-One Days in the Confederate Army,* ed. Bell I. Wiley (Jackson, Tenn.: McCowat-Mercer Press, 1954), (entries of 4 and 6 June), 130; James A. L. Fremantle, *The Fremantle Diary,* ed. Walter Lord (Boston: Little, Brown and Company, 1954), 125.

20. Buck, *Cleburne and His Division,* 128; Govan to Fullerton, 22 May 1984, War Department Park Commission Papers, box 1, folder 1, Chickamauga and Chattanooga National Military Park Library.

21. Connelly, *Autumn of Glory,* 118.

22. Samuel T. Foster, *One of Cleburne's Command: The Civil War Reminiscences and Diary of Capt. Samuel T. Foster, Granbury's Texas Brigade, C.S.A.,* ed. Norman D. Brown (Austin: University of Texas Press, 1980), 43.

23. Hardee to Bragg, 5 June 1863, O.R., I, 23(2):862.

24. Connelly, *Autumn of Glory,* 116–25.

25. Buck to Lucy Buck, 12 June 1863, Buck Papers, SHC, UNC; PRC to Hardee, 26 May 1863, Patrick Cleburne Letters, Doug Schanz Collection (private), Roanoke, Virginia.

26. Liddell to Benham, 1 August 1863, O.R., I, 23(1):588.

27. PRC to Anderson (AAG), 3 August 1863, O.R, I, 23(1):586–87.

28. P. Snyder (6th Arkansas) to G. A. Williams, 28 July 1863, and Liddell to Benham, 1 August 1863, both in O.R., I, 23(1):597, 591.

29. Coleman Diary, 30 June 1863, SHC, UNC; PRC to Anderson (AAG), 3 August 1863, O.R., I, 23(1):587; Heartsill, *Fourteen Hundred and Ninety-One Days* (entry for 2 July), 137.

30. Hardee to Mackall, 27 April 1863, Special Orders no. 97, and Hardee to Stewart, 26 June 1863 (8:30 P.M.), all in O.R., I, 23(2):796, 797, 886; W. B. Richmond Notes, O.R., I, 23(1):618–21; I. W. Avery, "Patrick Ronayne Cleburne," *Kennesaw Gazette,* 15 May 1887, 4.

31. PRC to Hardee, 27 June 1863, Mackall to Polk, 27 June 1863 (10:00 P.M.), and PRC to Hardee, 13 July 1863, all in O.R., I, 23(2):888, 907; W. B. Richmond Notes, O.R., I, 23(1):619–21.

32. Jim Turner, "Co. G, 6th Texas Infantry, CSA, from 1861 to 1865," *Texana* 12 (1974): 161; Heartsill, *Fourteen Hundred and Ninety-One Days* (entry of 27 June), 133.

33. Buck, *Cleburne and His Command,* 133; W. T. Wilson, "Hardships of Bragg's Retreat," *CV* 28 (1920): 51.

34. Heartsill, *Fourteen Hundred and Ninety-One Days* (entry of 6 July), 137; T. B. Roy to Stewart, 5 July 1863, and D. H. Poole to Stewart, 8 July 1863, O.R., I, 23(2):901, 904–5.

35. H. J. Cheney, "Reminiscences of War Incidents," *CV* 18 (1910): 517–18.

36. Ibid.

37. Seddon to Bragg, 14 July 1863, and Seddon to D. H. Hill, 14 July 1863, both in O.R., I, 23(2):908–9.

38. Daniel H. Hill, "Chickamauga, The Great Battle of the West," *B&L,* 3:639; Peter Cozzens, *This Terrible Sound: The Battle of Chickamauga* (Urbana: University of Illinois Press, 1992), 27–28.

39. Bragg to D. H. Hill, 4 September 1863, O.R., I, 30(4):594.

40. D. H. Hill to Jack (AAG), n.d., O.R., I, 30(2):137; Foster, *One of Cleburne's Command*, 50.

41. From the organization's constitution, quoted in Howell Purdue and Elizabeth Purdue, *Pat Cleburne, Confederate General* (Hillsboro, Texas: Hill Junior College Press, 1973), 229n; W. F. Douglas, "A Sketch of Maj. Gen. P. R. Cleburne," *The Land We Love* 2 (1867): 462.

42. Buck to Lucy Buck, 29 August and 8 August 1863, Buck Papers, SHC, UNC.

43. Connelly, *Autumn of Glory*, 169; Buck to Lucy Buck, 29 August 1863, Buck Papers, SHC, UNC. D. H. Hill remained convinced that the Yankees *did* intend to cross above Chattanooga, but that they were forced "to abandon their original plan" thanks to the "vigilant and determined men" of Cleburne's Division (Hill to Jack [AAG], n.d., O.R., I, 30[2]:137).

44. PRC to D. H. Hill, 5 September 1863 (10:00 P.M.), O.R., I, 30(4):601.

CHAPTER EIGHT. BARREN VICTORY: THE BATTLE OF CHICKAMAUGA

1. Jim Turner, "Co. G, 6th Texas Infantry, CSA, from 1861 to 1865," *Texana* 12 (1974): 162; Sam R. Watkins, *"Co. Aytch," Maury Grays, First Tennessee Regiment* (Wilmington, N.C.: Broadfoot Publishing Company, 1987), 155; Irving A. Buck, *Cleburne and His Command* (Dayton, Ohio: Morningside Bookshop, 1992), 135.

2. W. W. Mackall to D. H. Hill, 9 September 1863, Joseph E. Johnston Collection (JO 317), HEH Library.

3. Daniel H. Hill, "Chickamauga, The Great Battle of the West," *B&L*, 3:645–46; D. H. Hill to Jack (AAG), n.d., O.R., I, 30(2):137–38; Hill to Mackall, 10 September 1863 (4:25 A.M.), O.R., I, 30(2):300.

4. PRC to D. H. Hill, 10 September 1863 (6:00 P.M.), D. H. Hill Papers, VSLA.

5. Calhoun Benham, "Major-Gen. P. R. Cleburne," *Kennesaw Gazette*, 1 April 1889, 2; Glenn Tucker, *Chickamauga: Bloody Battle in the West* (New York: Konecky and Konecky, 1994), 69–70.

6. Hindman to Brent (AAG), 25 October 1863, and Brent to Hindman, 10 September 1863 (6:00 P.M.), both in O.R., I, 30(2):294, 300; Diane Neal and Thomas W. Kremm, *Lion of the South: General Thomas C. Hindman* (Macon, Ga.: Mercer University Press, 1993), 166–67; Peter Cozzens, *This Terrible Sound: The Battle of Chickamauga* (Urbana: University of Illinois Press, 1992), 71–72.

7. Calhoun Benham, "Major-Gen. P. R. Cleburne," *Kennesaw Gazette*, 15 March 1889, 2; Buck, *Cleburne and His Command*, 139n; Bragg to Cooper, 28 December 1863, O.R., I, 30(2):29–30.

8. D. H. Hill to Jack (AAG), n.d., O.R., I, 30(2):138–39.

9. Coleman Diary, 11 September 1863, SHC, UNC; Benham, "Major-Gen. P. R. Cleburne," *Kennesaw Gazette*, 15 March 1889, 2; Charges and Specifications preferred against Maj. Gen. T. C. Hindman, O.R., I, 30(2):310.

10. Thomas L. Connelly, *Autumn of Glory* (Baton Rouge: Louisiana State University Press, 1971), 177–82; Cozzens, *This Terrible Sound*, 71–75.

11. Mackall to Hindman, 11 September 1863 (11:00 A.M.), O.R., I, 30(2):296.

Hill blamed the failure on "Bragg's ignorance of the condition of the roads, the obstructions at Dug Gap, and the position of the enemy" (Hill, "Chickamauga," 642).

12. Buck, *Cleburne and His Command,* 136n.

13. D. H. Hill to Jack (AAG), n.d., and Lucius Polk to Buck, 10 October 1863, both in O.R., I, 30(2):140, 176; Buck, *Cleburne and His Command,* 144–45; Cozzens, *This Terrible Sound,* 263.

14. William E. Bevins, *Reminiscences of a Private,* ed. Daniel E. Sutherland (Fayetteville: University of Arkansas Press, 1992), 135; James L. Nichols and Frank Abbott, eds., "Reminiscences of Confederate Service by Wiley A. Washburn," *AHQ* 35 (Spring 1976): 57.

15. PRC to Anderson (AAG), 18 October 1863, O.R., I, 30 (2):153; St. John R. Liddell, *Liddell's Record,* ed. Nathaniel C. Hughes, Jr. (Dayton, Ohio: Morningside House, 1985), 143.

16. PRC to Anderson (AAG), 18 October 1863, O.R., I, 30(2):154; Archer Anderson, "Campaign and Battle of Chickamauga," *SHSP* 9 (1881): 409; Bevins, *Reminiscences,* 135.

17. Benham, "Major-Gen. P. R. Cleburne," *Kennesaw Gazette,* 1 April 1889, 2; D. H. Hill to Jack (AAG), n.d., O.R., I, 30(2):140.

18. Reports of Colonels Adams, Breedlove, and Lowrey, O.R., I, 30(2):165–71; Report of Lieutenant Key, 6 October 1863, ibid., 186; Samuel T. Foster, *One of Cleburne's Command,* ed. Norman D. Brown (Austin: University of Texas Press, 1980), 54; Cozzens, *This Terrible Sound,* 266–69.

19. Buck, *Cleburne and His Command,* 146; Foster, *One of Cleburne's Command,* 54.

20. Tucker, *Chickamauga,* 188–92; John B. Gordon, *Reminiscences of the Civil War* (New York: Charles Scribner's Sons, 1981), 204–5; Yeatman Memoirs, p. 5, Confederate Collection, TSLA.

21. Henry Freeman, "Chickamauga," Henry Freeman Papers, Wyoming Historical Society.

22. Statement of Captain J. F. Wheliss, O.R., I, 30(2):61–62.

23. Jack (AAG) to Cleburne and Breckinridge, 20 September 1863 (5:30 A.M.), and Wheliss Statement, both in O.R., I, 30(2):52, 61–62; D. H. Hill to Jack (AAG), n.d., OR, I, 30(2):137–41.

24. Connelly, *Autumn of Glory,* 216–20; Cozzens, *This Terrible Sound,* 305–9. There was much subsequent confusion and disagreement about the timing of the breakfast visits to Cleburne's headquarters by Wheliss, Polk, and Bragg. Hill later claimed that Wheliss arrived at 7:25, but Polk claimed that he had received Hill's reply by 7:00. Hill was eager to demonstrate that he did not get orders to attack until late in the morning; Polk hoped to prove that the delay was mainly Hill's fault. See Hill, "Chickamauga," *B&L,* 3:653, and W. W. Polk, "General Polk at Chickamauga," *B&L,* 3:662. See also Y. R. LeMonnier, "Gen. Leonidas Polk at Chickamauga," *CV* 24 (1916): 17–18.

25. Gordon, *Reminiscences,* 206.

26. PRC to Anderson (AAG), 18 October 1863, O.R., I, 30(2):155.

27. Wood to Buck, 9 October 1863, and PRC to Anderson (AAG), 18 October 1863, both in O.R., I, 30(2):156, 161; Cozzens, *This Terrible Sound,* 342–44.

28. Foster, *One of Cleburne's Command* (undated entry), 52.

29. Mark P. Lowery Autobiography, USAMHI; Cozzens, *This Terrible Sound,* 316.

30. W. W. Heartsill, *Fourteen Hundred and Ninety-One Days in the Confederate Army*, ed. Bell I. Wiley (Jackson, Tenn.: McCowat-Mercer Press, 1954), 152; W. W. Carnes, "Chickamauga," *SHSP* 14 (1886): 403.

31. Douglas to Hearne, 6 October 1863, and Lucius Polk to Buck, 10 October 1863, both in O.R., I, 30(2):145, 156, 177, 196–97; Heartsill, *Fourteen Hundred and Ninety-One Days*, 154.

32. Heartsill, *Fourteen Hundred and Ninety-One Days*, 154; PRC to Anderson (AAG), 18 October 1863, O.R., I, 30(2):156; Hill to Jack (AAG), n.d., O.R., I, 30(2):145; Buck, *Cleburne and His Command*, 152–53.

33. Edwin C. Bearss, "Pat Cleburne, Stonewall Jackson of the West" (M.A. thesis, Indiana University, 1954), 84.

34. William M. Polk, *Leonidas Polk*, 2 vols. (London: Longmans, Green and Company, 1915), 2:280–81.

35. Thomas L. Livermore, *Numbers and Losses in the Civil War in America* (Bloomington: Indiana University Press, 1957), 105; Buck, *Cleburne and His Command*, 154–55; Hill to Jack (AAG), n.d., O.R., I, 30(2):146.

36. Buck, *Cleburne and His Command*, 157; Forrest to Polk, 21 September 1863 (9:00 A.M.), O.R., I, 30(4):681; PRC to Hill, 22 and 25 September 1863, D. H. Hill Papers, VSLA.

37. The authorship of this document has provoked much speculation. Longstreet assumed that Hill wrote it because Hill kept it at his headquarters and because Longstreet received the petition from Hill. Hill, however, denied authorship. The key evidence is the location of Buckner's signature on the paper and the fact that his name was followed by those of two of his three brigade commanders. See the discussion of this question in Connelly, *Autumn of Glory*, 235–40.

38. Buckner et al. to Davis, 4 October 1863, D. H. Hill Papers, VSLA; Liddell, *Liddell's Record*, 151–52.

39. Liddell, *Liddell's Record*, 152.

40. Connelly, *Autumn of Glory*, 241–46. Buck claims that Cleburne attended this meeting and avowed that the army had lost its confidence in Bragg and that "a change was absolutely necessary." Buck admits, however, that his account was based on memory and hearsay, and no other account places Cleburne at the meeting. Although Buck no doubt accurately represents Cleburne's views, it is unlikely that he presented them at this meeting (*Cleburne and His Command*, 158–59).

41. Bragg to Davis, 11 October 1863, O.R., I, 30(2):148; PRC to Hill, 15 October 1863, D.H. Hill Papers, VSLA. See also Hill to Cooper, 13 November 1863, and Cooper to Hill, 20 November 1863, both in O.R., I, 30(2):150–51.

42. PRC to Anderson (AAG), 18 October 1863, O.R., I, 30(2):156.

43. Benham to Alexander, 21 December 1863, Peter W. Alexander Collection, Columbia University; Wood to Buck (AAG), 9 October 1863, O.R., I, 30(2):160.

44. Learned H. Mangum, "Death of General Pat. R. Cleburne," in Thomas A. Head, *Campaigns and Battles of the Sixteenth Regiment, Tennessee Volunteers* (Nashville, Tenn.: Cumberland Presbyterian Publishing House, 1885), 375; Liddell, *Liddell's Record*, 161.

CHAPTER NINE. STONEWALL OF THE WEST

1. Philip D. Stephenson, *The Civil War Memoir of Philip Daingerfield Stephenson, D.D.*, ed. Nathaniel C. Hughes, Jr. (Conway: University of Central Arkansas Press, 1995), 135; Jim Turner, "Co. G, 6th Texas Infantry, CSA, from 1861 to 1865," *Texana* 12 (1974): 165; Peter Cozzens, *The Shipwreck of Their Hopes: The Battles for Chattanooga* (Urbana: University of Illinois Press, 1994), 119–20; Wiley Sword, *Mountains Touched with Fire: Chattanooga Besieged, 1863* (New York: St. Martin's Press, 1995), 105–11; Samuel T. Foster, *One of Cleburne's Command*, ed. Norman D. Brown (Austin: University of Texas Press, 1980), 58.

2. Lee is quoted in Irving A. Buck, *Cleburne and His Command* (Dayton, Ohio: Morningside Bookshop, 1992), 294. Although historians have generally credited Davis with coining the phrase "Stonewall of the West," what he actually wrote was that Cleburne's men "followed him with the implicit confidence that in another army was given to Stonewall Jackson" (Jefferson Davis, *Rise and Fall of the Confederate Government*, 2 vols. [New York: D. Appleton, 1881], 2:577).

3. Lowrey Autobiography, USAMHI; Ezra J. Warner, *Generals in Gray: Lives of the Confederate Commanders* (Baton Rouge: Louisiana State University Press, 1959), 281–83; St. John R. Liddell, *Liddell's Record*, ed. Nathaniel C. Hughes, Jr. (Dayton, Ohio: Morningside House, 1977), 149.

4. Liddell, *Liddell's Record*, 161.

5. Thomas L. Connelly, *Autumn of Glory* (Baton Rouge: Louisiana State University Press, 1971), 253–61; Jeffry D. Wert, *General James Longstreet* (New York: Simon and Schuster, 1993), 334–35.

6. Special Orders no. 306, 30 November 1863, O.R., I, 31(3):767; Bragg to Davis, 31 October 1863, O.R., I, 51(2):557.

7. Bragg to Davis, 20 November 1863, and Longstreet to Bragg, 21 November 1863, both in O.R., I, 31(2):667, 732.

8. PRC to Falconer (AAG), n.d., O.R., I, 31(2):745–46.

9. Judith Lee Hallock, *Braxton Bragg and Confederate Defeat*, vol. 2 (Tuscaloosa: University of Alabama Press, 1991), 127; Cozzens, *Shipwreck of Their Hopes*, 149–50; Sword, *Mountains Touched with Fire*, 25–26.

10. Buck, *Cleburne and His Command*, 163; PRC to Falconer (AAG), n.d., O.R., I, 31(2):746.

11. PRC to Falconer (AAG), n.d., O.R., I, 31(2):747; Cozzens, *Shipwreck of Their Hopes*, 152.

12. Robert D. Goforth, "Sherman and Cleburne at Tunnel Hill: The Myth of the Inevitability of Confederate Defeat at Chattanooga, November 23–25, 1863" (M.A. thesis, East Carolina University, 1992), 70–71.

13. Cozzens, *Shipwreck of Their Hopes*, 153.

14. Ibid., 154.

15. PRC to Falconer (AAG), n.d., O.R., I, 31(2):747; Stephenson, *Civil War Memoir*, 140; Irving A. Brock [Buck], "Cleburne and His Division at Missionary Ridge and Ringgold Gap," *SHSP* 8 (1880): 466.

16. Buck, *Cleburne and His Command*, 466–67.

17. James M. McCaffrey, *This Band of Heroes: Granbury's Texas Brigade, C.S.A.* (Austin: Eakin Press, 1985), 88; Cozzens, *Shipwreck of Their Hopes*, 198. See also

James Lee McDonough, *Chattanooga: A Death Grip on the Confederacy* (Knoxville: University of Tennessee Press, 1984), 143–60.

18. J. H. Bingham, "How Errors Become 'Historic Facts,'" *CV* 12 (1904): 172; Connelly, *Autumn of Glory*, 275; Cozzens, *Shipwreck of Their Hopes*, 211; Sword, *Mountains Touched with Fire*, 237–39; PRC to Falconer (AAG), n.d., O.R., I, 31(2): 749; William C. Davis, *The Orphan Brigade: The Kentucky Confederates Who Couldn't Go Home* (Garden City, N.Y.: Doubleday, 1980), 198.

19. Cummins, Bingham, and others cite an earlier hour for the first Federal attack, but Cleburne is quite specific that it began at 10:30. Bingham, "How Errors Become Facts," 172; PRC to Falconer (AAG), O.R., I, 31(2):749; Foster, *One of Cleburne's Command*, 62–63.

20. PRC to Falconer (AAG), n.d., O.R., I, 31(2):750.

21. Ibid.; Cozzens, *Shipwreck of Their Hopes*, 215; Sword, *Mountains Touched with Fire*, 248–54.

22. PRC to Falconer (AAG), n.d., O.R., I, 31(2):750–51.

23. Cumming to Reeve (AAG), 5 December 1863, O.R., I, 31(2):734–35.

24. Brock [Buck], "Cleburne and His Division," 468; Cozzens, *Shipwreck of Their Hopes*, 240; Sword, *Mountains Touched with Fire*, 257.

25. PRC to Falconer (AAG), n.d., O.R., I, 31(2):752.

26. James Cooper Nisbit, *Four Years on the Firing Line*, ed. Bell I. Wiley (Jackson, Tenn.: McCowat-Mercer Press, 1963), 123; PRC to Falconer (AAG), n.d., O.R., I, 31(2):753.

27. PRC to Falconer (AAG), n.d., O.R., I, 31(2):753.

28. Cozzens, *Shipwreck of Their Hopes*, 348–49.

29. Buck, *Cleburne and His Command*, 174–75.

30. Ibid., 175–76.

31. Ibid., 177, 177n.

32. Brent (AAG) to PRC, 27 December 1863 (3:00 A.M.), O.R., I, 31(2):754; William E. Bevins, *Reminiscences of a Private*, ed. Daniel E. Sutherland (Fayetteville: University of Arkansas Press, 1992), 145; W. W. Gibson, "Reminiscences of Ringgold Gap," *CV* 12 (1904): 526; James L. Nichols and Frank Abbott, eds., "Reminiscences of Confederate Service by Wiley A. Washburn," *AHQ* 35 (Spring 1976): 60; Kennard to Hearne (AAG), 2 December 1863, O.R., I, 31(2):775–76.

33. Circular, 25 and 26 November 1863, and PRC to Brent (AAG), 9 December 1863, both in O.R., I, 31(2):679–80, 754.

34. Murray's Report, 2 December 1863, and Goldthwaithe to Buck, 7 December 1863, both in O.R., I, 31(2):764, 758–60; Stephenson, *Civil War Memoir*, 144.

35. PRC to Brent (AAG), 9 December 1863, Granbury to Buck, 3 December 1863, and Polk to Buck, 3 December 1863, all in O.R., I, 31(2):754, 773–74, 760–61.

36. PRC to Brent (AAG), 9 December 1863, O.R., I, 31(2):754.

37. Govan to Buck, 3 December 1863, and Murray to Sawrie (Acting AAG), 2 December 1863, both in O.R., I, 31(2):763, 764–65; P. D. Stephenson, "Reminiscences of the Last Campaign of the Army of Tennessee, from May 1864 to January 1865," *SHSP* 12 (1884): 38–39; Stephenson, *Civil War Memoir*, 144–46; W. W. Gibson, "Reminiscences of Ringgold Gap," 526; Buck, *Cleburne and His Command*, 181; Turner, "Co. G, 6th Texas Infantry," 170.

38. Polk to Buck, 3 December 1863, O.R., I, 31(2):760–61.

39. Lowrey Autobiography, USAMHI.

40. Lowrey to Buck, 3 December 1863, and PRC to Brent (AAG), 9 December 1863, both in O.R., I, 31(2):768–69, 756; Gibson, "Reminiscences of Ringgold Gap," 526.

41. PRC to Brent (AAG), 9 December 1863, O.R., I, 31(2):757; Buck, *Cleburne and His Command*, 183.

42. PRC to Brent (AAG), 9 December 1863, O.R., I, 31(2):757.

43. Ibid.

44. Gibson, "Reminiscences of Ringgold Gap," 527.

45. PRC to Brent (AAG), 9 December 1863, and Polk to Buck, 3 December 1863, both in O.R., I, 31(2):757, 761; Stephenson, *Civil War Memoir*, 147; Yeatman Memoir, p. 6, Confederate Collection, TSLA; Sword, *Mountains Touched with Fire*, 349.

46. Bragg to Wright, 14 December 1863, Marcus J. Wright Papers, folder 9, SHC, UNC; Bragg to Cooper, 29 and 30 November 1863, Cooper to Bragg, 30 November 1863, Joint Resolution of Congress (no. 16), 9 February 1864, and Geary to Butterfield, 15 December 1863, all in O.R., I, 31(2):682, 666, 758, 403.

47. PRC to Brant (AAG), 9 December 1863, O.R., I, 31(2):755; Wirt Armistead Cate, ed., *Two Soldiers: The Campaign Diaries of Thomas F. Key, C.S.A., and Robert F. Campbell, U.S.A.* (Chapel Hill: University of North Carolina Press, 1938), 8–9 (entry for 9 December 63), hereafter cited as Key Diary.

48. Liddell, *Liddell's Record*, 161.

CHAPTER TEN. "A PLAN WHICH WE BELIEVE
WILL SAVE OUR COUNTRY"

1. PRC to Robert Cleburne, 7 May 1861, Cleburne Papers, U.Ark.

2. PRC to Robert Cleburne, n.d., Cleburne Papers, U.Ark.

3. PRC to Robert Cleburne, 7 May 1861, Cleburne Papers, U.Ark.

4. Key Diary, 9 December 1863, 8–9.

5. J. G. Randall and David Herbert Donald, *The Civil War and Reconstruction*, 2d ed. (Lexington, Mass.: D. C. Heath, 1969), 3–6.

6. In February 1865, the Confederacy extended the upper age limit for the draft to fifty. On Confederate morale and desertions, see Thomas's report, 15 January 1864, O.R., I, 31(2):124, and Key Diary, 12 January 1864, 24. Samuel T. Foster, *One of Cleburne's Command*, ed. Norman D. Brown (Austin: University of Texas Press, 1980), diary entry of July 1863, 49.

7. St. John R. Liddell, *Liddell's Record*, ed. Nathaniel C. Hughes, Jr. (Dayton, Ohio: Morningside House, 1985), 120; Diane Neal and Thomas W. Kremm, *Lion of the South: General Thomas C. Hindman* (Macon, Ga.: Mercer University Press, 1993), 185–86; Dudley Taylor Cornish, *The Sable Arm: Black Troops in the Union Armies, 1861–1865* (Lawrence: University Press of Kansas, 1987), 114.

8. Buck to the Richmond *Times-Dispatch*, January 1896, printed in Irving A. Buck, *Cleburne and His Command* (Dayton, Ohio: Morningside Bookshop, 1992), 188–89.

9. On army morale, see Sam R. Watkins, *"Co. Aytch," Maury Grays, First Tennessee Regiment* (Wilmington, N.C.: Broadfoot Publishing Company, 1987), 132, and

Buck to My Dear Sister, 3 January 1864, Buck Papers, SHC, UNC. The conversation with Key is in Key Diary, 28 December 1863 and 10 April 1864, 16–17, 70.

10. Buck, *Cleburne and His Command,* 189; D. H. Poole to Walker, 2 January 1864, in Walker to Davis, 12 January 1864, O.R., I, 52(2):595.

11. Anderson to Polk, 14 January 1864, O.R., I, 52(2):598.

12. These and subsequent quotations are all from Cleburne's "Memorial," printed in O.R., I, 52(2):586–92.

13. Ibid. The planter was James Henry Hammond on the floor of Congress in December 1835; quoted in William Lee Miller, *Arguing About Slavery: The Great Battle in the United States Congress* (New York: Alfred A. Knopf, 1996), 136.

14. Walker to Davis, 12 January 1864, and Anderson to Polk, 14 January 1864, both in O.R., I, 52(2):598–99. See also Steven Ambrose, "By Enlisting Negroes Could the South Still Win the War?" *CWTI* 3 (January 1965): 16–21; Steve Davis, "That Extraordinary Document: W. H. T. Walker and Patrick Cleburne's Emancipation Proposal," *CWTI* 16 (December 1977): 14–20; Thomas R. Hay, "The South and the Arming of the Slaves," *MVHR* 4 (June 1919): 34–73; and Barbara C. Ruby, "General Patrick Cleburne's Proposal to Arm Southern Slaves," *AHQ* 20 (Fall 1971): 193–212. The only book-length study of the issue is the compilation of documents edited by Robert F. Durden entitled *The Gray and the Black: The Confederate Debate on Emancipation* (Baton Rouge: Louisiana State University Press, 1972).

15. J. B. Cumming, "Sketch of General Walker," *CV* 10 (1902): 404–7; Liddell, *Liddell's Record,* 137; Buck, *Cleburne and His Command,* 189–90; Thomas L. Connelly, *Autumn of Glory* (Baton Rouge: Louisiana State University Press, 1971), 319–20.

16. Walker to Hindman, 9 January 1964, Hindman to Johnston, 9 January 1864, and Walker to Davis, 12 January 1864, all in O.R., I, 52(2):593–94, 595.

17. James Cooper Nisbet, *Four Years on the Firing Line,* ed. Bell I. Wiley (Jackson, Tenn.: McCowat-Mercer Press, 1963), 172–73; James M. McPherson, *What They Fought For, 1861–1865* (Baton Rouge: Louisiana State University Press, 1994), 51.

18. Charles E. Nash, *Biographical Sketches of Gen. Pat Cleburne and Gen. T. C. Hindman* (Dayton, Ohio: Morningside Bookshop, 1977), 19–22, 111.

19. Nathaniel Cheairs Hughes, Jr., *General William J. Hardee* (Baton Rouge: Louisiana State University Press, 1965), 186–87.

20. Ibid., 188–89; Howell Purdue and Elizabeth Purdue, *Pat Cleburne, Confederate General* (Hillsboro, Texas: Hill Junior College Press, 1973), 284–86.

21. Mobile *Daily Advertiser and Register,* 15 and 22 January 1864, 2; Purdue and Purdue, *Pat Cleburne,* 285–87; Robert Tarleton to Dear Miss Sallie, 18 February 1864, Tarleton Family Papers, folder 4, Yale.

22. Mobile *Daily Advertiser and Register,* 24 January 1864, 3. In March, Cleburne wrote Sallie Lightfoot that Sue had kept him waiting "six weeks" for an answer. Back-dating the letter suggests that he first proposed on or about 21 January 1864, or just before he left Mobile to return to Dalton. PRC to Sallie Lightfoot, 11 March 1864, Tarleton Family Papers, folder 9, Yale; Nash, *Biographical Sketches,* 111–12.

23. Buck to My Darling Sister, 23 January 1864, Buck Papers, SHC, UNC; Key Diary, 31 January 1864, 32; PRC to Rowe Webster, 31 January 1864, Webster Family Papers, TSLA; A. S. Colyar to A. S. Marks, n.d., in E. L. Drake, ed., *The Annals of Tennessee and Early Western History* (1878), 1:51.

24. Stephens to Davis, 22 January 1864, in Michael Perman, ed., *Major Problems in the Civil War and Reconstruction* (Lexington, Mass: D. C. Heath, 1991), 283–84; William C. Davis, *Jefferson Davis, the Man and His Hour* (New York: Harper-Collins, 1991), 541; Seddon to Johnston, 24 January 1864, O.R., I, 52(2):606–7.

25. Key Diary, 3 February 1864, 33; Johnston to Hardee et al., 31 January 1864, O.R., I, 52(2):608. The first public appearance of Cleburne's "Memorial" on arming slaves was in the 1 June 1888 issue of the *Kennesaw Gazette*.

26. Judith L. Hallock, *Braxton Bragg and Confederate Defeat,* vol. 2 (Tuscaloosa: University of Alabama Press, 1991), 180; Bragg to Marcus J. Wright, 6 February and 6 March 1864, folder 5, Wright Papers, SHC, UNC; General Orders no. 23, 24 February 1864, O.R., I, 32(2):799.

27. Buck to Lucy Buck, 9 February 1864, Buck Papers, SHC, UNC.

28. Ibid.; Buck, *Cleburne and His Command,* 187; John C. Hammond, *With Honor Untarnished: The Story of the First Arkansas Infantry Regiment, Confederate States Army* (Little Rock, Ark.: Pioneer Press, 1961), 110. The number of troops in Cleburne's Division increased from 5,359 on 20 December 1863 to 7,117 on 20 January 1864. See O.R., I, 31(3):850, and 32(2):586.

29. Albert Castel, *Decision in the West: The Atlanta Campaign of 1864* (Lawrence: University Press of Kansas, 1992), 47; Polk to Johnston, 3 February 1864, and Johnston to Polk, 3 February 1864, both in O.R., I, 32(2):662.

30. Johnston to Hardee, 23 February 1864, O.R., I, 32(2):799; Buck to Lucie Buck, 3 March 1864, Buck Papers, SHC, UNC; Johnston to Cooper, 20 October 1864, O.R., I, 32(1):477; Flavel C. Barber, *Holding the Line: The Third Tennessee Infantry, 1861–1864,* ed. Robert H. Ferrell (Kent, Ohio: Kent State University Press, 1994), entry of 26 February 1864, 162 (hereafter referred to as Flavel Barber Diary).

31. Robert Tarleton to Sallie Lightfoot, 22 February 1864 (folder 4), 2 March 1864 (folder 5), and 21 July 1864 (folder 9), all in Tarleton Family Papers, Yale.

32. Buck to My Dear Lucie, 3 March 1864, Buck Papers, SHC, UNC.

33. Robert Tarleton to Sallie Lightfoot, 11 March 1864, and PRC to Sallie Lightfoot, 11 March 1864, both in folder 5, Tarleton Family Papers, Yale.

34. Robert Tarleton to Sallie Lightfoot, 18 and 29 March 1864, folders 5 and 6, Tarleton Family Papers, Yale.

35. Cleburne was never a serious candidate for the command of Hindman's Corps. After Johnston assumed command of the army, he wanted to create a third corps, but rather than promote Cleburne, he asked Davis first for W. H. C. Whiting, then Mansfield Lovell. Davis turned down both Johnston's recommendation and his request and instead sent Hood to replace Hindman. Hindman was miffed and offered to resign. See Craig L. Symonds, *Joseph E. Johnston* (New York: W. W. Norton, 1992), 252, and Neal and Kremm, *Lion of the South,* 190. For Hood, see Richard M. McMurry, *John Bell Hood and the War for Southern Independence* (Lexington: University Press of Kentucky, 1982). The quote is from Philip D. Stephenson, *The Civil War Memoir of Philip Daingerfield Stephenson, D.D.,* ed. Nathaniel C. Hughes, Jr. (Conway: University of Central Arkansas Press, 1995), 209.

36. General Orders no. 5, 8 January 1864, O.R., I, 32(2):530–35; Frank S. Roberts, "In Winter Quarters at Dalton, Ga., 1863–64," *CV* 26 (1918): 274.

37. Stephenson, *Civil War Memoir,* 168.

38. Steve Davis, "The Great Snow Battle of 1864," *CWTI* 15 (June 1976): 34.

39. Key Diary, 31 March 1864, 66; Flavel Barber Diary, 7 April 1864, 174–75; John S. Jackman, *Diary of a Confederate Soldier,* ed. William C. Davis (Columbia: University of South Carolina Press, 1990), 112.

40. Key Diary, 19 April 1864, 72; Buck to My Dear Lucie, 3 March 1864, Buck Papers, SHC, UNC.

CHAPTER ELEVEN. FROM DALTON TO
THE CHATTAHOOCHEE

1. The precise number of troops available to Johnston in the spring of 1864 was a topic of dispute at the time and remains so today. Johnston's critics argue that his army's strength in May was nearly 53,000, not the 42,000 he claimed, and that the addition of reinforcements from Polk's Army of the Mississippi and elsewhere gave him as many as 84,000 men by June (see, for example, E. C. Dawes, "The Confederate Strength in the Atlanta Campaign," *B&L,* 4:281–83). These figures are unquestionably high, but then Johnston's own estimates are very likely low. He did not help his case by making distinctions, which are sometimes unclear, between those "present for duty" and the number of "effectives." His January 1864 returns, for example, listed 40,642 "effectives," but an "aggregate present" of 54,166 (O.R., I, 32[2]:586). The whole issue became tied up in army politics. Because President Davis dismissed Johnston in mid-July, it was important for the Davis-Bragg-Hood party to prove that Johnston had the *means* to conduct a successful defense and that he simply lacked the *will* to do so. That group, therefore, routinely chose to cite the highest figures available. The Johnston-Wigfall party just as routinely cited the lowest figure available to prove that Davis never gave Johnston the resources he needed to conduct an effective campaign.

2. PRC to Sellers (AAG), 16 August 1864, O.R., I, 38(3):721; Craig L. Symonds, *Joseph E. Johnston* (New York: W. W. Norton, 1992), 275–77; Albert Castel, *Decision in the West: The Atlanta Campaign of 1864* (Lawrence: University of Kansas Press, 1992), 134.

3. PRC to Sellers (AAG), 16 August 1864, and Johnston to Cooper, 20 October 1864, both in O.R., I, 38(3):721, 614; Nathaniel Cheairs Hughes, Jr., *General William J. Hardee* (Baton Rouge: Louisiana State University Press, 1965), 199–200.

4. Mackall to PRC, 9 May 1864 (6:30 A.M.), O.R., I, 38(4):681; PRC to Sellers (AAG), 16 August 1864, OR, I, 38(3):721; B. J. Hill to PRC, 9 May 1864, O.R., I, 38(4):682–83.

5. Symonds, *Joseph E. Johnston,* 277–78.

6. Buck to Granbury, 9 May 1864, O.R., I, 38(4):683; Samuel T. Foster, *One of Cleburne's Command,* ed. Norman D. Brown (Austin: University of Texas Press, 1980), diary entry of 10 May, 73; PRC to Sellers (AAG), 16 August 1864, O.R., I, 38(3):721; Irving A. Buck, *Cleburne and His Command* (Dayton, Ohio: Morningside Bookshop, 1992), 208.

7. Hood to Johnston, 11 May 1864 (8:00 A.M.), O.R., I, 38(4):686.

8. Cantey to Johnston, 11 May 1864, and PRC to T. B. Roy, 11 May 1864, both in O.R., I, 38(4):693; PRC to Sellers (AAG), 16 August 1864, O.R., I, 38(3):721.

9. PRC to Sellers (AAG), 16 August 1864, O.R., I, 38(3):721–22; Buck, *Cleburne and His Command,* 209; PRC to Hood, 11 May 1864 (2:00 P.M. and 5:00 P.M.), O.R., I, 38(4):696.

10. PRC to Sellers (AAG), 16 August 1864, O.R., I, 38(3):722; McPherson to Kilpatrick (1:00 A.M.), McPherson to Sherman (9:30 A.M.), and Kilpatrick to McPherson (11:00 A.M.), 12 May 1864, all in O.R., I, 38(4):139, 152, 153.

11. PRC to Polk, 12 May 1864, Joseph E. Johnston Papers (JO 317), HEH Library.

12. PRC to Sellers (AAG), 16 August 1864, O.R., I, 38(3):722.

13. Ibid.; Foster, *One of Cleburne's Command,* diary entry of 15 May, 76; Hughes, *General William J. Hardee,* 203.

14. PRC to Sellers (AAG), 16 August 1864, O.R., I, 38(3):722; Foster, *One of Cleburne's Command,* diary entry of 16 May, 77.

15. The Confederate counterattack on 16 May became known as the Battle of Rome Crossroads. Journal of Major Henry Hampton, entry of 16 May 1864, O.R., I, 38(3):704; PRC to Hardee, 17 May 1864, O.R., I, 38(4):721.

16. The best account of this campaign is Castel, *Decision in the West.* See also Richard M. McMurry, "The Atlanta Campaign: December 23, 1863, to July 18, 1864" (Ph.D. diss., Emory University, 1967); and William R. Scaife, *The Campaign for Atlanta* (Atlanta: William R. Scaife, 1993).

17. For the impact of this campaign on Confederate morale in the ranks, see the article by Richard McMurry, "Confederate Morale in the Atlanta Campaign of 1864," *GHQ* 54 (1970): 226–43. Foster, *One of Cleburne's Command,* diary entry of 24 May, 80.

18. Johnston to Lydia Johnston, 21 and 23 May 1864, MS2403, box 6, McLane-Fisher Family Papers, Maryland Historical Society; Symonds, *Joseph E. Johnston,* 296–301. The headquarters estimates came from Major General Mansfield Lovell, who was acting as a volunteer aide to Johnston. In fact, Sherman had suffered fewer than half the number of casualties estimated by Lovell.

19. Buck, *Cleburne and His Command,* 227. See also Charles E. Nash, *Biographical Sketches of Gen. Pat Cleburne and Gen. T. C Hindman* (Dayton, Ohio: Morningside Bookshop, 1977), 159; and Learned H. Mangum, "Death of General Pat R. Cleburne," in Thomas A. Head, *Campaigns and Battles of the Sixteenth Regiment, Tennessee Volunteers* (Nashville, Tenn.: Cumberland Presbyterian House Publishing, 1885), 375.

20. Learned H. Mangum, "General P. R. Cleburne," *Kennesaw Gazette,* 15 June 1887, 3; R. Tarleton to Sallie Lightfoot, 3 June 1864, folder 7, Tarleton Family Papers, Yale.

21. Basil W. Duke, *History of Morgan's Cavalry* (Bloomington: Indiana University Press, 1960), 518; D. H. Smith Report, 23 May 1864, O.R., I, 37(1):68. Cleburne received official notification of his brother's death about a month later outside Atlanta, but very likely he heard of it earlier.

22. Shelby Foote, *The Civil War, A Narrative* (New York: Random House, 1974), 3:318.

23. Foster, *One of Cleburne's Command,* diary entry of 25 May, 80.

24. T. B. Roy to PRC, 25 May 1864 (11:00 A.M.), O.R., I, 38(3):743; Buck, *Cleburne and His Command,* 218; Foster, *One of Cleburne's Command,* diary entry of 25 May, 80–81.

25. Foster, *One of Cleburne's Command,* diary entry of 27 May, 82.

26. PRC to Sellers (AAG), 30 May 1864, O.R., I, 38(3):724; Buck, *Cleburne and His Command,* 218–19; Calhoun Benham, "Major Gen. P. R. Cleburne," *Kennesaw Gazette,* 1 August 1889, 2.

27. PRC to Sellers (AAG), 30 May 1864, O.R., I, 38(3):724; Edward Bourne (private, 3d Confederate), "Govan's Brigade at New Hope Church," *CV* 31 (1923): 89.

28. Foster, *One of Cleburne's Command,* diary entry of 27 May, 82–83; PRC to Sellers (AAG), 30 May 1864, O.R., I, 38(3):724.

29. Richard M. McMurry, "The Hell Hole: New Hope Church," *CWTI* 11 (February 1973): 32–43; Bourne, "Govan's Brigade," 89.

30. Lowrey Autobiography, USAMHI; PRC to Sellers (AAG), 30 May 1864, O.R., I, 38(3):725; Buck, *Cleburne and His Command,* 219.

31. PRC to Sellers (AAG), 30 May 1864, O.R., I, 38(3):724.

32. Ibid.; Lowrey Autobiography, USAMHI.

33. PRC to Sellers (AAG), 30 May 1864, O.R., I, 38(3):725; Foster, *One of Cleburne's Command,* diary entry of 27 May, 85.

34. Jim Turner, "Co. G, 6th Texas Infantry, CSA, from 1861 to 1865," *Texana* 12 (1974): 172; Bourne, "Govan's Brigade," 89; Castel, *Decision in the West,* 241; Foster, *One of Cleburne's Command,* diary entry of 27 May, 88; PRC to Sellers (AAG), 30 May 1864, O.R., I, 38(3):726. Casualties are itemized in O.R., I, 38(3):687. Lowrey's Brigade suffered the most (183), while Polk's, which was on the left, suffered the least (8).

35. Castel, *Decision in the West,* 248–60, 267–74; McMurry, "The Atlanta Campaign," 178–79, 181–83; Howell Purdue and Elizabeth Purdue, *Pat Cleburne, Confederate General* (Hillsboro, Texas: Hill Junior College Press, 1973), 329–30.

36. Castel, *Decision in the West,* 274–77; McMurry, "The Atlanta Campaign," 188–91; Symonds, *Joseph E. Johnston,* 306–7; Buck, *Cleburne and His Command,* 222–26.

37. Sam R. Watkins, *"Co. Aytch," Maury Grays, First Tennessee Regiment* (Wilmington, N.C.: Broadfoot Publishing Company, 1987), 154–55; Buck, *Cleburne and His Command,* 224; James L. Nichols and Frank Abbott, eds., "Reminiscences of Confederate Service by Wiley A. Washburn," *AHQ* 35 (Spring 1976): 67; James Cooper Nisbet, *Four Years on the Firing Line,* ed. Bell I. Wiley (Jackson, Tenn.: McCowat-Mercer Press, 1963), 199; O.R., I, 38(3):662.

38. Andrew Malone Hill, "Personal Recollections of Andrew Malone Hill," *Alabama Historical Quarterly* 20 (Spring 1958): 90 (italics added).

39. W. T. Barnes, "An Incident of Kenesaw [sic] Mountain," *CV* 30 (1922): 48; Dennis Kelly, "The Battle of Kennesaw Mountain," *Blue and Gray Magazine* 6 (June 1989): 46; T. H. Maney, "Battle at Dead Angle on Kennesaw Line," *CV* 11 (1903): 159; Castel, *Decision in the West,* 309–11.

40. Castel, *Decision in the West,* 315.

41. R. M. Gray, "Reminiscences," SHC, UNC; Watkins, *"Co. Aytch,"* 159.

42. The words attributed here to Colonel Martin are an amalgam of those ascribed to him by two different witnesses: W. T. Barnes, a private in the 1st Arkansas, in "An Incident of Kennesaw Mountain," 48–49, and William E. Bevins, *Reminiscences of a Private,* ed. Daniel E. Sutherland (Fayetteville: University of Arkansas Press, 1992), 175. Colonel W. D. Pickett claimed that the initiative for this remarkable incident came from Lowrey's Brigade, but most contemporaries attribute it to Martin and the 1st Arkansas. In any event, Pickett was probably correct when he wrote, "Any brigade

of Cleburne's Division, or, in fact, of the Army of Tennessee, would have acted with the same promptness" ("The Dead Angle," *CV* 14 [1906]: 459).

43. JEJ to Cooper, 20 October 1864, O.R., I, 38(3):617. See the discussion of casualties at Kennesaw Mountain in Castel, *Decision in the West,* 319–20.

44. O.R., I, 38(3):676–80; Buck, *Cleburne and His Command,* 228 (emphasis in original).

45. Francis A. Shoup, "Dalton Campaign," *CV* 3 (1895): 262–65.

CHAPTER TWELVE. THE BATTLES FOR ATLANTA

1. Irving Buck, *Cleburne and His Command* (Dayton, Ohio: Morningside Bookshop, 1992), 229; Key Diary, 18 July 1864, 89; Samuel T. Foster, *One of Cleburne's Command,* ed. Norman D. Brown (Austin: University of Texas Press, 1980), entry of 18 July 64, 106–7; Philip D. Stephenson, *The Civil War Memoir of Philip Daingerfield Stephenson, D.D.,* ed. Nathaniel C. Hughes, Jr. (Conway: University of Central Arkansas Press, 1995), 209; James L. Nichols and Frank Abbott, eds., "Reminiscences of Confederate Service by Wiley A. Washburn," *AHQ* 35 (Spring 1976): 69.

2. Learned H. Mangum, "Death of General Cleburne," in Thomas A. Head, *Campaigns and Battles of the Sixteenth Regiment, Tennessee Volunteers* (Nashville, Tenn.: Cumberland Presbyterian House Publishing, 1885), 375; Mangum, "General P. R. Cleburne," *Kennesaw Gazette,* 15 June 1887, 4; Charles E. Nash, *Biographical Sketches of Gen. Pat Cleburne and Gen. T. C Hindman* (Dayton, Ohio: Morningside Bookshop, 1977), 159.

3. Hood to Seddon, 19 July 1864, O.R., I, 38(5):892.

4. See, for example, Paul Fessler, "The Case of the Missing Promotion: Historians and the Military Career of Major General Patrick Ronayne Cleburne, C.S.A.," *AHQ* 53 (Summer 1994): 211–31, and Slate L. Johnson, "Slavery and the Politics of Promotion: The Case of Major General Patrick R. Cleburne, C.S.A." (undergraduate honors thesis, U.S. Naval Academy, 1991).

5. Buck, *Cleburne and His Command,* 231; D. G. White to T. B. Roy, 6 April 1880, in T. B. Roy, "General Hardee and the Military Operations Around Atlanta," *SHSP* 8 (1880): 382.

6. Roy, "General Hardee Around Atlanta," 381–82. Many years later, Hood claimed that Cleburne had come to his headquarters following the battles for Atlanta and confided that prior to the attack Hardee had warned him "to be on the lookout for breastworks." Hood claimed this proved that Hardee "was wanting in that boldness requisite for offensive warfare" (John Bell Hood, *Advance and Retreat* [New York, 1880; reprinted DaCapo Press, 1993], 185–86). Roy's article, cited above, was intended to refute this charge. Roy, who was Hardee's chief of staff, solicited letters from several eyewitnesses, all of whom insisted that Hardee made no such statement. From a twentieth-century perspective, it is perhaps most interesting that virtually all involved felt that it would have been somehow inappropriate, even unmanly, for Hardee to issue such a caution.

7. Key Diary, 20 July 1864, 92; A. P. Mason (AAG) to Wheeler, misdated as 19 July 1864 (7:15 P.M.), O.R., I, 38(5):893.

8. Foster, *One of Cleburne's Command,* entry of 21 July 1864, 108–9; Nichols and

Abbott, eds., "Reminiscences of Confederate Service," 70; Smith to Buck, 5 August 1864, O.R., I, 38(3):746.

9. Foster, *One of Cleburne's Command,* 108-9; Buck, *Cleburne and His Command,* 233-34; Roy, "General Hardee Around Atlanta," 350; Mason (AAG) to PRC, 21 July 1864 (9:00 A.M.), O.R., I, 38(5):898; Hardee to Cooper, 5 April 1865, O.R., I, 38(3):699; Key Diary, 21 July 1864, 92-93.

10. T. B. Roy to PRC, 21 July 1864 (7:30 P.M. and 11:00 P.M.), O.R., I, 38(5): 899, 900; Jim Turner, "Co. G, 6th Texas Infantry, CSA, from 1861 to 1865," *Texana* 12 (1974): 175. See also Roy, "General Hardee Around Atlanta," 357.

11. Hood later wrote that his plan was "to throw Hardee, the same night, entirely to the rear and flank of McPherson—as Jackson was thrown, in a similar movement, at Chancellorsville" (John B. Hood, "The Defense of Atlanta," *B&L,* 4:338). Hood also claimed that his orders were for Hardee "to completely turn" McPherson's position and strike him in the rear. The burden of evidence, however, suggests that although these were his original orders, he modified them to allow Hardee discretion. See Nathaniel Cheairs Hughes, Jr., *General William J. Hardee* (Baton Rouge: Louisiana State University Press, 1965), 226.

12. W. E. Preston, "Memoirs of the War," 33d Alabama Papers, ADAH.

13. Foster, *One of Cleburne's Command,* entry of 22 July 1864, 111; Nichols and Abbott, eds., "Reminiscences of Confederate Service," 70-71; W. E. Preston, "Memoirs of the War," 33d Alabama Papers, ADAH; Calhoun Benham, "Major-Gen. P. R. Cleburne," *Kennesaw Gazette,* 15 October 1889, 2; G. A. William (AAG) to T. B. Roy, 14 March 1880, in Roy, "General Hardee Around Atlanta," 364; Key Diary, 22 July 1864, 94-95.

14. Govan to Buck, 30 July 1864, O.R., I, 38(3):737-41. Casualties had so reduced Govan's Brigade that there were barely 200 men in the two regiments that attacked the breastworks.

15. Buck, *Cleburne and His Command,* 284.

16. W. E. Preston, "Memoirs of the War," 33d Alabama Papers, ADAH; Smith to Buck, 5 August 1864, O.R., I, 38(3):747.

17. Lowrey did not mention the change of direction in his official report (O.R., I, 38[3]:731-33), but discusses it in some detail in his postwar "Autobiography" (USAMHI). The heatstroke is mentioned by both Lowrey and W. E. Preston, "Memoirs of the War," 33d Alabama Papers, ADAH.

18. Key Diary, 22 July 1864, 96; Sam R. Watkins, *"Co. Aytch," Maury Grays, First Tennessee Regiment* (Wilmington, N.C.: Broadfoot Publishing Company, 1987), 177.

19. G. W. Smith to Alexander (AAG), 28 July 1864, and Lowrey to Buck, 29 July 1864, both in O.R., I, 38(3):582, 732; Grenville Dodge, *The Battle of Atlanta and Other Campaigns* (Denver: Sage Books, 1965), 46; Albert Castel, *Decision in the West: The Atlanta Campaign of 1864* (Lawrence: University Press of Kansas, 1992), 402-3.

20. Key Diary, 23 July 1864, 99; W. E. Preston, "Memoirs of the War," 33d Alabama Papers, ADAH.

21. The next day, Hood revised his estimates and reported the capture of thirteen guns and eighteen stand of colors; Hood to Seddon, 22 and 23 July 1864, O.R., I, 38(5):900, 903. Smith to Buck, 5 August 1864, O.R., I, 38(3):747. Lowrey's comment is from his Autobiography, USAMHI.

22. The casualty estimates are from Castel, *Decision in the West* (p. 412), who does

not include the number of missing and argues for the lower figure, and Thomas L. Livermore, *Numbers and Losses in the American Civil War* (Bloomington: Indiana University Press, 1957), p. 123, who relies in part on Sherman's own estimates of Confederate casualties as being about 8,000.

23. Stephenson, *Civil War Memoir*, 212; W. E. Preston, "Memoirs of the War," 33d Alabama Papers, ADAH; PRC to Poole (AAG), 7 August 1864, O.R., I, 38(5):949; Castel, *Decision in the West*, 450. Olmstead replaced Colonel William Barkuloo on 2 August. He was unaware of Cleburne's poor opinion of him and later bragged about being a valued member of Cleburne's Division.

24. W. E. Preston, "Memoirs of the War," 33d Alabama Papers, ADAH; Key Diary, 24 July 1864, 100; General Field Orders no. 7, 25 July 1864, O.R., I, 38(5):909.

25. Key Diary, 27 July 1864, 100–102.

26. Buck, *Cleburne and His Command*, 247–48; exclamation point added.

27. Hood to Seddon, 28 July 1864, Hood to Davis, 2 August 1864, and Davis to Hood, 3 August 1864, all in O.R., I, 38(5):917, 940, 946.

28. Journal of F. A. Shoup, 7–9 August 1864, O.R., I, 38(3):690; W. E. Preston, "Memoirs of the War," 33d Alabama Papers, ADAH.

29. General Field Orders no. 14, 12 August 1864, O.R., I, 38(5):960.

30. T. O. Moore (private, 6th Texas), "Anecdotes of General Cleburne," *SHSP* 21 (1893): 301.

31. Hood to Davis, 9 August 1864, O.R., I, 38(5):951; Key Diary, 11 August 1864, 113.

32. General Field Orders no. 15, 15 August 1864, T. B. Roy to PRC, 12 August 1864, and Circular, 13 August 1864, all in O.R., I, 38(5):965, 958, 962. Foster, *One of Cleburne's Command*, diary entry of 13 August 1864, 121.

33. T. B. Roy to PRC, 18 August 1864, Hardee to PRC, 18 August 1864, Roy to PRC (11:50 A.M.), 19 August 1864, and Shoup to PRC (4:00 P.M. and 5:40 P.M.), 19 August 1864, all in O.R., I, 38(5):972, 973, 976.

34. Hood to PRC, 21 August 1864, O.R., I, 38(5):982; Mercer Diary, SHC, UNC; Foster, *One of Cleburne's Command*, diary entry of 29 August 1864, 121; Key Diary, 15, 20, 22, and 29 August 1864, 116, 118, 119, and 124.

35. Calhoun Benham, "Major-Gen. P. R. Cleburne," *Kennesaw Gazette*, 1 November 1889, 2.

36. Shoup (AAG) to Hardee, 31 August 1864 (3:00 A.M., 3:10 A.M., and 3:20 A.M.), O.R., I, 38(5):1006.

37. Castel, *Decision in the West*, 500.

38. Lowrey to Benham, 10 September 1864, and Maney to Buck, 28 September 1864, both in O.R., I, 38(3):708, 727; italics added. Also Olmstead to Palmer (AAG), 5 September 1864, and Lowrey to Buck, 10 September 1864, both in O.R., I, 38(3):755, 727.

39. Foster, *One of Cleburne's Command*, diary entry of 31 August 1864, 125–26; W. E. Preston, "Memoirs of the War," 33d Alabama Papers, ADAH; Lowrey to Benham, 10 September 1864, Granbury to Milner (AAG), 5 September 1864, and Olmstead to Palmer (AAG), 5 September 1864, all in O.R., I, 38(3):727, 744, 756.

40. Maney to Buck, 28 September 1864, O.R., I, 38(3):709.

41. Ibid., 711.

42. Ibid.; Hardee to Cooper, 5 April 1865, O.R., I, 38(3):701; Castel, *Decision in the West,* 450–51.

43. Shoup to Hardee, 31 August 1864 (6:00 P.M.), O.R., I, 38(3):701.

44. Benham, "Major-Gen. P. R. Cleburne," *Kennesaw Gazette,* 1 November 1889, 2; W. E. Preston, "Memoirs of the War," 33d Alabama Papers, ADAH.

45. Errol M. Clauss, "The Battle of Jonesboro," *CWTI* 7 (November 1968): 12; Benham, "Major-Gen. P. R. Cleburne," *Kennesaw Gazette,* 1 November 1889, 2.

46. George D. Van Horn, "Swett's Battery at Jonesboro," *CV* 11 (1903): 504; William E. Bevins, *Reminiscences of a Private,* ed. Daniel E. Sutherland (Fayetteville: University of Arkansas Press, 1992), 191; Foster, *One of Cleburne's Command,* diary entry of 1 September 1864, 127–28; Green (Govan's Brigade) to Buck, 5 September 1864, O.R., I, 38(3):741–43.

CHAPTER THIRTEEN. THE LAST CRUSADE

1. George Williams to Lucy Buck, 3 October 1864, Buck Papers, SHC, UNC; Hood to Bragg, 3 September 1864, O.R., I, 38(5):1016, 1021; Sue Tarleton to Sallie Lightfoot, 3 October 1864, folder 9, Tarleton Family Papers, Yale.

2. Mercer Diary, 2 September 1864, SHC, UNC; Key Diary, 1–2 September 1864, 127–28; Calhoun Benham, "Maj.-General P. R. Cleburne," *Kennesaw Gazette,* 1 November 1889, 3; W. E. Preston, "Memoirs of the War," 33d Alabama Papers, ADAH.

3. Hood to Bragg, 6 September 1864, O.R., I, 38(5):1023–24; Thomas L. Connelly, *Autumn of Glory* (Baton Rouge: Louisiana State University Press, 1971), 470–72.

4. Mercer Diary, 6 and 11 September 1864, SHC, UNC; W. E. Preston, "Memoirs of the War," 33d Alabama Papers, ADAH; Key Diary, 9 September 1864, 131; Army Returns, 10 September 1864, O.R., I, 39(2):828–29.

5. Key Diary, 15 September 1864, 134. Key wrote that Lowrey based his sermon on Psalm 15, but his description of it suggests that it was instead Psalm 18, which is quoted here.

6. Shoup Journal, 26 September 1864, O.R., I, 39(1):804; William E. Bevins, *Reminiscences of a Private,* ed. Daniel E. Sutherland (Fayetteville: University of Arkansas Press, 1992), 197; James L. Nichols and Frank Abbott, eds., "Reminiscences of Confederate Service by Wiley A. Washburn," *AHQ* 35 (Spring 1976): 73.

7. Connelly, *Autumn of Glory,* 471–72; Nathaniel Cheairs Hughes, Jr., *General William J. Hardee* (Baton Rouge: Louisiana State University Press, 1965), 246–48; Steven E. Woodworth, *Jefferson Davis and His Generals* (Lawrence: University Press of Kansas, 1990), 242; T. B. Roy, "General Hardee and Military Operations Around Atlanta," *SHSP* 8 (1880): 381–82; Irving Buck, *Cleburne and His Command* (Dayton, Ohio: Morningside Bookshop, 1992), 260.

8. Sue Tarleton to Sallie Lightfoot, 3 October 1864, folder 9, Tarleton Family Papers, Yale.

9. Samuel T. Foster, *One of Cleburne's Command,* ed. Norman D. Brown (Austin: University of Texas Press, 1980), diary entry for 3 October 1864, 137; W. E. Preston, "Memoirs of the War," 33d Alabama Papers, ADAH.

10. T. O. Moore (private, 6th Texas), "Anecdotes of General Cleburne," *SHSP* 21 (1893): 299–300.

11. Ibid.

12. Foster, *One of Cleburne's Command,* diary entry of 13–14 October 1864, 140.

13. Johnston's Report, 17 October 1864, O.R., I, 39(1):719; W. E. Preston, "Memoirs of the War," 33d Alabama Papers, ADAH; Buck, *Cleburne and His Command,* 262; Bevins, *Reminiscences,* 201.

14. W. E. Preston, "Memoirs of the War," 33d Alabama Papers, ADAH; Foster, *One of Cleburne's Command,* diary entry of 28 October 1864, 142.

15. Key Diary, 13–15 November 1864, 149–50; Foster, *One of Cleburne's Command,* diary entry of 15 November 1864, 144; Capers to Gordon (AAG), 4 January 1865, O.R., I, 45(1):735.

16. Brent (AAG) to Hood, 17 November 1864, Hood to Brent, 17 November 1864, and General Field Orders no. 35, 20 November 1864, all in O.R., I, 45(1):1215, 1227; Foster, *One of Cleburne's Command,* diary entry of 21 November 1864, 145; Hood letter, 21 November 1864, O.R., I, 45(1):1236.

17. Charles E. Nash, *Biographical Sketches of Gen. Pat Cleburne and Gen. T. C Hindman* (Dayton, Ohio: Morningside Bookshop, 1977), 160; W. E. Preston, "Memoirs of the War," 33d Alabama Papers, ADAH.

18. Buck, *Cleburne and His Command,* 266; W. E. Preston, "Memoirs of the War," 33d Alabama Papers, ADAH; Nichols and Abbott, eds., "Reminiscences of Confederate Service," 78–79.

19. Hood to Seddon, 11 December 1864, Walthall to Gale (AAG), 14 January 1865, both in O.R., I, 45(1):657, 719; S. C. Hardee, "Maj.-Gen. Patrick R. Cleburne," *CV* 12 (1904): 17.

20. Nichols and Abbott, eds., "Reminiscences of Confederate Service," 79; Hood to Seddon, 28 November 1864, O.R., I, 45(1):1254.

21. Lowrey Autobiography, USAMHI; Nichols and Abbott, eds., "Reminiscences of Confederate Service," 79; Memorandum of John S. R. Gregory, 4 November 1903, in Frank H. Smith, *History of Maury County, Tennessee* (N.p.: Maury County Historical Society, 1969), 237–38.

22. The most authoritative accounts of the skirmish at Spring Hill are Wiley Sword, *Embrace an Angry Wind: The Confederacy's Last Hurrah: Spring Hill, Franklin, and Nashville* (New York: Harper-Collins, 1992), published in paperback as *The Confederacy's Last Hurrah* (Lawrence: University Press of Kansas, 1993); J. P. Young, "Hood's Failure at Spring Hill," *CV* 16 (1908): 25–41; and Benjamin Franklin Cheatham, "The Lost Opportunity at Spring Hill," *SHSP* 9 (1881): 524–41. The quotation is from Learned H. Mangum, "The Death of Gen. Cleburne," in Thomas A. Head, *Campaigns and Battles of the Sixteenth Regiment, Tennessee Volunteers* (Nashville, Tenn.: Cumberland Presbyterian House Publishing, 1885), 373. See also Buck, *Cleburne and His Command,* 265.

23. Sword, *The Confederacy's Last Hurrah,* 126; Cheatham, "The Lost Opportunity," 525–26. Brown also believed that Spring Hill was the military objective and after the war wrote that he was ordered "to take Spring Hill" (Brown to Cheatham, 24 October 1881, in Cheatham, 538).

24. Nichols and Abbott, eds., "Reminiscences of Confederate Service," 80; Lowrey Autobiography, USAMHI.

25. Wood to Whipple, 10 January 1865, and Journal of the Fourth Army Corps (Union), 29 November 1864, both in O.R., I, 45(1):123, 148; Stanley Horn, "The Spring Hill Legend," *CWTI* 8 (April 1969): 26; Cheatham, "The Lost Opportunity," 525.

26. Mangum, "Death of Gen. Cleburne," 374.

27. Nichols and Abbott, eds., "Reminiscences of Confederate Service," 80; Cheatham, "The Lost Opportunity," 525–26.

28. Bate to Porter (AAG), 25 January 1865, O.R., I, 45(1):742.

29. Mangum, "Death of Gen. Cleburne," 374; S. D. Lee to J. F. H. Claibourne, 12 June 1878, Claibourne Papers, SHC, UNC; W. E. Preston, "Memoirs of the War," 33d Alabama Papers, ADAH. Cheatham wrote after the war that these orders came from Hood: "The Commanding General . . . informed me that he had concluded to wait till morning, and directed me to hold my command in readiness for an attack at daylight" ("Lost Opportunity," 526). Possibly, Hood believed that the turnpike was already occupied and that the attack the next morning would be on the *town* of Spring Hill.

30. Lee to Claibourne, 12 June 1878, Claibourne Papers, SHC, UNC.

31. Stewart to Cheatham, 8 February 1881, in Cheatham, "The Lost Opportunity," 533.

32. Horn argues that even if both Cleburne and Bate had occupied the pike, it would not have ensured success. He notes that there were 5,500 Federals in the town and nearly 20,000 approaching from Columbia. Cleburne and Bate would have been caught between superior forces. Seen from this view, there was no "lost opportunity" at Spring Hill; Horn, "The Spring Hill Legend," 32.

33. Brown to Cheatham, 24 October 1881, in Cheatham, "The Lost Opportunity," 539.

34. Govan is the source for this comment. In 1894 he rendered it as "Gen I will take the works or loose [*sic*] my life in the attempt." Thirteen years later in 1907 he recalled it as "I will take the enemy's works or fall in the attempt" (Govan to Fullerton, 22 May 1894, box 1, folder 1, War Department Park Commission Papers, Chickamauga and Chattanooga National Park Library; Govan to Buck, 3 September 1907, in Buck, *Cleburne and His Command,* 290–91).

35. Once again Govan is the source here; see the two letters cited above.

36. Isaac N. Shannon, "Sharpshooters with Hood's Army," *CV* 15 (1907): 124–25.

37. Ibid.

38. W. A. Washburn, "Cleburne's Division at Franklin," *CV* 13 (1905): 27; J. L. Boswell, "Confusing Gens. Loring and Lowrey at Franklin," *CV* 8 (1900): 12; David R. Logsdon, *Eyewitness at the Battle of Franklin* (Nashville, Tenn.: David R. Logsdon, 1988), 7.

39. Foster, *One of Cleburne's Command,* diary entry of 30 November 1864, 147; G. C. Phillips, "Witness to the Battle of Franklin," *CV* 14 (1906): 261–62; Joseph Boyce, "Missourians in Battle of Franklin," *CV* 24 (1916): 102; Washburn, "Cleburne's Division at Franklin," 27.

40. Jacob D. Cox, *The Battle of Franklin* (New York: Scribners, 1897), 67; John M. Schofield, *Forty-Six Years in the Army* (New York: Century Company, 1897), 233–34; Sword, *The Confederacy's Last Hurrah,* 197–98.

41. W. E. Preston, "Memoirs of the War," 33d Alabama Papers, ADAH.

42. Govan to Buck, 3 September 1907, in Buck, *Cleburne and His Command,* 291.

43. J. C. Dean, "The Battle of Franklin," *CV* 7 (1899): 27; D. H. Patterson, "Battle of Franklin," *CV* 9 (1901): 116–17; Phillips, "Witness to the Battle of Franklin," 261–62; Washburn, "Cleburne's Division at Franklin," 27–28; Mangum, "General P. R. Cleburne: A Sketch of His Early Life and His Last Battle," *Kennesaw Gazette,* 15 June 1887, 2–6.

44. William Preston Johnston, *The Life of Albert Sidney Johnston* (New York: D. Appleton, 1878), 354.

45. Patterson, "Battle of Franklin," 117; Frank A. Burr, with Talcott Williams, *The Battle of Franklin* (Philadelphia: Philadelphia Press, 1883), 18–19.

EPILOGUE

1. A photograph of these six bodies lying on the McGavock porch like so much cordwood was for many years believed to depict the six Confederate generals who lost their lives in the Battle of Franklin. "What an Old Lady Remembers About the Battle of Franklin," Sketches, Battle of Franklin, Confederate Collection, box 4, TSLA; Campbell H. Brown, "The Myth of the 5 Dead Rebel Generals," *CWTI* 8 (August 1969): 14–15.

2. Irving Buck, *Cleburne and His Command* (Dayton, Ohio: Morningside Bookshop, 1992), 289–94; Charles Todd Quintard, *Doctor Quintard, Chaplain C.S.A. and Second Bishop of Tennessee* (Sewanee, Tenn.: University Press, 1905), 116; Memorandum of John S. R. Gregory, in Frank H. Smith, *History of Maury County, Tennessee* (N.p.: Maury County Historical Society, 1969), 252; Howell Purdue and Elizabeth Purdue, *Pat Cleburne, Confederate Soldier* (Hillsboro, Texas: Hill Junior College Press, 1973), 430–33.

3. Hood to Seddon, 3 December 1864, O.R., I, 45(2):643–44. A second copy of this report on pp. 211–12 reads, "We captured *seven* stand of colors" (emphasis added).

4. Sarah W. Wiggins, ed., *Journals of Josiah Gorgas, 1857–1878* (Tuscaloosa: University of Alabama Press, 1995), 185; Mobile *Daily Advertiser and Register,* 20 October 1867.

5. George W. Gordon, "General P. R. Cleburne: Dedication of a Monument to His Memory at Helena, Arkansas, May 10, 1891," *SHSP* 18 (1890): 269.

6. William J. Hardee, "Maj. Gen. Patrick R. Cleburne," *CV* 12 (1904): 17.

SELECTED BIBLIOGRAPHY

MANUSCRIPT SOURCES

Alabama Department of Archives and History, Montgomery, Alabama
  33d Alabama Papers
Arkansas History Commission, Little Rock, Arkansas
  Patrick Cleburne Papers
William Pettus Buck Collection (private), Birmingham, Alabama
  Irving Buck Letters
Chickamauga-Chattanooga National Military Park Library
  War Department Park Commission Papers
Columbia University, New York, New York
  Peter W. Alexander Collection
Cork County Library, Cork, Ireland
  1845 Ordnance Survey Map of Ireland
Ruth Duemler Collection (private), Fresno, California
  William Cleburne Letters
Henry E. Huntington Library, San Marino, California
  Simon Bolivar Buckner Collection
  James W. Eldridge Collection
  Joseph E. Johnston Collection
Library of Congress, Washington, D.C.
  William J. Hardee Papers
Nora Lynch Collection (private), Ballincollig, Ireland
  John Hawkes Letters
Maryland Historical Society, Baltimore, Maryland
  McLane-Fisher Family Papers
National Archives, Washington, D.C. (Record Group 109)
  Compiled Service Records of Confederate General and Staff Officers, 1861–1865
  Letters Received by the Adjutant and Inspector General (AIGO), 1861–1865
  Letters Received by the Secretary of War, 1861–1865
  Muster and Pay Rolls, 1861–1865
William R. Perkins Library, Duke University, Durham, North Carolina
  Braxton Bragg Papers

304 Selected Bibliography

Doug Schanz Collection (private), Roanoke, Virginia
    Patrick Cleburne Letters
South Caroliniana Library, Charleston, South Carolina
    Diary of J. H. Steinmeyer
Tennessee State Library and Archives, Nashville, Tennessee
    Benjamin Franklin Cheatham Papers
    Confederate Collection
    Jill Knight Garrett Papers
    William Henry Harder Memoir
    Webster Family Papers
U.S. Military History Research Collection, U.S. Army War College, Carlisle Barracks,
    Pennsylvania
    Mark P. Lowrey Autobiography
University of Arkansas Libraries, Fayetteville, Arkansas
    Patrick Ronayne Cleburne Papers
    Richard Howell Purdue Collection
University of North Carolina, Chapel Hill, North Carolina, Southern Historical Col-
    lection, Manuscripts Division
    Irving Buck Papers
    J. F. H. Claiborne Papers
    D. Coleman Diary
    Daniel C. Govan Papers
    R. M. Gray Reminiscences
    William Whann Mackall Papers
    George A. Mercer Papers
    John R. Peacock Collection
    Henry C. Semple Papers
    Marcus J. Wright Papers
Virginia State Library and Archives, Richmond, Virginia
    Daniel Harvey Hill Papers
Western Reserve Historical Society, Cleveland, Ohio
    Braxton Bragg Papers
    David S. Stanley Manuscript
Wyoming Historical Society, Cheyenne, Wyoming
    Henry Freeman Papers
Yale University Library, New Haven, Connecticut
    Tarleton Family Papers

NEWSPAPERS

Chattanooga (Tennessee) *Rebel*
Cork (Ireland) *Constitution*
Cork (Ireland) *Examiner*
Helena (Arkansas) *Democratic Shield*
Helena (Arkansas) *Democratic Star*
Helena (Arkansas) *States Rights Democrat*

Kennesaw Gazette (Atlanta, Georgia)
Little Rock (Arkansas) *Gazette*
Little Rock (Arkansas) *Old Line Democrat*
Mobile (Alabama) *Daily Advertiser and Register*
The Nation (Dublin, Ireland)

OFFICIAL RECORDS AND PUBLISHED COLLECTIONS

Brady, W. Maziere. *Clerical and Parochial Records of Cork, Cloyne, and Ross.* Dublin: Alexander Thom, 1863.

Cole, J. H. *Church and Parish Records of the United Diocese of Cork, Cloyne, and Ross.* Cork: Guy, 1903.

DeBow, J. D. B., ed. *The Industrial Resources, etc. of the Southern and Western States.* 3 vols. New Orleans: DeBow's Review, 1852.

Journal of Both Sessions of the Convention of the State of Arkansas. Little Rock: Johnson and Yerkes, 1861.

Lewis, Samuel. *A Topographical Dictionary of Ireland with Historical and Statistical Descriptions.* 2 vols. London: S. Lewis and Company, 1837.

Lists of the Freemen and Freeholders, Alphabetically Arranged, Who Voted at the Cork Election, December 1826. Cork: J. Connor, 1827.

Perman, Michael, ed. *Major Problems in the Civil War and Reconstruction.* Lexington, Mass.: D. C. Heath, 1991.

U.S. Congress. *Report of the Superintendent of the Census.* Seventh census. Washington, D.C.: Robert Armstrong, 1853.

———. *Statistical View of the United States.* Seventh census. Washington, D.C.: A. O. P. Nicolson, 1854.

———. *War of the Rebellion. Official Records of the Union and Confederate Armies in the War of the Rebellion.* Series 4, 128 vols. Washington, D.C.: Government Printing Office, 1894–1922.

PUBLISHED MEMOIRS

Alexander, Edward Porter. *Fighting for the Confederacy.* Edited by Gary W. Gallagher. Chapel Hill: University of North Carolina Press, 1989.

Banks, R. W. *The Battle of Franklin, November 30, 1864.* Dayton, Ohio: Morningside Bookshop, 1988. First published 1908.

Barber, Flavel C. *Holding the Line: The Third Tennessee Infantry, 1861–1864.* Edited by Robert H. Ferrell. Kent, Ohio: Kent State University Press, 1994.

Bevins, William E. *Reminiscences of a Private.* Edited by Daniel E. Sutherland. Fayetteville: University of Arkansas Press, 1992.

Buck, Irving A. *Cleburne and His Command.* Dayton, Ohio: Morningside Bookshop, 1992. First published 1908.

Buck, Lucy Rebecca. *Sad Earth, Sweet Heaven: The Diary of Lucy Rebecca Buck During the War Between the States.* Edited by William P. Buck. Birmingham, Ala.: Buck Publishing Company, 1992.

Buell, Clarence, and Robert Johnson, eds. *Battles and Leaders of the Civil War.* 4 vols. New York: Thomas Yoseloff, 1956. First published 1887.

Cate, Wirt Armistead, ed. *Two Soldiers: The Campaign Diaries of Thomas F. Key, C.S.A., and Robert F. Campbell, U.S.A.* Chapel Hill: University of North Carolina Press, 1938.

Cox, Jacob D. *The Battle of Franklin.* New York: Scribners, 1897.

Dodge, Grenville. *The Battle of Atlanta and Other Campaigns, Addresses, etc.* Denver: Sage Books, 1965. First published 1911.

Douglas, Lucia R., ed. *Douglas's Texas Battery, CSA.* Tyler, Texas: Smith County Historical Society, 1966.

Duke, Basil W. *A History of Morgan's Cavalry.* Bloomington: Indiana University Press, 1960.

———. *Reminiscences of Basil W. Duke, C.S.A.* New York: Doubleday, 1911.

Fletcher, Elliott H. *The Civil War Letters of Captain Elliott H. Fletcher.* Edited by J. H. Atkinson. Bulletin no. 5. Little Rock, Ark: Pulaski County Historical Society, 1963.

Foster, Samuel T. *One of Cleburne's Command: The Civil War Reminiscences and Diary of Capt. Samuel T. Foster, Granbury's Texas Brigade, C.S.A.* Edited by Norman D. Brown. Austin: University of Texas Press, 1980.

Fremantle, Arthur J. L. *The Fremantle Diary.* Edited by Walter Lord. Boston: Little, Brown and Company, 1954.

French, Samuel G. *Two Wars: An Autobiography.* Nashville, Tenn.: Confederate Veteran, 1901.

Gordon, John B. *Reminiscences of the Civil War.* New York: Charles Scribner's Sons, 1981. First published 1903.

Head, Thomas A. *Campaigns and Battles of the Sixteenth Regiment, Tennessee Volunteers in the War Between the States.* Nashville, Tenn.: Cumberland Presbyterian Publishing House, 1885.

Heartsill, W. W. *Fourteen Hundred and Ninety-One Days in the Confederate Army.* Edited by Bell I. Wiley. Jackson, Tenn.: McCowat-Mercer Press, 1954.

Hood, John Bell. *Advance and Retreat: Personal Experiences in the United States and Confederate Armies.* New York: DaCapo Press, 1993. First published 1880.

Jackman, John S. *Diary of a Confederate Soldier: John S. Jackman of the Orphan Brigade.* Edited by William C. Davis. Columbia: University of South Carolina Press, 1990.

Liddell, St. John R. *Liddell's Record.* Edited by Nathaniel C. Hughes, Jr. Dayton, Ohio: Morningside House, 1985.

Nash, Charles E. *Biographical Sketches of Gen. Pat Cleburne and Gen. T. C. Hindman.* Dayton, Ohio: Morningside Bookshop, 1977. First published 1898.

Nisbet, James Cooper. *Four Years on the Firing Line.* Edited by Bell I. Wiley. Jackson, Tenn.: McCowat-Mercer Press, 1963.

Quintard, Charles Todd. *Doctor Quintard, Chaplain C.S.A. and Second Bishop of Tennessee.* Sewanee, Tenn.: University Press, 1905.

Schofield, John M. *Forty-Six Years in the Army.* New York: Century Company, 1897.

Shellenberger, John K. *The Battle of Spring Hill, Tennessee, November 29, 1864.* Cleveland: Arthur H. Clark Company, 1913.

Smith, Frank H. *History of Maury County, Tennessee.* N.p.: Maury County Historical Society, 1969.

Stanley, Henry Morton. *The Autobiography of Sir Henry Morton Stanley, G.C.B.* London: Sampson Low, Marston, and Company, 1909.

Stephenson, Philip D. *The Civil War Memoir of Philip Daingerfield Stephenson, D.D.* Edited by Nathaniel C. Hughes, Jr. Conway: University of Central Arkansas Press, 1995.

Watkins, Sam R. *"Co. Aytch," Maury Grays, First Tennessee Regiment, or A Side Show of the Big Show.* Wilmington, N.C.: Broadfoot Publishing Company, 1987. First published 1882.

Worsham, W. J. *The Old Nineteenth Tennessee Regiment, June 1861–April 1865.* Oxford, Miss.: Guild Bindery, 1992.

THESES AND DISSERTATIONS

Bearss, Edwin C. "Pat Cleburne, Stonewall Jackson of the West." Master's thesis, Indiana University, 1954.

Clauss, Errol M. "The Atlanta Campaign, 18 July–2 September, 1864." Ph.D. dissertation, Emory University, 1965.

Goforth, Robert D. "Sherman and Cleburne at Tunnel Hill: The Myth of the Inevitability of Confederate Defeat at Chattanooga, November 23–25, 1863." Master's thesis, East Carolina University, 1992.

Johnson, Slate L. "Slavery and the Politics of Promotion: The Case of Major General Patrick R. Cleburne, C.S.A." Undergraduate honors thesis, U.S. Naval Academy, 1991.

McMurry, Richard M. "The Atlanta Campaign: December 23, 1863 to July 18, 1864." Ph.D. dissertation, Emory University, 1967.

BOOKS

Boyce, D. George. *Nineteenth-Century Ireland: The Search for Stability.* Savage, Md.: Barnes and Noble, 1991.

Burr, Frank A., with Talcott Williams. *The Battle of Franklin.* Philadelphia: Philadelphia Press, 1883.

Calhoun, Robert M. *Evangelicals and Conservatives in the Early South, 1740–1861.* Columbia: University of South Carolina Press, 1988.

Castel, Albert. *Decision in the West: The Atlanta Campaign of 1864.* Lawrence: University Press of Kansas, 1992.

Connelly, Thomas L. *Army of the Heartland: The Army of Tennessee, 1861–1862.* Baton Rouge: Louisiana State University Press, 1967.

———. *Autumn of Glory: The Army of Tennessee, 1862–1865.* Baton Rouge: Louisiana State University Press, 1971.

Cornish, Dudley Taylor. *The Sable Arm: Black Troops in the Union Army, 1861–1865.* Lawrence: University Press of Kansas, 1987. First published 1956.

Cozzens, Peter. *No Better Place to Die: The Battle of Stones River.* Urbana: University of Illinois Press, 1990.

———. *The Shipwreck of Their Hopes: The Battles for Chattanooga.* Urbana: University of Illinois Press, 1994.

———. *This Terrible Sound: The Battle of Chickamauga.* Urbana: University of Illinois Press, 1992.

Daniel, Larry. *Cannoneers in Gray: The Field Artillery of the Army of Tennessee, 1861–1865.* University: University of Alabama Press, 1984.

———. *Soldiering in the Army of Tennessee: A Portrait of Life in a Confederate Army.* Chapel Hill: University of North Carolina Press, 1991.

Davis, William C. *Jefferson Davis, the Man and His Hour.* New York: Harper-Collins, 1991.

———. *The Orphan Brigade: The Kentucky Confederates Who Couldn't Go Home.* Garden City, N.Y.: Doubleday, 1980.

Donnelly, James S., Jr. *The Land and the People of Nineteenth Century Cork.* London: Routledge and Kegan Paul, 1975.

Dougan, Michael. *Confederate Arkansas: The People and the Politics of a Frontier State in Wartime.* University: University of Alabama Press, 1976.

Dufour, Charles. *Nine Men in Gray.* Lincoln: University of Nebraska Press, 1993. First published 1963.

Durden, Robert F., ed. *The Gray and the Black: The Confederate Debate on Emancipation.* Baton Rouge: Louisiana State University Press, 1972.

Foster, R. F. *Modern Ireland, 1600–1972.* London: Penguin Press, 1988.

Griffith, Paddy. *Battle Tactics of the Civil War.* New Haven: Yale University Press, 1987.

Hafendorfer, Kenneth A. *Perryville: Battle for Kentucky.* Louisville, Ky.: K H Press, 1991.

Hallock, Judith Lee. *Braxton Bragg and Confederate Defeat.* Vol. 2. Tuscaloosa: University of Alabama Press, 1991.

Hammock, John C. *With Honor Untarnished: The Story of the First Arkansas Infantry Regiment, Confederate States Army.* Little Rock, Ark.: Pioneer Press, 1961.

Hattaway, Herman. *General Stephen D. Lee.* Jackson: University Press of Mississippi, 1976.

Hay, Thomas Robson. "Pat Cleburne: Stonewall of the West." In Irving A. Buck, *Cleburne and His Command.* Dayton, Ohio: Morningside Bookshop, 1992. First published 1958.

Hughes, Nathaniel Cheairs, Jr. *General William J. Hardee: Old Reliable.* Baton Rouge: Louisiana State University Press, 1965.

Johnston, William Preston. *The Life of Albert Sidney Johnston.* New York: D. Appleton and Company, 1878.

Kee, Robert. *The Green Flag: The Turbulent History of the Irish National Movement.* New York: Delacorte Press, 1972.

Kelleher, George D. *Gunpowder to Guided Missiles: Ireland's War Industries, 1361–1986.* Cork: John F. Kelleher, 1992.

Livermore, Thomas L. *Numbers and Losses in the Civil War in America, 1861–1865.* Bloomington: Indiana University Press, 1957.

Losson, Christopher. *Tennessee's Forgotton Warriors: Frank Cheatham and His Confederate Division.* Knoxville: University of Tennessee Press, 1989.

Loveland, Anne C. *Southern Evangelicals and the Social Order, 1800–1860.* Baton Rouge: Louisiana State University Press, 1980.

McCaffrey, James M. *This Band of Heroes: Granbury's Texas Brigade, C.S.A.* Austin, Texas: Eakin Press, 1985.

McDonough, James Lee. *Chattanooga: A Death Grip on the Confederacy.* Knoxville: University of Tennessee Press, 1984.

————. *Shiloh: In Hell Before Night.* Knoxville: University of Tennessee Press, 1977.

————. *Stones River: Bloody Winter in Tennessee.* Knoxville: University of Tennessee Press, 1980.

————. *War in Kentucky: From Shiloh to Perryville.* Knoxville: University of Tennessee Press, 1994.

McDonough, James L., and James Pickett Jones. *War So Terrible: Sherman and Atlanta.* New York: W. W. Norton, 1987.

McDowell, R. B. *The Church of Ireland, 1869–1969.* London: Routledge and Kegan Paul, 1975.

MacIntyre, Angus. *The Liberator: Daniel O'Connor and the Irish Party, 1830–1847.* London: Hamish Hamilton, 1965.

McMurry, Richard M. *John Bell Hood and the War for Southern Independence.* Lexington: University Press of Kentucky, 1982.

McPherson, James M. *What They Fought For, 1861–1865.* Baton Rouge: Louisiana State University Press, 1994.

McWhiney, Grady. *Braxton Bragg and Confederate Defeat: Field Command.* Tuscaloosa: University of Alabama Press, 1991. First published 1969.

McWhiney, Grady, and Perry D. Jamieson. *Attack and Die: Civil War Military Tactics and the Southern Heritage.* University: University of Alabama Press, 1982.

Maguire, John F. *The Irish in America.* London: Longmans, Green, and Company, 1868.

Mathews, Donald G. *Religion in the Old South.* Chicago: University of Chicago Press, 1977.

Miller, William Lee. *Arguing About Slavery: The Great Battle in the United States Congress.* New York: Alfred A. Knopf, 1996.

Moneyhon, Carl H. *The Impact of the Civil War and Reconstruction on Arkansas: Persistence in the Midst of Ruin.* Baton Rouge: Louisiana State University Press, 1994.

Neal, Diane, and Thomas W. Kremm. *Lion of the South: General Thomas C. Hindman.* Macon, Ga.: Mercer University Press, 1993.

Parks, Joseph H. *General Edmund Kirby Smith, C.S.A.* Baton Rouge: Louisiana State University Press, 1954. Reprinted 1982.

————. *General Leonidas Polk, C.S.A., The Fighting Bishop.* Baton Rouge: Louisiana State University Press, 1962.

Polk, William M. *Leonidas Polk: Bishop and General.* 2 vols. London: Longmans, Green and Company, 1915.

Purdue, Howell, and Elizabeth Purdue. *Pat Cleburne, Confederate General.* Hillsboro, Texas: Hill Junior College Press, 1973.

Randall, J. G., and David Herbert Donald. *The Civil War and Reconstruction.* 2d ed. Lexington, Mass.: D. C. Heath, 1969.

Reynolds, James A. *The Catholic Emancipation Crisis in Ireland, 1823–1829.* New Haven: Yale University Press, 1954.

Robertson, William Glenn, et al. *Staff Ride Handbook for the Battle of Chickamauga, 18–20 September 1863.* Fort Leavenworth, Kans.: Combat Studies Institute, 1992.

Schrier, Arnold. *Ireland and the American Emigration, 1850–1900.* Minneapolis: University of Minnesota Press, 1958.

Stover, John F. *Iron Road to the West: American Railroads in the 1850s.* New York: Columbia University Press, 1978.

Sword, Wiley. *Embrace an Angry Wind: The Confederacy's Last Hurrah: Spring Hill, Franklin, and Nashville.* New York: Harper-Collins, 1992. Paperback, *The Confederacy's Last Hurrah: Spring Hill, Franklin, and Nashville.* Lawrence: University Press of Kansas, 1993.

———. *Mountains Touched with Fire: Chattanooga Besieged, 1863.* New York: St. Martins Press, 1995.

———. *Shiloh: Bloody April.* Dayton, Ohio: Morningside House, 1988. First published 1974.

Symonds, Craig L. *Joseph E. Johnston: A Civil War Biography.* New York: W. W. Norton, 1992.

Tucker, Glenn. *Chickamauga: Bloody Battle in the West.* New York: Konecky and Konecky, 1994. First published 1961.

Warner, Ezra J. *Generals in Gray: Lives of the Confederate Commanders.* Baton Rouge: Louisiana State University Press, 1959.

Woodham Smith, Cecil. *The Great Hunger: Ireland, 1845–1849.* New York: Harper and Row, 1962.

Woods, James M. *Rebellion and Realignment: Arkansas's Road to Secession.* Fayetteville: University of Arkansas Press, 1987.

Woodward, Llewellyn. *The Age of Reform, 1815–1870.* Vol. 13 of *The Oxford History of England.* Oxford: Clarendon Press, 1962. First published 1938.

Woodworth, Steven E. *Jefferson Davis and His Generals: The Failure of Confederate Command in the West.* Lawrence: University Press of Kansas, 1990.

ARTICLES

Ambrose, Stephen. "By Enlisting Negroes Could the South Still Win the War?" *Civil War Times Illustrated* 3 (January 1965): 16–21.

Anderson, Archer. "Campaign and Battle of Chickamauga." *Southern Historical Society Proceedings* 9 (1881): 385–418.

Atkinson, J. H., ed. "A Civil War Letter of Captain Elliott Fletcher, Jr." *Arkansas Historical Quarterly* 22 (Spring 1963): 49–54.

Avery, A. C. "Memorial Address on the Life and Character of Lieut.-General D. H. Hill." *Southern Historical Society Proceedings* 21 (1893): 110–50.

Avery, I. W. "Patrick Ronayne Cleburne." *Kennesaw Gazette,* 15 May 1887, 1–2.

Barnes, W. T. "An Incident of Kenesaw Mountain." *Confederate Veteran* 30 (1922): 48–49.

Benham, Calhoun. "Major-Gen. P. R. Cleburne, A Biography." *Kennesaw Gazette,* 1 January–15 November 1889.

Berry, J. M. "The Quiet Humor of Gen. Pat Cleburne." *Confederate Veteran* 12 (1904): 176.

Bingham, J. H. "How Errors Become 'Historic Facts.'" *Confederate Veteran* 12 (1904): 72–73.

Boyce, Joseph. "Missourians in Battle of Franklin." *Confederate Veteran* 24 (1916): 101–3, 138.

Brock. *See* Buck

Brown, Campbell H. "The Myth of the 5 Dead Rebel Generals." *Civil War Times Illustrated* 8 (August 1969): 14–15.

Buck, Irving A. "Cleburne and His Division at Missionary Ridge and Ringgold Gap." *Southern Historical Society Proceedings* 8 (1880): 464–75. The article, mistakenly, is listed as being by Irving A. Brock.

———. "Military View of Battle of Franklin." *Confederate Veteran* 17 (1909): 383.

Carnes, W. W. "At Missionary Ridge." *Confederate Veteran* 28 (1920): 185.

———. "Chickamauga." *Southern Historical Society Proceedings* 14 (1886): 398–407.

Carrigan, Alfred H. "Reminiscences of the Secession Convention." *Publications of the Arkansas Historical Association* 1 (1906): 301–12.

Cheatham, Benjamin Franklin. "The Lost Opportunity at Spring Hill—General Cheatham's Reply to General Hood." *Southern Historical Society Proceedings* 9 (1881): 524–41.

Cheney, H. J. "Reminiscences of War Incidents." *Confederate Veteran* 18 (1910): 517–19.

Claiborne, Thomas. "Battle of Perryville, Ky." *Confederate Veteran* 16 (1908): 225–27.

Clauss, Errol M. "The Battle of Jonesborough." *Civil War Times Illustrated* 7 (November 1968): 12–23.

Cleary, Martina, and Olive Driscoll. "Spedding's School and Hospital." *Journal of the Ballincollig Community School* (1985): 5–6.

Crownover, Sims. "The Battle of Franklin." *Tennessee Historical Quarterly* 14 (December 1955): 291–322.

Cumming, J. B. "Sketch of General Walker." *Confederate Veteran* 10 (1902): 404–7.

Cunningham, Sumner A. "Death of Gen. Strahl." *Confederate Veteran* 1 (1893): 31.

———. "Events Leading to the Battle." *Confederate Veteran* 18 (1910): 17–20.

———. "Gallant Mississippians at Chickamauga." *Confederate Veteran* 7 (1899): 546–47.

———. "Hood's View Point of Franklin." *Confederate Veteran* 11 (1903): 297.

Davis, Steve. "Atlanta Campaign: Hood Fights Desperately." *Blue and Gray Magazine* 6 (August 1989): 8–39, 45–62.

———. "The Great Snow Battle of 1864." *Civil War Times Illustrated* 15 (June 1976): 32–35.

———. "That Extraordinary Document: W. H. T. Walker and Patrick Cleburne's Emancipation Proposal." *Civil War Times Illustrated* 16 (December 1977): 14–20.

Dean, J. C. "The Battle of Franklin." *Confederate Veteran* 7 (1899): 27.

Dodd, W. O. "Reminiscences of Hood's Tennessee Campaign." *Southern Historical Society Proceedings* 9 (1881): 523.

Douglas, W. F. "A Sketch of Maj. Gen. P. R. Cleburne." *The Land We Love* 2 (1867): 460–63.

Everett, Lloyd T. "Patrick R. Cleburne, Prophet." *Tyler's Quarterly Historical and Genealogical Magazine* (27 January 1946): 206–20.

Gibson, W. W. "Reminiscences of Ringgold Gap." *Confederate Veteran* 12 (1904): 526–27.

Gist, W. W. "The Other Side at Franklin." *Confederate Veteran* 24 (1916): 13–15.

Gordon, George W. "General P. R. Cleburne: Dedication of a Monument to His

Memory at Helena, Arkansas, May 10, 1891." *Southern Historical Society Proceedings* 18 (1890): 260–72.

Grady, B. F. "Cleburne's Division at Missionary Ridge." *Confederate Veteran* 13 (1905): 28.

Hafendorfer, Kenneth A. "Major General Simon B. Buckner's Unpublished After-Action Report on the Battle of Perryville." *Civil War Regiments* 4 (1995): 50–64.

Hammond, Paul F. "General Kirby Smith's Campaign in Kentucky." *Southern Historical Society Proceedings* 9 (1881): 246–54.

Hardee, William J. "Maj. Gen. Patrick R. Cleburne." *Confederate Veteran* 12 (1904): 17.

———. "A Sketch of General Patrick R. Cleburne." *Southern Historical Society Proceedings* 31 (1903): 157.

Harley, S. C. "Govan's Brigade at Pickett's Mill." *Confederate Veteran* 12 (1904): 74–76.

Hassler, William W. "Stonewall of the West." *Civil War Times Illustrated* 10 (February 1972): 4–9, 44–47.

Hay, Thomas R. "The South and the Arming of the Slaves," *Mississippi Valley Historical Review* 4 (June 1919): 34–73.

Hill, Andrew Malone. "Personal Recollections of Andrew Malone Hill." *Alabama Historical Quarterly* 20 (Spring 1958): 85–91.

Horn, Stanley F. "Perryville." *Civil War Times Illustrated* 4 (February 1966): 4–11, 42–47.

———. "The Seesaw Battle of Stones River." *Civil War Times Illustrated* 2 (February 1964): 6–11, 34–39.

———. "The Spring Hill Legend." *Civil War Times Illustrated* 8 (April 1969): 20–32.

Jones, Charles E. "Foreign Born Generals in United States Army, 1861–1865." *Confederate Veteran* 26 (1918): 374.

Jones, James A. "About the Battle of Shiloh." *Confederate Veteran* 7 (1899): 556.

Kelly, Dennis. "The Battle of Kennesaw Mountain." *Blue and Gray Magazine* 6 (June 1989): 8–12, 16–30, 46–58.

Kelsey, Jasper. "The Battle of Shiloh." *Confederate Veteran* 25 (1917): 71–73.

Knight, F. W. "General Patrick Ronayne Cleburne." *Cork Historical and Archeological Society Journal* 21 (1915): 10–17.

Law, J. G. "Advance into Kentucky (Diary of Rev. J. G. Law)." *Southern Historical Society Proceedings* 12 (1884): 390–95.

Lee, Stephen D. "From Palmetto, Ga. to Defeat at Nashville." *Confederate Veteran* 16 (1908): 257–58.

LeMonnier, Y. R. "Gen. Leonidas Polk at Chickamauga." *Confederate Veteran* 24 (1916): 17.

Linder, Ethel. "Patrick Cleburne, Hero From Helena." *Arkansas Historical Quarterly* 4 (Spring 1945): 309–14.

Lindsay, R. H. "Seeing the Battle of Franklin." *Confederate Veteran* 9 (1901): 221.

Lowery, Mark P. "General M. P. Lowery: An Autobiography." *Southern Historical Society Proceedings* 16 (1888): 365–76.

M'Clure, Joe. "Wounded Texan's Trip Home on Crutches." *Confederate Veteran* 8 (1909): 161–62.

M'Dearman, [no first name]. "Private M'Dearman at Murfreesboro." *Confederate Veteran* 9 (1901): 306.

McDonough, James Lee. "The Battle at Franklin, Tennessee, November 30, 1864." *Blue and Gray Magazine* 2 (August–September 1984): 18–39.

McMurry, Richard M. "The Hell Hole: New Hope Church." *Civil War Times Illustrated* 11 (February 1973): 32–43.

———. "Kennesaw Mountain." *Civil War Times Illustrated* 8 (January 1970): 19–34.

M'Neilly, James H. "Franklin—Incidents of the Battle." *Confederate Veteran* 26 (1918): 116–17.

———. "In Winter Quarters at Dalton, Ga." *Confederate Veteran* 28 (1920): 130–33.

Maney, T. H. "Battle at Dead Angle on Kennesaw Line." *Confederate Veteran* 11 (1903): 159.

Mangum, Learned H. "General P. R. Cleburne, A Sketch of His Early Life and His Last Battle." *Kennesaw Gazette,* 15 June 1887, 2–6.

Milner, W. J. "Lieut. Gen. William Joseph Hardee." *Confederate Veteran* 22 (1914): 360–64.

Moneyhon, Carl H. "Economic Democracy in Antebellum Arkansas, Phillips County, 1850–1860." *Arkansas Historical Quarterly* 40 (Summer 1981): 2, 154–72.

Moore, T. O. "Anecdotes of General Cleburne." *Southern Historical Society Proceedings* 21 (1893): 299–301.

Nelson, H. K. "Dead Angle, or Devil's Elbow, Ga." *Confederate Veteran* 11 (1903): 321.

Patterson, D. H. "Battle of Franklin." *Confederate Veteran* 9 (1901): 116–17.

Peay, Austin. "The Battle of Dug Gap." *Confederate Veteran* 29 (1921): 182–83.

Phillips, G. C. "Witness to the Battle of Franklin." *Confederate Veteran* 14 (1906): 261–62.

Pickett, W. D. "The Dead Angle." *Confederate Veteran* 14 (1906): 458–59.

Randle, W. F. "Pat Cleburne's Early Career." *Confederate Veteran* 19 (1911): 212.

Rea, R. N. "A Mississippi Soldier of the Confederacy." *Confederate Veteran* 30 (1922): 287–88.

Rees, W. H. "Battle of New Hope Church." *Confederate Veteran* 11 (1903): 291.

———. "Cleburne's Men at Franklin." *Confederate Veteran* 9 (1901): 54.

Remington, J. D. "Cause of Hood's Failure at Spring Hill." *Confederate Veteran* 21 (1913): 569–70.

Ridley, B. L. "Camp Scenes Around Dalton." *Confederate Veteran* 10 (1902): 66–68.

———. "Southern Side at Chickamauga." *Confederate Veteran* 6 (1898): 514–17, 556–58.

Robert, Charles E. "At Murfreesboro Just Before the Battle." *Confederate Veteran* 16 (1908): 631–32.

Roberts, Frank S. "In Winter Quarters at Dalton, Ga., 1863–64." *Confederate Veteran* 26 (1918): 274–75.

Rone, John T. "First Arkansas Brigade at Chickamauga." *Confederate Veteran* 13 (1905): 166–67.

Roy, T. B. "General Hardee and the Military Operations Around Atlanta." *Southern Historical Society Proceedings* 8 (1880): 337–87.

Ruby, Barbara C. "General Patrick Cleburne's Proposal to Arm Southern Slaves." *Arkansas Historical Quarterly* 20 (Fall 1971): 193–212.

Schellenberger, John K. "The Fighting at Spring Hill, Tenn." *Confederate Veteran* 36 (1928): 100–103, 140–43, 188.

Searcher, Victor. "An Arkansas Druggist Defeats a Famous General." *Arkansas Historical Quarterly* 13 (Winter 1954): 249–56.

Secrist, Philip. "Scenes of Awful Carnage." *Civil War Times Illustrated* 10 (June 1971): 4–9, 45–48.

Shannon, Isaac N. "Sharpshooters with Hood's Army." *Confederate Veteran* 15 (1907): 123–26.

Shapard, E. "At Spring Hill and Franklin Again." *Confederate Veteran* 24 (1916): 138–39.

Smith, Harold T. "The Know-Nothings in Arkansas." *Arkansas Historical Quarterly* 34 (Winter 1975): 291–303.

Stephenson, Philip D. "Missionary Ridge." *Confederate Veteran* 21 (1913): 540–41.

———. "Reminiscences of the Last Campaign of the Army of Tennessee, from May 1864 to January 1865." *Southern Historical Society Proceedings* 12 (1884): 38–39.

Stewart, Alexander P. "A Critical Narrative." *Confederate Veteran* 16 (1908): 462–63.

Stiles, John C. "Confederate States Negro Troops." *Confederate Veteran* 23 (1915): 246–47.

Taylor, Lenette S. "Polemics and Partisanship: The Arkansas Press in the 1860 Election." *Arkansas Historical Quarterly* 44 (Winter 1985): 314–35.

Thompson, William C. "From Shiloh to Port Gibson." *Civil War Times Illustrated* 3 (October 1964): 20–25.

Tucker, Glenn. "The Battle of Chickamauga." *Civil War Times Illustrated* 8 (May 1964): 4–49.

Van Horn, George D. "Swett's Battery at Jonesboro." *Confederate Veteran* 11 (1903): 504.

Walker, Hugh F. "Bloody Franklin." *Civil War Times Illustrated* 3 (December 1964): 16–24.

Walz, Robert B. "Migration into Arkansas, 1820–1880: Incentives and Means of Travel." *Arkansas Historical Quarterly* 17 (Winter 1958): 309–24.

Washburn, Wiley A. "Cleburne's Division at Franklin." *Confederate Veteran* 13 (1905): 27–28.

———. "Reminiscences of Confederate Service by Wiley A. Washburn." Edited by James L. Nichols and Frank Abbott. *Arkansas Historical Quarterly* 35 (Spring 1976): 47–90.

Watkins, Sam R. "Dead Angle on the Kennessaw Line." *Confederate Veteran* 25 (1917): 166–67.

Wilson, W. T. "Hardships of Bragg's Retreat." *Confederate Veteran* 28 (1920): 51–52.

Young, J. P. "Hood's Failure at Spring Hill." *Confederate Veteran* 16 (1908): 25–41.

INDEX

A

Adams, John (Confederate general), 261
Alexander, Mark (PRC's law partner), 35–36, 39, 42
Allison, R. D. (Confederate colonel), 83
Anderson, Patton (Confederate general), 95, 189
Annebrook (Ronayne home in Ireland), 13
Army of Tennessee (Confederate), 1, 101–6, 196
  and Atlanta campaign, 221–41, 243
  and Chickamauga, Battle of, 143–51
  losses in, 183, 230
  morale in, 138–39, 183, 196
  politics in, 120–23, 131, 137, 153–57
  strength of, 293n1
Atlanta, Battle of. *See* Bald Hill, Battle of
Atlanta campaign, 221–41
  maps of, 227, 238

B

Bailey, Charlie (PRC's clerk), 103
Bald Hill, Battle of (22 July 1864), 221, 225–30, 297n11
Ballincollig Military Barricks (Ireland), 16, 21
Bate, William (Confederate general), 5, 65, 81, 200, 224
  and Franklin, Battle of, 258
  and PRC's Memorial, reaction to, 189–90
  and Shiloh, Battle of, 69, 72
  and Spring Hill, Tennessee, 252–55
Bausum, George (Confederate colonel), 213
Beauregard, P. G. T. (Confederate general), 62, 65, 82, 84, 248

dismissal of, 85
and Shiloh, Battle of, 68–77
Beechwood (Hardee's Wartrace headquarters), 125
Bell, John (U.S. senator), 43
Benham, Calhoun (PRC's chief of staff), 102, 112, 145, 195, 232, 236, 240, 242
  and PRC's Memorial, reaction to, 185, 187
Bostick, Joseph (Confederate major), 253
Bowling Green, Tennessee, 58–62
Bradley, Luther P. (Union general), 251–54
Bradley, Thomas H. (Arkansas militia general), 49–51, 52, 104
Bragg, Braxton (Confederate general), 63, 64–65, 85–86, 171, 195, 223
  and Army of Tennessee, 101–2, 116–18
  character of, 131, 136–37
  and Chattanooga, siege of, 158, 160–61, 166
  and Chickamauga, Battle of, 152–53
  criticism of in press, 116
  description of, 85, 120
  and Kentucky campaign, 86–98, 278n34
  and McLemore's Cove, 139–43
  and Murfreesboro, Battle of, 105–15
  relations with generals, 120–23, 128, 131, 141, 147–48, 153–57, 160–61, 287n40
  resignation of, 176, 182
  and Shiloh, Battle of, 66–76
  strategy of, 128–29, 130–33, 136–37
  unpopularity of, 104–5, 115–17, 120, 138–39, 281n35
Brandon, James (Confederate staff officer), 259
Bratton, Hugh (Confederate major), 84
Breckinridge, John C. (Confederate general), 43, 65, 159, 175

315